BIBLICAL
ARAMAIC

A READER & HANDBOOK

BIBLICAL
ARAMAIC

A READER & HANDBOOK

ARAMAIC TEXT

Biblia Hebraica Leningradensia
Edited by Aron Dotan

LEXICAL AND GRAMMATICAL APPARATUS

Donald R. Vance
George Athas
Yael Avrahami

VOCABULARY AND MORPHOLOGY LISTS

Jonathan G. Kline

HENDRICKSON
PUBLISHERS

Biblical Aramaic: A Reader & Handbook

© 2016 by Hendrickson Publishers Marketing, LLC
P. O. Box 3473
Peabody, Massachusetts 01961-3473
www.hendrickson.com

Aramaic text:
Biblia Hebraica Leningradensia is a fully revised and retypeset edition of
תורה נביאים וכתובים, published in 1973 by ADI Publishers Ltd. (Tel Aviv) and
the School of Jewish Studies of Tel Aviv University.
© 2001 Hendrickson Publishers, Inc.
P.O. Box 3473
Peabody, Massachusetts 01961-3473

ISBN 978-1-61970-891-4

All rights reserved. No part of this book may be reproduced or transmitted in
any form or by any means, electronic or mechanical, including photocopying,
recording, or by any information storage and retrieval system, without permission
in writing from the publisher.

Printed in the United States of America

First Printing—November 2016

TABLE OF CONTENTS

Introduction

The term "Hebrew Bible" is something of a misnomer. Of the 23,145 verses that make up its contents, 269 verses are not in Hebrew, but in Aramaic. This amounts to a little over one percent of the "Hebrew Bible" (usually known to Christians as the "Old Testament"). Yet it is a rather underprivileged one percent. Many students of the Bible have studied Hebrew and so have a way of navigating the majority of biblical texts. But when it comes to the Aramaic portions, few though they are, many have little to no facility for engaging directly with the texts. Biblical study thereby becomes impoverished.

In an attempt to address this, we have produced *Biblical Aramaic: A Reader & Handbook*. Our aim is to provide students of the Bible with an accessible means for interacting with its Aramaic portions in a simple and discrete package. The Aramaic texts of the Bible are presented in full and annotated with a reading apparatus that appears below the biblical text on each page. This reading apparatus contains lexical notes that analyze the words and phrases of the Aramaic biblical texts to facilitate understanding and translation of these passages. In addition to its "Reader" portion, this volume also contains a large number of word lists that have been carefully designed to help students master the vocabulary and grammar of Biblical Aramaic. The nature of these lists is described in detail below.

Short History of the Aramaic Language

Hebrew and Aramaic are closely related languages. Both belong to the Northwest branch of the Semitic language family. Within this Northwest branch are two broad language strands, Canaanite and Aramaic. The languages in the Canaanite strand include Hebrew, Ugaritic, Phoenician, Moabite, Ammonite, and Edomite. Aramaic represents the entirety of the second Northwest strand. Ironically, then, Aramaic was actually used far more widely than Hebrew in antiquity. Being a relatively minor language, Hebrew was mainly confined to the regions of ancient Israel and Judah. Aramaic, however, was a major language that was native to Syria (biblical "Aram")—a region covering the entire top curve of the "Fertile Crescent." This area extended from the Mediterranean coast in the west across to the land of Assyria on the Tigris River in the east, and from the mountains of Anatolia in the north to the Golan Heights south of Damascus.

The early first millennium BCE saw the rise and fall of numerous small states in this region, most of which used various forms of "Old Aramaic." These are our earliest attestations of the Aramaic language and come to us mainly in the form of monumental lapidary inscriptions. While they all represent the same language, they also exhibit considerable regional variety. This can be seen, for example, by comparing the Old Aramaic of the bilingual inscription on the statue from Tell Fekheriye with that of Bar Rakib.

From the eighth century BCE, the Neo-Assyrian Empire expanded and brought many of these small states under its sovereignty. This political reality brought Aramaic into use within the Neo-Assyrian Empire and beyond, which increased its utility. In 2 Kings 18:26 we have an interesting episode depicting the general of the invading Assyrian armies, the

Rabshakeh, addressing the residents of Jerusalem in Hebrew (literally, "Judean"). The officials of Hezekiah, king of Judah, ask the general to speak to them in Aramaic rather than Hebrew, so that Jerusalem's residents who are listening might not be demoralized by understanding the conversation. This episode demonstrates that, although Hebrew and Aramaic were related languages, they were not mutually intelligible. Yet, it was reasonable to expect society's elite to be proficient in the latter. In the late seventh century BCE, then, Aramaic was being widely used as a language of international diplomacy and trade.

This continued through the rise of the Neo-Babylonian Empire in the sixth century BCE. At this time, an interesting development in the Hebrew language occurred. Until this point, Hebrew writing had made use of its own particular script, based on the Phoenician alphabet. However, when the Babylonians exiled Hebrew-speaking Jews to Babylon in the sixth century BCE, it seems those Hebrew speakers began to adopt the Aramaic alphabetic script for writing Hebrew. While the original Hebrew script did not die out completely, the Aramaic script became the default script of the Hebrew language—a practice that was taken back to Jerusalem by those who eventually returned there. (In fact, the Jewish sages named this script "Assyrian," having full awareness of the transition of scripts.) This practice has persisted ever since. Thus many students are often surprised to discover that the Hebrew Bible is, perhaps ironically, written in the script of its "one percent" Aramaic (compare, for instance, English, which is written in the Latin script).

The Neo-Babylonian Empire gave way to the Persian Empire in 539 BCE. The Persians soon adopted Aramaic as their official language of administration. Hence, we call the Aramaic of this period "Imperial Aramaic," though it is sometimes known as "Official Aramaic" or "Standard Aramaic." The language had undergone some linguistic shifts from its Old Aramaic forms by this time. And though minute developments still occurred, its status as an official imperial language gave it considerable stability throughout this period, so that a standardized form of Aramaic was used throughout the Persian realm, from the cataracts of the Nile in Egypt to the mountains of Sogdiana in modern-day Tajikistan.

The Persian Empire fell to the Greeks in 330 BCE. Soon after, the Hellenistic kingdoms that had arisen from the conquests of Alexander the Great cemented Greek culture and language throughout the ancient Near East. Nonetheless, Aramaic continued to be used widely, entering a phase we know as "Middle Aramaic" (ca. 200 BCE–ca. 200 CE). Standardization of the language weakened, as Aramaic was no longer a language of official government. Regional Aramaic dialects developed throughout the Fertile Crescent as a result, especially during the Roman period. The Aramaic spoken by Jesus was one of these dialects. Explanations of biblical texts, known as *Targumim*, were produced in this era for Aramaic-speaking Jews. The Syriac dialect, with its own particular script, also developed during this period in northern Syria. Christians in this region translated the Old and New Testaments into this dialect, and their version became known as the *Peshitta* (Syriac for "simple" or "common").

Beyond this era, we move into the various forms of "Late Aramaic." Rabbinic Judaism conducted its theological discourse in some of these late forms. The "Classical Syriac" dialect became the language of Christian discourse and liturgy throughout most of the Fertile Crescent. To this day it continues to be the scriptural and liturgical language of Syriac Orthodox Christians (who call themselves "Assyrians").

As can be seen from this brief survey, Aramaic was a highly influential language for many centuries, not just in its native Syria, but across a wide array of territories. The advent of the Islamic empires in the Middle East from the seventh century CE onward signaled the rise of Arabic as an international language, and the native use of Aramaic thus began to decline. However, "Neo-Aramaic" dialects still survive to this day among small, isolated Christian minorities.

Aramaic Texts in the Bible

"Biblical Aramaic" is not a specific dialect or stage of the Aramaic language. Rather, it is a term that refers to the corpus of Aramaic texts found in the Bible. These appear in four groupings: (1) a two-word toponym in Genesis 30:47; (2) Jeremiah 10:11; (3) Daniel 2:4b–7:28; and (4) Ezra 4:8–6:18 and 7:12–26. Each of these texts is presented in this volume, but some brief comments about each are warranted by way of introduction.

It is difficult to classify the Aramaic of the two-word toponym (יְגַר שָׂהֲדוּתָא) in Genesis 30:47 due to its small sample size. It could technically belong to either Old Aramaic, Imperial Aramaic, or even Middle Aramaic. Within the narrative, the toponym is attributed to Laban, a native of Paddan Aram, which is usually located around the city of Haran in northern Syria. Being in the patriarchal narratives of Genesis, Laban is thus characterized as a native Aramaic speaker of the far distant past.

Jeremiah 10:11 is an interesting case that exhibits features of Old Aramaic, Imperial Aramaic, and even Hebrew, all in just fifteen words. This reflects the time of Jeremiah's composition and early transmission in the sixth century BCE. This period saw the increasing use of Aramaic in official capacities, cementing the distinction between Old Aramaic and Imperial Aramaic. Particularly noteworthy in the verse are the two occurrences of the word translated as "the earth." The first occurrence is in the Old Aramaic form (אַרְקָא), while the second presents the Imperial Aramaic form (אַרְעָא). This shift from ק to ע is one of the differences that distinguish these two stages of the language (such differences are called "isoglosses"). It is difficult to know whether the preservation of the two forms is deliberate or inadvertent, but this is nonetheless indicative of the linguistic transitions that occurred during the sixth century BCE.

The Aramaic texts of Daniel have generated considerable debate. The book begins in Hebrew, but switches to Aramaic at 2:4b. The text signals the change in language by the word אֲרָמִית, "Aramaic" (Daniel 2:4a), the exact force of which is not clear. Is it a textual note—"language switches to Aramaic here"—or is it part of the narrative stating that the Chaldeans spoke to King Nebuchadnezzar "in Aramaic"? The Aramaic portions then continue without interruption until the end of Daniel 7. This encompasses five distinct narrative episodes (Daniel 2–6) and the book's first apocalyptic vision (Daniel 7). Then, at Daniel 8:1, the text reverts to Hebrew with no notice whatsoever. The Aramaic portions therefore straddle the two distinct halves of the book (Daniel 1–6 and 7–12), which has long puzzled scholars.

There have been numerous attempts to explain this phenomenon. In 1882, A. A. Bevan proposed that Daniel had originally been written in Hebrew but that some parts were lost and subsequently replaced by an Aramaic translation.[1] This suggestion can in no way be proved, and it does not account for the transition between the Hebrew and Aramaic sections falling at very convenient "seams." Others have argued that the Hebrew of Daniel is of a rather poor quality, leading to the suggestion that Daniel was originally written in Aramaic and some parts of it subsequently translated into Hebrew.[2] Yet the motivation for such translation and its limited scope are not adequately explained. S. R. Driver proposed that the author of Daniel was consciously imitating the book of Ezra, which moves between

---

1. A. A. Bevan, *A Short Commentary on the Book of Daniel* (Cambridge: Cambridge University Press, 1882).

2. R. H. Charles, *A Critical and Exegetical Commentary on the Book of Daniel* (Oxford: Clarendon, 1929); H. L. Ginsberg, *Studies in Daniel* (New York: Jewish Theological Seminary, 1948); F. Hartman and A. A. Di Lella, *The Book of Daniel*, AB 23 (Garden City, NY: Doubleday, 1977). See critique by A. Lacoque, *The Book of Daniel*, trans. David Pellauer (Eugene, OR: Wipf & Stock, 1976).

Hebrew and Aramaic.[3] However, Ezra's Aramaic portions are logically delineated by their content (see discussion below), and Daniel's Aramaic section defies such neat categorization. Others have suggested that the two languages of Daniel appeal to the social status or ethnicity of two distinct audiences.[4] This proposal, though, does not account for the unity of the book, nor can it account for why the transition from one audience to another occurs mid-sentence (Daniel 2:4) and after one particular narrative episode (Daniel 2) has already begun. It is more plausible to suggest that Daniel's readership was bilingual rather than bifurcated. D. Valeta argues that the author of Daniel employed Aramaic for satirical purposes, such that the imperial court's own language is used to caricature it.[5] This may explain its use in Daniel's narrative episodes, but the Aramaic of the vision in Daniel 7 is a little harder to explain. Valeta's theory may have more traction if one proposes a complex development for the composition of Daniel that joins the vision of chapter 7 more closely to the preceding narratives. J. J. Collins argues that the Aramaic narratives in Daniel 2–6 appeared first, followed by an Aramaic introductory narrative and then the vision of Daniel 7. The introductory chapter, Collins surmises, was then translated into Hebrew when Daniel 8–12 was appended to the book, thus providing Daniel with a Hebrew frame.[6] The conceptual connections between Daniel 1 and Daniel 9, however, mean that these chapters were probably composed together in Hebrew.[7] Nonetheless, the Aramaic of Daniel 7 may signal that readers should associate the vision with the preceding narrative chapters as their ideological climax. In any case, we see that the Aramaic portions of Daniel are not easily explained. At the very least, they indicate a bilingual audience, and possibly also a complex compositional history and literary purpose.

The Aramaic of Daniel is arguably Imperial Aramaic, reflecting the standardized form of the language that prevailed during the Persian Empire and that persisted in large measure into the Hellenistic Era. J. J. Collins compares Daniel's Aramaic to that of other texts, such as the papyri from Elephantine in Egypt (late fourth century BCE) and the documents written by the Samarian refugees in the Wadi ed-Daliyeh caves (ca. 331 BCE). He observes that Daniel prefers late Imperial forms to early Imperial forms, though both are attested. He concludes that the Aramaic is closest to that of the Wadi ed-Daliyeh documents.[8] On the other hand, Z. Stefanovic has shown that the Aramaic of Daniel "contains a significant amount of material similar to O[ld] A[ramaic] texts."[9] It seems that the Aramaic of Daniel is a mixed bag and defies easy classification.

The book of Ezra is a unified work with Nehemiah. By convention, though, these are divided into two discrete "books." The Aramaic portions are found only in the Ezra "book," and not in Nehemiah. In 1900, S. R. Driver identified the Aramaic of Ezra as a "Western" dialect spoken in Palestine, which he viewed as identical to that of Daniel's Aramaic.[10] Leaving aside how unusual it would be for a Persian king, such as Darius or Artaxerxes, to write in a

---

3. S. R. Driver, *The Book of Daniel* (Cambridge: Cambridge University Press, 1900).

4. For example, H. H. Rowley, "The Bilingual Problem of Daniel," *ZAW* 50 (1932): 256–68; N. W. Porteous, *Daniel: A Commentary*, OTL (London: SCM, 1965); and M. Delcor, *Le Livre de Daniel* (Paris: Gabalda, 1971).

5. D. Valeta, *Lions and Ovens and Visions: A Satirical Reading of Daniel 1–6* (Sheffield: Sheffield Phoenix, 2008).

6. J. J. Collins, *Daniel*, Hermeneia (Minneapolis: Fortress, 1993).

7. G. Athas, "In Search of the Seventy 'Weeks' of Daniel 9," *JHS* 9.2 (2009).

8. Collins, *Daniel*.

9. Z. Stefanovic, *The Aramaic of Daniel in the Light of Old Aramaic*, JSOTSup 129 (Sheffield: Sheffield Academic, 1992), 108.

10. Driver, *Book of Daniel*.

dialect local to Palestine, the discoveries of the twentieth century proved that the Aramaic of the Persian Era did not consist of regional dialects, but rather of a standardized form across the empire. Thus, scholars today universally acknowledge the Aramaic of Ezra to be Imperial Aramaic. The book begins in Hebrew and switches to Aramaic at Ezra 4:8, where it begins quoting correspondence between Persian officials and King Artaxerxes (Ezra 4:8–22). More official correspondence is presented at Ezra 5:7b–6:12, this time between Persian officials and King Darius. This material is chronologically earlier than the preceding correspondence. This noted feature of Ezra's "narrative" therefore involves the Aramaic portions of the book. Though some debate the historical veracity of these quoted documents, they do accurately reflect the use of Imperial Aramaic in official correspondence during the Persian Empire. Ezra's Aramaic is not, however, limited to the quotation of official correspondence. Between and immediately after the letters are narrative comments that explain the context and outcomes of the correspondence. The section finishes with comments recounting the dedication of the Jerusalem temple, and then reverts to Hebrew at Ezra 6:19. One final portion of Aramaic occurs at 7:12–26, which is a letter from King Artaxerxes to Ezra, again demonstrating the official status of Aramaic.

Moving from Hebrew to Aramaic

Most students of the Bible who want to read its Aramaic portions have a knowledge of Biblical Hebrew. Much of this knowledge is easily transferable to Aramaic, because both languages belong to the Northwest branch of Semitic languages and so share many similar substructures and vocabulary. Both languages, for example, work with a three-consonant root system and use prefixed and suffixed verbal conjugations. Yet there are major differences between the languages. These differences exist in the structures, syntax, and vocabulary, so that one cannot simply assume a direct correspondence between the two languages. It is worth flagging some of the more important of these features, in order to facilitate the acquisition of Aramaic for those who already know Hebrew.

First, Hebrew and Aramaic have largely distinct vocabularies. For example, the word meaning "to go out" in Hebrew is יצא, but in Aramaic it is נפק. Also, there are some roots that have completely different meanings in the two languages. In Hebrew the root שׁכח means "to forget," but in Biblical Aramaic it means "to find." Also, since Biblical Aramaic consists largely, if not totally, of Imperial Aramaic, it contains many Persian loanwords—far more than Hebrew. That said, there are many words that Hebrew and Aramaic share in common, such as אבד ("to perish"), לבשׁ ("to be clothed"), and עַיִן ("eye").

There are significant pronunciation and spelling differences between Hebrew and Biblical Aramaic. For example, Hebrew tends to assimilate a נ that would end a syllable into the first consonant of the next syllable. Aramaic, however, tends not to assimilate נ. Thus, while Hebrew has חִטָּה ("wheat"), the Aramaic equivalent is חִנְטָה. At an early stage, Canaanite languages, including Hebrew, underwent a vowel shift that saw many long *ā* vowels become long *ō* vowels. Aramaic, not being a Canaanite language, did not undergo this "Canaanite shift." As a result, one tends to encounter more *a*-class vowels in Aramaic than in Hebrew. Thus, for example, the Aramaic equivalent of the Hebrew negative particle לֹא is לָא, and Hebrew שָׁלוֹם is שְׁלָם in Aramaic. This last example show another isogloss that distinguishes the two languages: Hebrew is marked by the lengthening of a vowel in the syllable immediately in front of the accent ("שָׁ), while Aramaic has reduction to *shewa* ("שְׁ).

We also see certain consonantal equivalencies between the two languages. That is, a particular consonant in Hebrew may often show up as a different consonant in Aramaic. This is

the result of each language having its own pronunciation trajectory, such as the one involving the Canaanite shift in Hebrew. These equivalent consonants tend to be related, because they are pronounced with very similar configurations of the mouth, breath, voice, or throat. For example, when pronouncing the sound /z/, the tongue is in almost the same position in the mouth as when pronouncing the sound /d/. This helps explain why, for instance, words that exhibit ז in Hebrew often exhibit ד in Biblical Aramaic (Proto-Semitic phoneme #17 in the table below).[11] The following table shows the consonantal development from Proto-Semitic (PS) to Hebrew (H) and Aramaic (A).[12]

	PS	H	A		PS	H	A		PS	H	A
1	ʾ	ʾ א	ʾ א	11	y	y י	y י	21	ʿ	ʿ ע	ʿ ע
2	b	b ב	b ב	12	k	k כ	k כ	22	p	p פ	p פ
3	g	g ג	g ג	13	š	š שׁ	š שׁ	23	ṣ	ṣ צ	ṣ צ
4	ḥ	ḥ ח	ḥ ח	14	ś	ś שׂ	s(ś) ס(שׂ)	24	ḍ	ṣ צ	ʿ (q) ע(ק)
5	d	d ד	d ד	15	l	l ל	l ל	25	q	q ק	q ק
6	h	h ה	h ה	16	m	m מ	m מ	26	r	r ר	r ר
7	w	w ו	w ו	17	ḏ	z ז	d(z) ד(ז)	27	ṯ	š שׁ	t ת
8	z	z ז	z ז	18	n	n נ	n נ	28	ṭ	ṣ צ	ṭ ט
9	ḫ	ḥ ח	ḥ ח	19	ẓ	ṣ צ	ṭ ט	29	ġ	ʿ ע	ʿ ע
10	ṭ	ṭ ט	ṭ ט	20	s	s ס	s ס	30	t	t ת	t ת

To illustrate, Hebrew שׁתר is Aramaic סתר (PS #14); Hebrew זָהָב is Aramaic דְּהַב (PS #17); Hebrew עֵצָה is Aramaic עֵטָה (PS #19); Hebrew אֶרֶץ is Aramaic אֲרַק and אֲרַע (PS #24); Hebrew שָׁלוֹשׁ is Aramaic תְּלָת (PS #27); and Hebrew צוּר is Aramaic טוּר (PS #28).

Turning to substantives (nouns, and nominal adjectives and participles), we see a few significant features that readers should note. First, there are the similarities. Like Hebrew, Aramaic has two grammatical genders (masculine and feminine) and three grammatical numbers (singular, dual, and plural). It also has the absolute and construct states for substantives. However, unlike Hebrew, Aramaic has no definite article. Instead, Aramaic achieves practical definition of a substantive by placing it in an "emphatic" (or "determined") state. This state is marked by the addition of a vocalic suffix with *mater lectionis* א (occasionally, a vocalic suffix with *mater lectionis* ה). Aramaic also has different markers of the plural. The following table demonstrates these particular distinctives.

	Singular Absolute	Singular Emphatic	Plural Absolute	Plural Emphatic
Masculine	טָב	טָבָא	טָבִין	טָבַיָּא
Feminine	טָבָה	טָבְתָּא	טָבָן	טָבָתָא

Another distinguishing feature of Aramaic is the conjunction דִּי. This particle can function as a relative pronoun ("who, which, that"; cf. Hebrew's אֲשֶׁר), a temporal marker

---

11. This is a very common linguistic phenomenon that is found throughout the world's languages, even to the present day.

12. See, e.g., S. Moscati, A. Spitaler, E. Ullendorff, and W. von Soden, *An Introduction to the Comparative Grammar of the Semitic Languages: Phonology and Morphology*, PLO 6 (Wiesbaden: Harrassowitz, 1980), 22–45, and C. H. Gordon, *Ugaritic Textbook*, AO 38 (Rome: Pontifical Biblical Institute, 1965), 25–35.

("when"; cf. Hebrew's temporal use of כִּי), a conjunction introducing an epexegetical com-
ment ("that"; cf. Hebrew's epexegetical use of כִּי), a causal conjunction ("because"; cf. Hebrew's causal use of כִּי), or a genitive particle ("of"; cf. Hebrew's construct state). It also
frequently appears in idiomatic expressions, such as כָּל־קֳבֵל דִּי ("because"). Its ubiquity may
initially be disconcerting for the beginner but is a testament to its versatility.

The nomenclature of the verb stems (or *binyanim*) differs between Hebrew and Aramaic.
Most of the stems correspond to each other. For example, the Peʻal stem is the Aramaic
equivalent of Hebrew's Qal stem; both represent their respective language's *Grundstamm*
(German for "base stem," from which we derive the linguistic name, "G stem"). However, not
every stem has its respective equivalent in the other language. The following table compares
the verb stems of Hebrew and Aramaic, showing equivalencies and differences.

Linguistic Name	Characteristic Features	Hebrew Stem	Aramaic Stem
G	Basic, active	Qal	Peʻal
Gp	Basic, passive	Qal passive	Peʻil
tG	Basic, middle/reciprocal	—	Hithpeʻel
N	Basic, middle/passive	Niphal	—
D	Doubling, active	Piel	Paʻʻel
Dp	Doubling, passive	Pual	Puʻʻal
tD	Doubling, middle/reciprocal	Hithpael	Hithpaʻʻal
H	Causative, active	Hiphil	Haphʻel or Aphʻel
Hp	Causative, passive	Hophal	Huphʻal
Š	Causative, active	—	Shaphʻel
Št	Causative, middle/reciprocal	—	Hishtaphʻal

Biblical Aramaic has no *wayyiqtol* verb. This prefix conjugation with *wāw* retentive
(also known as *wāw* consecutive or *wāw* progressive) is perhaps the distinguishing mark
of Hebrew narrative, but it is lacking in Aramaic.[13] Instead, Aramaic makes frequent use
of participles and suffix conjugations in narrative texts. In Aramaic prefix conjugations,
the subject prefixes are the same as in Hebrew. There are, however, slight differences in the
subject suffixes in certain forms of both prefix and suffix conjugations. Also, Aramaic has
only one form of the infinitive, whereas Hebrew distinguishes an infinitive absolute from an
infinitive construct. Hebrew and Aramaic have nearly equivalent direct object markers to
signal the accusative (Hebrew: אֵת; Aramaic: יָת), though Aramaic frequently employs the
prefixed preposition לְ as a direct object marker also.

Finally, Biblical Aramaic employs a deliberate grammatical irregularity. The Aramaic
verb "to be" is הוה (cf. Hebrew היה). When this root appears in the prefix conjugation with
a third-person masculine subject, the subject prefix י would ordinarily be added to the root.

---

13. Some argue that an Aramaic equivalent of the *wayyiqtol* verb existed in forms of Old Aramaic,
appealing to the Tel Dan Stele, Zakkur, and the Balaam texts from Deir ʻAlla as evidence. However, the
relevant forms in Tel Dan and Zakkur are either iterative or simple preterite uses of the prefix conjugation, and it is questionable whether the Deir ʻAlla texts should be classified as Aramaic at all (they are
more plausibly understood as presenting a distinct Canaanite dialect). In any case, Biblical Aramaic,
which is predominantly if not entirely Imperial Aramaic, does not exhibit a *wayyiqtol* equivalent.

However, the consonants of the resulting form are identical to the divine name—the *tetra-grammaton* (יהוה). In order to maintain the distinction of the divine name, in such cases the biblical scribes replaced the subject prefix י with לֹ, and sometimes replaced the final ה with א. The resultant forms, לֶהֱוֵה (e.g., Daniel 4:22) and לֶהֱוֵא (e.g., Ezra 4:12), are technically incorrect, but are a deliberate strategy to preserve the sanctity of the divine name.

How to Use *Biblical Aramaic: A Reader & Handbook*

To aid reading of the biblical texts, this book presents lexical notes on the same page as the text. These notes include parsing information and glosses, thus saving the reader the need to reach for a separate lexicon. Parsing and other technical information is abbreviated to allow the presentation of more text and information on each page. A list of all the abbreviations used in the lexical notes follows this Introduction. A key difference between *Biblical Aramaic: A Reader & Handbook* and its "parent" work, *Biblia Hebraica Stuttgartensia: A Reader's Edition* (or *BHS Reader*, for short), is that the *Reader & Handbook* does not use a specific code to present parsing details. The much smaller size of this volume permits the parsing details to be spelled out more fully, albeit in abbreviated form.

In the main, the glosses in the lexical notes come from *The Hebrew and Aramaic Lexicon of the Old Testament* (*HALOT*), though major English versions (especially NRSV and NJPS) were also consulted. Furthermore, the glosses are contextually filtered, meaning the reader does not need to work through an entire entry in a lexicon to find the gloss that is most appropriate to a given context. This also minimizes the risk of the "totality transfer" fallacy, in which a reader imports all the possible glosses in a lexical entry for a word into the given context. We have thus aimed to promote efficient, fluent, and responsible reading of the Bible's Aramaic texts.

Vocabulary that occurs twenty-five times or more is generally not analyzed in the lexical notes. Rather, these words and their glosses appear in a glossary at the end of the volume. These words do, however, receive attention in the lexical notes when other elements are brought to bear on them, such as the addition of a pronominal suffix. These instances are parsed, but a gloss is not usually given. This way, readers are encouraged to acquire the most common vocabulary, while still receiving some help for the more complicated occurrences. One key exception to this is the particle דִּי. Due to its versatility (see discussion above), every instance is analyzed in the lexical notes.

In order to further facilitate readers' mastery of the vocabulary and grammar of Biblical Aramaic, the "Reader" portion of this book is supplemented by an extensive array of word lists. These present the vocabulary of Biblical Aramaic (including both lexical and attested forms) in a variety of ways that are intended to maximize one's ability to learn, with efficiency and long-term retention, what these words mean and the forms in which they occur. Starting off this section of the book are two major frequency lists. The first list presents all the vocabulary in Biblical Aramaic that occurs two times or more, and the second list presents all the *hapax legomena* (words occurring only once). Because the Biblical Aramaic corpus is relatively small, it is not always useful to learn the lexical form of a word, which may occur rarely or even not at all. For this reason, the first of these lists provides the predominant form in which a word occurs when this is not the lexical form. For example, the entry for אַרְיֵה, "lion," notes that this word occurs in the emphatic plural, אַרְיָוָתָא, in nine of its ten occurrences. The second list provides both the lexical form and the attested form for each *hapax legomenon*. Thus the entry for גִּזְבַּר, "treasurer," provides both this lexical form and

the form in which this word is attested in the Bible, גִּזְבְרַיָּא, along with the latter's parsing, "noun mp emph."

When a word can occur as more than one part of speech, it is given in the first list (as well as in some of the lists described below) according to its frequency for each part of speech, with the word's total frequency listed in parentheses. For example, the word שַׂגִּיא occurs thirteen times in the Bible, functioning nine times as an adjective ("great") and four times as an adverb ("greatly"). When this word is listed as an adjective, the frequency is given as "9 (13)," which means that out of a total of thirteen occurrences the word functions as an adjective nine times; when it is listed as an adverb, this word's frequency is likewise given as "4 (13)." An exception to this way of denoting frequency occurs for a small number of frequently occurring words, such as וְ, which occurs 731 times and which can function as both a conjunction and a disjunctive. For such words, we have provided only the total number of the word's occurrences, not the number of occurrences for each part of speech.

Following the two major frequency lists described above is a set of lists that group all the vocabulary of Biblical Aramaic according to part of speech: verbs, common nouns, proper nouns, adjectives, pronouns, prepositions, numbers, adverbs, conjunctions, disjunctives, interjections, and particles. A final such list presents all the collocations (i.e., idiomatic phrases) found in Biblical Aramaic, such as בְּעֵל־טְעֵם, "chancellor, chief government official," and דִּי־לָא שָׁלוּ, "without fail" (indicating every verse in which each collocation occurs). The words in the part-of-speech lists are presented in order of the frequency with which they appear in the Bible, thereby allowing readers to focus on memorizing the forms that are the most common. For example, the pronouns אֲנָה, "I," and אַנְתְּ, "you (2ms)," occur in the Bible sixteen and fifteen times, respectively, whereas אַנְתּוּן, "you (2mp)," occurs only once. Consequently, the former two are found at the beginning of the pronouns list, while the latter is found at the end. Likewise, the following numbers are attested in Biblical Aramaic, in the following order of frequency: "one," "three," "four," "one hundred," "seven," "one thousand," "ten," "sixty," "ten thousand," "six," "thirty," "two," "twelve," and "twenty." By presenting all of these numbers together and in this order, the part-of-speech list devoted to numbers helps readers remember these words better than they might if they came across them interspersed randomly in a frequency list of vocabulary, and allows readers to focus their memorization efforts on the numbers that occur frequently (like "one" and "three," which together occur twenty-five times, as opposed to "two" and "six," each of which occurs only twice). Finally, the part-of-speech lists can assist readers in noticing relationships between or among words that they might not otherwise perceive. For example, the list of disjunctives allows readers to observe that there are two words in Biblical Aramaic whose basic meaning is "but," בְּרַם and לָהֵן.

The third set of lists presents all the attested forms for each verbal stem in Biblical Aramaic. These forms are listed according to conjugation and in the order of what we have judged to be the forms' "regularity" (i.e., the degree to which they adhere to or depart from the patterns evidenced by strong verbs). In addition, next to each form is an indication of all the verses in which the form appears, so that the student may easily reference these texts and see the forms in context. One of the frustrations that students of Biblical Aramaic can face in the classroom is that they may be instructed to memorize various paradigms—for example, the D prefix conjugation or the tG participle—that present only strong verb forms (which may or may not occur in the Bible) or that contain forms occurring once or twice but which are presented alongside other forms as if they occurred frequently. Worse, students are sometimes asked to learn "made-up" forms that do not actually occur in the Bible but that have been created to fill out paradigms to give them a sense of completeness. The lists in this book provide an antidote to these inefficient methods of learning Aramaic verbs,

which are not well suited to fostering students' long-term retention of the information. Thus, when readers consult the list of D stem suffix conjugation verbs, they will immediately notice that the Bible contains about the same number of 3ms and 3mp forms (seven and eight, respectively); that it contains comparatively fewer 2ms and 1cs forms (three each); and that it contains no 3fs, 2fs, 3fp, 2mp, 2fp, or 1cp forms. Therefore, this list indicates to students that they should concentrate on learning the 3ms and 3mp forms of the D stem suffix conjugation, spend a little time learning the 2ms and 1cs forms, and not worry about forms for the person/gender/number combinations that are not attested. In this way, students can use their time as efficiently as possible and gain confidence that the forms on which they concentrate are actually attested in the Bible, and that they are relatively common. Another way in which these verb lists are helpful is that, by grouping forms from the same stem and conjugation together, they allow students to learn quickly and easily what the distinguishing characteristics of these forms are. For example, the section on D infinitives lists the ten such forms that occur in the Bible. It takes only a few moments of scanning this list to ascertain that the distinguishing characteristics of the D infinitive are the presence of a *patach* under the first root consonant, doubling of the second root consonant, *qamets* under the second root consonant, and final *qamets hê* (or, a few times, *qamets aleph*). It is much easier to appreciate that these features are what define this verbal form when looking at a list of ten or a dozen such forms than when looking at one or two such forms (as they might be presented in a grammar) or, in fact, than when reading a descriptive sentence like the preceding one.

Following the lists that present verbal forms by stem is a set of lists that present verbal forms by type of root: I-א, I-נ, II-י, III-ה, etc. One example of the many kinds of facts that students can learn by studying these lists is that III-ה verbs end with some frequency not in ה but in א. When one comes across a statement like this ("some III-ה verbs end not in ה but in א"), it can be easy to forget; by contrast, when one views the list of III-ה verbs in this book and sees these many forms ending in א alongside similar forms ending in ה, this information is much easier to retain. To take another example, the list of I-נ verbs helps readers quickly ascertain that the first root consonant of such verbs does not usually assimilate, making these forms relatively easy to identify. The lists include geminate roots; roots whose first consonant undergoes metathesis with the preformative ת of the tG or tD stems; and the root סלק, which manifests peculiarities (assimilated ל, prefixed נ) in a few of its forms.

Next comes a final pair of verb lists. The first presents all the attested verb forms in Biblical Aramaic by the frequency with which they occur, and the second lists verbal roots according to the number of stems in which they are attested.

The sixth set of lists presents every suffixed form in Biblical Aramaic, organized by suffix (3ms, 3fs, 2ms, etc.), and within this organizational structure words are listed by part of speech. Thus, it takes only a few seconds of scanning the list of 2ms suffixed forms to understand that this suffix appears almost invariably as ךָ, regardless of the part of speech of the word (noun, preposition, or verb) to which it is suffixed. On the other hand, the list of 1cs suffixed forms indicates that this suffix manifests variety with respect to its form depending on whether it is attached to a singular or plural noun or to a verb. Again, facts like these, when presented primarily in the guise of grammatical principles, can be difficult to remember. When such facts are grasped by looking at the totality of attested forms that embody the principles, they are hard to forget.

A brief, seventh set of lists presents words that are easily confused: homonymns (words that sound identical, i.e., whose consonants and vowels are the same) and consonantal homographs (i.e., words whose consonants are identical but whose vowels differ). A final, eighth

set of lists presents loanwords in Biblical Aramaic, grouped by the language from which Aramaic borrowed them (Persian, Sumerian, Akkadian, Greek, or Hebrew).

All of the word lists found in this book are intended to complement the book's "Reader" portion. These two sections—the Reader and the word lists—are meant to mutually reinforce each other, and readers are encouraged to shuttle back and forth between the two. At the risk of being slightly reductionistic, it seems fair to say that learning to read a dead language well effectively boils down to (1) learning and reviewing the language's vocabulary and grammar (phonology, morphology, and syntax) and (2) regularly reading texts written in the language. These two activities need to be undertaken simultaneously throughout the process that begins with one's initial study of the language and culminates in mastery and the ability to read fluently. *Biblical Aramaic: A Reader & Handbook* has been designed as a "one-stop shop" to empower anyone who is studying, or who once studied, Biblical Aramaic to be able to read the Bible's Aramaic texts with comprehension, ease, and enjoyment, and to sustain the ability to do so over the long term.

A Note on the Biblical Text Used in This Book

Biblical Aramaic: A Reader & Handbook uses the biblical text presented in *Biblia Hebraica Leningradensia* (*BHL*).[14] Instances in which *BHL* differs from the original manuscript of *Codex Leningradensis* ("L") or the presentation of the text in *Biblia Hebraica Stuttgartensia* (*BHS*) are marked in the lexical notes, enabling the reader to trace any apparent discrepancies among the major editions of the Masoretic Text. These are relatively few in number and of minimal significance. *Biblical Aramaic: A Reader & Handbook* does not use the Masorah, except for instances of *Ketiv-Qere*. As a visual marker, any word with a *Ketiv-Qere* tradition is presented in the text without vowel points. Both the *Ketiv* and *Qere* forms (marked as "K" and "Q" respectively) are then given in the relevant lexical note in the reading apparatus. In order to facilitate ease of use, the word lists in this book do not generally deal with the differences between *Ketiv* and *Qere* forms; for simplicity's sake, and in order to reflect the vocalization tradition employed by the Masoretes, these lists are based primarily on *Qere* forms (though *Ketiv* forms are occasionally presented, and marked as such, in these lists as well).

Final Comments

The production of *Biblical Aramaic: A Reader & Handbook* follows on from our production of the *BHS Reader*. In some sense, then, this has all been one continuous scholarly journey that has taken the better part of a decade. In addition to the three of us who worked on the *BHS Reader* (Donald R. Vance, George Athas, and Yael Avrahami), we welcome the contribution of Jonathan Kline, who created the extensive word lists found after the Reader part of this volume. Jonathan is by no means new to our "team," having been an editor with Hendrickson during the final stages of the production of the *BHS Reader*. But he joins us now as a contributor to *Biblical Aramaic: A Reader & Handbook*. Once again, we have enjoyed the privilege of truly international and ecumenical cooperation, driven chiefly by Donald R. Vance. Our hope is that this volume increases the number and proficiency of readers engaging directly with the Bible's Aramaic texts.

---

14. Edited by Aron Dotan; Peabody, MA: Hendrickson, 2001.

ABBREVIATIONS

1	first person	*HALOT*	see Bibliography
2	second person	Heb	Hebrew
3	third person	Hp	Ho/Huphʻal (הָ/הֻפְעַל) stem
abs	absolute state	hypoth	hypothetical
acc	accusative or accusatival	impers	impersonal
adj	adjective	imv	imperative mood
adv	adverb	indef	indefinite
Akk	Akkadian	indep	independent
alt	alternative, alternate	inf	infinitive
Ass	Assyrian	interj	interjection
ATT.	attested	interr	interrogative
BDB	see Bibliography	intrans	intransitive
BHL	*Biblia Hebraica Leningradensia*	juss	jussive mood
BHS	*Biblia Hebraica Stuttgartensia*	K	*ketiv* variant
c	common	LEX.	lexical
card	cardinal number	loc	locative
caus	causal	lw	loanword
conj	conjunct, conjunction	m	masculine
CONJ.	conjugation	MN	month name
correl	correlative	n	noun
cstr	construct state	neg	negative
D	Paʻel (פִּעֵל) stem	NJPS	*Tanakh: The Holy Scriptures:*
def	definite		*The New JPS Translation according*
dem	demonstrative		*to the Traditional Hebrew Text.* The
dir	direct		Jewish Publication Society, 1985
dist	distal (i.e., far)	NRSV	New Revised Standard Version
disj	disjunctive	num	number
Dp	Puʻal (פֻּעַל) stem	obj	object
du	dual	p	plural
Ed	edition	part	particle
epex	epexegetical	PC	prefix conjugation
f	feminine	pers	personal
FREQ.	frequency	Pers	Persian
G	Peʻal (פְּעַל) stem	PGN	person/gender/number
gen	genitive or genitival	*pl. tan.*	*plurale tantum*
Gk	Greek		("only plural," i.e., a word that
GN	geographical name		occurs only in the plural)
Gp	Peʻil (פְּעִיל) stem	PN	personal name
H	A/Haphʻel (א/הַפְעֵל) stem	POS	part of speech
hapax	*hapax legomenon,*	prep	preposition
	a word that occurs only once	pron	pronoun

prox	proximal (i.e., near)	Sum	Sumerian
ptcp	participle	*s.v.*	*sub verbo*
purp	purpose		("under the word")
Q	*qere* variant	sx	suffix
rd	read or reads	*tan.*	see *pl. tan.*
rel	relative	tD	Hithpaʿal (הִתְפָּעַל) stem
s	singular	temp	temporal
sc	suffix conjugation	tG	Hithpeʿel (הִתְפְּעֵל) stem
Š	Shaphʿel (שַׁפְעֵל) stem	trans	transitive
Št	Hishtaphʿal (הִשְׁתַּפְעַל) stem	vb	verb
smthg	something	w/	with
subord	subordinating	=	equals, is the same as

Bibliography

BDB   Brown, Francis, Samuel R. Driver, and Charles A. Briggs. *A Hebrew and English Lexicon of the Old Testament.* Corrected ed. Oxford: Clarendon, 1953.

HALOT Koehler, Ludwig, Walter Baumgartner, and Johann J. Stamm. *The Hebrew and Aramaic Lexicon of the Old Testament.* Translated and edited under the supervision of M. E. J. Richardson. 5 vols. Leiden: Brill, 1994–2000.

THE BIBLICAL
ARAMAIC TEXTS

GENESIS בראשית

31 ⁴⁷ וַיִּקְרָא־לֹו לָבָ֔ן ⁿיְגַ֖ר ᶜשָׂהֲדוּתָ֑א ᶜᵇ וְֽיַעֲקֹ֔ב קָ֥רָא לֹ֖ו גַּלְעֵֽד׃

JEREMIAH ירמיהו

10 ¹¹ ᵃכִּדְנָה֙ ᵇתֵּאמְר֣וּן לְהֹ֔ום ᶜאֱלָ֣הַיָּ֔א ᵈדִּֽי־ᵉˢˢˢˢˢˢ שְׁמַיָּ֥א ᶠוְאַרְקָ֖א ᵍלָ֣א עֲבַ֑דוּ ʰיֵאבַ֧דוּ מֵֽאַרְעָ֛א ⁱוּמִן־תְּחֹ֥ות ᵏשְׁמַיָּ֖א ᶠאֵֽלֶּה׃ ˢ

Genesis 31:47

^{47ᵃ}noun ms cstr יְגַר hapax *heap*.
^ᵇnoun fs emph שָׂהֲדוּ hapax *witness, testimony*. ^{ᶜ⁻ᶜ}GN *Jegar-sahadutha* = *stone-monument witness*.

Jeremiah 10:11

^{11ᵃ}prox dem pron ms דְּנָה w/ prep כְּ *according to this, thus*. ^ᵇG PC 2mp אמר. ^ᶜprep לְ w/ 3mp gen sx. ^ᵈnoun mp emph אֱלָה. ^ᵉrel pron דִּי *who*. ^ᶠnoun mp emph שְׁמַיִן. ^ᵍnoun fs emph אֲרַק *earth, land*. ^ʰG sc 3mp עבד. ^ⁱG juss 3mp אבד *perish*. ^ʲnoun fs emph אֲרַע *earth, land*. ^ᵏprep תְּחֹות *under*. ^ˡprox dem pron mp אֵלֶּה *these*.

Daniel דניאל

2 ⁴ וַיְדַבְּרוּ הַכַּשְׂדִּים לַמֶּלֶךְ אֲרָמִית^a מַלְכָּא לְעָלְמִין^b חֱיִי^c אֱמַר^d חֶלְמָא^e לְעַבְדָיךְ^f וּפִשְׁרָא נְחַוֵּא^g׃ ⁵ עָנֵה^a מַלְכָּא וְאָמַר^b לכשדיא^c מִלְּתָא^d מִנִּי^e אַזְדָּא^f הֵן^g לָא תְהוֹדְעוּנַּנִי^h חֶלְמָא וּפִשְׁרֵהּ^j הַדָּמִין^k תִּתְעַבְדוּן^{ml} וּבָתֵּיכוֹןⁿ נְוָלִי^o יִתְּשָׂמוּן^p׃ ⁶ וְהֵן^a חֶלְמָא וּפִשְׁרֵהּ^b תְּהַחֲוֹן^c מַתְּנָן^e וּנְבִזְבָּה^f וִיקָר^g שַׂגִּיא^h תְּקַבְּלוּןⁱ מִן־קָדָמָי^j לָהֵן^k חֶלְמָא וּפִשְׁרֵהּ הַחֲוֹנִי^l׃ ⁷ עֲנוֹ^a תִנְיָנוּת^b וְאָמְרִין^c מַלְכָּא חֶלְמָא^d יֵאמַר^e לְעַבְדוֹהִי^f וּפִשְׁרָה נְהַחֲוֵה^g׃ ⁸ עָנֵה^a מַלְכָּא וְאָמַר^b מִן־יַצִּיב^c יָדַע^d אֲנָה^e דִּי^f עִדָּנָא^g אַנְתּוּן^h זָבְנִיןⁱ כָּל־קֳבֵל^j־^k דִּי^l חֲזֵיתוֹן^m דִּי אַזְדָּא^o מִנִּי^p מִלְּתָא^q׃

Daniel 2:4–7:28

4 ^aadj fs abs אֲרָמִי *Aramaic* Probably a scribal note indicating that the text switches to Aramaic here and stays such through Dan 7:28. BDB treats it as an adv, and the use in Ezra 4:7 (twice) supports this. Perhaps the form is to be understood as an adverbial accusative, …*in Aramaic*. ^bnoun mp abs עָלַם *eternity*. ^cG imv 2ms חיה *live*. ^dG imv 2ms אמר. ^enoun ms emph חֵלֶם *dream*. ^fK לְעַבְדָיךְ noun mp w/ 2ms gen sx, Q לְעַבְדָךְ noun ms w/ 2ms gen sx, both *slave, servant*. ^gD PC 1cp חוה *show, make known, declare*.

5 ^aG ptcp ms abs I ענה. ^bG ptcp ms abs אמר. ^cK לְכַשְׂדָּיֵא, Q לְכַשְׂדָּאֵי, both noun mp emph כַּשְׂדָּי *Babylonian astrologer* or *sage*. ^dnoun fs emph מִלָּה *word*. ^eprep מִן w/ 1cs gen sx. ^fadj fs abs אַזְדָּא Pers lw *publicly known* thus *irrevocable*. ^ghypoth conj הֵן *if*. ^hH PC 2mp ידע w/ 1cs acc sx. ⁱnoun ms emph חֵלֶם *dream*. ^jnoun ms פְּשַׁר w/ 3ms gen sx. ^knoun mp abs הַדָּם Pers lw *limb*. ^ltG PC 2mp עבד. ^{m–m}= *torn limb from limb*. ⁿnoun mp בַּיִת w/ 2mp gen sx. ^onoun fs abs נְוָלוּ Akk lw (?) *dunghill; latrine pit*. ^ptG PC 3mp שׂים.

6 ^ahypoth conj הֵן *if*. ^bnoun ms emph חֵלֶם *dream*. ^cnoun ms פְּשַׁר w/ 3ms gen sx. ^dH PC 2mp חוה *show, make known, declare*. ^enoun fp abs מַתְּנָה *gift*. ^fnoun fs abs נְבִזְבָּה *present, reward*. ^gnoun ms abs יְקָר *honor*. ^hadj ms abs שַׂגִּיא *great*. ⁱD PC 2mp קבל *receive*. ^jprep קֳדָם w/ 1cs gen sx. ^kconj I לָהֵן *therefore*. ^lH imv 2mp חוה w/ 1cs acc sx *show, make known, declare*.

7 ^aG SC 3mp I ענה. ^badv תִּנְיָנוּת hapax *second time, again*. ^cG ptcp mp abs אמר. ^dnoun ms emph חֵלֶם *dream*. ^eG juss 3ms אמר. ^fnoun mp עֲבֵד w/ 3ms gen sx *slave, servant*. ^gH PC 1cp חוה *show, make known, declare*.

8 ^aG ptcp ms abs I ענה. ^bG ptcp ms abs אמר. ^cnoun ms abs יַצִּיב w/ מִן = adv *certainly*. ^dG ptcp ms abs ידע. ^eindep pers pron 1cs אֲנָה *I*. ^fepex conj דִּי *that*. ^gnoun ms emph עִדָּן *time*. ^hindep pers pron 2mp אַנְתּוּן hapax *you*. ⁱG ptcp mp abs זבן hapax *buy*. ^j= לְ + כְּ *according to*. ^ksubord conj דִּי *that*. ^{l–l}= *because, since*. ^mG SC 2mp חזה *because*. ⁿcaus conj דִּי *because*. ^oadj fs abs אַזְדָּא Pers lw *publicly known* thus *irrevocable*. ^pprep מִן w/ 1cs gen sx. ^qnoun fs emph מִלָּה *word*.

9 דִּי הֵן־חֶלְמָא לָא תְהֹודְעֻנַּנִי חֲדָה־הִיא דָתְכֹון וּמִלָּה כִדְבָה
וּשְׁחִיתָה הִזְמִנְתּוּן לְמֵאמַר קָדָמַי עַד דִּי עִדָּנָא יִשְׁתַּנֵּא לָהֵן
חֶלְמָא אֱמַרוּ לִי וְאִנְדַּע דִּי פִשְׁרֵהּ תְּהַחֲוֻנַּנִי: 10 עֲנֹו כַשְׂדָּיֵא
קָדָם־מַלְכָּא וְאָמְרִין לָא־אִיתַי אֲנָשׁ עַל־יַבֶּשְׁתָּא דִּי מִלַּת מַלְכָּא
יוּכַל לְהַחֲוָיָה כָּל־קֳבֵל דִּי כָּל־מֶלֶךְ רַב וְשַׁלִּיט מִלָּה כִדְנָה לָא
שְׁאֵל לְכָל־חַרְטֹם וְאָשַׁף וְכַשְׂדָּי: 11 וּמִלְּתָא דִי־מַלְכָּה שָׁאֵל
יַקִּירָה וְאָחֳרָן לָא אִיתַי דִּי יְחַוִּנַּהּ קֳדָם מַלְכָּא לָהֵן אֱלָהִין דִּי
מְדָרְהֹון עִם־בִּשְׂרָא לָא אִיתֹוהִי: 12 כָּל־קֳבֵל דְּנָה מַלְכָּא בְּנַס
וּקְצַף שַׂגִּיא וַאֲמַר לְהֹובָדָה לְכֹל חַכִּימֵי בָבֶל: 13 וְדָתָא נֶפְקַת
וְחַכִּימַיָּא מִתְקַטְּלִין וּבְעֹו דָּנִיֵּאל וְחַבְרֹוהִי לְהִתְקְטָלָה:
פ

9 ᵃepex conj דִּי *that.* ᵇhypoth conj הֵן *if.* ᶜnoun ms emph חֵלֶם *dream.* ᵈH pc 2mp ידע w/ 1cs acc sx. ᵉcard w/ f noun חַד *one.* ᶠindep pers pron 3fs הִיא as copula *is.* ᵍnoun fs דָּת w/ 2mp gen sx, Pers lw *verdict.* ʰnoun fs abs מִלָּה *word.* ⁱnoun fs abs כִּדְבָה hapax *lie, false.* ʲGp ptcp fs abs שׁחת *corrupted, bad.* ᵏK הַזְמִנְתּוּן H sc 2mp or זמן הִזְדְּמִנְתּוּן tD sc 2mp; Q הִזְדַּמִּנְתּוּן [L, BHS] tG sc 2mp or הִזְדְּמִנְתּוּן [Ed] tD sc 2mp זמן, all *conspire.* ˡG inf אמר. ᵐprep קֳדָם w/ 1cs gen sx. ⁿtemp conj דִּי *that.* ᵒnoun ms emph עִדָּן *time.* ᵖtD pc 3ms שנה intrans *change.* �q conj I לָהֵן *therefore.* ʳnoun ms emph חֵלֶם *dream.* ˢG imv 2mp אמר. ᵗprep לְ w/ 1cs gen sx. ᵘG pc 1cs ידע [L "וְאַ, BHL* (?) "אִ; BHS "וְאַ, Ed "וְאִ]. ᵛepex conj דִּי *that.* ʷnoun ms פְּשַׁר w/ 3ms gen sx. ˣH pc 2mp חוה w/ 1cs acc sx *show, make known, declare.*

10 ᵃG sc 3mp I ענה K לְכַשְׂדָּיֵא, Q לְכַשְׂדָּיֵא, both noun mp emph כַּשְׂדָּי *Babylonian astrologer* or *sage.* ᶜG ptcp mp abs אמר. ᵈpart. of existence אִיתַי *there is.* ᵉnoun fs emph יַבֶּשָׁה hapax *dry land, earth.* ᶠrel pron דִּי *who, which, that.* ᵍnoun fs cs מִלָּה *word, thing.* ʰG pc 3ms יכל *be able.* ⁱH inf חוה *show, make known, declare.* ʲ= כְּ + לְ *according to.* ᵏsubord conj דִּי *that.* ˡ⁻ˡ= *because, since.* ᵐnoun ms cs

כֹּל. ⁿadj ms abs רַב *great.* ᵒadj ms abs שַׁלִּיט *powerful, mighty.* ᵖnoun fs abs מִלָּה *word, thing.* �q prox dem pron ms דְּנָה w/ prep כְּ *like this.* ʳG sc 3ms שׁאל *ask.* ˢnoun ms abs חַרְטֹם *magician* [Ed "טֹם; L, BHS, BHL* "טֹם;]. ᵗnoun ms abs אָשַׁף Akk lw *conjurer; exorcist.* ᵘnoun ms abs כַּשְׂדָּי *Babylonian astrologer* or *sage.*

11 ᵃnoun fs emph מִלָּה *thing.* ᵇrel pron דִּי *which, that.* ᶜnoun ms emph מֶלֶךְ. ᵈG ptcp ms abs שׁאל *ask.* ᵉadj fs abs יַקִּיר *difficult.* ᶠadj ms abs אָחֳרָן *another.* ᵍpart. of existence אִיתַי *there is.* ʰD pc 3ms חוה w/ 3fs acc sx *show, make known, declare.* ⁱprep II לָהֵן *except.* ʲnoun ms cstr מְדֹור w/ 3mp gen sx *dwelling.* ᵏnoun ms emph בְּשַׂר *flesh.* ˡpart. of existence אִיתַי w/ 3ms gen sx *it is.*

12 ᵃ= כְּ + לְ *according to.* ᵇprox dem pron ms דְּנָה *this.* ᶜ⁻ᶜ= *because of this, therefore.* ᵈG sc 3ms בנס hapax *be enraged.* ᵉG sc 3ms קצף hapax *be furious.* ᶠadj ms abs שַׂגִּיא as adv *greatly.* ᵍG sc 3ms אמר. ʰH inf אבד *kill.* ⁱnoun ms cstr כֹּל. ʲadj mp cstr חַכִּים *wise.*

13 ᵃnoun fs emph דָּת Pers lw *decree.* ᵇG sc 3fs נפק *go out* = *be issued.* ᶜadj mp emph חַכִּים *wise.* ᵈtD ptcp mp abs קטל *be killed.* ᵉG sc 3mp בעה *seek.* ᶠnoun mp חֲבַר w/ 3ms gen sx *friend, companion.* ᵍtG inf קטל *be killed.*

14 בֵּאדַ֣יִן דָּנִיֵּ֗אל הֲתִיב֙ עֵטָ֣א וּטְעֵ֔ם לְאַרְי֕וֹךְ רַב־טַבָּחַיָּ֖א
דִּ֣י מַלְכָּ֑א דִּ֥י נְפַ֛ק לְקַטָּלָ֖ה לְחַכִּימֵ֥י בָבֶֽל׃ 15 עָנֵ֣ה וְאָמַ֗ר
לְאַרְי֨וֹךְ שַׁלִּיטָ֜א דִּֽי־מַלְכָּ֗א עַל־מָ֞ה דָתָ֤א מְהַחְצְפָה֙ מִן־
קֳדָ֣ם מַלְכָּ֔א אֱדַ֗יִן מִלְּתָ֛א הוֹדַ֥ע אַרְי֖וֹךְ לְדָנִיֵּֽאל׃ 16 וְדָ֣נִיֵּ֔אל עַ֖ל
וּבְעָ֣ה מִן־מַלְכָּ֑א דִּ֚י זְמָ֣ן יִנְתֶּן־לֵ֔הּ וּפִשְׁרָ֖א לְהַֽחֲוָיָ֥ה לְמַלְכָּֽא׃

פ

17 אֱדַ֥יִן דָּֽנִיֵּ֖אל לְבַיְתֵ֣הּ אֲזַ֑ל וְ֠לַחֲנַנְיָ֨ה מִֽישָׁאֵ֧ל וַעֲזַרְיָ֛ה חַבְר֖וֹהִי
מִלְּתָ֥א הוֹדַֽע׃ 18 וְרַחֲמִ֗ין לְמִבְעֵא֙ מִן־קֳדָם֙ אֱלָ֣הּ שְׁמַיָּ֔א עַל־רָזָ֖ה
דְּנָ֑ה דִּ֣י לָ֤א יְהֹֽבְדוּן֙ דָּנִיֵּ֣אל וְחַבְר֔וֹהִי עִם־שְׁאָ֖ר חַכִּימֵ֥י בָבֶֽל׃
19 אֱדַ֗יִן לְדָנִיֵּ֛אל בְּחֶזְוָ֥א דִֽי־לֵֽילְיָ֖א רָזָ֣ה גֲלִ֑י אֱדַ֙יִן֙ דָּֽנִיֵּ֔אל בָּרִ֖ךְ
לֶאֱלָ֥הּ שְׁמַיָּֽא׃ 20 עָנֵ֤ה דָֽנִיֵּאל֙ וְאָמַ֔ר לֶהֱוֵ֨א שְׁמֵ֤הּ דִּֽי־אֱלָהָא֙
מְבָרַ֔ךְ מִן־עָלְמָ֖א וְעַ֣ד־עָלְמָ֑א דִּ֧י חָכְמְתָ֛א וּגְבֽוּרְתָ֖א דִּֽי לֵ֥הּ ־

---

14 ^atemp adv אֱדַ֫יִן (w/ בְּ) *immediately; then.*
^bH sc תוב trans *return.* ^cnoun fs abs
עֵטָה hapax *counsel.* ^dnoun ms abs טְעֵם
good taste. ^ePN *Arioch.* ^fadj ms cstr רַב
chief. ^gnoun mp emph טַבָּח hapax *execu-tioners, bodyguard.* ^hgen part דִּי *of.* ⁱrel
pron דִּי *who, that.* ^jG sc 3ms נפק *go out.*
^kD inf קטל *kill.* ^ladj mp cstr חַכִּים *wise.*

15 ^aG ptcp ms abs I ענה. ^bG ptcp ms abs אמר.
^cPN *Arioch.* ^dnoun ms emph שַׁלִּיט *offi-cial.* ^egen part דִּי *of.* ^fimpers interr pron
מָה *what.* ^{g–g}= *why? for what purpose?*
^hnoun fs emph דָּת Pers lw *decree.* ⁱH ptcp
fs abs חצף *be harsh.* ^jnoun fs emph מִלָּה
matter. ^kH sc 3ms ידע.

16 ^aG sc 3ms II עלל *enter.* ^bG sc 3ms בעה *seek, request.* ^cpurp conj דִּי *so that.* ^dnoun ms
abs זְמָן *time.* ^eG pc 3ms נתן *give.* ^fprep לְ w/
3ms gen sx. ^gH inf חוה *show, make known, declare.*

17 ^aL, *BHL** דָּנִיֵּ֖; *BHS*, Ed דָּֽנִיֵּ֖. ^bnoun ms
בַּיִת w/ 3ms gen sx. ^cG sc 3ms אזל *go.* ^dPN
Hananiah. ^ePN *Mishael.* ^fPN *Azariah.*
^gnoun mp emph חֲבַר w/ 3ms gen sx *friend, com-*

panion. ^hnoun fs emph מִלָּה *matter.* ⁱH sc
3ms ידע.

18 ^anoun mp abs רַחֲמִין hapax *compassion.*
^bG inf בעה *seek.* ^cnoun mp emph שְׁמַיָן. ^dnoun ms emph רָזָה Pers lw *secret, mys-tery.* ^eprox dem adj ms דְּנָה *this.* ^fpurp conj
דִּי *so that.* ^gH pc 3mp אבד *kill.* ^hnoun mp
חֲבַר w/ 3ms gen sx *friend, companion.*
ⁱnoun ms cstr שְׁאָר *rest.* ^jadj mp cstr חַכִּים
wise.

19 ^anoun ms emph חֵזוּ *vision.* ^bgen part דִּי
of. ^cnoun ms emph לֵילִי *night.* ^dnoun ms
emph רָזָה Pers lw *secret, mystery.* ^eGp
sc 3ms גלה *be revealed.* ^fD sc 3ms II ברך
bless. ^gnoun mp emph שְׁמַיָן.

20 ^aG ptcp ms abs I ענה. ^bG ptcp ms abs אמר.
^cG juss 3ms הוה. ^dnoun ms שֵׁם w/ 3ms gen
sx *name.* ^egen part דִּי *of.* ^fnoun ms emph
אֱלָה [so *BHS*, Ed; L, *BHL** אֱלָֽהּ]. ^gDp ptcp
ms abs II ברך *blessed.* ^hnoun ms emph עָלַם
eternity. ⁱcaus conj דִּי *because.* ^jnoun fs
emph חָכְמָה *wisdom.* ^knoun fs emph גְּבוּרָה
might. ^lrel pron דִּי *which, that.* ^mprep לְ w/
3ms gen sx. ^{n–n}= *his.*

הִיאᵒ׃ ²¹ וְהֽוּאᵃ מְהַשְׁנֵאᵇ עִדָּנַיָּאᶜ וְזִמְנַיָּאᵈ מְהַעְדֵּהᵉ מַלְכִין וּמְהָקֵים

מַלְכִין יָהֵבᵍ חָכְמְתָאʰ לְחַכִּימִיןⁱ וּמַנְדְּעָאʲ לְיָדְעֵיᵏ בִינָהˡ׃ ²² הֽוּאᵃ

גָּלֵאᵇ עַמִּיקָתָאᶜ וּמְסַתְּרָתָאᵈ יָדַעᵉ מָהᶠ בַחֲשׁוֹכָאᵍ וּנְהִירָאʰ עִמֵּהⁱ

שְׁרֵאʲ׃ ²³ לָךְ‖ᵃ אֱלָהּ אֲבָהָתִיᵇ מְהוֹדֵאᶜ וּמְשַׁבַּחᵈ אֲנָהᵉ דִּיᶠ חָכְמְתָאᵍ

וּגְבוּרְתָאʰ יְהַבְתְּ לִי וּכְעַןᵏ הֽוֹדַעְתַּנִיˡ דִּֽי־בְעֵינָאᵐ מִנָּךְⁿ דִּֽי־מִלַּתᵖ

מַלְכָּא הוֹדַעְתֶּֽנָא�q׃ ²⁴ כָּל־קֳבֵל דְּנָהᶜ‖ᵇ דָּנִיֵּאל עַלᵈ עַל־אַרְיוֹךְᵉ

דִּיᶠ מַנִּיᵍ מַלְכָּא לְהוֹבָדָהʰ לְחַכִּימֵי בָּבֶל אֲזַלʲ וְכֵןᵏ אֲמַר־לֵהᵐ

לְחַכִּימֵי בָּבֶל אַל־ⁿתְּהוֹבֵדᵒ קֳדָם מַלְכָּא הַעֵלְנִיᵖ וּפִשְׁרָא לְמַלְכָּא

אֲחַוֵּאq׃ ס ²⁵ אֱדַיִן אַרְיוֹךְᵈ בְּהִתְבְּהָלָהᵇ הַנְעֵלᶜ לְדָנִיֵּאל

קֳדָם מַלְכָּא וְכֵן אֲמַר־לֵהᵉ דִּֽי־הַשְׁכַּחַתʰ גְּבַרⁱ מִן־בְּנֵיʲ גָלוּתָאᵏ דִּי

יְהוּדᵐ דִּיⁿ פִּשְׁרָא לְמַלְכָּא יְהוֹדַעᵒ׃ ²⁶ עָנֵהᵃ מַלְכָּא וְאָמַרᵇ לְדָנִיֵּאל

---

20 ᵒindep pers pron 3fs הִיא as copula *are*.

21 ᵃindep pers pron 3ms הֽוּא *he*. ᵇH ptcp ms abs שנה trans *change*. ᶜnoun mp emph עִדָּן indicates time in general or a length of time such as a year *time*. ᵈnoun mp emph זְמָן indicates a point in time, a *moment*, or a set or fixed time such as the *date* of a recurring feast, or even the *time* of an appointment, e.g., the third hour. ᵉH ptcp ms abs עדה *remove, depose*. ᶠH ptcp ms abs קום. ᵍG ptcp ms abs יהב. ʰnoun fs emph חָכְמָה *wisdom*. ⁱadj mp abs חַכִּים *wise*. ʲnoun ms emph מִנְדַּע *knowledge*. ᵏG ptcp mp cstr ידע. ˡnoun fs abs בִּינָה hapax *understanding*.

22 ᵃindep pers pron 3ms הֽוּא *he*. ᵇG ptcp ms abs גלה *reveal*. ᶜadj fp emph עַמִּיק hapax *deep*. ᵈDp ptcp fp emph I סתר hapax *hidden*. ᵉG ptcp ms abs ידע. ᶠimpers correl pron מָה *that which, what*. ᵍnoun ms emph חֲשׁוֹךְ hapax *darkness*. ʰK וּנְהִירָא noun ms emph נְהִיר hapax *light*, Q וּנְהוֹרָא noun ms emph נְהוֹר hapax *light*. ⁱprep עִם w/ 3ms gen sx. ʲGp ptcp ms abs שרה *dwell*.

23 ᵃprep לְ w/ 2ms gen sx. ᵇnoun mp אַב w/ 1cs gen sx *father*. ᶜH ptcp ms abs ידה *give thanks*. ᵈD ptcp ms abs שבח *praise*.

ᵉindep pers pron 1cs אֲנָה *I*. ᶠrel pron דִּי *who, which, that*. ᵍnoun fs emph חָכְמָה *wisdom*. ʰnoun fs emph גְּבוּרָה *might*. ⁱG sc 2ms יהב. ʲprep לְ w/ 1cs gen sx. ᵏtransitional conj כְּעַן introduces new idea *now*. ˡH sc 2ms ידע w/ 1cs acc sx. ᵐG sc 1cp בעה *seek*. ⁿprep מִן w/ 2ms gen sx. ᵒcaus conj דִּי *because*. ᵖnoun fs cstr מִלָּה *word*. qH sc 2ms ידע w/ 1cp acc sx.

24 ᵃ= כְּ + לְ *according to*. ᵇprox dem pron ms דְּנָה *this*. ᶜ⁻ᶜ= *because of this, therefore*. ᵈG sc 3ms II עלל *enter*. ᵉPN *Arioch*. ᶠrel pron דִּי *who, that*. ᵍD sc 3ms מנה *appoint*. ʰH inf אבד *kill*. ⁱadj mp cstr חַכִּים *wise*. ʲG sc 3ms אזל *go*. ᵏadv כֵּן *thus*. ˡG sc 3ms אמר. ᵐprep לְ w/ 3ms gen sx. ⁿneg part אַל *not*. ᵒH juss 2ms אבד *kill*. ᵖH imv 2ms II עלל w/ 1cs acc sx *bring*. qD PC 1cs חוה *show, make known, declare*.

25 ᵃPN *Arioch*. ᵇnoun fs abs הִתְבְּהָלָה *haste*. ᶜH sc 3ms II עלל *bring*. ᵈadv כֵּן *thus*. ᵉG sc 3ms אמר. ᶠprep לְ w/ 3ms gen sx. ᵍepex conj דִּי *that*. ʰH sc 1cs שכח *find*. ⁱnoun ms abs גְּבַר *man, person*. ʲnoun mp cstr II בַּר *son*. ᵏnoun fs emph גָּלוּ *exile*. ˡgen part דִּי *of*. ᵐGN *Judah*. ⁿrel pron דִּי *who, that*. ᵒH PC 3ms ידע.

26 ᵃG ptcp ms abs I ענה. ᵇG ptcp ms abs אמר.

דִּיᵉ שְׁמֵהּᵈ בֵּלְטְשַׁאצַּרᵉ הַאִיתָיᶠ כָּהֵלᵍ לְהוֹדָעֻתַנִיʰ חֶלְמָאⁱ דִּי־חֲזֵיתʲ
וּפִשְׁרֵהּᵏ: 27 עָנֵהᵃ דָנִיֵּאל קֳדָם מַלְכָּא וְאָמַרᵇ רָזָהᶜ דִּי־מַלְכָּא שָׁאֵלᵈ
לָא חַכִּימִיןᶠ אָֽשְׁפִיןᵍ חַרְטֻמִּיןʰ גָּזְרִיןⁱ יָכְלִיןʲ לְהַחֲוָיָהᵏ לְמַלְכָּא: 28 בְּרַםᵃ
אִיתַיᵇ אֱלָהּ בִּשְׁמַיָּא גָּלֵאᵈ רָזִיןᵉ וְהוֹדַעᶠ לְמַלְכָּא נְבוּכַדְנֶצַּרᵍ מָהᵍ דִּי־
לֶהֱוֵאʲ בְּאַחֲרִיתᵏ יוֹמַיָּאˡ חֶלְמָ֥ᵐ וְחֶזְוֵיⁿ רֵאשָׁךᵒ עַֽל־מִשְׁכְּבָךᵖ דְּנָהᵟ
הֽוּא: פ

29 אַנְתָּהᵃ מַלְכָּא רַעְיוֹנָךᵇ עַל־מִשְׁכְּבָךᶜ סְלִקוּᵈ מָהᵉ דִּיᵍ לֶהֱוֵאʰ
אַחֲרֵיⁱ דְנָהʲ וְגָלֵאᵏ רָזַיָּאˡ הוֹדְעָךᵐ מָה־דִי לֶהֱוֵא: 30 וַאֲנָהᵃ לָא
בְחָכְמָהᵇ דִּי־אִיתַיᵈ בִּיᵉ מִן־כָּל־חַיַּיָּאᵍ רָזָאʰ דְּנָהⁱ גֱּלִיʲ לִי לְהֵןᵏ
עַל־דִּבְרַתᵐ דִּיⁿ פִּשְׁרָא לְמַלְכָּא יְהוֹדְעוּן וְרַעְיוֹנֵי לִבְבָךᵣ תִּנְדַּעᵣ:
31 אַנְתָּהᵃ מַלְכָּא חָזֵהᵇ הֲוַיְתᶜ וַאֲלוּᵈ צְלֵםᵉ חַדᶠ שַׂגִּיאᵍ צַלְמָאʰ דִּכֵּןⁱ

---

26 ᶜrel pron דִּי *who, that.* ᵈnoun ms שֵׁם w/ 3ms gen sx *name.* ᵉPN Belteshazzar. ᶠK הַֽאִיתָיִךְ, Q הַאִיתָי, both part. of existence אִיתַי w/ interr הַ and 2ms gen sx *are you?* ᵍG ptcp ms abs כהל *be able.* ʰH inf ידע w/ 1cs acc sx. ⁱnoun ms emph חֲלֵם *dream.* ʲG sc 1cs חזה. ᵏnoun ms פְּשַׁר w/ 3ms gen sx.

27 ᵃG ptcp ms abs I ענה. ᵇG ptcp ms abs אמר. ᶜnoun ms emph רָזָה Pers lw *secret, mystery.* ᵈrel pron דִּי *about which.* ᵉG ptcp ms abs שׁאל *ask.* ᶠadj mp abs חַכִּים *wise.* ᵍnoun mp abs אָשַׁף Akk lw *conjurer; exorcist.* ʰnoun mp abs חַרְטֹם *magician* [so BHS, Ed; L, BHL* טֻמִּין]. ⁱG ptcp mp abs גזר *diviner.* ʲG ptcp mp abs יכל *be able.* ᵏH inf חוה *show, make known, declare.*

28 ᵃdisj בְּרַם *but.* ᵇpart. of existence אִיתַי *there is.* ᶜnoun mp emph שְׁמַיִן. ᵈG ptcp ms abs גלה *revealer.* ᵉnoun mp abs רָזָה Pers lw *secret, mystery.* ᶠH sc 3ms ידע. ᵍimpers correl pron מָה *what.* ʰrel pron דִּי *which, that.* ⁱ⁻ⁱ= *that which; whatever.* ʲG pc 3ms הוה. ᵏnoun fs cstr אַחֲרִי *end.* ˡnoun mp emph יוֹם *day.* ᵐnoun ms חֲלֵם w/ 2ms gen sx *dream.* ⁿnoun mp cstr חֱזוּ *vision.* ᵒnoun ms רֵאשׁ w/ 2ms gen sx *head.* ᵖnoun ms מִשְׁכַּב w/ 2ms gen sx *bed.* ᵟprox dem pron ms דְּנָה *this.* ʳindep pers pron 3ms הוּא as copula *is.*

29 ᵃK אַנְתָּה, Q אַנְתְּ, both indep pers pron

2ms אַנְתְּ *you.* ᵇnoun ms רַעְיוֹן w/ 2ms gen sx *thought.* ᶜnoun ms מִשְׁכַּב w/ 2ms gen sx *bed.* ᵈG sc 3mp סלק *come up.* ᵉimpers correl pron מָה *what.* ᶠrel pron דִּי *which, that.* ᵍ⁻ᵍ= *that which; whatever.* ʰG pc 3ms הוה. ⁱprep אַחֲרֵי [HALOT] *after.* ʲprox dem pron ms דְּנָה *this.* ᵏG ptcp ms abs גלה *revealer.* ˡnoun mp emph רָזָה Pers lw *secret, mystery.* ᵐH sc 3ms ידע w/ 2ms acc sx.

30 ᵃindep pers pron 1cs אֲנָה *I.* ᵇnoun fs abs חָכְמָה *wisdom.* ᶜrel pron דִּי *who, which, that.* ᵈpart. of existence אִיתַי *there is.* ᵉprep בְּ w/ 1cs gen sx. ᶠnoun ms cstr כֹּל. ᵍadj mp emph I חַי *living.* ʰnoun ms emph רָזָה Pers lw *secret, mystery.* ⁱprox dem adj ms דְּנָה *this.* ʲGp sc 3ms גלה *be revealed.* ᵏprep לְ w/ 1cs gen sx. ˡdisj II לָהֵן *but.* ᵐnoun fs cstr דִּבְרָה *matter.* ⁿsubord conj דִּי *that.* ᵒ⁻ᵒ= *for the purpose of, for the sake of, that, so that.* ᵖH pc 3mp ידע. ᵟnoun mp cstr רַעְיוֹן *thought.* ʳnoun ms לְבַב w/ 2ms gen sx *heart.* ˢG pc 2ms ידע.

31 ᵃK אַנְתָּה, Q אַנְתְּ, both indep pers pron 2ms אַנְתְּ *you.* ᵇG ptcp ms abs חזה. ᶜG sc 2ms הוה. ᵈinterj אֲלוּ *behold!* ᵉnoun ms abs צְלֵם *statue.* ᶠcard w/ m noun חַד *one, a.* ᵍadj ms abs שַׂגִּיא *great.* ʰnoun ms emph צְלֵם *statue.* ⁱdist dem adj c, s דִּכֵּן *that.*

רַב‏ וְזִיוֵהּ‏ יַתִּיר‏ קָאֵם‏ לְקׇבְלָךְ‏ וְרֵוֵהּ‏ דְּחִיל‏: 32 הוּא‏ צַלְמָא‏
רֵאשֵׁהּ‏ דִּי־דְהַב‏ טָב‏ חֲדוֹהִי‏ וּדְרָעוֹהִי‏ דִּי כְסַף‏ מְעוֹהִי‏ וְיַרְכָתֵהּ‏
דִּי נְחָשׁ‏: 33 שָׁקוֹהִי‏ דִּי פַרְזֶל‏ רַגְלוֹהִי‏ מִנְּהוֹן‏ דִּי פַרְזֶל‏ וּמִנְּהוֹן‏
דִּי חֲסַף‏: 34 חָזֵה‏ הֲוַיְתָ‏ עַד‏ דִּי הִתְגְּזֶרֶת‏ אֶבֶן‏ דִּי־לָא‏ בִידַיִן‏
וּמְחָת‏ לְצַלְמָא‏ עַל־רַגְלוֹהִי‏ דִּי פַרְזְלָא‏ וְחַסְפָּא‏ וְהַדֵּקֶת‏ הִמּוֹן‏:
35 בֵּאדַיִן‏ דָּקוּ‏ כַחֲדָה‏ פַּרְזְלָא‏ חַסְפָּא‏ נְחָשָׁא‏ כַּסְפָּא‏ וְדַהֲבָא‏
וַהֲווֹ‏ כְּעוּר‏ מִן־אִדְּרֵי־קַיִט‏ וּנְשָׂא‏ הִמּוֹן‏ רוּחָא‏ וְכׇל־אֲתַר‏ לָא־
הִשְׁתֲּכַח‏ לְהוֹן‏ וְאַבְנָא‏ ׀ דִּי־מְחָת‏ לְצַלְמָא‏ הֲוָת‏ לְטוּר‏ רַב‏
וּמְלָת‏ כׇּל־אַרְעָא‏: 36 דְּנָה‏ חֶלְמָא‏ וּפִשְׁרֵהּ‏ נֵאמַר‏ קֳדָם־מַלְכָּא‏:
37 אַנתה‏ מַלְכָּא‏ מֶלֶךְ‏ מַלְכַיָּא‏ דִּי אֱלָהּ‏ שְׁמַיָּא‏ מַלְכוּתָא‏ חִסְנָא‏

31 jadj ms abs רַב great. knoun ms זִיו w/ 3ms gen sx brightness, radiance. ladj ms abs יַתִּיר extraordinary, excessive. mG ptcp ms abs קוּם. לְ + noun ms cstr קֳבֵל w/ 2ms gen sx to your front = before you. onoun ms רֵו w/ 3ms gen sx appearance. pGp ptcp ms abs דחל feared, fearsome.

32 adist dem adj ms הוּא that. bnoun ms emph צְלֵם statue. cnoun ms רֵאשׁ w/ 3ms gen sx head. dgen part דִּי of. enoun ms abs דְּהַב gold. fadj ms abs טָב good. gnoun ms emph חֲדֵה w/ 3ms gen sx hapax chest. hnoun fp דְּרָע w/ 3ms gen sx, hapax arm. inoun ms abs כְּסַף silver. jnoun mp מְעֵה w/ 3ms gen sx hapax belly. knoun fp יַרְכָה w/ 3ms gen sx hapax thigh. lnoun ms abs נְחָשׁ bronze.

33 anoun fp שָׁק w/ 3ms gen sx hapax shin, leg. bgen part דִּי of. cnoun ms abs פַּרְזֶל iron. dnoun fp רְגַל w/ 3ms gen sx foot. eK מִנְּהוֹן prep מִן w/ 3mp gen sx, Q מִנְּהֵין [BHS; Ed הֵן"; L, BHL* הֵן"] prep מִן w/ 3fp gen sx. fK וּמִנְּהוֹן prep מִן w/ 3mp gen sx, Q וּמִנְּהֵין [BHS הֵן"; Ed הֵן"; L, BHL* הֵן"] prep מִן w/ 3fp gen sx. gnoun ms abs חֲסַף clay.

34 aG ptcp ms abs חזה. bG sc 2ms הוה. ctemp conj דִּי that. dtG sc 3fs גזר be cut out. enoun fs abs אֶבֶן stone. frel pron דִּי which, that. g-g= (w/ בְּ) not by means of, without. hnoun fp abs יַד hand. iG sc 3fs מחא strike. jnoun ms emph צְלֵם statue. knoun fp רְגַל w/ 3ms gen sx foot. lgen

part דִּי of. mnoun ms emph פַּרְזֶל iron. nnoun ms emph חֲסַף clay. oH sc 3fs דקק pulverize. pindep pers pron 3mp הִמּוֹן as dir obj them.

35 atemp adv אֱדַיִן (w/ בְּ) immediately; then. bG sc 3mp דקק break. ccard w/ f noun חַד one, (w/ כְּ) as one, together. dnoun ms emph פַּרְזֶל iron. enoun ms emph חֲסַף clay. fnoun ms emph נְחָשׁ bronze. gnoun ms emph כְּסַף silver. hnoun ms emph דְּהַב gold. iG sc 3mp הוה. jnoun ms abs עוּר hapax chaff. knoun mp cstr אִדַּר hapax threshing floor. lnoun ms abs קַיִט hapax summer. mG sc 3ms נשא carry, lift. nindep pers pron 3mp הִמּוֹן as dir obj them. onoun fs emph רוּח wind. pnoun ms cstr כֹּל. qnoun ms abs אֲתַר place. rtG sc 3ms שכח be found. sprep לְ w/ 3mp gen sx. tnoun fs emph אֶבֶן stone. urel pron דִּי which, that. vG sc 3fs מחא strike. wnoun ms emph צְלֵם statue. xG sc 3fs הוה. ynoun ms abs טוּר mountain. zadj ms abs רַב great. aaG sc 3fs מלא fill. bbnoun fs emph אֲרַע earth.

36 aprox dem pron ms דְּנָה this. bnoun ms emph חֵלֶם dream. cnoun ms פְּשַׁר w/ 3ms gen sx. dG pc 1cp אמר.

37 aK אַנתָּה, Q אַנְתְּ, both indep pers pron 2ms אַנְתְּ you. bnoun mp emph מֶלֶךְ. crel pron דִּי who, that. dnoun mp emph שְׁמַיִן. enoun fs emph מַלְכוּ kingship, sovereignty. fnoun ms emph חֲסֵן [BDB חֲסַן] power.

וְתִקְפָּ֖א֮ וְיִקָרָ֑א֒ יְהַב־לָ֑ךְ 38 וּבְכָל־דִּ֣י דָֽאֲרִ֩ין בְּֽנֵי־אֲנָשָׁ֨א חֵיוַ֤ת בָּרָא֙ וְעוֹף־שְׁמַיָּ֔א יְהַ֣ב בִּידָ֔ךְ וְהַשְׁלְטָ֖ךְ בְּכָלְּה֑וֹן אַ֥נְתְּה־ה֖וּא רֵאשָׁ֥ה דִּֽי דַהֲבָֽא׃ 39 וּבַתְרָ֗ךְ תְּק֛וּם מַלְכ֥וּ אָחֳרִ֖י אֲרַ֣ע מִנָּ֑ךְ וּמַלְכ֨וּ תְלִיתָ֤יָא אָחֳרִי֙ דִּ֣י נְחָשָׁ֔א דִּ֥י תִשְׁלַ֖ט בְּכָל־אַרְעָֽא׃ 40 וּמַלְכוּ֙ רְבִיעָיָ֔ה תֶּהֱוֵ֥א תַקִּיפָ֖ה כְּפַרְזְלָ֑א כָּל־קֳבֵ֞ל דִּ֧י פַרְזְלָ֛א מְהַדֵּ֥ק וְחָשֵׁ֖ל כֹּ֑לָּא וּֽכְפַרְזְלָ֞א דִּֽי־מְרָעַ֣ע כָּל־אִלֵּ֗ין תַּדִּ֖ק וְתֵרֹֽעַ׃ 41 וְדִֽי־חֲזַ֜יְתָה רַגְלַיָּ֣א וְאֶצְבְּעָתָ֗א מִנְּהֵ֞ן חֲסַ֤ף דִּֽי־פֶחָר֙ וּמִנְּהֵ֣ן פַּרְזֶ֔ל מַלְכ֥וּ פְלִיגָ֖ה תֶּהֱוֵ֑ה וּמִן־נִצְבְּתָ֤א דִֽי פַרְזְלָא֙ לֶֽהֱוֵא־בַ֔הּ כָּל־קֳבֵ֣ל דִּ֤י חֲזַ֙יְתָה֙ פַּ֣רְזְלָ֔א מְעָרַ֖ב בַּחֲסַ֥ף טִינָֽא׃ 42 וְאֶצְבְּעָת֙ רַגְלַיָּ֔א מִנְּהֵ֥ן פַּרְזֶ֖ל וּמִנְּהֵ֣ן חֲסַ֑ף מִן־קְצָת֙ מַלְכוּתָא֙ תֶּהֱוֵ֣ה

---

37 ᵍnoun ms emph תְּקֹף hapax *strength.* ʰnoun ms emph יְקָר *honor.* ⁱG sc 3ms יְהַב. ʲprep לְ w/ 2ms gen sx.

38 ᵃnoun ms cstr כֹּל. ᵇrel pron דִּי *who, which, that.* ᶜK דָּאֲרִין, Q דְּיָרִין, both G ptcp mp abs דור *dwell.* ᵈnoun mp cstr II בַּר *son.* ᵉ⁻ᵉ= *human beings.* ᶠnoun fs cstr חֵיוָה *animal.* ᵍnoun ms emph I בַּר *field.* ʰ⁻ʰ= *wild animal.* ⁱnoun ms cstr עוֹף *bird.* ʲnoun mp emph שְׁמַיִן. ᵏG sc 3ms יְהַב. ˡnoun fs יַד w/ 2ms gen sx *hand.* ᵐH sc 3ms שלט w/ 2ms acc sx *make rule.* ⁿnoun ms כֹּל w/ 3mp gen sx. ᵒK אַנְתָּה, Q אַנְתְּ, both indep pers pron 2ms *you.* ᵖindep pers pron 3ms הוּא as copula *are.* �q noun ms emph רֵאשׁ *head.* ʳgen part דִּי *of.* ˢnoun ms emph דְּהַב *gold.*

39 ᵃprep בָּאתַר w/ 2ms gen sx *after.* ᵇG pc 3fs קוּם. ᶜnoun fs abs מַלְכוּ *kingdom.* ᵈadj fs abs אָחֳרִי *another.* ᵉK אַרְעָא noun fs emph אֲרַע *earth, land;* Q אֲרַע noun ms abs = prep *beneath, inferior.* ᶠprep מִן w/ 2ms gen sx *than you.* ᵍK תְּלִיתָיָא, Q תְּלִיתָאָה [Ed תְּלִי״], both adj fs abs תְּלִיתָי *third.* ʰgen part דִּי *of.* ⁱnoun ms emph נְחָשׁ *bronze.* ʲrel pron דִּי *which, that.* ᵏG pc 3fs שלט *rule.* ˡnoun ms cstr כֹּל. ᵐnoun fs emph אֲרַע *earth, land.*

40 ᵃnoun fs abs מַלְכוּ *kingdom.* ᵇK רְבִיעָיָה, Q רְבִיעָאָה, both adj fs abs רְבִיעָי *fourth.* ᶜG pc 3fs הוה. ᵈadj fs abs תַּקִּיף *strong.* ᵉnoun ms emph פַּרְזֶל *iron.* ᶠ= כְּ + לְ *according to.* ᵍsubord conj דִּי *that.* ʰ⁻ʰ= *because, since.*

ⁱH ptcp ms abs דקק *pulverize.* ʲG ptcp ms abs חֲשַׁל hapax *smash.* ᵏnoun ms emph כֹּל. ˡrel pron דִּי *which, that.* ᵐD ptcp ms abs רעע *crush.* ⁿnoun ms cstr כֹּל. ᵒprox dem pron cp אִלֵּין *these.* ᵖH pc 3fs דקק *pulverize.* q G pc 3fs רעע *crush.*

41 ᵃcaus conj דִּי *because.* ᵇG sc 2ms חזה. ᶜnoun fp emph רְגַל *foot.* ᵈnoun fp emph אֶצְבַּע *toe.* ᵉK מִנְּהוֹן prep מִן w/ 3mp gen sx, Q מִנְּהֵן prep מִן w/ 3fp gen sx. ᶠnoun ms abs חֲסַף *clay.* ᵍgen part דִּי *of.* ʰnoun ms abs פֶּחָר hapax *potter.* ⁱK וּמִנְּהוֹן prep מִן w/ 3mp gen sx, Q וּמִנְּהֵן [BHS; L, BHL* הֵן״]; Ed הֵן״] prep מִן w/ 3fp gen sx. ʲnoun ms abs פַּרְזֶל *iron.* ᵏnoun fs abs מַלְכוּ *kingdom.* ˡGp ptcp fs abs פלג hapax *divided.* ᵐG pc 3fs הוה. ⁿnoun fs emph נִצְבָּה hapax *hardness, strength.* ᵒgen part דִּי *of* [So L, BHL*, Ed; BHS דִּי]. ᵖnoun ms emph פַּרְזֶל *iron.* q G pc 3ms הוה. ʳprep בְּ w/ 3fs gen sx. ˢ= כְּ + לְ *according to.* ᵗconj דִּי *that.* ᵘ⁻ᵘ= *because, since.* ᵛDp ptcp ms abs ערב *mixed.* ʷnoun ms cstr חֲסַף *clay.* ˣnoun ms emph טִין *unfired pottery.*

42 ᵃnoun fp cstr אֶצְבַּע *toe.* ᵇnoun fp emph רְגַל *foot.* ᶜK מִנְּהוֹן prep מִן w/ 3mp gen sx, Q מִנְּהֵן [Ed הֵן״], prep מִן w/ 3fp gen sx. ᵈnoun ms abs פַּרְזֶל *iron.* ᵉK וּמִנְּהוֹן prep מִן w/ 3mp gen sx, Q וּמִנְּהֵן [Ed הֵן״] prep מִן w/ 3fp gen sx. ᶠnoun ms abs חֲסַף *clay.* ᵍnoun fs cstr קְצָת *end.* ʰnoun fs emph מַלְכוּ *kingdom.* ⁱG pc 3fs הוה.

43 דִּיᵃ חֲזַ֙יְתָᵇ פַּרְזְלָאᶜ מְעָרַ֖בᵈ בַּחֲסַ֣ףᵉ תַּקִּיפָ֑הᵏ וּמִנַּהּᵏ תֶּהֱוֵה֙ תְּבִירָ֔הᵐ:
טִינָאᶠ מִתְעָֽרְבִ֤ין לֶֽהֱוֺן֙ᵍ בִּזְרַ֣ע אֲנָשָׁ֔א וְלָֽא־לֶהֱוֺ֥ןʰ דָּֽבְקִ֖יןʲ דְּנָ֣הᵏ עִם־
דְּנָ֑הᵏ הֵֽא־כְדִ֥יⁿᵐ פַרְזְלָ֖אᵒ לָ֥א מִתְעָרַ֥ב עִם־חַסְפָּֽאᵖ: 44 וּֽבְיוֹמֵיהוֹן֙ᵃ
דִּיᵇ מַלְכַיָּ֣אᶜ אִנּ֗וּןᵈ יְקִים֩ᵉ אֱלָ֨הּ שְׁמַיָּ֜אᶠ מַלְכוּ֙ᵍ דִּֽי־לְעָלְמִ֣יןʰ לָ֣א
תִתְחַבַּ֔לʲ וּמַלְכוּתָ֕הᵏ לְעַ֥םˡ אָחֳרָֽןᵐ לָ֖א תִשְׁתְּבִ֑קⁿ תַּדִּ֣קᵒ וְתָסֵ֤יףᵖ כָּל־ᵍ
אִלֵּ֣יןʳ מַלְכְוָתָ֔אˢ וְהִ֖יאᵗ תְּק֥וּםᵘ לְעָלְמַיָּֽאᵛ: 45 כָּל־ᵃקֳבֵ֣לᵇ דִּֽי־חֲזַ֡יְתָᵈ דִּ֣י
מִטּוּרָאᶠ אִתְגְּזֶ֩רֶת֩ᵍ אֶ֨בֶןʰ דִּֽי־לָ֜אʲ בִידַ֗יִןᵏ וְֽהַדֶּ֡קֶתᵐ פַּרְזְלָ֣א נְחָשָׁאⁿ
חַסְפָּאᵒ כַּסְפָּ֣אᵖ וְדַהֲבָ֗אᵠ אֱלָ֤הּ רַ֣בᵈ הוֹדַ֣עᵗ לְמַלְכָּ֔א מָ֛הᵂ דִּ֥יᵛ לֶהֱוֵ֖אˣ
אַחֲרֵ֣יʸ דְּנָ֑הᶻ וְיַצִּ֥יבᵃᵃ חֶלְמָ֖אᵃᵃ וּמְהֵימַ֥ןᵇᵇ פִּשְׁרֵֽהּᶜᶜ: ᵈᵈ
פ
46 בֵּ֠אדַיִןᵃ מַלְכָּ֤א נְבֽוּכַדְנֶצַּר֙ᵇ נְפַ֣ל עַל־אַנְפּ֔וֹהִיᶜ וּלְדָנִיֵּ֖אל סְגִ֑דᵈ וּמִנְחָה֙ᵉ
וְנִ֣יחֹחִ֔יןᶠ אֲמַ֖רᵍ לְנַסָּ֥כָהʰ לֵֽהּʲ: 47 עָנֵה֩ᵃ מַלְכָּ֨א לְדָנִיֵּ֜אל וְאָמַ֗רᵇ מִן־קְשֹׁטᶜ

---

42 ʲadj fs abs תַּקִּיף *strong.* ᵏprep מִן w/ 3fs gen sx. ˡG PC 3fs הוה. ᵐGp ptcp fs abs תבר hapax *fragile, brittle.*

43 ᵃK דִּי, Q וְדִי caus conj דִּי *because.* ᵇG SC 2ms חזה. ᶜnoun ms emph פַּרְזֶל *iron.* ᵈDp ptcp ms abs ערב *mixed.* ᵉnoun ms cstr חֲסַף *clay.* ᶠnoun ms emph טִין *unfired pottery.* ᵍtD ptcp mp abs ערב *intermingle.* ʰG PC 3mp הוה. ʲnoun ms abs זְרַע hapax *seed.* ʲG ptcp mp abs דבק hapax *stick together.* ᵏprox dem pron ms דְּנָה *this.* ˡdem part הֵא hapax *behold!* ᵐsubord conj (כְּ + דִּי) כְּדִי *when.* ⁿ⁻ⁿ= *just as* [rd (?) as conj הֵאךְ־דִּי = הֵיךְ־דִּי *just as*]. ᵒnoun ms emph פַּרְזֶל *iron.* ᵖtD ptcp ms abs ערב *intermingle.* ᵠnoun ms emph חֲסַף *clay.*

44 ᵃnoun mp יוֹם w/ 3mp gen sx *day.* ᵇgen part דִּי *of.* ᶜnoun mp emph מֶלֶךְ *king.* ᵈdist dem adj cp אִנּוּן *those.* ᵉH PC 3ms קום. ᶠnoun mp emph שְׁמַיִן. ᵍnoun fs abs מַלְכוּ *kingdom.* ʰrel pron דִּי *which, that.* ʲnoun mp abs עָלַם *eternity.* ʲtD PC 3fs חבל *be destroyed.* ᵏnoun fs emph מַלְכוּ *kingdom.* ˡnoun ms abs עַם *people.* ᵐadj ms abs אָחֳרָן *another.* ⁿtG PC 3fs שבק *be left* (w/ לְ) *to.* ᵒH PC 3fs דקק *pulverize.* ᵖH PC 3fs סוף *bring to an end, annihilate.* ᵠnoun ms cstr כֹּל. ʳprox dem adj cp אִלֵּין *these.* ˢnoun fp emph מַלְכוּ. ᵗindep pers pron 3fs הִיא *she, it.* ᵘG PC 3fs קום. ᵛnoun mp emph עָלַם *eternity.*

45 ᵃ= כְּ + לְ *according to.* ᵇsubord conj דִּי *that.* ᶜ⁻ᶜ= *because, since.* ᵈG SC 2ms חזה. ᵉepex conj דִּי *that.* ᶠnoun ms emph טוּר *mountain.* ᵍtG SC 3fs גזר *cut out.* ʰnoun fs abs אֶבֶן *stone.* ʲrel pron דִּי *which, that.* ʲ⁻ʲ= (w/ בְּ) *not through, without.* ᵏnoun fd abs יַד *hand.* ˡH SC 3fs דקק *pulverize* [L, BHS, BHL* (?) וְהַדֶּקֶת; Ed וְֽהַדֶּקֶת]. ᵐnoun ms emph פַּרְזֶל *iron.* ⁿnoun ms emph נְחָשׁ *bronze.* ᵒnoun ms emph חֲסַף *clay.* ᵖnoun ms emph כְּסַף *silver.* ᵠnoun ms emph דְּהַב *gold.* ʳnoun ms abs אֱלָהּ *God.* ˢadj ms abs רַב *great.* ᵗH SC 3ms ידע. ᵘi-mpers correl pron מָה *what.* ᵛrel pron דִּי *which, that.* ᵂ⁻ᵂ= *that which; whatever.* ˣG PC 3ms הוה. ʸprep אַחֲרֵי [HALOT] *after.* ᶻprox dem pron ms דְּנָה *this.* ᵃᵃadj ms abs יַצִּיב *certain.* ᵇᵇnoun ms emph חֵלֶם *dream.* ᶜᶜHp ptcp ms abs אמן *trustworthy.* ᵈᵈnoun ms פְּשַׁר w/ 3ms gen sx.

46 ᵃtemp adv אֱדַיִן (w/ בְּ) *immediately; then.* ᵇG SC 3ms נפל *fall.* ᶜnoun mp אֲנַף w/ 3ms gen sx *face.* ᵈG SC 3ms סגד *prostrate oneself, bow down to the ground.* ᵉnoun fs abs מִנְחָה *grain offering.* ᶠnoun mp abs נִיחוֹחַ *soothing sacrifice; incense offering.* ᵍG SC 3ms אמר. ʰD inf נסך hapax *pour out = offer.* ʲprep לְ w/ 3ms gen sx.

47 ᵃG ptcp ms abs I ענה. ᵇG ptcp ms abs אמר. ᶜnoun ms abs קְשֹׁט *truth.*

דִּי^{ed} אֱלָהֲכוֹן הוּא^g אֱלָהּ אֱלָהִין וּמָרֵא מַלְכִין וְגָלֵה רָזִין דִּי^k יְכֵלְתָּ^l
לְמִגְלֵא^m רָזָהⁿ דְנָה^o: ⁴⁸ אֱדַיִן מַלְכָּא לְדָנִיֵּאל רַבִּי^a וּמַתְּנָן רַבְרְבָן^c
שַׂגִּיאָן^d יְהַב^e־לֵהּ^f וְהַשְׁלְטֵהּ^g עַל כָּל^h־מְדִינַתⁱ בָּבֶל וְרַב^j־סִגְנִין^k עַל
כָּל^h־חַכִּימֵי^l בָּבֶל: ⁴⁹ וְדָנִיֵּאל בְּעָא^a מִן־מַלְכָּא וּמַנִּי^b עַל עֲבִידְתָּא^c דִּי^d
מְדִינַת^e בָּבֶל לְשַׁדְרַךְ^f מֵישַׁךְ^g וַעֲבֵד נְגוֹ^h וְדָנִיֵּאל בִּתְרַעⁱ מַלְכָּא: פ

3 ¹ נְבוּכַדְנֶצַּר מַלְכָּא עֲבַד^a צְלֵם^b דִּי^c־דְהַב^d רוּמֵהּ^e אַמִּין^f שִׁתִּין^g
פְּתָיֵהּ^h אַמִּין^f שֵׁתⁱ אֲקִימֵהּ^j בְּבִקְעַת^k דּוּרָא^l בִּמְדִינַת^m בָּבֶל:
² וּנְבוּכַדְנֶצַּר מַלְכָּא שְׁלַח^a לְמִכְנַשׁ^b׀ לַאֲחַשְׁדַּרְפְּנַיָּא^c סִגְנַיָּא^d
וּפַחֲוָתָא^e אֲדַרְגָּזְרַיָּא^f גְּדָבְרַיָּא^g דְּתָבְרַיָּא^h תִּפְתָּיֵאⁱ וְכֹל^j שִׁלְטֹנֵי^k
מְדִינָתָא^l לְמֵתֵא^m לַחֲנֻכַּתⁿ צַלְמָא^o דִּי^p הֲקֵים^q נְבוּכַדְנֶצַּר מַלְכָּא:
³ בֵּאדַיִן^a מִתְכַּנְּשִׁין^b אֲחַשְׁדַּרְפְּנַיָּא^c סִגְנַיָּא^d וּפַחֲוָתָא^e אֲדַרְגָּזְרַיָּא^f
גְּדָבְרַיָּא^g דְּתָבְרַיָּא^h תִּפְתָּיֵאⁱ וְכֹל^j שִׁלְטֹנֵי^k מְדִינָתָא^l לַחֲנֻכַּת^m

---

47 ^dsubord conj דִּי *that.* ^{e–e}= *truly.* ^fnoun ms
אֱלָהּ w/ 2mp gen sx. ^gindep pers pron 3ms
הוּא *he.* ^hnoun ms cstr מָרֵא *lord.* ⁱG ptcp
ms abs גלה *reveal.* ^jnoun mp abs רָז Pers
lw *secret, mystery.* ^kcaus conj דִּי *because.*
^lG sc 2ms יכל *be able.* ^mG inf גלה *reveal.*
ⁿnoun ms emph רָזָה Pers lw *secret, mys-
tery.* ^oprox dem adj ms דְּנָה *this.*

48 ^aD sc 3ms רבה *make great, promote.*
^bnoun fp abs מַתְּנָה *gift.* ^cadj fp abs רַב
many. ^dadj fp abs שַׂגִּיא *very.* ^eG sc 3ms
יהב. ^fprep לְ w/ 3ms gen sx. ^gH sc 3ms שׁלט
w/ 3ms acc sx *make rule.* ^hnoun ms cstr
כֹּל. ⁱnoun fs cstr מְדִינָה *district, province.*
^jadj ms cstr רַב *chief.* ^knoun mp abs סְגַן
prefect. ^ladj mp cstr חַכִּים *wise.*

49 ^aG sc 3ms בעה *seek, request.* ^bD sc 3ms
מנה *appoint.* ^cnoun fs emph עֲבִידָה *administration.* ^dgen part דִּי *of.* ^enoun fs cstr
מְדִינָה *district, province.* ^fPN *Shadrach.*
^gPN *Meshach.* ^{h–h}PN *Abednego.* ⁱnoun ms
cstr תְּרַע *door, gate.*

3

¹ ^aG sc 3ms עבד. ^bnoun ms abs צְלֵם *statue.*
^cgen part דִּי *of.* ^dnoun ms abs דְּהַב *gold.*
^enoun ms רוּם w/ 3ms gen sx *height.*
^fnoun fp abs אַמָּה *cubit.* ^gcard שִׁתִּין *sixty.*
^hnoun ms פְּתָי w/ 3ms gen sx *width.* ⁱcard

w/ f noun שֵׁת *six.* ^jH sc 3ms קום w/ 3ms
acc sx. ^knoun fs cstr בִּקְעָה hapax *plain,
broad valley.* ^lGN *Dura.* ^mnoun fs cstr
מְדִינָה *province.*

² ^aG sc 3ms שׁלח *send.* ^bG inf כנשׁ *assemble.*
^cnoun mp emph אֲחַשְׁדַּרְפַּן Pers lw *satrap.*
^dnoun mp emph סְגַן *prefect.* ^enoun mp
emph פֶּחָה *governor.* ^fnoun mp emph
אֲדַרְגָּזֵר Pers lw *counselor.* ^gnoun mp emph
גְּדָבַר Pers lw *treasurer.* ^hnoun mp emph
דְּתָבַר Pers lw *judge.* ⁱnoun mp emph תִּפְתָּי
magistrate. ^jnoun ms cstr כֹּל. ^knoun mp
cstr שִׁלְטוֹן *official.* ^lnoun fs emph מְדִינָה
district, province. ^mG inf אתה *come.*
ⁿnoun fs cstr חֲנֻכָּה *dedication.* ^onoun ms
emph צְלֵם *statue.* ^prel pron דִּי *who, which,
that.* ^qH sc 3ms קום.

³ ^atemp adv אֱדַיִן (w/ בְּ) *immediately; then.*
^btD ptcp mp abs כנשׁ *assemble.* ^cnoun mp
emph אֲחַשְׁדַּרְפַּן Pers lw *satrap.* ^dnoun mp
emph סְגַן *prefect.* ^enoun mp emph פֶּחָה
governor. ^fnoun mp emph אֲדַרְגָּזֵר Pers lw
counselor. ^gnoun mp emph גְּדָבַר *treasurer.* ^hnoun mp emph דְּתָבַר Pers lw *judge.*
ⁱnoun mp emph תִּפְתָּי *magistrate.* ^jnoun ms
cstr כֹּל. ^knoun mp cstr שִׁלְטוֹן *official.* ^lnoun fs
emph מְדִינָה *district, province.* ^mnoun fs cstr
חֲנֻכָּה *dedication.*

צַלְמָאⁿ דִּיˢ הֲקֵיםᴾ נְבוּכַדְנֶצַּר מַלְכָּא וְקָאֲמִין לָקֳבֵל צַלְמָאˢ דִּי

הֲקֵיםᴾ נְבוּכַדְנֶצַּר: 4 וְכָרוֹזָאᵃ קָרֵᵇא בְחָיִלᶜ לְכוֹןᵈ אָמְרִיןᵉ עַמְמַיָּאᶠ

עַמְמַיָּאᵍ וְלִשָּׁנַיָּאʰ: 5 בְּעִדָּנָאᵃ דִּי־תִשְׁמְעוּןᵇ קָלᵈ קַרְנָאᵉ מַשְׁרוֹקִיתָאᶠ

קִיתְרוֹסᵍ סַבְּכָאʰ פְּסַנְתֵּרִיןⁱ סוּמְפֹּנְיָהʲ וְכֹלᵏ זְנֵיˡ זְמָרָאᵐ תִּפְּלוּןⁿ

וְתִסְגְּדוּןᵒ לְצֶלֶםᴾ דַּהֲבָא דִּיˢ הֲקֵים נְבוּכַדְנֶצַּר מַלְכָּא: 6 וּמַן־דִּי⁻ᶜᵇ

לָא יִפֵּלᵈ וְיִסְגֻּדᵉ בַּהּ־שַׁעֲתָא יִתְרְמֵאʰ לְגוֹא־אַתּוּןⁱ נוּרָאᵏ יָקִדְתָּאˡ:

7 כָּל־קֳבֵלᵃ דְּנָהᶜᵇ בֵּהּ־זִמְנָאᵉ כְּדִיᶠ שָׁמְעִיןᵍ כָּל־עַמְמַיָּאʰ קָלʲ קַרְנָאᵏ

מַשְׁרוֹקִיתָאˡ קִיתָרֹסᵐ שַׂבְּכָאⁿ פְּסַנְטֵרִיןᵒ וְכֹלʰ זְנֵי זְמָרָאᵖ נָפְלִיןᑫ

כָּל־עַמְמַיָּאˢ אֻמַיָּא וְלִשָּׁנַיָּאᵘ סָגְדִיןᵛ לְצֶלֶםᵂ דַּהֲבָאˣ דִּיʸ הֲקֵיםᶻ

נְבוּכַדְנֶצַּר מַלְכָּא: 8 כָּל־קֳבֵלᵃ דְּנָהᶜᵇ בֵּהּ־זִמְנָאᵈ קְרִבוּᵉ גֻּבְרִיןᶠ

---

3 ⁿnoun ms emph צְלֵם *statue.* ᵒrel pron דִּי *who, which, that.* ᴾH sc 3ms קום. ᑫK וְקָאֲמִין, Q וְקָיְמִין, both G ptcp mp abs קום. ʳ לְ + noun ms cstr קֳבֵל *to the front of = before.* ˢnoun ms emph צְלֵם *statue.*

4 ᵃnoun fs emph כָּרוֹז *hapax, Pers lw herald.* ᵇG ptcp ms abs קרא *cry out, shout.* ᶜnoun ms abs חַיִל *power.* ᵈprep לְ w/ 2mp gen sx. ᵉG ptcp mp abs אמר. ᶠnoun mp emph עַם *people.* ᵍnoun fp emph אֻמָּה *nation.* ʰnoun mp emph לְשָׁן *tongue.*

5 ᵃnoun ms emph עִדָּן *time.* ᵇtemp conj דִּי *that, when.* ᶜG pc 2mp שמע *hear.* ᵈnoun ms cstr קָל *sound.* ᵉnoun fs emph קֶרֶן *horn.* ᶠnoun fs emph מַשְׁרוֹקִי *pipe.* ᵍK קִיתְרוֹס, Q קַתְרֹס, both noun ms abs קיתרס Gk. lw *kitharos, zither.* ʰnoun fs abs variant spelling of שַׂבְּכָא *trigon.* ⁱnoun ms abs פְּסַנְתֵּרִין Gk. lw *psalterion.* ʲnoun fs abs סוּמְפֹּנְיָה Gk. lw *symphonia.* ᵏnoun ms cstr כֹּל. ˡnoun mp cstr זַן *type, kind.* ᵐnoun ms emph זְמָר *musical instrument.* ⁿG pc 2mp נפל *fall.* ᵒG pc 2mp סגד *prostrate oneself, bow down to the ground.* ᴾnoun ms cstr צְלֵם *statue.* ᑫnoun ms emph דְּהַב *gold.* ʳrel pron דִּי *which, that.* ˢH sc 3ms קום.

6 ᵃpers indef pron מַן *who.* ᵇrel pron דִּי *who.* ᶜ⁻ᶜ= *whoever.* ᵈG pc 3ms נפל *fall.* ᵉG pc 3ms סגד *prostrate oneself, bow down to the ground.* ᶠprep בְּ w/ 3fs gen sx. ᵍnoun fs

---

emph שָׁעָה *hour = moment.* ʰtG pc 3ms רמה *be thrown.* ⁱnoun ms cstr גַּו *midst.* ʲnoun ms cstr אַתּוּן Akk lw *furnace.* ᵏnoun fs emph נוּר *fire.* ˡG ptcp fs emph יקד *burn.*

7 ᵃ= בְּ + לְ *according to.* ᵇprox dem pron ms דְּנָה *this.* ᶜ⁻ᶜ= *because of this, therefore.* ᵈprep בְּ w/ 3ms gen sx. ᵉnoun ms emph זְמַן *time, moment.* ᶠtemp conj כְּדִי (כְּ + דִּי) *when.* ᵍG ptcp mp abs שמע *hear.* ʰnoun ms cstr כֹּל. ⁱnoun mp emph עַם *people.* ʲnoun ms cstr קָל *sound.* ᵏnoun fs emph קֶרֶן *horn.* ˡnoun fs emph מַשְׁרוֹקִי *pipe.* ᵐK קִיתָרֹס, Q קַתְרֹס, both noun ms abs קיתרס Gk. lw *kitharos, zither.* ⁿnoun fs abs שַׂבְּכָא *trigon.* ᵒnoun ms abs פְּסַנְתֵּרִין Gk. lw *psalterion.* ᴾnoun mp cstr זַן *type, kind.* ᑫnoun ms emph זְמַר *musical instrument.* ʳG ptcp mp abs נפל *fall.* ˢnoun mp emph עַם *people.* ᵗnoun fp emph אֻמָּה *nation.* ᵘnoun mp emph לְשָׁן *tongue.* ᵛG ptcp mp abs סגד *prostrate oneself, bow down to the ground.* ᵂnoun ms cstr צְלֵם *statue.* ˣnoun ms emph דְּהַב *gold.* ʸrel pron דִּי *which, that.* ᶻH sc 3ms קום.

8 ᵃ= בְּ + לְ *according to.* ᵇprox dem pron ms דְּנָה *this.* ᶜ⁻ᶜ= *because of this, therefore.* ᵈprep בְּ w/ 3ms gen sx. ᵉnoun ms emph זְמַן *time.* ᶠG sc 3mp קרב *approach.* ᵍnoun mp abs גְּבַר *man, person.*

כְּשְׂדָּאִין֙ ʰוַאֲכַ֣לוּ i קַרְצֵיה֔וֹן k דִּי֖ j יְהוּדָיֵ֑א kj 9 עֲנוֹ֙ a וְאָ֣מְרִ֔ין b לִנְבוּכַדְנֶצַּ֖ר
מַלְכָּ֑א מַלְכָּ֖א לְעָלְמִ֥ין c חֱיִֽי d 10 אַ֣נְתָּה a מַלְכָּא֮ שָׂ֣מְתָּ טְעֵם֒ b דִּ֣י c כָל־ e
אֱנָ֡שׁ דִּֽי־יִשְׁמַ֡ע g קָ֣ל h קַרְנָ֣א i מַ֠שְׁרוֹקִיתָא j קִיתָרֹס֙ k שַׂבְּכָ֤א l פְּסַנְתֵּרִין֙ m
וְסִיפֹנְיָ֔ה n וְכֹ֖ל o זְנֵ֣י p זְמָרָ֑א יִפֵּ֥ל q וְיִסְגֻּ֖ד r לְצֶ֥לֶם s דַּהֲבָֽא t 11 וּמַן־דִּי־ c cb
לָ֥א יִפֵּ֖ל d וְיִסְגֻּ֑ד e יִתְרְמֵ֕א f לְגֽוֹא־g אַתּ֥וּן h נוּרָ֖א i יָקִֽדְתָּֽא j 12 אִיתַ֞י a גֻּבְרִ֣ין b
יְהוּדָאיִ֗ן c דִּֽי־מַנִּ֤יתָ d אָֽתְהוֹן e עַל־עֲבִידַת֙ g מְדִינַ֣ת h בָּבֶ֔ל שַׁדְרַ֥ךְ i מֵישַׁ֖ךְ j
וַעֲבֵ֣ד נְג֑וֹ k גֻּבְרַיָּ֣א l אִלֵּ֗ךְ m לָא־שָׂ֤מֽוּ n עליך o מַלְכָּא֙ טְעֵ֔ם p לאלהיך q
לָ֣א פָֽלְחִ֔ין r וּלְצֶ֧לֶם s דַּהֲבָ֛א t דִּ֥י הֲקֵ֖ימְתָּ u לָ֥א סָֽגְדִֽין v 13 בֵּאדַ֤יִן a
נְבוּכַדְנֶצַּר֙ בִּרְגַ֣ז b וַחֲמָ֔ה c אֲמַר֙ d לְהַיְתָיָ֔ה e לְשַׁדְרַ֥ךְ f מֵישַׁ֖ךְ g וַעֲבֵ֣ד נְג֑וֹ h
בֵּאדַ֛יִן a גֻּבְרַיָּ֥א i אִלֵּ֖ךְ j הֵיתָ֥יוּ k קֳדָ֖ם מַלְכָּֽא 14 עָנֵ֤ה a נְבֻֽכַדְנֶצַּר֙ וְאָמַ֣ר b

---

8 ʰnoun mp abs כַּשְׂדָּי *Babylonian astrologer or sage.* iG sc 3mp אכל *eat.* jnoun mp קְרַץ w/ 3mp gen sx Akk lw *bits.* k‑k= *slander* (w/ דִּי) *someone; accuse.* lgen part דִּי *of.* mnoun mp emph יְהוּדִי *Jew; Judean.*

9 aG sc 3mp i ענה. bG ptcp mp abs אמר. cnoun mp abs עָלַם *eternity.* dG imv 2ms חיה *live.*

10 aK אַנְתָּה, Q אַנְתְּ, both indep pers pron 2ms אַנְתְּ *you.* bG sc 2ms שׂים. cnoun ms abs טְעֵם *statement.* depex conj דִּי *that.* enoun ms cstr כֹּל *all.* frel pron דִּי *who, that.* gG pc 3ms שׁמע *hear.* hnoun ms cstr קָל *sound.* inoun fs emph קֶרֶן *horn.* jnoun fs emph מַשְׁרוֹקִי *pipe.* kK קִיתָרוֹס, Q קַתְרוֹס, both noun ms abs קיתרס Gk. lw *kitharos, zither.* lnoun fs abs שַׂבְּכָא *trigon.* mnoun ms abs פְּסַנְתֵּרִין Gk. lw *psalterion.* nK וְסִיפֹנְיָה, Q וְסוּפֹנְיָה, both noun fs abs סוּמְפֹנְיָה Gk. lw *symphonia.* onoun mp cstr זַן *type, kind.* pnoun ms emph זְמָר *musical instrument.* qG pc 3ms נפל *fall.* rG pc 3ms סגד *prostrate oneself, bow down to the ground.* snoun ms cstr צֶלֶם *statue.* tnoun ms emph דְּהַב *gold.*

11 apers indef pron מַן *who.* brel pron דִּי *who, that.* c‑c= *whoever.* dG pc 3ms נפל *fall.* eG pc 3ms סגד *prostrate oneself, bow down to the ground.* ftG pc 3ms רמה *be thrown.*

gnoun ms cstr גּוֹ *midst.* hnoun ms cstr אַתּוּן Akk lw *furnace.* inoun fs emph נוּר *fire.* jG ptcp fs emph יקד *burn.*

12 apart. of existence אִיתַי *there are.* bnoun mp abs גְּבַר *man, person.* cnoun mp abs יְהוּדִי *Jew; Judean.* drel pron דִּי *who, that.* eD sc 2ms מנה *appoint.* fsign def dir obj יָת w/ 3mp gen sx hapax *whom.* gnoun fs cstr עֲבִידָה *administration.* hnoun fs cstr מְדִינָה *district, province.* iPN Shadrach. jPN Meshach. k‑kPN Abednego. lnoun mp emph גְּבַר *man, person.* mdist dem adj cp אִלֵּךְ *those.* nG sc 3mp שׂים. oK עֲלַיִךְ, Q עֲלָךְ, both prep עַל־ w/ 2ms gen sx. pnoun ms abs טְעֵם *good taste, deference.* qK לֵאלָהַיִךְ, noun mp w/ 2ms gen sx, Q לֵאלָהָךְ, noun ms w/ 2ms gen sx אֱלָהּ *God.* rG ptcp mp abs פלח *serve.* snoun ms cstr צֶלֶם *statue.* tnoun ms emph דְּהַב *gold.* uH sc 2ms קום. vG ptcp mp abs סגד *prostrate oneself, bow down to the ground.*

13 atemp adv אֱדַיִן (w/ בְּ) *immediately; then.* bnoun ms abs רְגַז hapax *rage.* cnoun fs abs חֲמָה *fury.* dG sc 3ms אמר. eH inf אתה *bring.* fPN Shadrach. gPN Meshach. h‑hPN Abednego. inoun mp emph גְּבַר *man, person.* jdist dem adj cp אִלֵּךְ *those.* kHp sc 3mp אתה *be brought.*

14 aG ptcp ms abs i ענה. bG ptcp ms abs אמר.

לְהוֹן הַצְדָּ֨אd שַׁדְרַ֤ךְe מֵישַׁךְ֙f וַעֲבֵ֣ד נְג֔וֹg לֵֽאלָהַ֗יh לָ֤א אִֽיתֵיכוֹן֙i פָּֽלְחִ֔יןj

וּלְצֶ֧לֶםk דַּהֲבָ֛אl דִּ֥יm הֲקֵ֖ימֶתc לָ֥א סָֽגְדִֽיןn׃ °15 כְּעַ֞ןa הֵ֧ןb אִֽיתֵיכ֣וֹן עֲתִידִ֗יןc

דִּ֣יd בְעִדָּנָ֡אe דִּֽי־תִשְׁמְע֡וּןf קָ֣לg קַרְנָ֣אh מַשְׁרוֹקִיתָ֣אi קיתרסֹ֩k קִיתָרֹ֜סl שַׂבְּכָ֤אm

פְּסַנְתֵּרִין֙n וְסוּמְפֹּ֣נְיָ֔הo וְכֹ֖לp זְנֵ֣יq זְמָרָ֑אr תִּפְּל֣וּןs וְתִסְגְּדוּן֮t לְצַלְמָ֣אu

דִּֽי־עַבְדֵת֒w וְהֵ֣ןx לָ֣א תִסְגְּד֔וּןy בַּהּ־שַׁעֲתָ֣הz תִּתְרְמ֗וֹןaa לְגֽוֹא־bb

אַתּ֨וּןcc נוּרָ֤אdd יָקִֽדְתָּא֙ee וּמַן־ff ה֣וּאgg אֱלָ֔הhh דִּ֥יii יְשֵׁיזְבִנְכ֖וֹןjj מִן־יְדָֽיii׃

16 עֲנ֗וֹa שַׁדְרַ֤ךְb מֵישַׁךְ֙c וַעֲבֵ֣דd נְג֔וֹe וְאָֽמְרִ֖יןf לְמַלְכָּ֑א נְבֽוּכַדְנֶצַּ֕ר

לָֽא־חַשְׁחִ֨יןg אֲנַ֧חְנָהh עַל־דְּנָ֛הi פִּתְגָ֖םi לַהֲתָבוּתָֽךְj׃ 17 הֵ֣ן אִיתַ֗יa

אֱלָהַ֙נָא֙b דִּֽי־אֲנַ֣חְנָאd פָֽלְחִ֔יןe יָכִ֖לg לְשֵׁיזָבוּתַ֑נָאh מִן־אַתּ֛וּןi נוּרָ֥אj

יָקִֽדְתָּ֖אk וּמִן־יְדָ֥ךְl מַלְכָּ֖א יְשֵׁיזִֽבm׃ 18 וְהֵ֣ןa לָ֔א יְדִ֥יעַb לֶהֱוֵֽא־c לָ֖ךְd

14 cprep לְ w/ 3mp gen sx. dadv צְדָא w/ interr ה, hapax *is it true that?* ePN Shadrach. fPN Meshach. g-gPN Abednego. hnoun mp אֱלָה w/ 1cs gen sx. ipart. of existence אִיתַי w/ 2mp gen sx *you are.* jG ptcp mp abs פלח *serve.* knoun ms cstr צְלֵם *statue.* lnoun ms emph דְּהַב *gold.* mrel pron דִּי *which, that.* nH sc 1cs קום. oG ptcp mp abs סגד *prostrate oneself, bow down to the ground.*

15 atransitional conj כְּעַן introduces new idea *now.* bhypoth conj הֵן *if.* cpart. of existence אִיתַי w/ 2mp gen sx *you are.* dadj mp abs עֲתִיד hapax *ready.* epurp conj דִּי *so that.* fnoun ms emph עִדָּן *time.* gtemp conj דִּי *that, when.* hG PC 2mp שמע *hear.* inoun ms cstr קָל *sound.* jnoun fs emph קֶרֶן *horn.* kK מַשְׁרוֹקִי *pipe.* lK קיתרֹס, Q קַתְרֹס [L no Q; BHS, Ed רֹס״], both noun ms abs קיתרֹס Gk. lw *kitharos, zither.* mnoun fs abs שַׂבְּכָא *trigon.* nnoun ms abs פְּסַנְתֵּרִין Gk. lw *psalterion.* onoun fs abs סוּמְפֹּנְיָה Gk. lw *symphonia.* pnoun ms cstr כֹּל. qnoun mp cstr זַן *type, kind.* rnoun ms emph זְמָר *musical instrument.* sG PC 2mp נפל *fall.* tG PC 2mp סגד *prostrate oneself, bow down to the ground.* unoun ms emph צְלֵם *statue.* vrel pron דִּי *which, that.* wG sc 1cs עבד. xhypoth conj

14 (cont.) הֵן *if.* yprep בְּ w/ 3fs gen sx. znoun fs emph שָׁעָה *hour = moment.* aaG PC 2mp רמה *be thrown.* bbnoun ms cstr גַּו *midst.* ccnoun ms cstr אַתּוּן Akk lw *furnace.* ddnoun fs emph נוּר *fire.* eeG ptcp fs emph יקד *burn.* ffpers interr pron מַן *who?* ggindep pers pron 3ms הוּא as copula *is.* hhrel pron דִּי *who, that.* [So Ed; L, BHS, BHL* דֵּי]. iiŠ PC 3ms שיזב w/ 2mp acc sx *rescue.* jjnoun fp יַד w/ 1cs gen sx *hand.*

16 aG sc 3mp I ענה. bPN Shadrach. cPN Meshach. d-dPN Abednego. eG ptcp mp abs אמר. fG ptcp mp abs חשח hapax *need.* gindep pers pron 1cp אֲנַחְנָה *we.* hprox dem adj ms דְּנָה *this.* inoun ms abs פִּתְגָם Pers lw *word, answer.* jH inf תוב w/ 2ms acc sx trans *give a reply* (w/ sx) *to.*

17 ahypoth conj הֵן *if.* bpart. of existence אִיתַי *there is.* cnoun ms אֱלָה w/ 1cp gen sx. drel pron דִּי *who, that.* eindep pers pron 1cp אֲנַחְנָה *we.* fG ptcp mp abs פלח *serve.* gG ptcp ms abs יכל *be able.* hŠ inf שיזב w/ 1cp acc sx *rescue.* inoun ms cstr אַתּוּן Akk lw *furnace.* jnoun fs emph נוּר *fire.* kG ptcp fs emph יקד *burn.* lnoun fs יַד w/ 2ms gen sx *hand.* mŠ PC 3ms שיזב *rescue.*

18 ahypoth conj הֵן *if.* bGp ptcp ms abs ידע. cG juss 3ms הוה. dprep לְ w/ 2ms gen sx.

מַלְכָּא דִּי לֵאלָהָיךְ לָא־אִיתַֽינָאg פָלְחִיןh וּלְצֶלֶםi דַּהֲבָאj דִּי

הֲקֵימְתָּ לָא נִסְגֻּֽדm: ס 19 בֵּאדַ֫יִןa נְבוּכַדְנֶצַּר הִתְמְלִיb

חֱמָאc וּצְלֵם אַנְפּֽוֹהִיe אשׁתנוf עַל־שַׁדְרַךְg מֵישַׁךְh וַעֲבֵד נְגוֹ עָנֵהj

וְאָמַרk לְמֵזֵאl לְאַתּוּנָאm חַד־שִׁבְעָה po עַל דִּי חֲזֵהr לְמֵזְיֵהּs:

20 וּלְגֻבְרִיןa גִּבָּֽרֵי־חַֽילb דִּי בְחַֽילֵהּe אֲמַרf לְכַפָּתָהg לְשַׁדְרַךְh

מֵישַׁךְi וַעֲבֵד נְגוֹ לְמִרְמֵאk לְאַתּוּן נוּרָאl יָקִֽדְתָּאm: 21 בֵּאדַ֫יִןa

גֻּבְרַיָּאb אִלֵּךְc כְּפִתוּd בְּסַרְבָּלֵיהוֹןe פטישׁיהוֹןf וְכַרְבְּלָתְהוֹןg

וּלְבֻשֵׁיהוֹןh וּרְמִיוi לְגוֹא־אַתּוּןj נוּרָאk יָקִֽדְתָּאl: 22 כָּל־קֳבֵלc דְּנָהcb

מִן־דִּיe מִלַּתf מַלְכָּא מַחְצְפָהg וְאַתּוּנָאh אֵזֵהi יַתִּֽירָאj גֻּבְרַיָּאk

אִלֵּךְl דִּיm הַסִּקוּn לְשַׁדְרַךְo מֵישַׁךְp וַעֲבֵד נְגוֹq קַטִּל הִמּוֹןs שְׁבִיבָאt

---

18 eepex conj דִּי *that*. fK לֵאלָהָיךְ noun mp, Q לֵאלָהָךְ noun ms, both אֱלָהּ w/ 2ms gen sx. gK אִיתַֽינָא, Q אִיתַֽנָא, both part. of existence אִיתַי w/ 1cp gen sx *we are*. hG ptcp mp abs פלח *serve*. inoun ms cstr צְלֵם *statue*. jnoun ms emph דְּהַב *gold*. krel pron דִּי *which, that*. lH sc 2ms קום. mG pc 1cp סגד *prostrate oneself, bow down to the ground*.

19 atemp adv אֱדַיִן (w/ בְּ) *immediately; then*. btG sc 3ms מלא *be filled*. cnoun fs abs חֱמָה *fury*. dnoun ms cstr צְלֵם *image*. enoun mp אֲנַף w/ 3ms gen sx *face*. fK אֶשְׁתַּנּוּ tD sc 3mp, Q אֶשְׁתַּנִּי tD sc 3ms, both שׁנה intrans *change*. gPN Shadrach. hPN Meshach. i–iPN Abednego. jG ptcp ms abs ענה. kG ptcp ms abs אמר. lG inf אזה *heat, stoke*. mnoun ms emph אַתּוּן Akk lw *furnace*. ncard w/ m noun חַד *one*, as multiplicative *times*. ocard w/ m noun שְׁבַע *seven*. p–p= *seven times*. qrel pron דִּי *that which*. rGp ptcp ms abs חזה *seen = normal*. sG inf אזה w/ 3ms acc sx *heat, stoke*.

20 anoun mp abs גְּבַר *man, person*. bnoun mp cstr גְּבַר hapax *hero, warrior, strong man*. cnoun ms abs חַיִל *power*. drel pron דִּי *who, which, that*. enoun ms חַיִל w/ 3ms gen sx *army*. fG sc 3ms אמר. gD inf כפת *tie up*. hPN Shadrach. iPN Meshach. j–jPN Abednego. kG inf רמה *throw*. lnoun ms cstr אַתּוּן

Akk lw *furnace*. mnoun fs emph נוּר *fire*. nG ptcp fs emph יקד *burn*.

21 atemp adv אֱדַיִן (w/ בְּ) *immediately; then*. bnoun mp emph גְּבַר *man, person*. cdist dem adj cp אִלֵּךְ *those*. dGp sc 3mp כפת *be tied up*. enoun mp סַרְבָּל w/ 3mp gen sx Pers lw *trousers (?); coat (?)*. fK פַּטִּישֵׁיהוֹן, Q פַּטְּשֵׁיהוֹן, both noun mp פַּטִּישׁ w/ 3mp gen sx Pers lw (?) hapax *garment; shirt (?); trousers (?)*. gnoun fp כַּרְבְּלָה w/ 3mp gen sx hapax, Akk lw *cap, hat*. hnoun mp לְבוּשׁ w/ 3mp gen sx *clothing*. iGp sc 3mp רמה *be thrown*. jnoun ms cstr גַּו *midst*. knoun ms cstr אַתּוּן Akk lw *furnace*. lnoun fs emph נוּר *fire*. mG ptcp fs emph יקד *burn* [L, BHS יְקִֽ; Ed יְקִֽ].

22 a= כְּ + לְ *according to*. bprox dem pron ms דְּנָה *this*. c–c= *therefore*. dsubord conj דִּי *that*. e–e*from that = because*. fnoun fs cstr מִלָּה *word*. gH ptcp fs abs חצף *be harsh*. hnoun ms emph אַתּוּן Akk lw *furnace*. iGp ptcp ms abs אזה *heat, stoke*. jadv יַתִּיר *excessively*. knoun mp emph גְּבַר *man, person*. ldist dem adj cp אִלֵּךְ *those*. mrel pron דִּי *who, that*. nH sc 3mp סלק *bring up*. oPN Shadrach. pPN Meshach. q–qPN Abednego. rD sc 3ms קטל *kill*. sindep pers pron 3mp הִמּוֹן as dir obj *them*. tnoun ms emph שְׁבִיב *flame*.

דִי נוּרָֽאʳ: 23 וְגֻבְרַיָּאᵃ אִלֵּךְᵇ תְּלָתֵּהוֹןᶜ שַׁדְרַךְᵈ מֵישַׁךְᵉ וַעֲבֵד נְגוֹ
נְפַ֫לוּᵍ לְגֽוֹא־אַתּוּןʰ־נוּרָאⁱ יָקִֽדְתָּאᵏ מְכַפְּתִֽיןˡ: פ

24 אֱדַ֫יִן נְבוּכַדְנֶצַּר מַלְכָּאᵇ תְּוַהᵃ וְקָםᵇ בְּהִתְבְּהָלָהᶜ עָנֵהᵈ וְאָמַרᵉ
לְהַדָּֽבְרוֹהִיᶠ הֲלָאᵍ גֻבְרִיןʰ תְּלָתָהⁱ רְמֵ֫ינָאʲ לְגוֹא־נוּרָאᵏ מְכַפְּתִיןˡ
עָנַ֫יִןⁿ וְאָמְרִיןᵒ לְמַלְכָּאᵖ יַצִּיבָֽאᵠ מַלְכָּא: 25 עָנֵהᵃ וְאָמַרᵇ הָא־אֲנָהᵈ
חָזֵהᵉ גֻּבְרִ֫ין אַרְבְּעָהᵍ שְׁרַ֫יִןʰ מַהְלְכִיןⁱ בְּגֽוֹא־נוּרָאʲ וַחֲבָלᵏ לָא־אִיתַ֫יⁿ
בְּהוֹןⁿ וְרֵוֵהᵒ דִּי רֽבִיעָיָאᵖ דָּמֵהᵠ לְבַר־אֱלָהִֽיןˢ: ס 26 בֵּאדַ֫יִןᵃ
קְרֵבᵇ נְבוּכַדְנֶצַּר לִתְרַעᶜ אַתּוּןᵈ נוּרָאᵉ יָקִֽדְתָּאᶠ עָנֵהᵍ וְאָמַרʰ שַׁדְרַ֫ךְⁱ
מֵישַׁ֫ךְʲ וַעֲבֵד־נְגוֹᵏ עַבְדֽוֹהִיˡ דִּֽי־אֱלָהָאᵐ עִלָּיָאⁿ פֻּקוּᵒ וֶאֱתוֹᵖ בֵּאדַ֫יִןᵠ
נָֽפְקִיןᵣ שַׁדְרַךְⁱ מֵישַׁךְʲ וַעֲבֵד נְגוֹᵏ מִן־גּֽוֹאˢ נוּרָֽאᵉ: 27 וּֽמִתְכַּנְּשִׁיןᵃ
אֲחַשְׁדַּרְפְּנַיָּאᵇ סִגְנַיָּאᶜ וּפַחֲוָתָאᵈ וְהַדָּֽבְרֵיᵉ מַלְכָּא חָזַ֫יִןᶠ לְגֻבְרַיָּאᵍ

---

22 ᵘgen part דִּי *of.* ᵛnoun fs emph נוּר *fire.*
23 ᵃnoun mp emph גְּבַר *man, person.* ᵇdist
dem adj cp אִלֵּךְ *those.* ᶜcard w/ m noun
תְּלָת w/ 3mp gen sx *the three of them.* ᵈPN
Shadrach. ᵉPN *Meshach.* ᶠ⁻ᶠPN *Abednego.* ᵍG sc 3mp נפל *fall.* ʰnoun ms cstr גּו
midst. ⁱnoun ms cstr אַתּוּן Akk lw *furnace.*
ʲnoun fs emph נוּר *fire.* ᵏG ptcp fs emph
יקד *burn.* ˡDp ptcp mp abs כפת *tied up.*
24 ᵃG sc 3ms תוה hapax *be astonished, star-
tled, horrified.* ᵇG sc 3ms קום. ᶜnoun fs
abs הִתְבְּהָלָה *haste.* ᵈG ptcp ms abs I ענה.
ᵉG ptcp ms abs אמר. ᶠnoun mp abs הַדָּבָר w/
3ms gen sx Pers lw *companion.* ᵍneg part
לָא w/ interr ה. ʰnoun mp abs גְּבַר *man,
person.* ⁱcard w/ m noun תְּלָת *three.* ʲG sc
1cp רמה *throw.* ᵏnoun ms cstr גּו *midst.*
ˡnoun fs emph נוּר *fire.* ᵐDp ptcp mp abs
כפת *tied up.* ⁿG ptcp mp abs I ענה. ᵒG ptcp
mp abs אמר. ᵖadj fs abs יַצִּיב adv *certainly.*
25 ᵃG ptcp ms abs I ענה. ᵇG ptcp ms abs אמר.
ᶜdem part הָא hapax *behold! look!* ᵈindep
pers pron 1cs אֲנָה *I.* ᵉG ptcp ms abs חזה.
ᶠnoun mp abs גְּבַר *man, person.* ᵍcard
w/ m noun אַרְבַּע *four.* ʰGp ptcp mp abs
שרה *untied.* ⁱH ptcp mp abs הלך *walk.*
ʲnoun ms cstr גּו *midst.* ᵏnoun fs emph נוּר

fire. ˡnoun ms abs חֲבָל *harm.* ᵐpart. of existence אִיתַי *there is.* ⁿprep בְּ w/ 3mp gen
sx. ᵒnoun ms רֵו w/ 3ms gen sx *appearance.* ᵖgen part דִּי *of.* ᵠK רְבִיעָיָא, Q
רְבִיעָאָה [Ed רְבִיעָי], both adj ms emph רְבִיעָי *fourth.*
ʳG ptcp ms abs דמה *resemble.* ˢnoun ms
cstr II בַּר *son.* This cstr chain is indefinite,
a divine being.
26 ᵃtemp adv אֱדַיִן (w/ בְּ) *immediately; then.*
ᵇG sc 3ms קרב *approach.* ᶜnoun ms cstr
תְּרַע *door, opening.* ᵈnoun ms cstr אַתּוּן
Akk lw *furnace.* ᵉnoun fs emph נוּר *fire.* ᶠG
ptcp fs emph יקד *burn.* ᵍG ptcp ms abs I
ענה. ʰG ptcp ms abs אמר. ⁱPN *Shadrach.*
ʲPN *Meshach.* ᵏ⁻ᵏPN *Abednego.* ˡnoun mp
עֲבֵד w/ 3ms gen sx *slave, servant.* ᵐgen
part דִּי *of.* ⁿK עֶלְיָא, Q עִלָּאָה, both noun ms
emph עִלָּי *most high.* ᵒG imv 2mp נפק *exit.*
ᵖG imv 2mp אתה *come.* ᵠG ptcp mp abs
נפק *exit.* ʳnoun ms cstr גּו *midst.* ˢnoun fs
emph נוּר *fire.*
27 ᵃtD ptcp mp abs כנש *assemble.* ᵇnoun mp
emph אֲחַשְׁדַּרְפַּן Pers lw *satrap.* ᶜnoun mp
emph סְגַן *prefect.* ᵈnoun mp emph פֶּחָה
governor. ᵉnoun mp cstr הַדָּבָר Pers lw
companion. ᶠG ptcp mp abs חזה. ᵍnoun mp
emph גְּבַר *man, person.*

אֵלֵּ֨ךְ דִּ֤י לָֽא־שְׁלֵ֨ט נוּרָ֜א בְּגֶשְׁמְהוֹן֙ וּשְׂעַ֤ר רֵאשְׁהוֹן֙ לָ֣א הִתְחָרַ֔ךְ
וְסָרְבָּלֵיהוֹן֙ לָ֣א שְׁנ֔וֹ וְרֵ֥יחַ נ֖וּר לָ֥א עֲדָ֖ת בְּהֽוֹן׃ 28 עָנֵ֨ה נְבֽוּכַדְנֶצַּ֜ר
וְאָמַ֗ר בְּרִ֤יךְ אֱלָהֲהוֹן֙ דִּֽי־שַׁדְרַ֤ךְ מֵישַׁךְ֙ וַעֲבֵ֣ד נְג֔וֹ דִּֽי־שְׁלַ֤ח
מַלְאֲכֵהּ֙ וְשֵׁיזִ֣ב לְעַבְד֔וֹהִי דִּ֣י הִתְרְחִ֣צֽוּ עֲל֑וֹהִי וּמִלַּ֤ת מַלְכָּא֙
שַׁנִּ֔יו וִיהַ֣בוּ גֶשְׁמֵיה֗וֹן דִּ֠י לָֽא־יִפְלְח֤וּן וְלָֽא־יִסְגְּדוּן֙ לְכָל־אֱלָ֔הּ
לָהֵ֖ן לֵאלָֽהֲהֽוֹן׃ 29 וּמִנִּי֮ שִׂ֣ים טְעֵם֒ דִּי֩ כָל־עַ֨ם אֻמָּ֜ה וְלִשָּׁ֗ן
דִּֽי־יֵאמַ֤ר שָׁלָה֙ עַ֣ל אֱלָהֲה֗וֹן דִּֽי־שַׁדְרַ֤ךְ מֵישַׁךְ֙ וַעֲבֵ֣ד נְג֔וֹא
הַדָּמִ֣ין יִתְעֲבֵ֗ד וּבַיְתֵ֛הּ נְוָלִ֥י יִשְׁתַּוֵּ֖ה כָּל־קֳבֵ֣ל דִּ֣י לָ֤א אִיתַ֨י
אֱלָ֣הּ אָחֳרָ֔ן דִּֽי־יִכֻּ֥ל לְהַצָּלָ֖ה כִּדְנָֽה׃ 30 בֵּאדַ֣יִן מַלְכָּ֗א הַצְלַ֛ח
לְשַׁדְרַ֥ךְ מֵישַׁ֛ךְ וַעֲבֵ֥ד נְג֖וֹ בִּמְדִינַ֥ת בָּבֶֽל׃
פ
31 נְבוּכַדְנֶצַּ֣ר מַלְכָּ֗א לְֽכָל־עַֽמְמַיָּ֞א אֻמַּיָּ֧א וְלִשָּׁנַיָּ֛א דִּֽי־דָאֲרִ֥ין בְּכָל־

---

27 ᵸdist dem adj cp אֵלֵּךְ *those*. ⁱrel pron דִּי *who, that*. ʲG sc 3ms שלט *have power* (w/ בְּ) *over*. ᵏnoun ms emph נוּר *fire*. ˡnoun ms גֶשֶׁם w/ 3mp gen sx *body* [so Ed Q, K "גֶּשְׁמֵיה"]. ᵐnoun ms cstr שְׂעַר *hair*. ⁿnoun ms רֵאשׁ w/ 3mp gen sx *head*. ᵒtD sc 3ms חרך *hapax be singed*. ᵖnoun mp סַרְבָּל w/ 3mp gen sx Pers lw *trousers* (?); *coat* (?) [Ed "וְסָרְבְּ; L, BHL*, BHS "וְסַרְ]. �ۊG sc 3mp שׁנה *intrans change; change color*. ʳnoun ms cstr רֵיחַ *hapax smell, odor*. ˢnoun ms abs נוּר *fire*. ᵗG sc 3fs עדה *touch* (w/ בְּ). ᵘprep בְּ w/ 3mp gen sx.

28 ᵃG ptcp ms abs I ענה. ᵇG ptcp ms abs אמר. ᶜGp ptcp ms abs II ברך *blessed*. ᵈnoun ms אֱלָהּ w/ 3mp gen sx. ᵉgen part דִּי *of*. ᶠPN *Shadrach*. ᵍPN *Meshach*. ʰ⁻ʰPN *Abednego*. ⁱrel pron דִּי *who, that*. ʲG sc 3ms שלח *send*. ᵏnoun ms מַלְאַךְ w/ 3ms gen sx *messenger, angel*. ˡŠ sc 3ms שׁיזב *rescue*. ᵐnoun mp עֲבֵד w/ 3ms gen sx *slave, servant*. ⁿtG sc 3mp רחץ *hapax trust* (w/ עַל־) *in*. ᵒprep עַל־ w/ 3ms gen sx. ᵖnoun fs cstr מִלָּה *word*. ۊD sc 3mp שׁנה *trans change = violate*. ʳG sc 3mp יהב. ˢK גֶשְׁמֵיהוֹן noun mp גֶּשֶׁם w/ 3mp gen sx, Q גֶשְׁמְהוֹן noun ms גֶשֶׁם w/ 3mp gen sx, both *body*. ᵗpurp conj דִּי *so that*. ᵘG pc 3mp פלח *serve*. ᵛG pc 3mp סגד *prostrate oneself, bow down to the ground*. ʷnoun ms cstr כֹּל. ˣprep II לָהֵן

except. ʸnoun ms אֱלָהּ w/ 3mp gen sx.

29 ᵃprep מִן w/ 1cs gen sx. ᵇGp sc 3ms שִׂים. ᶜnoun ms abs טְעֵם *statement*. ᵈepex conj דִּי *that*. ᵉnoun ms cstr כֹּל. ᶠnoun ms abs עַם *people*. ᵍnoun fs abs אֻמָּה *nation*. ʰnoun ms abs לִשָּׁן *tongue*. ⁱrel pron דִּי *who, that*. ʲG pc 3ms אמר. ᵏK שָׁלָה, Q שָׁלוּ, both noun fs abs שָׁלוּ *negligence = blasphemy*. ˡnoun ms אֱלָהּ w/ 3mp gen sx. ᵐgen part דִּי *of*. ⁿPN *Shadrach*. ᵒPN *Meshach*. ᵖ⁻ᵖPN *Abednego*. ۊnoun mp abs הַדָּם Pers lw *limb*. ʳtG pc 3ms עבד. ˢ⁻ˢ= *torn limb from limb*. ᵗnoun ms בַּיִת w/ 3ms gen sx. ᵘnoun fs abs נְוָלוּ Akk lw (?) *dunghill; latrine pit*. ᵛtD pc 3ms שׁוה *be turned into*. ʷ= כְּ + לְ *according to*. ˣsubord conj דִּי *that*. ʸ⁻ʸ= *because, since*. ᶻpart. of existence אִיתַי *there is*. ᵃᵃadj ms abs אָחֳרָן *another*. ᵇᵇG pc 3ms יכל *be able*. ᶜᶜH inf נצל *deliver*. ᵈᵈprox dem pron ms דְּנָה w/ prep כְּ *like this, thus*.

30 ᵃtemp adv אֱדַיִן (w/ בְּ) *immediately; then*. ᵇH sc 3ms צלח *promote*. ᶜPN *Shadrach*. ᵈPN *Meshach*. ᵉ⁻ᵉPN *Abednego*. ᶠnoun fs cstr מְדִינָה *district, province*.

31 ᵃnoun ms cstr כֹּל. ᵇnoun mp emph עַם *people*. ᶜnoun fp emph אֻמָּה *nation*. ᵈnoun mp emph לִשָּׁן *tongue*. ᵉrel pron דִּי *who, that*. ᶠK דָּאֲרִין, Q דָּיְרִין [Ed "דָּ], both G ptcp mp abs דור *dwell*.

אַרְעָאᵍ שְׁלָמְכוֹןʰ יִשְׂגֵּאᶦ׃ ³² אָתַיָּאᵃ וְתִמְהַיָּאᵇ דִּי עֲבַדᵈ עִמִּיᵉ אֱלָהָא
עִלָּיָאᶠ שְׁפַרᵍ קָדָמַי לְהַחֲוָיָהʰ׃ ³³ אָתוֹהִיᵃ כְּמָה רַבְרְבִין וְתִמְהוֹהִיᵈ
כְּמָה תַקִּיפִיןᵇ מַלְכוּתֵהᶜ מַלְכוּתᵉ עָלַםᵍ וְשָׁלְטָנֵהᶦ עִם־דָּרᵏ וְדָרᵏʲ׃

4 ¹ אֲנָהᵃ נְבוּכַדְנֶצַּר שְׁלֵהᵇ הֲוֵיתᶜ בְּבֵיתִיᵈ וְרַעְנַןᵉ בְּהֵיכְלִיᶠ׃ ² חֵלֶםᵃ
חֲזֵיתᵇ וִידַחֲלִנַּנִיᶜ וְהַרְהֹרִיןᵈ עַל־מִשְׁכְּבִי וְחֶזְוֵיᶠ רֵאשִׁי יְבַהֲלֻנַּנִיʰ׃
³ וּמִנִּיᵃ שִׂיםᵇ טְעֵםᶜ לְהַנְעָלָהᵈ קָדָמַי לְכֹל חַכִּימֵיᶠ בָבֶל דִּי־פְשַׁרʰ
חֶלְמָאᶦ יְהוֹדְעֻנַּנִי׃ ⁴ בֵּאדַיִןᵃ עָלֲלִיןᵇ חַרְטֻמַיָּאᶜ אָשְׁפַיָּאᵈ כַּשְׂדָּיֵאᵉ
וְגָזְרַיָּאᶠ וְחֶלְמָאᵍ אָמַרʰ אֲנָהᶦ קָדָמֵיהוֹןʲ וּפִשְׁרֵהᵏ לָא־מְהוֹדְעִיןˡ לִי׃
⁵ וְעַדᵃ אָחֳרֵיןᵃ עַלᶜ קָדָמַי דָּנִיֵּאל דִּי־שְׁמֵהᵈ בֵּלְטְשַׁאצַּרᵍ כְּשֻׁםʰ
אֱלָהִיᶦ וְדִי רוּחַ־אֱלָהִיןʲ קַדִּישִׁיןᵏ בֵּהˡ וְחֶלְמָאᵐ קָדָמוֹהִיⁿ אַמְרֵתᵒ׃

---

31 ᵍnoun fs emph אֲרַע *earth, land.* ʰnoun ms
שְׁלָם w/ 2mp gen sx *peace.* ᶦG juss 3ms
שְׂגָא *become great, grow.*

32 ᵃnoun mp emph אָת *sign.* ᵇnoun mp emph
תְּמַה *wonder.* ᶜrel pron דִּי *which, that.* ᵈG
sc 3ms עֲבַד. ᵉprep עִם w/ 1cs gen sx *in con-
nection with me.* ᶠK עִלָּיָא, Q עֶלְאָה, both
noun ms emph עִלָּי *most high.* ᵍG sc 3ms
שְׁפַר *be pleasant, pleasing.* ʰprep קֳדָם w/
1cs gen sx [so Ed; L, BHS ״קֳ]. ᶦH inf חֲוָה
show, make known, declare.

33 ᵃnoun mp אָת w/ 3ms gen sx *sign.* ᵇimpers
correl pron מָה + כְּ *how!* ᶜadj mp abs רַב
great. ᵈnoun mp תְּמַה w/ 3ms gen sx *wonder.* ᵉadj mp abs תַּקִּיף *powerful, mighty.*
ᶠnoun fs מַלְכוּ w/ 3ms gen sx *kingdom.*
ᵍnoun fs cstr מַלְכוּ *kingdom.* ʰnoun ms
abs עָלַם *eternity.* ᶦnoun ms שָׁלְטָן w/ 3ms
gen sx *empire; dominion.* ʲnoun ms abs דָּר
generation. ᵏ⁻ᵏ= *from generation to generation.*

4

1 ᵃindep pers pron 1cs אֲנָה *I.* ᵇadj ms abs
שְׁלֵה hapax *at ease, carefree.* ᶜG sc 1cs הוה.
ᵈnoun ms בַּיִת w/ 1cs gen sx. ᵉadj ms abs
רַעְנַן hapax *flourishing, happy.* ᶠnoun ms
הֵיכַל w/ 1cs gen sx *palace.*

2 ᵃnoun ms abs חֵלֶם *dream.* ᵇG sc 1cs חזה.
ᶜD pc 3ms דחל w/ 1cs acc sx *frighten.*
ᵈnoun mp abs הַרְהֹר hapax *imaginations,
fantasies.* ᵉnoun ms מִשְׁכַּב w/ 1cs gen sx

---

bed. ᶠnoun mp cstr חֱזוּ *vision.* ᵍnoun ms
רֵאשׁ w/ 1cs gen sx *head.* ʰD pc 3mp בהל
w/ 1cs acc sx *terrify.*

3 ᵃprep מִן w/ 1cs gen sx. ᵇGp sc 3ms שִׂים.
ᶜnoun ms abs טְעֵם *statement.* ᵈH inf II עלל
bring. ᵉprep קֳדָם w/ 1cs gen sx. ᶠnoun ms
cstr כֹּל. ᵍadj mp cstr חַכִּים *wise.* ʰpurp conj
דִּי *so that.* ᶦnoun ms emph חֵלֶם *dream.* ʲH
pc 3mp ידע w/ 1cs acc sx.

4 ᵃtemp adv אֱדַיִן (w/ בְּ) *immediately; then.*
ᵇK עָלֲלִין, Q עָלֲלִין, both G ptcp mp abs II עלל
enter. ᶜnoun mp emph חַרְטֹם *magician.*
ᵈnoun mp emph אָשַׁף Akk lw *conjurer; exorcist.* ᵉK כַּשְׂדָּיֵא, Q כַּשְׂדָּאֵי, both noun mp
emph כַּשְׂדָּי *Babylonian astrologer* or *sage.*
ᶠG ptcp mp emph גזר *diviner.* ᵍnoun ms
emph חֵלֶם *dream.* ʰG ptcp ms abs אמר.
ᶦindep pers pron 1cs אֲנָה *I.* ʲprep קֳדָם w/
3mp gen sx. ᵏnoun ms פְּשַׁר w/ 3ms gen sx.
ˡH ptcp mp abs ידע. ᵐprep לְ w/ 1cs gen sx.

5 ᵃadv אָחֳרֵין hapax *at last; eventually.* ᵇ⁻ᵇ=
finally. ᶜG sc 3ms II עלל *enter.* ᵈprep קֳדָם
w/ 1cs gen sx. ᵉrel pron דִּי *who, that.*
ᶠnoun ms שֵׁם w/ 3ms gen sx *name.* ᵍPN
Belteshazzar [so BHS; Ed ״בְּ; L, BHL*
״בֵּלְטְ]. ʰnoun ms cstr שֵׁם *name.* ᶦnoun ms
אֱלָה w/ 1cs gen sx. ʲnoun fs cstr רוּחַ *spirit.*
ᵏadj mp abs קַדִּישׁ *holy.* ˡprep בְּ w/ 3ms gen
sx. ᵐnoun ms emph חֵלֶם *dream.* ⁿprep
קֳדָם w/ 3ms gen sx. ᵒG sc 1cs אמר.

6 בֵּלְטְשַׁאצַּרᵃ רַבᵇ חַרְטֻמַיָּאᶜ דִּי׀ דᵈ אֲנָהᵉ יִדְעֵתᶠ דִּי רוּחַʰ אֱלָהִין
קַדִּישִׁיןᵏ בָּךְ וְכָל־רָזˡ לָא־אָנֵסᵐ לָךְⁿ חֶזְוֵי חֶלְמִי דִי־חֲזֵיתᵖ וּפִשְׁרֵהᑫ
אֱמַרˢ: 7 וְחֶזְוֵיᵃ רֵאשִׁיᵇ עַל־מִשְׁכְּבִיᶜ
חָזֵהᵈ הֲוֵיתᵉ

      וַאֲלוּᶠ אִילָןᵍ   בְּגוֹאʰ אַרְעָאⁱ   וְרוּמֵהʲ שַׂגִּיאᵏ:

8 רְבָהᵃ אִילָנָאᵇ וּתְקִףᶜ
      וְרוּמֵהᵈ יִמְטֵאᵉ לִשְׁמַיָּאᶠ   וַחֲזוֹתֵהᵍ לְסוֹףʰ כָּל־אַרְעָאⁱ:

9 עָפְיֵהᵃ שַׁפִּירᵇ וְאִנְבֵּהᶜ שַׂגִּיאᵈ   וּמָזוֹןᵉ לְכֹלָּא־בֵהᵍ
תְּחֹתוֹהִיʰ תַּטְלֵל׀ חֵיוַתʲ בָּרָאˡᵏ
וּבְעַנְפוֹהִיᵐ יְדֻרוּןⁿ צִפֲּרֵי שְׁמַיָּאᵖ   וּמִנֵּהᑫ יִתְּזִין כָּל־בִּשְׂרָאˢ:

10 חָזֵהᵃ הֲוֵיתᵇ בְּחֶזְוֵיᶜ רֵאשִׁיᵈ עַל־מִשְׁכְּבִיᵉ וַאֲלוּᶠ עִירᵍ וְקַדִּישʰ מִן־
שְׁמַיָּאⁱ נָחִתʲ: 11 קָרֵאᵃ בְחַיִלᵇ וְכֵןᶜ אָמַרᵈ

---

6 ᵃPN *Belteshazzar.* ᵇadj ms cstr רַב *chief.* ᶜnoun mp emph חַרְטֹם *magician.* ᵈrel pron דִּי *who, which, that.* ᵉindep pers pron 1cs אֲנָה *I.* ᶠG SC 1cs ידע. ᵍepex conj דִּי *that.* ʰnoun fs cstr רוּחַ *spirit.* ⁱadj mp abs קַדִּישׁ *holy.* ʲprep בְּ w/ 2ms gen sx. ᵏnoun ms cstr כֹּל. ˡnoun ms abs רָזֶה Pers lw *secret, mystery.* ᵐG ptcp ms abs אנס hapax *be too difficult for.* ⁿprep לְ w/ 2ms gen sx. ᵒnoun mp cstr חֱזוּ *vision.* ᵖnoun ms חֵלֶם w/ 1cs gen sx *dream.* ᑫG SC 1cs חזה. ʳnoun ms פְּשַׁר w/ 3ms gen sx. ˢG imv 2ms אמר.

7 ᵃnoun mp cstr חֱזוּ *vision.* ᵇnoun ms רֵאשׁ w/ 1cs gen sx *head.* ᶜnoun ms מִשְׁכַּב w/ 1cs gen sx *bed.* ᵈG ptcp ms abs חזה. ᵉG SC 1cs הוה. ᶠinterj אֲלוּ *behold!* ᵍnoun ms abs אִילָן *tree.* ʰnoun ms cstr גַּו *midst.* ⁱnoun fs emph אֲרַע *earth, land.* ʲnoun ms רוּם w/ 3ms gen sx *height.* ᵏadj ms abs שַׂגִּיא *great.*

8 ᵃG SC 3ms רבה *grow.* ᵇnoun ms emph אִילָן *tree.* ᶜG SC 3ms תקף *become strong.* ᵈnoun ms רוּם w/ 3ms gen sx *height.* ᵉG PC 3ms מטא *reach.* ᶠnoun mp emph שְׁמַיִן. ᵍnoun fs חֲזוֹת w/ 3ms gen sx *visibleness, ability to be seen (?); branches, canopy of a tree (?).* ʰnoun ms cstr סוֹף *end.* ⁱnoun ms

cstr כֹּל. ʲnoun fs emph אֲרַע *earth, land.*

9 ᵃnoun ms עֲפִי w/ 3ms gen sx *leaves.* ᵇadj ms abs שַׁפִּיר *beautiful.* ᶜnoun ms אֲנַב w/ 3ms gen sx *fruit.* ᵈadj ms abs שַׂגִּיא *abundant.* ᵉnoun ms abs מָזוֹן *food.* ᶠnoun ms emph כֹּל. ᵍprep בְּ w/ 3ms gen sx. ʰprep תְּחוֹת w/ 3ms gen sx *under.* ⁱH PC 3fs טלל hapax *find shade.* ʲnoun fs cstr חֵיוָה *animal.* ᵏnoun ms emph בַּר ᴵ *field.* ˡ⁻ˡ= *wild animal.* ᵐnoun mp עֲנַף w/ 3ms gen sx *bough, branches.* ⁿK יְדֻרוּן G PC 3mp דור, Q יְדֻרָן G PC 3fp דור, both *dwell.* ᵒnoun fp cstr צְפַר *bird.* ᵖnoun mp emph שְׁמַיִן. ᑫprep מִן w/ 3ms gen sx. ʳtG PC 3ms זון hapax *be fed.* ˢnoun ms cstr כֹּל. ᵗnoun ms emph בְּשַׂר *flesh.*

10 ᵃG ptcp ms abs חזה. ᵇG SC 1cs הוה. ᶜnoun mp cstr חֱזוּ *vision.* ᵈnoun ms רֵאשׁ w/ 1cs gen sx *head.* ᵉnoun ms מִשְׁכַּב w/ 1cs gen sx *bed.* ᶠinterj אֲלוּ *behold!* ᵍnoun ms abs עִיר *watcher.* ʰadj ms abs קַדִּישׁ *holy.* ⁱnoun mp emph שְׁמַיִן. ʲG ptcp ms abs נחת *descend.*

11 ᵃG ptcp ms abs קרא *cry out, shout.* ᵇnoun ms abs חַיִל *power.* ᶜadv כֵּן *thus.* ᵈG ptcp ms abs אמר.

גֹּדּוּ^e אִֽילָנָא^f וְקַצִּצוּ עַנְפֿוֹהִי^h   אַתַּרוּⁱ עָפְיֵהּ^j וּבַדַּרוּ^k אִנְבֵּהּ^l

תְּנֻד^m חֵיוְתָאⁿ מִן־תַּחְתּֽוֹהִי^o   וְצִפְּרַיָּא^p מִן־עַנְפֽֿוֹהִי:

¹² בְּרַם^a עִקַּר^b שָׁרְשֽׁוֹהִי^c בְּאַרְעָא^d שְׁבֻקוּ^e

וּבֶֽאֱסוּר^f דִּֽי־פַרְזֶל^g וּנְחָשׁⁱ   בְּדִתְאָא^j דִּֽי בָרָא^k

וּבְטַל^l שְׁמַיָּא^m יִצְטַבַּעⁿ   וְעִם־חֵיוְתָא^o חֲלָקֵהּ^p בַּעֲשַׂב אַרְעָֽא:^d

¹³ לִבְבֵהּ^a מִן־אֲנוֹשָׁא^b יְשַׁנּוֹן^c וּלְבַב^d חֵיוָה^e יִתְיְהִב^f לֵהּ^g וְשִׁבְעָה^h

עִדָּנִיןⁱ יַחְלְפוּן^j עֲלֽוֹהִי:^k   ¹⁴ בִּגְזֵרַת^a עִירִין^b פִּתְגָמָא^c וּמֵאמַר^d קַדִּישִׁין^e

שְׁאֵלְתָא^f עַד־דִּבְרַת^g דִּֽי^h יִנְדְּעוּןⁱ⁻ⁱ חַיַּיָּא^k דִּֽי־שַׁלִּיט^m עִלָּיָאⁿ בְּמַלְכוּת^o

אֲנוֹשָׁא^p וּלְמַן־דִּֽי^{q-r} יִצְבֵּא^{s-s} יִתְּנִנַּהּ^t וּשְׁפַל^v אֲנָשִׁים^w יְקִים^x עֲלַֽיהּ:^y

¹⁵ דְּנָה^a חֶלְמָא^b חֲזֵית^c אֲנָה^d מַלְכָּא^e נְבֽוּכַדְנֶצַּר וְאַנְתָּה^e בֵּלְטְשַׁאצַּר^f

---

11 ^eG imv 2mp גדד *chop down.* ^fnoun ms emph אִילָן *tree.* ^gD imv 2mp קצץ hapax *cut off, lop off.* ^hnoun mp עֲנַף w/ 3ms gen sx *bough, branches.* ⁱH imv 2mp נתר hapax *strip off.* ^jnoun ms עֳפִי w/ 3ms gen sx *leaves.* ^kD imv 2mp בדר hapax *scatter.* ^lnoun ms אֵנֶב w/ 3ms gen sx *fruit.* ^mG juss 3fs נוד hapax *flee.* ⁿnoun fs emph חֵיוָה *animal.* ^oprep תְּחוֹת w/ 3ms gen sx *under.* ^pnoun fp emph צְפַר *bird.*

12 ^adisj בְּרַם *but, however.* ^bnoun ms cstr עִקַּר *stump.* ^cnoun mp שְׁרֵשׁ w/ 3ms gen sx *root.* ^dnoun fs emph אֲרַע *earth, land.* ^eG imv 2mp שבק *leave.* ^fnoun ms abs אֱסוּר *band.* ^ggen part דִּי *of.* ^hnoun ms abs פַּרְזֶל *iron.* ⁱnoun ms abs נְחָשׁ *bronze.* ^jnoun ms emph דֶּתֶא *grass.* ^knoun ms emph בַּר *field.* ^lnoun ms cstr טַל *dew.* ^mnoun mp emph שְׁמַיִן *heaven.* ⁿtD juss 3ms צבע *be drenched.* ^onoun fs emph חֵיוָה *animal.* ^pnoun ms חֲלָק w/ 3ms gen sx *portion, lot.* ^qnoun ms cstr עֲשַׂב *vegetation, plants.* The phrase ^{q-d} may be an in-text gloss for the phrase ^{j-k}.

13 ^anoun ms לְבַב w/ 3ms gen sx *heart.* ^bK אֲנוֹשָׁא, Q אֲנָשָׁא, both noun ms emph אֱנָשׁ. ^cD juss 3mp שנה trans *change.* ^dnoun ms cstr לְבַב *heart.* ^enoun fs abs חֵיוָה *animal.* ^ftG juss 3ms יהב ^gprep לְ w/ 3ms gen sx. ^hcard

w/ m noun שְׁבַע *seven.* ⁱnoun mp abs עִדָּן indicates time in general or a length of time such as a year *season, time.* ^jG juss 3mp חלף *pass over.* ^kprep עַל w/ 3ms gen sx.

14 ^anoun fs cstr גְּזֵרָה *decree.* ^bnoun mp abs עִיר *watcher.* ^cnoun ms emph פִּתְגָם Pers lw *word, sentence.* ^dnoun ms cstr מֵאמַר *word, command.* ^eadj mp abs קַדִּישׁ *holy.* ^fnoun fs emph שְׁאֵלָה hapax *decision.* ^gnoun fs cstr דִּבְרָה *matter.* ^hsubord conj דִּי *that.* ⁱ⁻ⁱ= *for the purpose of, for the sake of, that, so that.* ^jG PC 3mp ידע. ^kadj mp emph חַי *living.* ^lepex conj דִּי *that.* ^madj ms abs שַׁלִּיט *sovereign; mighty.* ⁿK עֶלְיָא, Q עִלָּאָה, both noun ms emph עִלִּי *most high.* ^onoun fs cstr מַלְכוּ *kingdom.* ^pK אֲנוֹשָׁא, Q אֲנָשָׁא, both noun ms emph אֱנָשׁ. ^qpers indef pron מַן *who.* ^rrel pron דִּי *who, that.* ^{s-s}= *whoever.* ^tG PC 3ms צבה *desire, wish.* ^uG PC 3ms נתן w/ 3fs acc sx *give.* ^vnoun ms cstr שְׁפַל *low, lowest.* ^wnoun mp abs אֱנָשׁ *human.* Heb ending! ^xH PC 3ms קום. ^yK עֲלַיהּ, Q עֲלַהּ, both prep עַל w/ 3fs gen sx.

15 ^aprox dem pron ms דְּנָה *this.* ^bnoun ms emph חֵלֶם *dream.* ^cG sc 1cs חזה. ^dindep pers pron 1cs אֲנָה *I.* ^eK וְאַנְתָּה, Q וְאַנְתְּ, both indep pers pron 2ms אַנְתְּ *you.* ^fPN Belteshazzar [so BHS, Ed בֵּ; L, BHL* בֵּלְטְ].

פִּשְׁרָא᷍ᵍ אֱמַר| כָּל־קֳבֵל᷍ᵏ דִּי|ᵏʲⁱ כָּל־חַכִּימֵי᷍ᵐ מַלְכוּתִי לָא־יָכְלִין᷍ᵒ
פִּשְׁרָא לְהוֹדָעֻתַנִיᵖ וְאַנְתָּהᑫ כָּהֵלˢ דִּי רוּחַᵗ אֱלָהִין־קַדִּישִׁיןᵘ בָּךְᵛ:
אֱדַיִן᷍ᵃ דָּנִיֵּאל דִּי־שְׁמֵהᵇ בֵּלְטְשַׁאצַּרᶜ אֶשְׁתּוֹמַםᵈ כְּשָׁעָהᵉ חֲדָהᶠ 16
וְרַעְיֹנֹהִיᵍ יְבַהֲלֻנֵּהּʰ עָנֵהⁱ מַלְכָּא וְאָמַרʲ בֵּלְטְשַׁאצַּר חֶלְמָאᵏ וּפִשְׁרָאˡ
אַל־ᵐיְבַהֲלָךְⁿ עָנֵהᵒ בֵלְטְשַׁאצַּרᵖ וְאָמַרʲ מָרִאⁱ חֶלְמָאᵏ לְשָׂנְאַיִךְᑫ
וּפִשְׁרֵהʳ לְעָרָיִךְˢ: אִילָנָאᵃ דִּי חֲזַיְתָᵇ דִּי רְבָהᵈ וּתְקִףᵉ וְרוּמֵהᶠ 17
יִמְטֵאᵍ לִשְׁמַיָּאʰ וַחֲזוֹתֵהⁱ לְכָל־אַרְעָאᵏ: וְעָפְיֵהᵃ שַׁפִּירᵇ וְאִנְבֵּהᶜ 18
שַׂגִּיאᵈ וּמָזוֹןᵉ לְכֹלָּא־בֵהᶠᵍ תְּחֹתֹוֹהִיʰ תְּדוּרⁱ חֵיוַתʲ בָּרָאᵏˡ וּבְעַנְפֹוֹהִיᵐ
יִשְׁכְּנָןⁿ צִפֲּרֵיᵒ שְׁמַיָּאᵖ: אַנְתָּהᵃ הוּאᵇ מַלְכָּא דִּי רְבַיְתᵈ וּתְקֵפְתְּᵉ 19
וּרְבוּתָךְᶠ רְבָתᵍ וּמְטָת לִשְׁמַיָּאʰ וְשָׁלְטָנָךְʲ לְסוֹףᵏ אַרְעָאˡ: וְדִי᷍ᵃ חֲזָהᵇ 20

15 ᵍnoun ms פְּשַׁר w/ 3ms gen sx [Ed K פִּשְׁרָא noun ms emph, Q פִּשְׁרֵהּ noun ms w/ 3ms gen sx]. ʰG imv 2ms אמר. ⁱ= לְ + כְּ = *according to.* ʲsubord conj דִּי *that.* ᵏ⁻ᵏ= *because, since.* ˡnoun ms cstr כֹּל. ᵐadj mp cstr חַכִּים *wise.* ⁿnoun fs מַלְכוּ w/ 1cs gen sx *kingdom.* ᵒG ptcp mp abs יכל *be able.* ᵖH inf ידע w/ 1cs acc sx. ᑫK וְאַנְתָּה, Q וְאַנְתָּ, both indep pers pron 2ms אַנְתְּ *you.* ʳG ptcp ms abs כהל *be able.* ˢcaus conj דִּי *because.* ᵗnoun ms emph רוּחַ *spirit.* ᵘadj mp abs קַדִּישׁ *holy.* ᵛprep בְּ w/ 2ms gen sx.

16 ᵃrel pron דִּי *who, that.* ᵇnoun ms שֵׁם w/ 3ms gen sx *name.* ᶜPN Belteshazzar [so BHS; Ed בֵּ″; L, BHL* בֵּלְטְ׳]. ᵈD PC 1cs שמם hapax *be appalled.* ᵉnoun fs abs שָׁעָה *hour = moment.* ᶠcard w/ f noun חַד *one, a.* ᵍnoun mp רַעְיֹן w/ 3ms gen sx *thought.* ʰD PC 3mp בהל w/ 3ms acc sx *terrify.* ⁱG ptcp ms abs ı ענה. ʲG ptcp ms abs אמר. ᵏnoun ms emph חֵלֶם *dream.* ˡnoun ms פְּשַׁר w/ 3ms gen sx [so BHS; L, BHL* וּפִ׳; Ed K פִּשְׁרָא noun ms emph, Q פִּשְׁרֵהּ noun ms w/ 3ms gen sx]. ᵐneg part אַל *not.* ⁿD juss 3ms בהל w/ 2ms acc sx *terrify.* ᵒPN Belteshazzar [so BHS; Ed בֵּ″. ᵖK מָרִאי, Q מָרִי, both noun ms מָרֵא w/ 1cs gen sx *lord.* ᑫK לְשָׂנְאַיִךְ G ptcp mp, Q לְשָׂנְאָךְ G ptcp ms, both שׂנא w/ 2ms acc sx hapax *hater, enemy.* ʳnoun ms פְּשַׁר w/ 3ms gen sx. ˢK לְעָרָיִךְ noun mp, Q לְעָרָךְ noun ms, both עָר w/ 2ms gen sx hapax *adversary.*

17 ᵃnoun ms emph אִילָן *tree.* ᵇrel pron דִּי *which, that.* ᶜG sc 2ms חזה. ᵈG sc 3ms רבה *grow.* ᵉG sc תקף *become strong.* ᶠnoun ms רוּם w/ 3ms gen sx *height.* ᵍG PC 3ms מטא *reach.* ʰnoun mp emph שְׁמַיִן. ⁱnoun fs חֲזוֹת w/ 3ms gen sx *visibleness, ability to be seen (?); branches, canopy of a tree (?).* ʲnoun ms cstr כֹּל. ᵏnoun fs emph אֲרַע *earth, land.*

18 ᵃnoun ms עֳפִי w/ 3ms gen sx *foliage.* ᵇadj ms abs שַׁפִּיר *beautiful.* ᶜnoun ms אֵנֶב w/ 3ms gen sx *fruit.* ᵈadj ms abs שַׂגִּיא *abundant.* ᵉnoun ms abs מָזוֹן *food.* ᶠnoun ms emph כֹּל. ᵍprep בְּ w/ 3ms gen sx. ʰprep תְּחוֹת w/ 3ms gen sx *under.* ⁱG PC 3fs דור *dwell.* ʲnoun fs cstr חֵיוָה *animal.* ᵏnoun ms emph ı בַּר *field.* ˡ⁻ˡ= *wild animal.* ᵐnoun mp עֲנַף w/ 3ms gen sx *branches.* ⁿG PC 3fp שׁכן *dwell.* ᵒnoun fp cstr צְפַר *bird.* ᵖnoun mp emph שְׁמַיִן.

19 ᵃK אַנְתָּה, Q אַנְתְּ, both indep pers pron 2ms אַנְתְּ *you.* ᵇdist dem pron ms הוּא *that* tree. ᶜcaus conj דִּי *because.* ᵈK רְבַיְתָ, Q רְבַת, both G sc 2ms רבה *grow, become great.* ᵉG sc 2ms תקף *grow strong.* ᶠnoun fs רְבוּ w/ 2ms gen sx *greatness.* ᵍG sc 3fs רבה *grow, become great.* ʰG sc 3fs מטא *reach.* ⁱnoun mp emph שְׁמַיִן. ʲnoun ms שָׁלְטָן w/ 2ms gen sx *empire; dominion.* ᵏnoun ms cstr סוֹף *end.* ˡnoun fs emph אֲרַע *earth.*

20 ᵃcaus conj דִּי *because.* ᵇG sc 3ms חזה.

מַלְכָּא עִירᶜ וְקַדִּישׁᵈ נָחֵתᵉ| מִן־שְׁמַיָּאᶠ וְאָמַרᵍ גֹּדּוּʰ אִילָנָאⁱ וְחַבְּלוּהִיʲ

בְּרַםᵏ עִקַּרˡ שָׁרְשׁוֹהִיᵐ בְּאַרְעָאⁿ שְׁבֻקוּᵒ וּבֶאֱסוּרᵖ דִּי־פַרְזֶלʳ וּנְחָשˢ

בְּדִתְאָאᵗ דִּי בָרָאᵘ וּבְטַלᵛ שְׁמַיָּא יִצְטַבַּעᵂ וְעִם־חֵיוַתˣ בָּרָאʸ חֲלָקֵהᶻ

עַדᵇᵇ דִּי־שִׁבְעָהᵇᵇᵃᵃ עִדָּנִיןᶜᶜ יַחְלְפוּןᵈᵈ עֲלוֹהִיᵉᵉ ᶠᶠ: 21 דְּנָהᵃ פִשְׁרָא מַלְכָּא

וּגְזֵרַתᵇ עֶלְיָא הִיאᵈ דִּי מְטָתᶠ עַל־מָרִאיᵍ מַלְכָּא: 22 וְלָךְᵃ טָרְדִיןᵇ

מִן־אֲנָשָׁא וְעִם־חֵיוַתᶜ בָּרָאᵉ לֶהֱוֵהᵍ מְדֹרָךְʰ וְעִשְׂבָּאʰ כְתוֹרִיןⁱ|

לָךְᵃ יְטַעֲמוּן וּמִטַּל שְׁמַיָּאᵏ לָךְˡ מְצַבְּעִיןᵐ וְשִׁבְעָהⁿ עִדָּנִיןᵒ יַחְלְפוּן

עֲלָיךְᵖ עַדᵖ דִּי־תִנְדַּעʳ דִּי־שַׁלִּיטˢ עֶלָּיָאᵛ בְּמַלְכוּתᵂ אֲנָשָׁאˣ וּלְמַן־דִּיʸ

יִצְבֵּאᵃᵃ יִתְּנִנַּהּᵇᵇ: 23 וְדִיᵃ אֲמַרוּ לְמִשְׁבַּקᶜ עִקַּרᵈ שָׁרְשׁוֹהִיᵉ דִּיᶠ אִילָנָאᵍ

---

20 ᶜnoun ms abs עִיר *watcher*. ᵈadj ms abs קַדִּישׁ *holy*. ᵉG ptcp ms abs נחת *descend*. ᶠnoun mp emph שְׁמַיִן. ᵍG ptcp ms abs אמר. ʰG imv 2mp גדד *chop down*. ⁱnoun ms emph אִילָן *tree*. ʲD imv 2mp חבל w/ 3ms acc sx *destroy*. ᵏdisj בְּרַם *but, however*. ˡnoun ms cstr עִקַּר *stump*. ᵐnoun mp שְׁרֹשׁ w/ 3ms gen sx *root*. ⁿnoun fs emph אֲרַע *earth, land*. ᵒG imv 2mp שבק *leave*. ᵖnoun ms abs אֱסוּר *band*. ᑫgen part דִּי *of*. ʳnoun ms abs פַּרְזֶל *iron*. ˢnoun ms abs נְחָשׁ *bronze*. ᵗnoun ms emph דֶּתֶא *grass*. ᵘnoun ms emph I בַּר *field*. ᵛnoun ms cstr טַל *dew*. ᵂtD juss 3ms צבע *be drenched*. ˣnoun fs cstr חֵיוָה *animal*. ʸ⁻ʸ= *wild animal*. ᶻnoun ms חֲלָק w/ 3ms gen sx *portion, lot*. ᵃᵃtemp conj דִּי *that*. ᵇᵇ⁻ᵇᵇ= *until*. ᶜᶜcard w/ m noun שְׁבַע *seven*. ᵈᵈnoun mp abs עִדָּן indicates time in general or a length of time such as a year *season, time*. ᵉᵉG PC 3mp חלף *pass over*. ᶠᶠprep עַל־ w/ 3ms gen sx.

21 ᵃprox dem pron ms דְּנָה *this*. ᵇnoun fs cstr גְּזֵרָה *decree*. ᶜK עֶלְיָא, Q עֶלְאָה, both noun ms emph עֶלִי *most high*. ᵈindep pers pron 3fs הִיא *she, it*. ᵉrel pron דִּי *which, that*. ᶠG SC 3fs מטא *reach, affect*. ᵍK מָרִאי, Q מָרִי, both noun ms מָרֵא w/ 1cs gen sx *lord*.

22 ᵃprep לְ w/ 2ms gen sx. ᵇG ptcp mp abs טרד *drive away*. This and the other plural verbs in this verse (ʲ and ᵐ) have unexpressed plural subjects which impy non-human agency and are the equivalents of passives. ᶜnoun fs cstr חֵיוָה *animal*. ᵈnoun ms emph I בַּר *field*. ᵉ⁻ᵉ= *wild animal*. ᶠG PC 3ms הוה. ᵍnoun ms מְדוֹר w/ 2ms gen sx *dwelling*. ʰnoun ms emph עֲשַׂב *vegetation, plants*. ⁱnoun mp abs תּוֹר *bull*. ʲD PC 3mp טעם *feed*. ᵏnoun ms cstr טַל *dew*. ˡnoun mp emph שְׁמַיִן. ᵐD ptcp mp abs צבע *drench*. ⁿcard w/ m noun שְׁבַע *seven*. ᵒnoun mp abs עִדָּן indicates time in general or a length of time such as a year *season, time*. ᵖG PC 3mp חלף *pass over*. ᑫK עֲלַיִךְ, Q עֲלָךְ, both prep עַל w/ 2ms gen sx. ʳtemp conj דִּי *that*. ˢG PC 2ms ידע. ᵗepex conj דִּי *that*. ᵘadj ms abs שַׁלִּיט *sovereign; mighty*. ᵛK עֶלְיָא, Q עֶלָּאָה, both noun ms emph עֶלִי *most high*. ᵂnoun fs cstr מַלְכוּ *kingdom*. ˣpers indef pron מַן *who*. ʸrel pron דִּי *who, that*. ᶻ⁻ᶻ= *whoever*. ᵃᵃG PC 3ms צבה *desire, wish*. ᵇᵇG PC 3ms נתן w/ 3fs acc sx *give*.

23 ᵃcaus conj דִּי *because*. ᵇG SC 3mp אמר. ᶜG inf שבק *leave*. ᵈnoun ms cstr עִקַּר *stump*. ᵉnoun mp שְׁרֹשׁ w/ 3ms gen sx *root*. ᶠgen part דִּי *of*. ᵍnoun ms emph אִילָן *tree*.

מַלְכוּתָ֣ךְ ᵸ לָ֔ךְ ᶦ קַיָּמָ֖ה ʲ מִן־דִּ֣י ᴸᴷ תִנְדַּ֑ע ᵐ דִּ֥י שַׁלִּטִ֖ן ᵒ שְׁמַיָּֽא ᴾ׃ 24 לָהֵ֣ן ᵃ מַלְכָּ֗א מִלְכִּי ᵇ יִשְׁפַּ֣ר עֲלָ֔ךְ ᶜ וַחֲטָיָךְ ᵈ וַחֲטָיָךְ ᵉ בְּצִדְקָ֣ה ᶠ פְרֻ֗ק ᵍ וַעֲוָיָתָךְ ᵸ בְּמִחַ֣ן ᶦ עֲנָ֑יִן ʲ הֵ֛ן ᵏ תֶּהֱוֵ֥א ᴸ אַרְכָ֖ה ᵐ לִשְׁלֵוְתָֽךְ ᴺ׃ 25 כֹּ֖לָּא ᵃ מְטָ֑א ᵇ עַל־נְבוּכַדְנֶצַּ֖ר מַלְכָּֽא׃ ᴾ

26 לִקְצָ֖ת ᵃ יַרְחִ֣ין ᵇ תְּרֵי־עֲשַׂ֑ר ᶜ עַל־הֵיכַ֤ל ᵈ מַלְכוּתָא֙ ᵉ דִּ֣י בָבֶ֔ל מְהַלֵּ֖ךְ ᵍ הֲוָֽה ᵸ׃ 27 עָנֵ֤ה ᵃ מַלְכָּא֙ וְאָמַ֔ר ᵇ הֲלָ֥א ᶜ דָֽא־הִ֖יא ᵈ בָּבֶ֣ל רַבְּתָ֑א ᵉ דִּֽי־אֲנָ֤ה ᵍ בֱנַיְתַהּ֙ ᵸ לְבֵ֣ית ᶦ מַלְכ֔וּ ʲ בִּתְקַ֥ף ᵏ חִסְנִ֖י ˡ וְלִיקָ֥ר ᵐ הַדְרִֽי ᵑ׃ 28 ע֗וֹד ᵃ מִלְּתָא֙ ᵇ בְּפֻ֣ם ᶜ מַלְכָּ֔א קָ֖ל ᵈ מִן־שְׁמַיָּ֣א ᵉ נְפַ֑ל ᶠ לָ֤ךְ ᵍ אָֽמְרִין֙ ᵸ נְבוּכַדְנֶצַּ֣ר מַלְכָּ֔א מַלְכוּתָ֖ה ᶦ עֲדָ֥ת מִנָּֽךְ ʲ׃ 29 וּמִן־אֲנָשָׁא֩ ᵏ לָ֨ךְ ᵃ טָֽרְדִ֜ין ᵇ וְעִם־חֵיוַ֧ת ᶜ בָּרָ֣א ᵉ ᵈ מְדֹרָ֗ךְ ᶠ עִשְׂבָּ֤א ᵍ כְתוֹרִין֙ ᵸ יְטַעֲמ֣וּן ᶦ לָ֔ךְ וְשִׁבְעָ֥ה ʲ עִדָּנִ֖ין ᵏ יַחְלְפ֣וּן ˡ עֲלָ֑יִךְ ᵐ

---

23 ᵸnoun fs מַלְכוּ w/ 2ms gen sx *kingdom.* ᶦprep לְ w/ 2ms gen sx. ʲadj fs abs קַיָּם *enduring, reestablished.* ᵏtemp conj דִּי *that.* ˡ⁻ˡ= *after, as soon as.* ᵐG PC 2ms ידע. ᵑepex conj דִּי *that.* ᵒadj mp abs שַׁלִּיט *sovereign.* ᴾnoun mp emph שְׁמַיִן.

24 ᵃconj לָהֵן *therefore.* ᵇnoun ms מֶלַךְ w/ 1cs gen sx hapax *advice.* ᶜG juss 3ms שׁפר *be pleasant, pleasing.* ᵈK עֲלַיִךְ, Q עֲלָךְ, both prep עַל־ w/ 2ms gen sx. ᵉK וַחֲטָיִךְ noun mp, Q וַחֲטָאָךְ noun ms, both w/ חֲטִי w/ 2ms gen sx *sin.* ᶠnoun fs abs צִדְקָה hapax *righteousness, charity.* ᵍG imv 2ms פרק hapax *wipe away; ransom.* ᵸnoun fp עֲוָיָה w/ 2ms gen sx hapax *iniquity.* ᶦG inf חנן *show mercy, grace.* ʲadj mp abs עֲנֵה hapax *poor, miserable.* ᵏhypoth conj הֵן *whether (or not).* ˡG PC 3fs הוה *there may be.* ᵐnoun fs abs אַרְכָה *a lengthening.* ᵑnoun fs שְׁלֵוָה w/ 2ms gen sx hapax *ease, serenity.*

25 ᵃnoun ms emph כֹּל. ᵇG SC 3ms מטא *reach, come upon, happen to.*

26 ᵃnoun fs cstr קְצָת *end.* ᵇnoun mp abs יְרַח *month.* ᶜ⁻ᶜcard w/ f noun תְּרֵי־עֲשַׂר *twelve.* ᵈnoun ms cstr הֵיכַל *palace.* ᵉnoun fs emph מַלְכוּ *kingship, sovereignty; kingdom.* ᶠgen part דִּי *of.* ᵍD ptcp ms abs הלך *walk.* ᵸG SC 3ms הוה.

27 ᵃG ptcp ms abs I ענה. ᵇG ptcp ms abs אמר. ᶜneg part לָא w/ interr ה. ᵈprox dem pron fs דָּא *this.* ᵉindep pers pron 3fs הִיא as copula *is.* ᶠadj fs emph רַב *great.* ᵍrel pron דִּי *which, that.* ᵸindep pers pron 1cs אֲנָה *I.* ᶦG SC 1cs בנה w/ 3fs acc sx *(re)build.* ʲnoun ms cstr בֵּית. ᵏnoun fs abs מַלְכוּ *kingship, sovereignty; kingdom.* ˡnoun ms cstr תְּקָף hapax *strength, might.* ᵐnoun ms חֶסֶן [BDB] חֵסֶן w/ 1cs gen sx *power, might.* ᵑnoun ms abs יְקָר *honor.* ᵒnoun ms הֲדַר w/ 1cs gen sx *majesty.*

28 ᵃadv עוֹד hapax *still.* ᵇnoun fs emph מִלָּה *word.* ᶜnoun ms cstr פֻּם *mouth.* ᵈnoun ms abs קָל *voice.* ᵉnoun mp emph שְׁמַיִן. ᶠG SC 3ms נפל *fall.* ᵍprep לְ w/ 2ms gen sx. ᵸG ptcp mp abs אמר. ᶦnoun fs emph מַלְכוּ *kingship, sovereignty; kingdom.* ʲG SC 3fs עדה *pass (w/ מִן) away from.* ᵏprep מִן w/ 2ms gen sx.

29 ᵃprep לְ w/ 2ms gen sx, marks direct object. ᵇG ptcp mp abs טרד *drive away.* ᶜnoun fs cstr חֵיוָה *animal.* ᵈnoun ms emph I בַּר *field.* ᵉ⁻ᵉ= *wild animal.* ᶠnoun ms מְדוֹר w/ 2ms gen sx *dwelling.* ᵍnoun ms emph עֲשַׂב *vegetation, plants.* ᵸnoun mp abs תּוֹר *bull.* ᶦD PC 3mp טעם *feed.* ʲcard w/ m noun שְׁבַע *seven.* ᵏnoun mp abs עִדָּן indicates time in general or a length of time such as a year *season, time.* ˡG PC 3mp חלף *pass over.* ᵐK עֲלַיִךְ, Q עֲלָךְ, both prep עַל־ w/ 2ms gen sx.

עַד דִּי־תִנְדַּעᵒ דִּי־שַׁלִּיטᵖ עִלָּיאᵠ בְּמַלְכוּתᶳ אֲנָשָׁאᵗ וּלְמַן־דִּיᵘ יִצְבֵּא

יִתְּנִנַּהᵡ: ³⁰ בַּהּ־שַׁעֲתָא מִלְּתָא סָפַתᵈ עַל־נְבוּכַדְנֶצַּרᵉ וּמִן־אֲנָשָׁא

טְרִידᵉ וְעִשְׂבָּא כְתוֹרִין יֵאכֻלᵍ וּמִטַּל שְׁמַיָּא גִּשְׁמֵהᵏ יִצְטַבַּע עַד

דִּיᵐ שַׂעְרֵהⁿ כְּנִשְׁרִין רְבָה וְטִפְרוֹהִי כְצִפְּרִין: ³¹ וְלִקְצָת יוֹמַיָּה

אֲנָה נְבוּכַדְנֶצַּרᵈ עַיְנַיᵉ לִשְׁמַיָּא נִטְלֵת וּמַנְדְּעִי עֲלַי יְתוּב וּלְעִלָּיאᵏ

בָּרְכֵתᵏ וּלְחַי עָלְמָאᵐ שַׁבְּחֵתⁿ וְהַדְּרֵתᵒ דִּי שָׁלְטָנֵהᵖ שָׁלְטָן עָלַם

וּמַלְכוּתֵהᵗ עִם־דָּרᵘ וְדָר: ³² וְכָל־דָּאֲרֵי אַרְעָא כְּלָה חֲשִׁיבִין

וּכְמִצְבְּיֵהᵍ עָבֵד בְּחֵיל שְׁמַיָּא וְדָאֲרֵי אַרְעָא וְלָא אִיתַי דִּי־יְמַחֵא

בִידֵהᵐ וְיֵאמַר לֵהᵒ מָה עֲבַדְתָּ: ³³ בַּהּ־זִמְנָא מַנְדְּעִי יְתוּב

עֲלַי וְלִיקַר מַלְכוּתִי הַדְרִי וְזִיוִי יְתוּב עֲלַי וְלִי הַדָּבְרַי וְרַבְרְבָנַי

29 ⁿtemp conj דִּי *that*. ᵒG PC 2ms ידע. ᵖepex conj דִּי *that*. ᵠnoun ms abs שַׁלִּיט *sovereign*. ʳK עִלָּיא, Q עִלָּאָה, both noun ms emph עִלָּי *most high*. ˢnoun fs cstr מַלְכוּ *kingdom*. ᵗpers indef pron מַן *who*. ᵘrel pron דִּי *who, that*. ᵛ⁻ᵛ= *whoever*. ʷG PC 3ms צבה *desire, wish*. ˣG PC 3ms נתן w/ 3fs acc sx *give*.

30 ᵃprep בְּ w/ 3fs gen sx. ᵇnoun fs emph שָׁעָה *hour = moment*. ᶜnoun fs emph מִלָּה *word*. ᵈG SC 3fs סוף *be fulfilled*. ᵉGp SC 3ms טרד *be driven away*. ᶠnoun ms emph עֲשַׂב *vegetation, plants*. ᵍnoun mp abs תּוֹר *bull*. ʰG PC 3ms אכל *eat*. ⁱnoun ms cstr טַל *dew*. ʲnoun mp emph שְׁמַיִן. ᵏnoun ms w/ 3ms gen sx *body*. ˡD PC 3ms צבע *be soaked*. ᵐtemp conj דִּי *that*. ⁿnoun ms שְׂעַר w/ 3ms gen sx *hair*. ᵒnoun mp abs נְשַׁר *eagle*. ᵖG SC 3ms רבה *grow*. ᵠnoun fp טְפַר w/ 3ms gen sx *nail*. ʳnoun fp abs צְפַר *bird*.

31 ᵃnoun fs cstr קְצָת *end*. ᵇnoun mp emph יוֹם *day*. ᶜindep pers pron 1cs אֲנָה *I*. ᵈnoun fp עַיִן w/ 1cs gen sx *eye*. ᵉnoun mp emph שְׁמַיִן. ᶠG SC 1cs נטל *lift*. ᵍnoun ms מַנְדַּע w/ 1cs gen sx *knowledge*. ʰprep עַל w/ 1cs gen sx. ⁱG PC 3ms תוב intrans *return*. The PC here indicates action simultaneous to the preceding vb. ʲK וּלְעִלָּיא, Q וּלְעִלָּאָה, both noun ms emph עִלָּי *most high*. ᵏD SC 1cs II ברך *bless*. ˡnoun ms cstr I חַי *living one*. ᵐnoun ms emph עָלַם *eternity*. ⁿD SC 1cs שבח *praise*. ᵒD SC 1cs הדר *glorify*. ᵖcaus

conj דִּי *because*. ᵠnoun ms שָׁלְטָן w/ 3ms gen sx *empire; dominion*. ʳnoun ms cstr שָׁלְטָן *empire; dominion*. ˢnoun ms abs עָלַם *eternity*. ᵗnoun fs מַלְכוּ w/ 3ms gen sx *kingship, sovereignty; kingdom*. ᵘnoun ms abs דָּר *generation*. ᵛ⁻ᵛ= *from generation to generation*.

32 ᵃnoun ms cstr כֹּל. ᵇK דָּאֲרֵי, Q דָּיְרֵי [Ed ″דָּיְ], both G ptcp mp cstr דור *dwell*. ᶜnoun fs emph אֲרַע *earth, land*. ᵈלָא + כְּ *as nothing*. ᵉGp ptcp mp abs חשב hapax *be thought of*. ᶠG inf צבה w/ 3ms gen sx *desire, wish*. ᵍG ptcp ms abs עבד. ʰnoun ms cstr חַיִל *army*. ⁱnoun mp emph שְׁמַיִן. ʲK וְדָאֲרֵי, Q וְדָיְרֵי [Ed ″וְדָיְ], both G ptcp mp cstr דור *dwell*. ᵏpart. of existence אִיתַי *there is*. ˡrel pron דִּי *who, that*. ᵐD PC 3ms מחא *strike* (w/ בְּ) smthg, *deflect*. ⁿnoun fs יַד w/ 3ms gen sx *hand*. ᵒG PC 3ms אמר. ᵖprep לְ w/ 3ms gen sx. ᵠimpers interr pron מָה *what?* ʳG SC 2ms עבד.

33 ᵃprep בְּ w/ 3ms gen sx. ᵇnoun ms emph זְמַן *time*. ᶜnoun ms מַנְדַּע w/ 1cs gen sx *knowledge*. ᵈG PC 3ms תוב intrans *return*. ᵉprep עַל w/ 1cs gen sx. ᶠnoun ms cstr יְקָר *honor*. ᵍnoun fs מַלְכוּ w/ 1cs gen sx *kingdom*. ʰnoun ms הֲדַר w/ 1cs gen sx *majesty*. ⁱnoun ms זִיו w/ 1cs gen sx *splendor*. ʲprep לְ w/ 1cs gen sx. ᵏnoun mp הַדָּבָר w/ 1cs gen sx Pers lw *companion*. ˡnoun mp רַבְרְבָנִין w/ 1cs gen sx *lord*.

יִבְעֹ֑וֹן ᵐ וְעַל־מַלְכוּתִ֖י הָתְקְנַ֑ת ᵒ וּרְב֥וּ ᴾ יַתִּירָ֖ה ᑫ הוּסְפַ֥ת ʳ לִֽי ˢ׃ ³⁴ כְּעַ֣ן ᵃ
אֲנָ֣ה ᵇ נְבוּכַדְנֶצַּ֡ר מְשַׁבַּ֣ח ᶜ וּמְרוֹמֵ֣ם ᵈ וּמְהַדַּר ᵉ לְמֶ֣לֶךְ שְׁמַיָּ֑א ᶠ דִּ֥י ᵍ כָל־ʰ
מַעֲבָד֨וֹהִי ʰ קְשֹׁ֜ט ⁱ וְאֹרְחָתֵ֣הּ ʲ דִּ֑ין ᵏ וְדִ֥י ᵐ מַהְלְכִ֣ין ᵐ בְּגֵוָ֖ה ᵐ יָכִ֥ל ᵒ לְהַשְׁפָּלָֽה ᴾ׃
פ

5 ¹ בֵּלְשַׁאצַּ֣ר ᵃ מַלְכָּ֗א ᵇ עֲבַד ᵇ לְחֶ֣ם ᵇ רַ֔ב ᶜ לְרַבְרְבָנ֖וֹהִי ᵉ אֲלַ֑ף ᶠ וְלָקֳבֵ֥ל ᵍ
אַלְפָּ֖א ʰ חַמְרָ֥א ⁱ שָׁתֵֽה ʲ׃ ² בֵּלְשַׁאצַּ֣ר ᵃ אֲמַ֣ר ᵃ | בִּטְעֵ֣ם ᵇ חַמְרָ֗א ᶜ לְהַיְתָיָה ᵈ
לְמָאנֵ֣י ᶠ דַּהֲבָ֣א ᵍ וְכַסְפָּ֗א ᵍ דִּ֤י ʰ הַנְפֵּק ʲ נְבוּכַדְנֶצַּ֣ר אֲב֔וּהִי ᵏ מִן־הֵיכְלָ֖א ˡ
דִּ֣י ᵐ בִירוּשְׁלֶ֑ם וְיִשְׁתּ֣וֹן ᵐ בְּה֗וֹן ⁿ מַלְכָּא֙ ᵒ וְרַבְרְבָנ֔וֹהִי ᴾ שֵׁגְלָתֵ֖הּ ᴾ וּלְחֵנָתֵֽהּ ᑫ׃
³ בֵּאדַ֗יִן ᵃ הַיְתִ֙יו ᵇ מָאנֵ֣י ᶜ דַהֲבָ֔א ᵈ דִּ֣י ᵉ הַנְפִּ֗קוּ ᶠ מִן־הֵיכְלָ֛א ᵍ דִּי־בֵ֥ית ᵍ
אֱלָהָ֖א ʰ דִּ֣י ⁱ בִירוּשְׁלֶ֑ם וְאִשְׁתִּ֣יו ᵏ בְּה֗וֹן ʲ מַלְכָּא֙ ˡ וְרַבְרְבָנ֔וֹהִי ˡ שֵׁגְלָתֵ֖הּ ˡ
וּלְחֵנָתֵֽהּ ᵐ׃ ⁴ אִשְׁתִּ֖יו ᵃ חַמְרָ֑א ᵇ וְשַׁבַּ֙חוּ ᶜ לֵֽאלָהֵ֥י ᶜ דַהֲבָ֛א ᵈ וְכַסְפָּ֖א ᵉ

---

33 ᵐD PC 3mp בעה *seek.* ⁿnoun fs מַלְכוּ w/ 1cs
gen sx *kingdom.* ᵒHp sc 3fs תקן hapax *be
reestablished.* ᴾnoun fs abs רְבוּ *greatness.*
ᑫadj fs abs יַתִּיר *extraordinary, excessive.*
ʳHp sc 3fs יסף hapax *be added.* ˢprep לְ w/
1cs gen sx.

34 ᵃtransitional conj כְּעַן *introduces new idea
now.* ᵇindep pers pron 1cs אֲנָה *I.* ᶜD ptcp
ms abs שבח *praise.* ᵈD ptcp ms abs רום
exalt, extol. ᵉD ptcp ms abs הדר *glorify.*
ᶠnoun mp emph שְׁמַיִן. ᵍcaus conj דִּי *because.* ʰnoun ms cstr כֹּל. ⁱnoun mp abs מַעֲבָד
w/ 3ms gen sx hapax *work, deed.* ʲnoun ms
abs קְשֹׁט *truth.* ᵏnoun fp אֹרַח w/ 3ms gen
sx *path.* ˡnoun ms abs דִּין *justice.* ᵐH ptcp
mp abs הלך *walk.* ⁿnoun fs abs גֵּוָה hapax
pride. ᵒG ptcp ms abs יכל *be able.* ᴾH inf
שפל *humiliate.*

5

1 ᵃPN *Belshazzar.* ᵇG sc 3ms עבד. ᶜnoun ms
abs לְחֶם hapax *feast.* ᵈadj ms abs רַב *great.*
ᵉnoun mp רַבְרְבָנִין w/ 3ms gen sx *lord.*
ᶠcard ms abs אֲלַף *a thousand.* ᵍלְ + noun ms
cstr קֳבֵל *to the front of = before.* ʰcard ms
emph אֲלַף *the thousand.* ⁱnoun ms emph
חֲמַר *wine.* The emphatic state is used here
for general designation. ʲG ptcp ms abs
שתה *drink.*

2 ᵃPN *Belshazzar.* ᵇG sc 3ms אמר. ᶜnoun ms
cstr טְעֵם *taste.* ᵈnoun ms emph חֲמַר *wine.*
ᵉH inf אתה *bring.* ᶠnoun mp cstr מָאן *vessel.* ᵍnoun ms emph דְּהַב *gold.* ʰnoun ms
emph כְּסַף *silver.* ⁱrel pron דִּי *which, that.*
ʲH sc 3ms נפק *bring out.* ᵏnoun ms אֲב w/
3ms gen sx *father.* ˡnoun ms emph הֵיכַל
temple. ᵐG PC 3mp שתה *drink* (w/ בְּ)
from. ⁿprep בְּ w/ 3mp gen sx. ᵒnoun mp
רַבְרְבָנִין w/ 3ms gen sx *lord.* ᴾnoun fp שֵׁגַל
w/ 3ms gen sx Akk lw *second-tier wife;
concubine.* ᑫnoun fp לְחֵנָה w/ 3ms gen sx
Akk lw *consort.*

3 ᵃtemp adv אֱדַיִן (w/ בְּ) *immediately; then.*
ᵇH sc 3mp אתה *bring.* ᶜnoun mp cstr
מָאן *vessel.* ᵈnoun ms emph דְּהַב *gold.* ᵉrel
pron דִּי *who, which, that.* ᶠH sc 3mp נפק
bring out. ᵍnoun ms emph הֵיכַל *temple,
sanctuary.* ʰgen part דִּי *of.* ⁱG sc 3mp שתה
drink (w/ בְּ) *from.* ʲprep בְּ w/ 3mp gen
sx. ᵏnoun mp רַבְרְבָנִין w/ 3ms gen sx *lord.*
ˡnoun fp שֵׁגַל w/ 3ms gen sx Akk lw *second-tier wife; concubine.* ᵐnoun fp לְחֵנָה
w/ 3ms gen sx Akk lw *consort.*

4 ᵃG sc 3mp שתה *drink.* ᵇnoun ms emph
חֲמַר *wine.* ᶜD sc 3mp שבח *praise.*
ᵈnoun ms emph דְּהַב *gold.* ᵉnoun ms
emph כְּסַף *silver.*

נְחָשָׁאᶠ פַּרְזְלָאᵍ אָעָאʰ וְאַבְנָאⁱ: 5 בַּהּ־אשַׁעֲתָהᵇ נְפַקוּ אֶצְבְּעָןᶜ דִּי־

יַד־אֱנָשᶠ וְכָתְבָן לָקֳבֵלʰ נֶבְרַשְׁתָּאⁱ עַל־גִּירָאʲ דִּי־כְתַל הֵיכְלָאᵏ דִּי

מַלְכָּא וּמַלְכָּא חָזֵהᵐ פַּסⁿ יְדָהᵒ דִּי כָתְבָהᵖ: 6 אֱדַיִן מַלְכָּא זִיוֺהִיᵃ

שְׁנוֺהִיᵇ וְרַעְיֹנֹהִיᶜ יְבַהֲלוּנֵּהᵈ וְקִטְרֵיᵉ חַרְצֵהᶠ מִשְׁתָּרַיִןᵍ וְאַרְכֻבָּתֵהʰ

דָּא לְדָאⁱ נָקְשָׁןʲ: 7 קָרֵאᵃ מַלְכָּא בְּחַיִלᵇ לְהֶעָלָה לְאָשְׁפַיָּאᶜ כַּשְׂדָּיאᵈ

וְגָזְרַיָּאᵉ עָנֵהᵍ מַלְכָּא וְאָמַר| לְחַכִּימֵי בָבֶל דִּי כָל־אֱנָשᵏ דִּי־יִקְרֵהᵐ

כְּתָבָהⁿ דְּנָהᵒ וּפִשְׁרֵהᵖ יְחַוִּנַּנִי אַרְגְּוָנָאʳ יִלְבַּשˢ והמונכאᵗ דִּי־דַהֲבָא

עַל־צַוְּארֵהʷ וְתַלְתִּיˣ בְּמַלְכוּתָאʸ יִשְׁלַטᶻ:ₛ 8 אֱדַיִן עלליןᵃ

כֹּל חַכִּימֵיᵇ מַלְכָּא וְלָא־כָהֲלִיןᵈ כְּתָבָאᵉ לְמִקְרֵאᶠ וּפִשְׁרָאᵍ לְהוֹדָעָהʰ

לְמַלְכָּא: 9 אֱדַיִן מַלְכָּא בֵלְשַׁאצַּרᵃ שַׂגִּיאᵇ מִתְבָּהַלᶜ וְזִיוֺהִיᵈ שָׁנַיִןᵉ

4 ᶠnoun ms emph נְחָשׁ *bronze.* ᵍnoun ms emph פַּרְזֶל *iron.* ʰnoun ms emph אָע *timber.* ⁱnoun fs emph אֶבֶן *stone.*

5 ᵃprep בְּ w/ 3fs gen sx. ᵇnoun fs emph שָׁעָה *hour = moment.* ᶜK נְפַקוּ G sc 3mp, נפק Q נְפָקָה G sc 3fp, both נפק *come out.* ᵈnoun fp abs אֶצְבַּע *finger.* ᵉgen part דִּי *of.* ᶠnoun fs cstr יַד *hand.* ᵍG ptcp fp abs כתב *write.* Participle here indicates action simultaneous with main verb ᶜ. ʰלְ + noun ms cstr קֳבֵל *to the front of =* *before.* ⁱnoun fs emph נֶבְרְשָׁה hapax, Pers lw *lampstand.* ʲnoun ms emph גִּיר hapax *plaster.* ᵏnoun ms abs כְּתַל *wall.* ˡnoun ms emph הֵיכַל *palace.* ᵐG ptcp ms abs חזה. ⁿnoun ms cstr פַּס *palm.* ᵒnoun fs emph יַד *hand.* ᵖrel pron דִּי *which, that.* ᑫG ptcp fs abs כתב *write.*

6 ᵃnoun mp זִיו w/ 3ms gen sx *splendor, radiance.* ᵇG sc 3mp שנה w/ 3ms acc sx intrans *changed on him.* ᶜnoun mp רַעְיֹן w/ 3ms gen sx *thought* [so Ed; L, BHL*, BHS וְרַע″]. ᵈD pc 3mp בהל w/ 3ms acc sx *terrify.* ᵉnoun mp cstr קְטַר *knot = joint.* ᶠnoun ms חֲרַץ w/ 3ms gen sx hapax *hip.* ᵍtD ptcp mp abs שׁרה *giving way.* ʰnoun fp אַרְכֻּבָּה w/ 3ms gen sx hapax *knee.* ⁱprox dem pron fs דָּא *this.* ʲG ptcp fp abs נקשׁ hapax *knock.*

7 ᵃG ptcp ms abs קרא *cry out.* ᵇnoun ms abs חַיִל *power.* ᶜH inf II עלל *bring* (w/ לְ)

smthg. ᵈnoun mp emph אָשַׁף Akk lw *exorcist.* ᵉK כַּשְׂדָּיֵא, Q כַּשְׂדָּאֵי, both noun mp emph כַּשְׂדָּי *Babylonian astrologer* or *sage.* ᶠG ptcp mp emph גזר *diviner.* ᵍG ptcp ms abs I ענה. ʰG ptcp ms abs אמר. ⁱadj mp cstr חַכִּים *wise.* ʲepex conj דִּי *that.* ᵏnoun ms cstr כֹּל. ˡrel pron דִּי *who, that.* ᵐG pc 3ms קרא *read.* ⁿnoun ms emph כְּתָב *writing.* ᵒprox dem adj ms דְּנָה *this.* ᵖnoun ms פְּשַׁר w/ 3ms gen sx. ᑫD pc 3ms חוה w/ 1cs acc sx *make known* [so BHS, Ed; L, BHL*, יְחַוִּ″]. ʳnoun ms emph אַרְגְּוָן Akk lw *purple.* ˢG pc 3ms לבשׁ *wear.* ᵗK וְהַמְנִיכָא, Q וְהַמּוֹנְכָא, both noun ms emph הַמְנַךְ Pers lw *necklace, chain.* ᵘgen part דִּי *of.* ᵛnoun ms emph דְּהַב *gold.* ʷnoun ms צַוַּאר w/ 3ms gen sx *neck.* ˣnoun ms תַּלְתָּא w/ 1cs gen sx Akk calque *triumvir* (official of the third rank), *rank third.* ʸnoun fs emph מַלְכוּ *kingdom.* ᶻG pc 3ms שלט *rule.*

8 ᵃK עָלְלִין, Q עָלִּין [L, BHS עָ″; Ed עַ″], both G ptcp mp abs II עלל *enter.* ᵇnoun ms cstr כֹּל. ᶜadj mp cstr חַכִּים *wise.* ᵈG ptcp mp abs כהל *be able.* ᵉnoun ms emph כְּתָב *writing.* ᶠG inf קרא *read.* ᵍK וּפִשְׁרָא noun ms emph וּפִשְׁרָה, Q פְּשַׁר noun ms w/ 3ms gen sx. ʰH inf ידע.

9 ᵃPN *Belshazzar.* ᵇadj ms abs שַׂגִּיא as adv *very.* ᶜtD ptcp ms abs בהל *be terrified.* ᵈnoun mp זִיו w/ 3ms gen sx *splendor, radiance.* ᵉG ptcp mp abs שנה intrans *changed.*

עֲלוֹהִי וְרַבְרְבָנוֹהִי מִשְׁתַּבְּשִׁיןᵍ: 10 מַלְכְּתָאᵃ לָקֳבֵלᵇ מִלֵּיᶜ מַלְכָּא
וְרַבְרְבָנוֹהִיᵈ לְבֵית מִשְׁתְּיָאᵉ עַלַּתᶠ עֲנָתᵍ מַלְכְּתָא וַאֲמֶרֶתʰ מַלְכָּא
לְעָלְמִין חֱיִיʲ אַלᵏ־יְבַהֲלוּךְˡ רַעְיוֹנָךְᵐ וְזִיוָיךְⁿ אַל־יִשְׁתַּנּוֹ: 11 אִיתַיᵃ
גְּבַרᵇ בְּמַלְכוּתָךְᶜ דִּיᵈ רוּחַᵉ אֱלָהִין קַדִּישִׁיןᶠ בֵּהᵍ וּבְיוֹמֵיʰ אֲבוּךְⁱ
נַהִירוּʲ וְשָׂכְלְתָנוּᵏ וְחָכְמָהˡ כְּחָכְמַתᵐ־אֱלָהִין הִשְׁתְּכַחַת בֵּהⁿ וּמַלְכָּא
נְבֻכַדְנֶצַּר אֲבוּךְᵒ רַבᵖ חַרְטֻמִּין אָשְׁפִין כַּשְׂדָּאִיןᵖ גָּזְרִיןᵍ הֲקִימֵהʳ
אֲבוּךְⁱ מַלְכָּא: 12 כָּלᶜ־קֳבֵל דִּיᵇ רוּחַ | יַתִּירָהᵉ וּמַנְדַּע וְשָׂכְלְתָנוּᵍ
מְפַשַּׁרʰ חֶלְמִיןⁱ וַאֲחַוָיַתʲ אֲחִידָןᵏ וּמְשָׁרֵאˡ קִטְרִיןᵐⁿ הִשְׁתְּכַחַתᵒ בֵּהᵖ
בְּדָנִיֵּאל דִּי־מַלְכָּא שָׂם־שְׁמֵהˢ בֵּלְטְשַׁאצַּרᵗ כְּעַןᵘ דָּנִיֵּאל יִתְקְרֵיᵛ
וּפִשְׁרָה יְהַחֲוֵהʷ:
פ

13 בֵּאדַיִןᵃ דָּנִיֵּאל הֻעַלᵇ קֳדָם מַלְכָּא עָנֵהᶜ מַלְכָּא וְאָמַרᵈ לְדָנִיֵּאל
אַנְתְּᵉ הוּאᶠ דָנִיֵּאל דִּי־ᵍמִן־בְּנֵיʰ גָלוּתָאⁱ דִּי יְהוּדᵏ דִּי הַיְתִיˡ מַלְכָּא

---

9 ᶠprep עַל־ w/ 3ms gen sx. ᵍnoun mp רַבְרְבָנִין w/ 3ms gen sx *lord*. ʰtD ptcp mp abs שבש hapax *be perplexed*.

10 ᵃnoun fs emph מַלְכָּה *queen*. ᵇלְ + noun ms cstr קֳבֵל *in the face of* = *because*. ᶜnoun fp cstr מִלָּה *word*. ᵈnoun mp רַבְרְבָנִין w/ 3ms gen sx *lord*. ᵉnoun ms emph מִשְׁתֵּא hapax *banquet*. ᶠK עֲלַלַת, Q עֲלַת, both G sc 3fs II עלל *enter*. ᵍG sc 3fs I ענה אמר. ʰG sc 3fs אמר. ⁱnoun mp abs עָלַם *eternity*. ʲG imv 2ms חיה *live*. ᵏneg part אַל *not*. ˡD juss 3mp בהל w/ 2ms acc sx *terrify*. ᵐnoun ms רַעְיוֹן w/ 2ms gen sx *thought*. ⁿK וְזִיוָיך noun mp, Q וְזִינָךְ noun ms, both זִיו w/ 2ms gen sx *radiance*. ᵒtD juss 3mp שנה *be changed*.

11 ᵃpart. of existence אִיתַי *there is*. ᵇnoun ms abs גְּבַר *man*. ᶜnoun fs מַלְכוּ w/ 2ms gen sx *kingdom*. ᵈrel pron דִּי *who, that*. ᵉnoun ms cstr רוּחַ *spirit*. ᶠadj mp abs קַדִּישׁ *holy*. ᵍprep בְּ w/ 3ms gen sx. ʰnoun mp cstr יוֹם *day*. ⁱnoun ms אַב w/ 2ms gen sx *father*. ʲnoun fs abs נַהִירוּ *enlightenment*. ᵏnoun fs abs שָׂכְלְתָנוּ *prudence, insight*. ˡnoun fs abs, ᵐnoun fs cstr חָכְמָה *wisdom*. ⁿtG sc 3fs שכח *be found*. ᵒadj ms cstr רַב *chief*. ᵖnoun mp abs חַרְטֹם *magician*. ᵍnoun mp abs אָשַׁף Akk lw *exorcist*.

ʳnoun mp abs כַּשְׂדָּי *Babylonian astrologer* or *sage*. ˢG ptcp mp abs גזר *diviner*. ᵗH sc 3ms קום w/ 3ms acc sx.

12 ᵃ= כְּ + לְ *according to*. ᵇsubord conj דִּי *that*. ᶜ⁻ᶜ= *because, since*. ᵈnoun fs abs רוּחַ *spirit*. ᵉadj fs abs יַתִּיר *extraordinary*. ᶠnoun ms abs מַנְדַּע *knowledge*. ᵍnoun fs abs שָׂכְלְתָנוּ *insight*. ʰD ptcp ms cstr פשר *interpret*. ⁱnoun mp abs חֵלֶם *dream*. ʲH inf חוה *make known*. ᵏnoun fp abs אֲחִידָה hapax *riddle*. ˡD ptcp ms cstr שׁרה *loosen*. ᵐnoun mp abs קְטַר *knot*. ⁿ⁻ⁿ= *solve problems*. ᵒtG sc 3fs שכח *be found*. ᵖprep בְּ w/ 3ms gen sx. ᵍrel pron דִּי *who, that*. ʳG sc 3ms שׂים. ˢnoun ms שֵׁם w/ 3ms gen sx *name*. ᵗPN Belteshazzar. ᵘtransitional conj or temp adv כְּעַן *now*. ᵛtD juss 3ms קרא *be called*. ʷH pc 3ms חוה *make known*.

13 ᵃtemp adv אֱדַיִן (w/ בְּ) *immediately; then*. ᵇHp sc 3ms II עלל *be brought*. ᶜG ptcp ms abs I ענה. ᵈG ptcp ms abs אמר. ᵉK אַנְתָּה, Q אַנְתְּ, both indep pers pron 2ms אַנְתְּ *you*. ᶠindep pers pron 3ms הוּא as copula *are*. ᵍrel pron דִּי *who, that*. ʰnoun mp cstr II בַּר *son*. ⁱnoun fs emph גָּלוּ *exile*. ʲgen part דִּי *of*. ᵏGN Judah. ˡH sc 3ms אתה *bring*.

אֲבִ֫יᵐ מִן־יְהֽוּדᵑ: ¹⁴ וְשִׁמְעֵ֫תᵃ עֲלָ֫יךְᵇ דִּיᶜ ר֫וּחᵈ אֱלָהִ֫ין בָּ֫ךְᵉ וְנַהִיר֫וּᶠ

וְשָׂכְלְתָנ֫וּᵍ וְחָכְמָ֫הʰ יַתִּיר֫הᶦ הִשְׁתְּכַ֫חַתʲ בָּֽךְ: ¹⁵ וּכְעַ֫ןᵃ הֻעַ֫לּוּᵇ קָֽדָמַ֫יᶜ

חַכִּֽימַיָּ֫אᵈ אָֽשְׁפַיָּ֫אᵉ דִּֽי־כְתָבָ֫הᵍ דְנָ֫הʰ יִקְר֫וֹןᶦ וּפִשְׁר֫הʲ לְהוֹדָעֻתַ֫נִיᵏ

וְלָֽא־כָהֲלִ֫יןˡ פְּשַׁר־מִלְּתָ֫אᵐ לְהַֽחֲוָיָֽהᵑ: ¹⁶ וַאֲנָ֫הᵃ שִׁמְעֵ֫תᵇ עֲלָ֫יךְᶜ דִּֽי־ᵈ

תוּכַ֫לᵉ פִּשְׁרִ֫יןᶠ לְמִפְשַׁ֫רᵍ וְקִטְרִ֫יןʰ לְמִשְׁרֵ֫אᶦ כְּעַ֫ן הֵ֫ןᵏ תּוּכַ֫לˡ כְּתָבָ֫אᵐ

לְמִקְרֵ֫אᵒ וּפִשְׁרֵ֫הᵖ לְהוֹדָעֻתַ֫נִיᵃ אַרְגְּוָנָ֫אˢ תִּלְבַּ֫שᵗ וְהַמֽוֹנְכָ֫אᵘ דִֽי־ᵘ⁻

דַהֲבָ֫אᵛ עַֽל־צַוְּארָ֫ךְᵂ וְתַלְתָּ֫אˣ בְּמַלְכוּתָ֫אʸ תִּשְׁלַֽטᶻ:
פ

¹⁷ בֵּאדַ֫יִןᵃ עָנֵ֫הᵇ דָֽנִיֵּ֫אל וְאָמַ֫רᶜ קֳדָ֫ם מַלְכָּ֫א מַתְּנָתָ֫ךְᵈ לָ֫ךְ לֶֽהֶוְיָ֫ןᵉ

וּנְבָֽזְבְּיָתָ֫ךְᵈ לְאָחֳרָ֫ןᵍ הַ֫ב בְּרַ֫ם כְּתָבָ֫אʲ אֶקְרֵ֫אᵏ לְמַלְכָּ֫אˡ וּפִשְׁרָ֫א

אֲהוֹדְעִנַּֽהᵐ: ¹⁸ אַ֫נְתָהᵃ מַלְכָּ֫א אֱלָהָ֫א עִלָּיָ֫אᵇ מַלְכוּתָ֫אᶜ וּרְבוּתָ֫אᵈ

וִיקָרָ֫אᵉ וְהַדְרָ֫הᶠ יְהַ֫בᵍ לִנְבֻכַדְנֶצַּ֫ר אֲב֫וּךְʰ: ¹⁹ וּמִן־רְבוּתָ֫אᵃ דִּ֫יᵇ יְהַב־ᶜ

---

13 ᵐnoun ms אַב w/ 1cs gen sx *father*. ᵑGN *Judah*.

14 ᵃG sc 1cs שמע *hear*. ᵇK עֲלָיִךְ, Q עֲלָךְ, both prep עַל־ w/ 2ms gen sx. ᶜepex conj דִּי *that*. ᵈnoun ms cstr רוּחַ *spirit*. ᵉprep בְּ w/ 2ms gen sx. ᶠnoun fs abs נַהִירוּ *enlightenment*. ᵍnoun fs abs שָׂכְלְתָנוּ *prudence, insight*. ʰnoun fs abs חָכְמָה *wisdom*. ᶦadj fs abs יַתִּיר *extraordinary*. ʲtG sc 3fs שכח *be found*.

15 ᵃtransitional conj כְּעַן introduces new idea *now*. ᵇHp sc 3mp II עלל *be brought*. ᶜprep קֳדָם w/ 1cs gen sx. ᵈadj mp emph חַכִּים *wise*. ᵉnoun mp emph אַשָׁף Akk lw *conjurer; exorcist*. ᶠpurp conj דִּי *so that*. ᵍnoun ms emph כְּתָב *writing*. ʰprox dem adj ms דְּנָה *this*. ᶦG pc 3mp קרא *read*. ʲnoun ms פְּשַׁר w/ 3ms gen sx. ᵏH inf ידע w/ 1cs acc sx. ˡG ptcp mp abs כהל *be able*. ᵐnoun fs emph מִלָּה *word*. ᵑH inf חוה *show, declare*.

16 ᵃindep pers pron 1cs אֲנָה *I*. ᵇG sc 1cs שמע *hear*. ᶜK עֲלָיִךְ, Q עֲלָךְ, both prep עַל־ w/ 2ms gen sx. ᵈepex conj דִּי *that*. ᵉK תּוּכַל G pc 2ms, Q תִּכּוּל [Ed תֻּכַּל], both G pc 2ms יכל *be able*. ᶠnoun mp abs פְּשַׁר *interpretation*. ᵍG inf פשׁר *interpret*. ʰnoun mp abs קְטַר *knot*. ᶦG inf שׁרה *loosen*. ʲ⁻ʲ= *solve problems*. ᵏtransitional conj כְּעַן introduces new idea *now*. ʰhypoth conj הֵן *if*. ᵐK תּוּכַל Q תִּכּוּל [Ed תֻּכַּל], both G pc 2ms

---

יכל *be able*. ᵑnoun ms emph כְּתָב *writing*. ᵒG inf קרא *read*. ᵖnoun ms פְּשַׁר w/ 3ms gen sx. ᵃH inf ידע w/ 1cs acc sx. ʳnoun ms emph אַרְגְּוָן Akk lw *purple*. ˢG pc 2ms לבשׁ *wear*. ᵗK וְהַמְנִיכָא Q וְהַמֽוֹנְכָא, both noun ms emph הַמוּנֵךְ Pers lw *necklace, chain*. ᵘgen part דִּי *of*. ᵛnoun ms emph דְּהַב *gold*. ᵂnoun ms צַוַּאר w/ 2ms gen sx *neck*. ˣnoun ms abs תַּלְתָּא Akk calque *triumvir* (official of the third rank), *rank third*. ʸnoun fs emph מַלְכוּ *kingdom*. ᶻG pc 2ms שלט *rule*.

17 ᵃtemp adv אֱדַיִן (w/ בְּ) *immediately; then*. ᵇG ptcp ms abs I ענה. ᶜG ptcp ms abs אמר. ᵈnoun fp מַתְּנָה w/ 2ms gen sx *gift*. ᵉprep לְ w/ 2ms gen sx. ᶠG juss 3fp הוה. ᵍnoun fp נְבִזְבָּה w/ 2ms gen sx *present, reward*. ʰadj ms abs אָחֳרָן *another*. ᶦG imv 2ms יהב. ʲdisj בְּרַם *but, however*. ᵏnoun ms emph כְּתָב *writing*. ˡG pc 1cs קרא *read*. ᵐH pc 1cs ידע w/ 3ms acc sx.

18 ᵃK אַנְתָה, Q אַנְתְּ, both indep pers pron 2ms *you*. ᵇKעִלָּיָא,Qעִלָּאָה, both noun ms emph עִלָּי *most high*. ᶜnoun fs emph מַלְכוּ *kingship; kingdom*. ᵈnoun fs emph רְבוּ *greatness*. ᵉnoun ms emph יְקָר *honor*. ᶠnoun ms emph הֲדַר *majesty*. ᵍG sc 3ms יהב. ʰnoun ms abs אַב w/ 2ms gen sx *father*.

19 ᵃnoun fs emph רְבוּ *greatness*. ᵇrel pron דִּי *which, that*. ᶜG sc 3ms יהב.

לֵהּ⁽ᵈ⁾ כָּל⁽ᵉ⁾ עַֽמְמַיָּא⁽ᶠ⁾ אֻמַּיָּא⁽ᵍ⁾ וְלִשָּׁנַיָּא⁽ʰ⁾ הֲוֹו⁽ⁱ⁾ זָאֲעִין⁽ʲ⁾ וְדָחֲלִין⁽ᵏ⁾ מִן־קֳדָמ֑וֹהִי
דִּֽי־הֲוָה⁽ᵐ⁾ צָבֵא⁽ⁿ⁾ הֲוָא⁽ᵒ⁾ קָטֵ֔ל⁽ᵖ⁾ וְדִֽי־הֲוָה⁽ᵐ⁾ צָבֵא⁽ⁿ⁾ הֲוָה⁽ᵒ⁾ מַחֵ֑א⁽ᑫ⁾ וְדִֽי־
הֲוָה⁽ᵐ⁾ צָבֵא⁽ⁿ⁾ הֲוָה⁽ᵒ⁾ מָרִ֔ים⁽ʳ⁾ וְדִֽי־הֲוָה⁽ᵐ⁾ צָבֵא⁽ⁿ⁾ הֲוָה⁽ᵒ⁾ מַשְׁפִּֽיל⁽ˢ⁾׃ 20 וּכְדִי⁽ᵃ⁾
רִם⁽ᵇ⁾ לִבְבֵהּ⁽ᶜ⁾ וְרוּחֵהּ⁽ᵈ⁾ תִּֽקְפַת⁽ᵉ⁾ לַהֲזָדָה⁽ᶠ⁾ הָנְחַת⁽ᵍ⁾ מִן־כָּרְסֵא⁽ʰ⁾ מַלְכוּתֵהּ⁽ⁱ⁾
וִיקָרָה⁽ʲ⁾ הֶעְדִּיו⁽ᵏ⁾ מִנֵּֽהּ⁽ˡ⁾׃ 21 וּמִן־בְּנֵי⁽ᵃ⁾ אֲנָשָׁא⁽ᵇ⁾ טְרִ֔יד⁽ᶜ⁾ וְלִבְבֵהּ⁽ᵈ⁾ ׀ עִם־
חֵיוְתָא⁽ᵉ⁾ שַׁוִּי⁽ᶠ⁾ וְעִם־עֲרָדַיָּא⁽ᵍ⁾ מְדוֹרֵהּ⁽ʰ⁾ עִשְׂבָּא⁽ⁱ⁾ כְתוֹרִין⁽ʲ⁾ יְטַֽעֲמוּנֵּהּ⁽ᵏ⁾ וּמִטַּל⁽ˡ⁾
שְׁמַיָּא⁽ᵐ⁾ גִּשְׁמֵהּ⁽ⁿ⁾ יִצְטַבַּ֑ע⁽ᵒ⁾ עַד⁽ᵖ⁾ דִּֽי־יְדַ֗ע⁽ᑫ⁾ דִּֽי־שַׁלִּיט⁽ʳ⁾ אֱלָהָא⁽ˢ⁾ עִלָּיָא⁽ᵗ⁾
בְּמַלְכוּת⁽ᵘ⁾ אֲנָשָׁא⁽ᵛ⁾ וּלְמַן־דִּֽי⁽ʷ⁾ יִצְבֵּה⁽ʸ⁾ יְהָקֵים⁽ᶻ⁾ עֲלַֽהּ⁽ˣʷ⁾׃ 22 וְאַנְתְּה⁽ᵃ⁾
בְּרֵהּ⁽ᵇ⁾ בֵּלְשַׁאצַּר⁽ᶜ⁾ לָא⁽ᵈ⁾ הַשְׁפֵּלְתְּ⁽ᵉ⁾ לִבְבָךְ⁽ᶠ⁾ כָּל־קֳבֵ֔ל⁽ᵍ⁾ דִּי⁽ʰ⁾ כָּל־דְּנָה⁽ʲ⁾
יְדַֽעְתָּ⁽ᵏ⁾׃ 23 וְעַל⁽ᵃ⁾ מָֽרֵא־שְׁמַיָּא⁽ᵇ⁾ ׀ הִתְרוֹמַ֗מְתָּ⁽ᶜ⁾ וּלְמָֽאנַיָּא⁽ᵈ⁾ דִֽי־בַיְתֵהּ⁽ᶠ⁾

---

19 ^dprep לְ w/ 3ms gen sx. ^enoun ms cstr
כֹּל. ^fnoun mp emph עַם *people.* ^gnoun fp
emph אֻמָּה *nation.* ^hnoun mp emph לִשָּׁן
tongue. ⁱG sc 3mp הוה. ^jK זָאֲעִין, Q זָיְעִין,
both G ptcp mp abs זוע *tremble.* ^kG ptcp
mp abs דחל *fear.* ^lprep קֳדָם w/ 3ms gen sx.
^mrel pron דִּי *he who; whoever.* ⁿG sc 3ms
הוה. ^oG ptcp ms abs צבה *desire, wish.* ^pG
ptcp ms abs קטל *kill.* ^qH ptcp ms abs חיה
let live. ^rH ptcp ms abs רום *exalt.* ^sH ptcp
ms abs שפל *bring low.*

20 ^atemp conj (כְּ + דִּי) *when.* ^bG sc 3ms
רום *be high.* ^cnoun ms לְבַב w/ 3ms gen sx
heart. ^dnoun fs רוּחַ w/ 3ms gen sx *wind.*
^eG sc 3fs תקף *become strong.* ^fH inf זוד
hapax *be arrogant; act presumptuously.*
^gHp sc 3ms נחת *be brought down, deposed.*
^hnoun ms cstr כָּרְסֵא *throne.* ⁱnoun fs מַלְכוּ
w/ 3ms gen sx *kingship, sovereignty; king-
dom.* ^jnoun ms emph יְקָר *honor.* ^kH sc
3mp עדה *remove.* ^lprep מִן w/ 3ms gen sx.

21 ^anoun mp cstr II בַּר *son.* ^{b–b}*human beings.*
^cGp sc 3ms טרד *be driven away.* ^dnoun ms
לְבַב w/ 3ms gen sx *heart.* ^enoun fs emph חֵיוָה
animal. ^fK שַׁוִּה Gp sc 3ms שוה *become
like,* Q שַׁוִּיו [Ed; L, *BHS, BHL** שַׁוִּי] D sc
3mp שוה *make the same as.* ^gnoun mp

emph עֲרָד hapax *wild donkey.* ^hnoun ms
מְדוֹר w/ 3ms gen sx *dwelling.* ⁱnoun ms
emph עֲשַׂב *vegetation, plants.* ^jnoun mp
abs תּוֹר *bull.* ^kD pc 3mp טעם w/ 3ms acc
sx *feed.* ^lnoun ms cstr טַל *dew.* ^mnoun mp
emph שְׁמַיָּן. ⁿnoun ms גְּשֶׁם w/ 3ms gen
sx *body.* ^otD juss 3ms צבע *be drenched.*
^ptemp conj דִּי *that.* ^qG sc 3ms ידע. ^repex
conj דִּי *that.* ^sadj ms abs שַׁלִּיט *sovereign.*
^tK עִלַּי, Q עִלָּאָה, both noun ms emph
most high. ^unoun fs cstr מַלְכוּ *kingdom.*
^vpers indef pron מַן *who.* ^wrel pron דִּי *who,
that.* ^{x–x}= *whoever.* ^yG pc 3ms צבה *desire,
wish.* ^zH pc 3ms קום. ^{aa}K עֲלַיֵהּ prep עַל w/
3ms gen sx, Q עֲלַהּ prep עַל w/ 3fs gen sx.

22 ^aK וְאַנְתָּה, Q וְאַנְתְּ, both indep pers pron
2ms אַנְתְּ *you.* ^bnoun ms II בַּר w/ 3ms gen
sx *son.* ^cPN *Belshazzar.* ^dH sc 2ms שפל
humble. ^enoun ms לְבַב w/ 2ms gen sx
heart. ^f= כְּ + לְ *according to.* ^gconj דִּי *that.*
^{h–h}= *though, although.* ⁱnoun ms cstr כֹּל.
^jprox dem pron ms דְּנָה *this.* ^kG sc 2ms
ידע.

23 ^anoun ms cstr מָרֵא *lord.* ^bnoun mp
emph שְׁמַיָן. ^ctD sc 2ms רום *exalt oneself.*
^dnoun mp emph מָאן *vessel.* ^egen part דִּי
of. ^fnoun ms בַּיִת w/ 3ms gen sx.

הֵיתָיו֩ g קָדָמָיךְ h וְאַנְתָּה i וְרַבְרְבָנָיךְ j שֵׁגְלָתָךְ k וּלְחֵנָתָךְ l חַמְרָא m
שָׁתַיִן n בְּהוֹן o וְלֵאלָהֵי כַסְפָּא־ p וְדַהֲבָא q נְחָשָׁא r פַרְזְלָא s אָעָא t
וְאַבְנָא u דִּי v לָא־חָזַיִן w וְלָא־שָׁמְעִין x וְלָא יָדְעִין y שַׁבַּחְתָּ z וְלֵאלָהָא
דִּי־נִשְׁמְתָךְ aa בִּידֵהּ bb וְכָל־אֹרְחָתָךְ cc לֵהּ dd לָא הַדַּרְתָּ ff 24 בֵּאדַיִן a
מִן־קָדָמוֹהִי שְׁלִיחַ c פַּסָּא d דִּי־יְדָא e וּכְתָבָא g דְּנָה h רְשִׁים i 25 וּדְנָה a
כְּתָבָא b דִּי רְשִׁים d מְנֵא e מְנֵא תְּקֵל f וּפַרְסִין g 26 דְּנָה a פְּשַׁר־מִלְּתָא b
מְנֵא d מְנָה־אֱלָהָא e מַלְכוּתָךְ וְהַשְׁלְמַהּ f 27 תְּקֵל a תְּקִילְתָּה b בְּמֹאזַנְיָא c
וְהִשְׁתְּכַחַתְּ d חַסִּיר e 28 פְּרֵס a פְּרִיסַת מַלְכוּתָךְ b וִיהִיבַת לְמָדַי e וּפָרָס f 29 בֵּאדַיִן a | אֲמַר b בֵּלְשַׁאצַּר c וְהַלְבִּשׁוּ d לְדָנִיֵּאל אַרְגְּוָנָא e וְהַמְונְכָא f

---

23 gH sc 3mp אתה *bring.* hK קָדָמָיךְ, Q קָדָמָךְ, both prep קֳדָם w/ 2ms gen sx. iK וְאַנְתָּה, Q וְאַנְתְּ, both indep pers pron 2ms אַנְתְּ *you.* jK וְרַבְרְבָנָיךְ, Q וְרַבְרְבָנָךְ, both noun mp רַבְרְבָנִין w/ 2ms gen sx *lord.* knoun fp שֵׁגָל w/ 2ms gen sx Akk lw *second-tier wife; concubine.* lnoun fp לְחֵנָה w/ 2ms gen sx Akk lw *consort, concubine, prostitute.* mnoun ms emph חֲמַר *wine.* nG ptcp mp abs שתה *drink* (w/ בְּ) *from.* oprep בְּ w/ 3mp gen sx. pnoun ms emph כְּסַף *silver.* qnoun ms emph דְּהַב *gold.* rnoun ms emph נְחָשׁ *bronze.* snoun ms emph פַּרְזֶל *iron.* tnoun ms emph אָע *wood.* unoun fs emph אֶבֶן *stone.* vrel pron דִּי *who, which, that.* wG ptcp mp abs חזה *see.* xG ptcp mp abs שמע *hear.* yG ptcp mp abs ידע *know.* zD sc 2ms שבח *praise.* aanoun fs נִשְׁמָה w/ 2ms gen sx hapax *breath.* bbnoun fs יַד w/ 3ms gen sx *hand.* ccnoun ms cstr כֹּל. ddnoun fp אֹרַח w/ 2ms gen sx *path.* eeprep לְ w/ 3ms gen sx. ffD sc 2ms הדר *glorify.*

24 atemp adv אֱדַיִן (w/ בְּ) *immediately; then.* bprep קֳדָם w/ 3ms gen sx. cGp sc 3ms שלח *sent* [so Ed; L, BHS, BHL* שְׁלִיחַ]. dnoun ms emph פַּס *palm.* egen part דִּי *of.* fnoun fs emph יַד *hand.* gnoun ms emph כְּתָב *writing.* hprox dem adj ms דְּנָה *this.* iGp sc 3ms רשם *be written, inscribed.*

25 aprox dem pron ms דְּנָה *this.* bnoun ms emph כְּתָב *writing.* crel pron דִּי *which, that.* dGp sc 3ms רשם *be written.* enoun ms abs מְנֵא Sum lw, weight measure *mina,*

or Gp ptcp ms abs מנה *counted; MENE.* fnoun ms abs תְּקֵל *weight measure shekel,* or pun on תְּקִיל Gp ptcp ms abs תקל *weighed; TEKEL.* gnoun mp abs (noun m dual?) פְּרֵס Akk lw, volume measure *peres,* weight measure *one-half mina; one-half shekel; PARSIN (UPHARSIN, NJPS).*

26 aprox dem pron ms דְּנָה *this.* bnoun fs emph מִלָּה *word.* cnoun ms abs מְנֵא Sum lw, weight measure *mina,* or Gp ptcp ms abs מנה *counted; MENE.* dG sc 3ms מנה *count.* enoun fs מַלְכוּ w/ 2ms gen sx *kingship, sovereignty; kingdom.* fH sc 3ms שלם w/ 3fs acc sx *compete, finish off.*

27 anoun ms abs תְּקֵל *weight measure shekel,* or pun on תְּקִיל Gp ptcp ms abs תקל *weighed; TEKEL.* bGp sc 2ms תקל *hapax be weighed.* cnoun mp emph מֹאזְנָא *hapax balance.* dtG sc 2ms שכח *be found.* eadj ms abs חַסִּיר *hapax lacking.*

28 anoun ms abs פְּרֵס Akk lw, volume measure *peres,* weight measure *one-half mina; one-half shekel; PARSIN (UPHARSIN, NJPS).* bGp sc 3fs פרס *hapax be divided.* cnoun fs מַלְכוּ w/ 2ms gen sx *kingdom.* dGp sc 3fs יהב. eGN *Media.* fGN *Persia.*

29 atemp adv אֱדַיִן (w/ בְּ) *immediately; then.* bG sc 3ms אמר. cPN *Belshazzar.* dH sc 3mp לבש *clothe.* enoun ms emph אַרְגְּוָן Akk lw *purple.* fK וְהַמְונְכָא, Q וְהַמְונְכָא, both noun ms emph הַמְונֵךְ Pers lw *necklace, chain.*

דִּי־דַהֲבָאʰ עַל־צַוְּארֵהּⁱ וְהַכְרִזוּʲ עֲלֹוהִיᵏ דִּי־לֶהֱוֵאᵐ שַׁלִּיטⁿ תַּלְתָּאᵒ
בְּמַלְכוּתָאᴾ: 30 בֵּהּᵃ בְּלֵילְיָאᶜᵇ קְטִילᵈ בֵּלְאשַׁצַּרᵉ מַלְכָּא כַשְׂדָּיָאᶠ: פ

6 ¹ וְדָרְיָ֫וֶשׁᵃ מָדָיאᵇ קַבֵּלᶜ מַלְכוּתָאᵈ כְּבַרᵉ שְׁנִיןᶠ שִׁתִּיןᵍ וְתַרְתֵּֽיןⁱʰ:
² שְׁפַרᵃ קֳדָםᵇ דָּרְיָ֫וֶשׁᶜ וַהֲקִיםᵈ עַל־מַלְכוּתָא לַאֲחַשְׁדַּרְפְּנַיָּאᵉ
מְאָהᶠ וְעֶשְׂרִיןᵍ דִּי לֶהֱוֹןʰ בְּכָל־מַלְכוּתָאⁱ: ³ וְעֵלָּאᵃ מִנְּהֹוןᵇ סָרְכִיןᶜ
תְּלָתָאᵈ דִּי דָנִיֵּאלᵉ חַד־מִנְּהֹוןᶠ דִּי־לֶהֱוֹןᵍ אֲחַשְׁדַּרְפְּנַיָּאʰ אִלֵּֽיןⁱ
יָהֲבִין לְהֹוןʲ טַעְמָאᵏ וּמַלְכָּא לָא־לֶהֱוֵאᵐ נָזִקⁿ: ⁴ אֱדַ֫יִן דָּנִיֵּאל דְּנָהᵃ
הֲוָאᵇ מִתְנַצַּחᶜ עַל־סָרְכַיָּאᵈ וַאֲחַשְׁדַּרְפְּנַיָּאᵉ כָּל־קֳבֵלᶠ דִּיᵍ רֽוּחʰ
יַתִּירָאⁱ בֵּהּ וּמַלְכָּא עֲשִׁיתˡ לַהֲקָמוּתֵהּᵐ עַל־כָּל־מַלְכוּתָאᵒ: ⁵ אֱדַ֫יִן
סָרְכַיָּאᵃ וַאֲחַשְׁדַּרְפְּנַיָּאᵇ הֲוֹוᶜ בָעַיִןᵈ עִלָּהᵉ לְהַשְׁכָּחָהᶠ לְדָנִיֵּאל מִצַּדᵍ

---

29 ᵍgen part דִּי *of.* ʰnoun ms emph דְּהַב *gold.* ⁱnoun ms emph צַוָּאר w/ 3ms gen sx *neck.* ʲH sc 3mp כרז hapax *herald, proclaim.* ᵏprep עַל־ w/ 3ms gen sx. ˡepex conj דִּי *that.* ᵐG PC 3ms הוה. ⁿadj ms abs שַׁלִּיט *sovereign; mighty.* ᵒnoun ms abs תַּלְתָּא Akk calque *triumvir* (official of the third rank), *rank third.* ᴾnoun fs emph מַלְכוּ *kingdom.*

30 ᵃprep בְּ w/ 3ms gen sx. ᵇnoun ms emph לֵילֵי *night.* ᶜ⁻ᶜ= *in this very night.* ᵈGp sc 3ms קטל *be killed.* ᵉPN *Belshazzar.* ᶠK בַּשְׂדָּיָא, Q כַּשְׂדָּאָה, both noun ms emph כַּשְׂדָּי *Chaldean.*

6

1 ᵃPN *Darius.* ᵇK מְדָיָא, Q מָדָאָה [Ed ״מָ] noun ms emph מָדָי *Mede.* ᶜD sc 3ms קבל *receive.* ᵈnoun fs emph מַלְכוּ *kingdom.* ᵉnoun ms cstr II בַּר *son.* ᶠnoun fp abs I שְׁנָה *year.* ᵍcard שִׁתִּין *sixty.* ʰcard w/ f noun תְּרֵין *two.* ⁱ⁻ⁱ= *being about sixty-two years old.*

2 ᵃG sc 3ms שפר *be pleasant, pleasing.* ᵇPN *Darius.* ᶜH sc 3ms קום. ᵈnoun fs emph מַלְכוּ *kingdom.* ᵉnoun mp emph אֲחַשְׁדַּרְפַּן Pers lw *satrap.* ᶠcard מְאָה *hundred.* ᵍcard עֶשְׂרִין hapax *twenty.* ʰrel pron דִּי *who, that.* ⁱG PC 3mp הוה. ʲnoun ms cstr כֹּל.

3 ᵃprep עֵלָּא hapax *over.* ᵇprep מִן w/ 3mp gen sx. ᶜnoun mp abs סָרֵךְ Pers lw, high offi-

cial *president.* ᵈcard w/ m noun תְּלָת *three.* ᵉrel pron דִּי *who, that.* ᶠcard w/ m noun חַד *one.* ᵍG PC 3mp הוה. ʰnoun mp emph אֲחַשְׁדַּרְפַּן Pers lw *satrap.* ⁱprox dem adj cp אִלֵּין *these.* ʲG ptcp mp abs יהב. ᵏprep לְ w/ 3mp gen sx. ˡnoun ms abs טְעֵם *statement, report.* ᵐG PC 3ms הוה. ⁿG ptcp ms abs נזק *come to grief* (HALOT); *be damaged.*

4 ᵃprox dem adj ms דְּנָה *this.* Perhaps = *our Daniel.* ᵇG sc 3ms הוה. ᶜtD ptcp ms abs נצח hapax *distinguish oneself, surpass.* ᵈnoun mp emph סָרֵךְ Pers lw, *high official president.* ᵉnoun mp emph אֲחַשְׁדַּרְפַּן Pers lw *satrap.* ᶠ= כְּ + לְ *according to.* ᵍconj דִּי *that.* ʰ⁻ʰ= *because, since.* ⁱnoun fs abs רוּחַ *spirit.* ʲadj fs abs יַתִּיר *extraordinary, superior.* ᵏprep בְּ w/ 3ms gen sx. ˡGp ptcp ms abs עשׁת hapax *intend* active sense. ᵐH inf קום w/ 3ms acc sx. ⁿnoun ms cstr כֹּל. ᵒnoun fs emph מַלְכוּ *kingship, sovereignty; kingdom.*

5 ᵃnoun mp emph סָרֵךְ Pers lw, high official *president.* ᵇnoun mp emph אֲחַשְׁדַּרְפַּן Pers lw *satrap.* ᶜG sc 3mp הוה. ᵈG ptcp mp abs בעה *seek.* ᵉnoun fs abs עִלָּה [עַלָּא HALOT] *cause, pretext.* ᶠH inf שׁכח *find.* ᵍnoun ms cstr צַד *side = perspective.*

מַלְכוּתָאʰ וְכָל־עִלָּהⁱ וּשְׁחִיתָהʲ לָא־יָכְלִיןˡ לְהַשְׁכָּחָהᵐ כָּל־קֳבֵלᵖ

דִּי־מְהֵימַןᵖᵒ הוּאʳ וְכָל־שָׁלוּˢ וּשְׁחִיתָהⁱ לָא הִשְׁתְּכַחַתᵗ עֲלוֹהִיⱽ׃

6 אֱדַיִן גֻּבְרַיָּאª אִלֵּךְᵇ אָמְרִיןᶜ דִּי לָא נְהַשְׁכַּחᵉ לְדָנִיֵּאל כָּל־

עִלָּאᵍ לָהֵןʰ הַשְׁכַּחְנָהʲ עֲלוֹהִיᵏ בְּדָתˡ אֱלָהֵהᵐ׃ ס 7 אֱדַיִןʰ

סָרְכַיָּאª וַאֲחַשְׁדַּרְפְּנַיָּאᵇ אִלֵּןᶜ הַרְגִּשׁוּᵈ עַל־מַלְכָּא וְכֵן אָמְרִיןᵍ לֵהᵍ

דָּרְיָוֶשׁʰ מַלְכָּא לְעָלְמִיןⁱ חֱיִיʲ׃ 8 אִתְיָעַטוּª כֹּל׀ סָרְכֵי מַלְכוּתָאᵈ

סִגְנַיָּאᵉ וַאֲחַשְׁדַּרְפְּנַיָּאᶠ הַדָּבְרַיָּאᵍ וּפַחֲוָתָאʰ לְקַיָּמָהⁱ קְיָםʲ מַלְכָּא

וּלְתַקָּפָהᵏ אֱסָרˡ דִּי כָל־דִּי־יִבְעֵהᵠ בָעוּᵖ מִן־כָּל־אֱלָהᵒ וֶאֱנָשˣ

עַד־יוֹמִיןⁱ תְּלָתִיןˢ לָהֵןᵗ מִנָּךְᵘ מַלְכָּא יִתְרְמֵאⱽ לְגֹבʷ אַרְיָוָתָאˣ׃ 9 כְּעַןª

מַלְכָּא תְּקִיםᵇ אֱסָרָאᶜ וְתִרְשֻׁםᵈ כְּתָבָאᵉ דִּי לָא לְהַשְׁנָיָהᵍ כְּדָת־ʰ

מָדַיⁱ וּפָרַסʲ דִּי־לָא תֶעְדֵּאᵏ׃ 10 כָּל־קֳבֵלªᵇ דְּנָהᶜᵇ מַלְכָּאᶜ דָּרְיָוֶשׁᵈ רְשַׁםᵉ

---

5 ʰnoun fs emph מַלְכוּ *kingdom.* ⁱnoun ms cstr כָּל. ʲnoun fs abs עִלָּה [עִלָּא *HALOT*] *cause, pretext.* ᵏGp ptcp fs abs שׁחת *corrupted* or *bad thing.* ˡG ptcp mp abs יכל *be able.* ᵐH inf שׁכח *find.* ⁿ= כְּ + לְ *according to.* ᵒsubord conj דִּי *that.* ᵖ⁻ᵖ= *because, since.* ᵠHp ptcp ms abs אמן *trustworthy.* ʳindep pers pron 3ms הוּא *he.* ˢnoun fs abs שָׁלוּ *negligence.* ᵗGp ptcp fs abs שׁחת *corrupted* or *bad thing.* ᵘtG sc 3fs שׁכח *be found.* ⱽprep עַל w/ 3ms gen sx.

6 ªnoun mp emph גְּבַר *man, person.* ᵇdist dem adj cp אִלֵּךְ *those.* ᶜG ptcp mp abs אמר. ᵈepex conj דִּי *that.* ᵉH PC 1cp שׁכח *find.* ᶠprox dem adj ms דְּנָה *this.* Perhaps = *our Daniel.* ᵍnoun fs cstr כָּל. ʰnoun fs abs עִלָּה [עִלָּא *HALOT*] *cause, pretext.* ⁱdisj II לָהֵן *unless.* ʲH sc 1cp שׁכח *find.* ᵏprep עַל־ w/ 3ms gen sx. ˡnoun fs cstr דָּת Pers lw *law.* ᵐnoun ms אֱלָה w/ 3ms gen sx.

7 ªnoun mp emph סְרַךְ Pers lw, high official *president.* ᵇnoun mp emph אֲחַשְׁדַּרְפַּן Pers lw *satrap.* ᶜprox dem adj cp אִלֵּין *these.* ᵈH sc 3mp רגשׁ *throng* [= *conspire (?)*]. ᵉadv כֵּן *thus.* ᶠG ptcp mp abs אמר. ᵍprep לְ w/ 3ms gen sx. ʰPN *Darius.* ⁱnoun mp abs עָלַם *eternity.* ʲG imv 2ms חיה *live.*

8 ªtD sc 3mp יעט *consult together.* ᵇnoun ms cstr כֹּל. ᶜnoun mp cstr סְרַךְ Pers lw, high official *president.* ᵈnoun fs emph מַלְכוּ *kingdom.* ᵉnoun mp emph סְגַן *prefect.* ᶠnoun mp emph אֲחַשְׁדַּרְפַּן Pers lw *satrap.* ᵍnoun mp emph הַדָּבַר Pers lw *companion.* ʰnoun mp emph פֶּחָה *governor.* ⁱD inf קום. ʲnoun ms cstr קְיָם *statute.* ᵏD inf תקף *strengthen; enforce.* ˡnoun ms abs אֱסָר *prohibition.* ᵐepex conj דִּי *that.* ⁿrel pron דִּי *who, that.* ᵒG PC 3ms בעה *request.* ᵖnoun fs abs בָּעוּ *request.* ᵠ⁻ᵠ= *pray.* ʳnoun mp abs יוֹם *day.* ˢcard תְּלָתִין *thirty.* ᵗprep II לָהֵן *except.* ᵘprep מִן w/ 2ms gen sx. ⱽtG G 3ms רמה *be thrown.* ʷnoun ms cstr גֹּב *den.* ˣnoun mp emph אַרְיֵה *lion.*

9 ªtransitional conj כְּעַן introduces new idea *now.* ᵇH PC 2ms קום. ᶜnoun ms emph אֱסָר *prohibition.* ᵈG PC 2ms רשׁם *sign.* ᵉnoun ms emph כְּתָב *document.* ᶠrel pron דִּי *which, that.* ᵍH inf שׁנה trans *change.* ʰnoun fs cstr דָּת Pers lw *law.* ⁱGN *Media.* ʲGN *Persia.* ᵏG PC 3fs עדה *be annulled.*

10 ª= כְּ + לְ *according to.* ᵇprox dem pron ms דְּנָה *this.* ᶜ⁻ᶜ= *because of this, therefore.* ᵈPN *Darius.* ᵉG sc 3ms רשׁם *sign.*

כְּתָבָאᶠ וֶאֱסָרָא: 11 וְדָנִיֵּאל כְּדִיᵃ יְדַעᵇ דִּי־רְשִׁיםᶜ כְּתָבָאᵈ עַלᵉ לְבַיְתֵהᶠ לְבַיְתֵהᵍ
וְכַוִּיןʰ פְּתִיחָןⁱ לֵהʲ בְּעִלִּיתֵהᵏ נֶגֶדˡ יְרוּשְׁלֶם וְזִמְנִיןᵐ תְּלָתָהⁿ בְּיוֹמָאᵒ
הוּאᵖ| בָּרֵךְۛ עַל־בִּרְכוֹהִיⁱ וּמְצַלֵּאˢ וּמוֹדֵאᵗ קֳדָם אֱלָהֵהᵘ כָּל־קֳבֵלˣ
דִּי־ᵂˣʸ הֲוָאʸ עָבֵדᶻ מִן־קַדְמַתᵃᵃ דְּנָהᵇᵇ: ᶜᶜᵇᵇ ס   12 אֱדַיִןᵃ גֻּבְרַיָּאᵃ אִלֵּךְᵇ
הַרְגִּשׁוּᶜ וְהַשְׁכַּחוּᵈ לְדָנִיֵּאל בָּעֵאᵉ וּמִתְחַנַּןᶠ קֳדָם אֱלָהֵהᵍ: 13 בֵּאדַיִןᵃ
קְרִיבוּᵇ וְאָמְרִיןᶜ קֳדָם־מַלְכָּאᵈ עַל־אֱסָרᵈ מַלְכָּא הֲלָאᵉ אֱסָרᵈ רְשַׁמְתָּᶠ
דִּי כָל־אֱנָשʰ דִּי־יִבְעֵהʲ מִן־כָּל־אֱלָהʰ וֶאֱנָשׁ עַד־יוֹמִיןᵏ תְּלָתִיןˡ לָהֵןᵐ
מִנָּךְⁿ מַלְכָּא יִתְרְמֵאᵒ לְגוֹבᵖ אַרְיָוָתָאᵠ עָנֵהⁱ מַלְכָּא וְאָמַרˢ יַצִּיבָאᵗ
מִלְּתָאᵘ כְּדָת־מָדַיʷ וּפָרַס דִּי־ʸלָא תֶעְדֵּאᶻ: 14 בֵּאדַיִןᵃ עֲנוֹᵇ וְאָמְרִיןᶜ
קֳדָם מַלְכָּאᵈ דִּי דָנִיֵּאלᵉ דִּי מִן־בְּנֵיᶠ גָלוּתָאᵍ דִּי יְהוּדʰ לָא־שָׂםⁱ עֲלָיִךְⁱ
מַלְכָּא טְעֵםˡ וְעַל־אֱסָרָאᵐ דִּי רְשַׁמְתָּⁿ וְזִמְנִיןᵒ תְּלָתָהᵖ בְּיוֹמָאᵠ בָּעֵאⁱ

10 ᶠnoun ms emph כְּתָב *document.* ᵍnoun ms emph אֱסָר *prohibition.*

11 ᵃtemp conj (כְּ + דִי) כְּדִי *when.* ᵇG sc 3ms ידע. ᶜepex conj דִּי *that.* ᵈGp sc 3ms רשם *be signed.* ᵉnoun ms emph כְּתָב *document.* ᶠG sc 3ms II עלל *enter.* ᵍnoun ms cstr בֵּית w/ 3ms gen sx. ʰnoun fp abs כַּוָּה hapax *window.* ⁱGp ptcp fp abs פתח *be opened.* ʲprep לְ w/ 3ms gen sx. ᵏnoun fs עֲלִי w/ 3ms gen sx hapax *upstairs room.* ˡprep נֶגֶד hapax *toward.* ᵐnoun mp abs זְמַן *set time, appointment.* ⁿcard w/ m noun תְּלָת *three.* ᵒnoun ms emph יוֹם *day.* ᵖindep pers pron 3ms הוּא *he.* ᵠG ptcp ms abs I ברך hapax *kneel.* ⁱnoun fp abs בְּרַךְ w/ 3ms gen sx hapax *knee.* ˢD ptcp ms abs צלה *pray.* ᵗH ptcp ms abs ידה *give thanks.* ᵘnoun ms אֱלָה w/ 3ms gen sx. ᵛ= כְּ + לְ *according to.* ʷconj דִּי *that.* ˣ⁻ˣ= *because, since.* ʸG sc 3ms הוה. ᶻG ptcp ms abs עבד. ᵃᵃnoun fs cstr קַדְמָה *earlier time than.* ᵇᵇprox dem pron ms דְּנָה *this* [so BHS, Ed; L, BHL* ה″]. ᶜᶜ⁻ᶜᶜ*he was doing from before this = he had always done so.*

12 ᵃnoun mp emph גְּבַר *man, person.* ᵇdist dem adj cp אִלֵּךְ *those.* ᶜH sc 3mp רגש *throng* [= *conspire* (?)]. ᵈH sc 3mp שכח *find.* ᵉG ptcp ms abs בעה *request = pray.* ᶠtD ptcp ms abs חנן *seek mercy,*

grace. ᵍnoun ms אֱלָה w/ 3ms gen sx.

13 ᵃtemp adv אֱדַיִן (w/ בְּ) *immediately; then.* ᵇG sc 3mp קרב *approach.* ᶜG ptcp mp abs אמר. ᵈnoun ms abs אֱסָר *prohibition.* ᵉneg part לָא w/ interr ה. ᶠG sc 2ms רשם *sign.* ᵍepex conj דִּי *that.* ʰnoun ms cstr כֹּל. ⁱrel pron דִּי *who, that.* ʲG pc 3ms בעה *seek.* ᵏnoun mp abs יוֹם *day.* ˡcard תְּלָתִין *thirty.* ᵐprep II לָהֵן *except.* ⁿprep מִן w/ 2ms gen sx. ᵒtG pc 3ms רמה *be thrown.* ᵖnoun ms cstr גֹּב *den.* ᵠnoun mp emph אַרְיֵה *lion.* ⁱG ptcp ms abs I ענה. ˢG ptcp ms abs אמר. ᵗadj fs abs יַצִּיב *certain; firm.* ᵘnoun fs emph מִלָּה *word.* ᵛnoun fs cstr דָּת Pers lw *law.* ʷGN *Media.* ˣGN *Persia.* ʸrel pron דִּי *which, that.* ᶻG pc 3fs עדה *pass away, be annulled.*

14 ᵃtemp adv אֱדַיִן (w/ בְּ) *immediately; then.* ᵇG sc 3mp I ענה. ᶜG ptcp mp abs אמר. ᵈepex conj דִּי *that.* ᵉrel pron דִּי *who, which, that.* ᶠnoun mp cstr II בַּר *son.* ᵍnoun fs emph גָּלוּ *exile.* ʰgen part דִּי *of.* ⁱGN *Judah.* ʲG sc 3ms שים *set.* ᵏK עֲלַיִךְ, Q עֲלָךְ, both prep עַל־ w/ 2ms gen sx. ˡnoun ms abs טְעֵם *good taste, deference.* ᵐnoun ms emph אֱסָר *prohibition.* ⁿG sc 2ms רשם *sign.* ᵒnoun mp abs זְמַן *set time.* ᵖcard w/ m noun תְּלָת *three.* ᵠnoun ms emph יוֹם *day.* ⁱG ptcp ms abs בעה *request.*

בְּעוּתֵהּ[ts]: 15 אֱדַיִן מַלְכָּא כְּדִי[b] מִלְּתָא[c] שְׁמַע[b] בְּאֵשׁ[d] שַׂגִּיא[c] עֲלוֹהִי[f]

וְעַל דָּנִיֵּאל שָׂם[g] בָּל[h] לְשֵׁיזָבוּתֵהּ[i] וְעַד מֶעָלֵי[j] שִׁמְשָׁא[k] הֲוָא[l] מִשְׁתַּדַּר[m]

לְהַצָּלוּתֵהּ: 16 בֵּאדַיִן[a] גֻּבְרַיָּא[b] אִלֵּךְ[c] הַרְגִּשׁוּ[d] עַל־מַלְכָּא וְאָמְרִין

לְמַלְכָּא דַּע[e] מַלְכָּא דִּי־דָת[g] לְמָדַי[i] וּפָרַס[j] דִּי־כָל־אֱסָר[k] וּקְיָם[m] דִּי־

מַלְכָּא יְהָקֵים[o] לָא לְהַשְׁנָיָה[p]: 17 בֵּאדַיִן[a] מַלְכָּא אֲמַר[b] וְהַיְתִיו לְדָנִיֵּאל

וּרְמוֹ[d] לְגֻבָּא[e] דִּי[f] אַרְיָוָתָא[g] עָנֵה[h] מַלְכָּא וְאָמַר[i] לְדָנִיֵּאל אֱלָהָךְ[k] דִּי[k]

אַנְתָּה[l] פָּלַח[m]־לֵהּ[n] בִּתְדִירָא[o] הוּא[p] יְשֵׁיזְבִנָּךְ[q]: 18 וְהֵיתָיִת[a] אֶבֶן[b] חֲדָה[c]

וְשֻׂמַת[d] עַל־פֻּם[e] גֻּבָּא[f] וְחַתְמַהּ[g] מַלְכָּא בְּעִזְקְתֵהּ[h] וּבְעִזְקָת[i] רַבְרְבָנוֹהִי[j]

דִּי[k] לָא־תִשְׁנֵא[l] צְבוּ[m] בְּדָנִיֵּאל: 19 אֱדַיִן אֲזַל[a] מַלְכָּא לְהֵיכְלֵהּ[b] וּבָת[c]

טְוָת[d] וְדַחֲוָן[e] לָא־הַנְעֵל[f] קָדָמוֹהִי[g] וְשִׁנְתֵהּ[h] נַדַּת[i] עֲלוֹהִי[j]: 20 בֵּאדַיִן[a]

---

14 [s]noun fs בְּעוּ w/ 3ms gen sx *request.* [t–t]= *pray.*

15 [a]temp conj כְּדִי (כְּ + דִּי) *when.* [b]noun fs emph מִלָּה *word.* [c]G sc 3ms שְׁמַע *hear.* [d]adj ms abs שַׂגִּיא as adv *very.* [e]G sc 3ms בּאשׁ hapax *be bad, evil to* (w/ עַל). [f]prep עַל w/ 3ms gen sx. [g]G sc 3ms שׂים. [h]noun ms abs בָּל hapax *mind.* [i]Š inf שֵׁיזָב w/ 3ms acc sx *rescue.* [j]adj mp cstr מֶעָל hapax *entering* = *setting.* [k]noun ms emph שְׁמַשׁ hapax *sun.* [l]G sc 3ms הוה. [m]tD ptcp ms abs שׁדר hapax *exert, make every effort.* [n]H inf נצל w/ 3ms acc sx *deliver.*

16 [a]temp adv אֱדַיִן (w/ בְּ) *immediately; then.* [b]noun mp emph גְּבַר *man, person.* [c]dist dem adj cp אִלֵּךְ *those.* [d]H sc 3mp רגשׁ *throng* [= *conspire* (?)]. [e]G ptcp mp abs אמר. [f]G imv 2ms ידע. [g]epex conj דִּי *that.* [h]noun fs abs דָּת Pers lw *law.* [i]GN *Media.* [j]GN *Persia.* [k]noun ms cstr כֹּל. [l]noun ms abs אֱסָר *prohibition.* [m]noun ms abs קְיָם *statute.* [n]rel pron דִּי *which, that.* [o]H PC 3ms קום. [p]H inf שׁנה trans *change.*

17 [a]temp adv אֱדַיִן (w/ בְּ) *immediately; then.* [b]G sc 3ms אמר. [c]H sc 3mp אתה *bring.* [d]G sc 3mp רמה *throw.* [e]noun ms emph גֹּב *den.* [f]gen part דִּי *of.* [g]noun mp emph אַרְיֵה *lion.* [h]G ptcp ms abs I ענה. [i]G ptcp ms abs אמר. [j]noun ms אֱלָהּ w/ 2ms gen sx. [k]rel

---

pron דִּי *who, that.* [l]K אַנְתָּה, Q אַנְתְּ, both indep pers pron 2ms אַנְתְּ *you.* [m]G ptcp ms abs פלח *serve.* [n]prep לְ w/ 3ms gen sx. [o]noun fs emph תְּדִיר as adv *continually.* [p]indep pers pron 3ms הוּא *he.* [q]Š PC 3ms שׁיזב w/ 2ms acc sx *rescue.*

18 [a]Hp sc 3fs אתה *be brought.* [b]noun fs abs אֶבֶן *stone.* [c]card w/ f noun חַד *one, a.* [d]Gp sc 3fs שׂים. [e]noun ms cstr פֻּם *mouth.* [f]noun ms emph גֹּב *den.* [g]G sc 3ms חתם w/ 3fs acc sx hapax *seal.* [h]noun fs עִזְקָה w/ 3ms gen sx *signet ring.* [i]noun fs cstr עִזְקָה *signet ring.* [j]noun mp רַבְרְבָנִין w/ 3ms gen sx *lord.* [k]purp conj דִּי *so that.* [l]G PC 3fs שׁנה intrans *change.* [m]noun fs abs צְבוּ hapax *thing, matter.*

19 [a]G sc 3ms אזל *go.* [b]noun ms הֵיכַל w/ 3ms gen sx *palace.* [c]G sc 3ms בית hapax *spend the night.* [d]noun fs abs טְוָת = adv, hapax *fasting.* [e]noun fp abs דַּחֲוָה hapax *food* (?), *table* (?); *concubine* (?), *dancing girl* (?); *diversion* (?). [f]H sc 3ms II עלל *bring.* [g]prep קֳדָם w/ 3ms gen sx. [h]noun fs II שְׁנָה w/ 3ms gen sx hapax *sleep.* [i]G sc 3fs נדד hapax *flee.* [j]prep עַל w/ 3ms gen sx. For this use, compare English *she walked out on him.*

20 [a]temp adv אֱדַיִן (w/ בְּ) *immediately; then.*

מַלְכָּא בִּשְׁפַרְפָּרָאᵇ יְקוּםᶜ בְּנָגְהָאᵈ וּבְהִתְבְּהָלָהᵉ לְגֻבָּא דִּי־אַרְיָוָתָאʰ
אֲזַל׃ 21 וּכְמִקְרְבֵהּᵃ לְגֻבָּאᵇ לְדָנִיֵּאל בְּקָלᶜ עֲצִיבᵈ זְעִקᵉ עָנֵהᶠ מַלְכָּא
וְאָמַרᵍ לְדָנִיֵּאל דָּנִיֵּאל עֲבֵדʰ אֱלָהָא חַיָּאⁱ דִּי־אנתה‍ʲ אֲלָהָ‍ᵏ דִּי‍ᵏ אנתה‍ˡ פָּלַח‍ᵐ־
לֵהּⁿ בִּתְדִירָאᵒ הַיְכֵל לְשֵׁיזָבוּתָ‍ᵏᵖ מִן־אַרְיָוָתָא‍ᵠ׃ 22 אֱדַיִן דָּנִיֵּאל עִם‍ᵃ־
מַלְכָּא מַלִּל‍ᵇ מַלְכָּא לְעָלְמִין‍ᶜ חֱיִי‍ᵈ׃ 23 אֱלָהִי‍ᵃ שְׁלַח‍ᵇ מַלְאֲכֵה‍ᶜ וּסֲגַר‍ᵈ
פֻּם‍ᵉ אַרְיָוָתָא וְלָא חַבְּלוּנִי‍ᵍ כָּל־קֳבֵל‍ʰ דִּי‍ʲⁱ קָדָמוֹהִי זָכוּ‍ᵏ הִשְׁתְּכַחַת
לִי‍ˡ וְאַף‍ᵒ קָדָמָ‍ᵏᵖ מַלְכָּא חֲבוּלָה‍ᵠ לָא עַבְדֵת‍ʳ׃ 24 בֵּאדַיִן‍ᵃ מַלְכָּא שַׂגִּיא‍ᵇ
טְאֵב‍ᶜ עֲלוֹהִי‍ᵈ וּלְדָנִיֵּאל אֲמַר‍ᵉ לְהַנְסָקָה‍ᶠ מִן־גֻּבָּא‍ᵍ וְהֻסַּק‍ʰ דָּנִיֵּאל מִן־
גֻּבָּא‍ᵍ וְכָל־חֲבָל‍ⁱ לָא־הִשְׁתְּכַח‍ᵏ בֵּהּ‍ˡ דִּי‍ᵐ הֵימִן‍ⁿ בֵּאלָהֵהּ‍ᵒ׃ 25 וַאֲמַר‍ᵃ
מַלְכָּא וְהַיְתִיו‍ᵇ גֻּבְרַיָּא‍ᶜ אִלֵּךְ‍ᵈ דִּי‍ᵉ־אֲכַלוּ‍ᶠ קַרְצוֹהִי‍ʰᵍ דִּי דָנִיֵּאל
וּלְגֹב‍ʲ אַרְיָוָתָא‍ᵏ רְמוֹ‍ˡ אִנּוּן‍ᵐ בְּנֵיהוֹן‍ⁿ וּנְשֵׁיהוֹן‍ᵒ וְלָא־מְטוֹ‍ᵖ לְאַרְעִית‍ᵠ

20 ᵇnoun ms emph שְׁפַרְפָּר hapax *dawn*. ᶜG PC 3ms קום. ᵈnoun ms emph נְגַהּ hapax *first light*. This appears to be an in-text gloss for ᶜ. ᵉnoun fs abs הִתְבְּהָלָה *haste*. ᶠnoun ms emph גֹּב *den*. ᵍgen part דִּי *of*. ʰnoun mp emph אַרְיֵה *lion*. ⁱG SC 3ms אזל *go*.

21 ᵃG inf קרב w/ 3ms gen sx *after he approached*. ᵇnoun ms emph גֹּב *den*. ᶜnoun ms abs קָל *voice*. ᵈadj ms abs עֲצִיב hapax *anxious (?), sad (?)*. ᵉG SC 3ms זעק hapax *yell*. ᶠG ptcp ms abs I ענה. ᵍG ptcp ms abs אמר. ʰnoun ms cstr עֲבֵד *slave, servant*. ⁱnoun ms emph I חַי *living*. ʲnoun ms emph אֱלָהּ w/ 2ms gen sx *god, deity*. ᵏrel pron דִּי *who, which, that*. ˡK אנתה, Q אַנְתְּ, both indep pers pron 2ms אַנְתְּ *you*. ᵐG ptcp ms abs פלח *serve*. ⁿprep לְ w/ 3ms gen sx. ᵒnoun fs emph תְּדִיר as adv *continually*. ᵖG PC 3ms יכל w/ interr ה *be able*. ᵠŠ inf שיזב w/ 2ms acc sx *rescue*. ʳnoun mp emph אַרְיֵה *lion*.

22 ᵃL, BHL*, BHS דָּנִיֵּ֫אל; Ed דָּנִיֵּאל. ᵇD SC 3ms מלל *speak*. ᶜnoun mp abs עָלַם *eternity*. ᵈG imv 2ms חיה *live*.

23 ᵃnoun ms emph אֱלָהּ w/ 1cs gen sx. ᵇG SC 3ms שלח *send*. ᶜnoun ms מַלְאַךְ w/ 3ms gen sx *angel*. ᵈG SC 3ms סגר hapax *close, shut*. ᵉnoun ms cstr פֻּם *mouth*. ᶠnoun mp emph אַרְיֵה *lion*. ᵍD SC 3mp חבל w/ 1cs acc sx *destroy*. ʰ= כְּ + לְ *according to*. ⁱconj דִּי *that*.

ʲ-ʲ= *because, since*. ᵏprep קֳדָם w/ 3ms gen sx. ˡnoun fs abs זָכוּ *innocence*. ᵐtG SC 3fs שכח *be found*. ⁿprep לְ w/ 1cs gen sx. ᵒconj אַף *also*. ᵖK קָדָמַיִךְ, Q קָדָמָךְ, both prep קֳדָם w/ 2ms gen sx. ᵠnoun fs abs חֲבוּלָה hapax *wrong, harm, crime*. ʳG SC 1cs עבד.

24 ᵃtemp adv אֱדַיִן (w/ בְּ) *immediately; then*. ᵇadj ms abs שַׂגִּיא *very*. ᶜG SC 3ms טאב hapax *be good to* (w/ עַל) X = X *was glad*. ᵈprep עַל w/ 3ms gen sx. ᵉG SC 3ms אמר. ᶠH inf סלק *bring up*. ᵍnoun ms emph גֹּב *den*. ʰHp SC 3ms סלק *be brought up*. ⁱnoun ms cstr כֹּל. ʲnoun ms abs חֲבָל *harm*. ᵏtG SC 3ms שכח *be found*. ˡprep בְּ w/ 3ms gen sx. ᵐcaus conj דִּי *because*. ⁿH SC 3ms אמן *believe, trust*. ᵒnoun ms אֱלָהּ w/ 3ms gen sx.

25 ᵃG SC 3ms אמר. ᵇH SC 3mp אתה *bring*. ᶜnoun mp emph גְּבַר *man, person*. ᵈdist dem adj cp אִלֵּךְ *those*. ᵉrel pron דִּי *who, which, that*. ᶠG SC 3mp אכל *eat*. ᵍnoun mp קְרַץ w/ 3ms gen sx Akk lw *bits*. ʰ-ʰ= *slander* (w/ דִּי) *someone; accuse*. ⁱgen part דִּי *of*. ʲnoun ms cstr גֹּב *den*. ᵏnoun mp emph אַרְיֵה *lion*. ˡG SC 3mp רמה *throw*. ᵐindep pers pron 3mp אִנּוּן *they*. ⁿnoun mp II בַּר w/ 3mp gen sx *son*. ᵒnoun fp נְשִׁין w/ 3mp gen sx hapax *wife*. ᵖG SC 3mp מטא *reach*. ᵠnoun fs cstr אַרְעִי hapax *bottom*.

גֻּבָּאʳ עַדʳˢ דִּי־שְׁלִטוּᵗ בְהוֹןᵘ אַרְיָוָתָאᵛ וְכָל־ᵂגַּרְמֵיהוֹןˣ הַדִּקוּʸ׃ 26 בֵּאדַיִןᵃ

דָּרְיָוֶשׁᵇ מַלְכָּאᶜ כְּתַבᶜ לְכָל־ᵈעַמְמַיָּאᵉ אֻמַיָּאᶠ וְלִשָּׁנַיָּאᵍ דִּי־ᵈדָאֲרִיןⁱ

בְּכָל־ᵈאַרְעָאʲ שְׁלָמְכוֹןᵏ יִשְׂגֵּאˡ׃ 27 מִן־קֳדָמַיᵃ שִׂיםᵇ טְעֵםᶜ דִּי|ᵈ בְּכָל־ᵉ

שָׁלְטָןᶠ מַלְכוּתִיᵍ לֶהֱוֹןʰ זָאעִיןⁱ וְדָחֲלִיןʲ מִן־קֳדָםᵏ אֱלָהֵהˡ דִּי־ᵏדָנִיֵּאל

דִּיᵐ־הוּאⁿ| אֱלָהָא חַיָּאᵒ וְקַיָּםᴾ לְעָלְמִיןᵠ

וּמַלְכוּתֵהʳ דִּי־ˢלָא תִתְחַבַּלᵗ וְשָׁלְטָנֵהᵘ עַד־סוֹפָאᵛ׃

28 מְשֵׁיזִבᵃ וּמַצִּלᵇ וְעָבֵדᶜ אָתִיןᵈ וְתִמְהִיןᵉ בִּשְׁמַיָּאᶠ וּבְאַרְעָאᵍ

דִּי שֵׁיזִבʰ לְדָנִיֵּאל מִן־יַדʲ אַרְיָוָתָאᵏ׃

29 וְדָנִיֵּאל דְּנָהᵃ הַצְלַחᵇ בְּמַלְכוּתᶜ דָּרְיָוֶשׁᵈ וּבְמַלְכוּת כּוֹרֶשׁᵉ

פָּרְסָיאᶠ׃
פ

7 1 בִּשְׁנַתᵃ חֲדָהᵇ לְבֵלְאשַׁצַּרᶜ מֶלֶךְ בָּבֶל דָּנִיֵּאל חֵלֶםᵈ חֲזָהᵉ וְחֶזְוֵיᶠ

רֵאשֵׁהᵍ עַל־מִשְׁכְּבֵהʰ בֵּאדַיִןⁱ חֶלְמָאʲ כְתַבᵏ רֵאשׁˡ מִלִּיןᵐ אֲמַרⁿ׃

---

25 ʳnoun ms emph גֻּב *den.* ˢtemp conj דִּי *that.* ᵗG sc 3mp שְׁלַט *rule.* ᵘprep בְּ w/ 3mp gen sx. ᵛnoun mp emph אַרְיֵה *lion.* ᵂnoun ms cstr כֹּל. ˣnoun mp גְּרַם w/ 3mp gen sx hapax *bone.* ʸH sc 3ms דְּקַק *pulverize.*

26 ᵃtemp adv אֱדַיִן (w/ בְּ) *immediately; then.* ᵇPN *Darius.* ᶜG sc 3ms כְּתַב *write.* ᵈnoun ms cstr כֹּל. ᵉnoun mp emph עַם *people.* ᶠnoun fp emph אֻמָּה *nation.* ᵍnoun mp emph לִשָּׁן *tongue.* ʰrel pron דִּי *who, that.* ⁱK דָּאֲרִין, Q דָּיְרִין [Ed דָּ֫], both G ptcp mp abs דּוּר *dwell.* ʲnoun fs emph אֲרַע *earth, land.* ᵏnoun ms שְׁלָם w/ 2mp gen sx *peace.* ˡG juss 3ms שְׂגָא *become great, grow.*

27 ᵃprep קֳדָם w/ 1cs gen sx. ᵇGp sc 3ms שִׂים. ᶜnoun ms abs טְעֵם *statement.* ᵈepex conj דִּי *that.* ᵉnoun ms cstr כֹּל. ᶠnoun ms cstr שָׁלְטָן *empire; dominion.* ᵍnoun fs מַלְכוּ w/ 1cs gen sx *kingdom.* ʰG pc 3mp הֲוָה. ⁱK זָאעִין, Q זָיְעִין, both G ptcp mp abs זוּע *tremble.* ʲG ptcp mp abs דְּחַל *fear.* ᵏnoun ms אֱלָה w/ 3ms gen sx. ˡgen part דִּי *of.* ᵐcaus conj דִּי *because.* ⁿindep pers pron 3ms הוּא *he.* ᵒadj ms emph חַי *living.* ᴾadj ms abs קַיָּם *enduring.* ᵠnoun mp abs עָלַם *eternity.* ʳnoun fs מַלְכוּ w/ 3ms gen sx *kingdom.* ˢrel pron דִּי *that which.* ᵗD pc 3fs חֲבַל *be*

destroyed. ᵘnoun ms שָׁלְטָן w/ 3ms gen sx *empire; dominion.* ᵛnoun ms emph סוֹף *end.*

28 ᵃŠ ptcp ms abs שֵׁיזִב *rescue.* ᵇH ptcp ms abs נְצַל *deliver.* ᶜG ptcp ms abs עֲבַד. ᵈnoun mp abs אָת *sign.* ᵉnoun mp abs תְּמַהּ *wonder.* ᶠnoun mp emph שְׁמַיִן. ᵍnoun fs emph אֲרַע *earth, land.* ʰcaus conj דִּי *because, for.* ⁱŠ sc 3ms שֵׁיזִב *rescue.* ʲnoun fs cstr יַד *hand.* ᵏnoun mp emph אַרְיֵה *lion.*

29 ᵃprox dem adj ms דְּנָה *this.* Perhaps = *our Daniel.* ᵇH sc 3ms צְלַח *prosper.* ᶜnoun fs cstr מַלְכוּ *reign; kingdom.* ᵈPN *Darius.* ᵉPN *Cyrus.* ᶠK פָּרְסָיא, Q פָּרְסָאֵה, both noun ms emph פָּרְסִי *Persian.*

7

1 ᵃnoun fs cstr שְׁנָה *year.* ᵇcard w/ f noun חַד *one.* ᶜPN *Belshazzar.* ᵈnoun ms abs חֵלֶם *dream.* ᵉG sc 3ms חֲזָה. ᶠnoun mp cstr חֱזוּ *vision.* ᵍnoun ms רֵאשׁ w/ 3ms gen sx *head.* ʰnoun ms מִשְׁכַּב w/ 3ms gen sx *bed.* ⁱtemp adv אֱדַיִן (w/ בְּ) *immediately; then.* ʲnoun ms emph חֵלֶם *dream.* ᵏG sc 3ms כְּתַב *write.* ˡnoun ms cstr רֵאשׁ *head; recapitulation, summary* or *start, beginning.* ᵐnoun fp abs מִלָּה *prophetic word.* ⁿG sc 3ms אֲמַר.

2 עֲנֵה[a] דָנִיֵּאל וְאָמַר[b] חָזֵה[c] הֲוֵית[d] בְּחֶזְוִי[e] עִם־לֵֽילְיָא[f] וַאֲרוּ[g] אַרְבַּע[h]
רוּחֵי[i] שְׁמַיָּא[j] מְגִיחָן[k] לְיַמָּא[l] רַבָּא[m]: 3 וְאַרְבַּע[a] חֵיוָן[b] רַבְרְבָן[c] סָלְקָן[d] מִן־
יַמָּא[e] שָׁנְיָן[f] דָּא[g] מִן־דָּא: 4 קַדְמָיְתָא[a] כְאַרְיֵה[b] וְגַפִּין[c] דִּי־נְשַׁר[d] לַהּ[e]
חָזֵה[g] הֲוֵית[h] עַד דִּי־מְּרִיטוּ[j] גַפַּיהּ[k] וּנְטִילַת[l] מִן־אַרְעָא[m] וְעַל־רַגְלַיִן[n]
כֶּאֱנָשׁ הָקִימַת[o] וּלְבַב[p] אֱנָשׁ יְהִיב[q] לַהּ: 5 וַאֲרוּ[a] חֵיוָה[b] אָחֳרִי[c] תִנְיָנָה[d]
דָּמְיָה[e] לְדֹב[f] וְלִשְׂטַר־חַד[g] הֳקִמַת[h] וּתְלָת[i] עִלְעִין[j] בְּפֻמַּהּ[k] בֵּין[m] שִׁנַּיהּ[n]
וְכֵן[o] אָמְרִין[p] לַהּ[q] קוּמִי[r] אֲכֻלִי[s] בְּשַׂר[t] שַׂגִּיא[u]: 6 בָּאתַר[a] דְּנָה[b] חָזֵה[c]
הֲוֵית[d] וַאֲרוּ[e] אָחֳרִי[f] כִּנְמַר[g] וְלַהּ[h] גַּפִּין[i] אַרְבַּע[j] דִּי־עוֹף[l] עַל־גַּבַּיהּ[m]
וְאַרְבְּעָה[n] רֵאשִׁין[o] לְחֵיוְתָא[p] וְשָׁלְטָן[q] יְהִיב[r] לַהּ: 7 בָּאתַר[a] דְּנָה[b] חָזֵה[c]
הֲוֵית[d] בְּחֶזְוֵי[e] לֵילְיָא[f] וַאֲרוּ[g] חֵיוָה[h] רביעיה[i] דְחִילָה[j] וְאֵימְתָנִי[k] וְתַקִּיפָא[l]

2 [a]G ptcp ms abs I עֲנֵה. [b]G ptcp ms abs אֲמַר. [c]G ptcp ms abs חֲזֵה. [d]G sc 1cs הֲוָה. [e]noun ms חֱזוּ w/ 1cs gen sx *vision*. [f]noun ms emph לֵילִי *night*. [g]interj אֲרוּ *behold!* [h]card w/ f noun אַרְבַּע *four*. [i]noun mp cstr רוּחַ *wind*. [j]noun mp emph שְׁמַיִן. [k]H ptcp fp abs גוח hapax *stir up*. [l]noun ms emph יַם *sea*. [m]adj ms emph רַב *great*.

3 [a]card w/ f noun אַרְבַּע *four*. [b]noun fp abs חֵיוָה *animal, beast*. [c]adj fp abs רַב *great*. [d]G ptcp fp abs סלק *come up*. [e]noun ms emph יַם *sea*. [f]G ptcp fp abs שׁנה *be different*. [g]prox dem pron fs דָּא *this*.

4 [a]noun fs emph קַדְמַי *earliest, first*. [b]noun ms abs אַרְיֵה *lion*. [c]noun mp abs גַּף *wing*. [d]gen part דִּי *of*. [e]noun ms abs נְשַׁר *eagle*. [f]prep לְ w/ 3fs gen sx. [g]G ptcp ms abs חֲזֵה. [h]G sc 1cs הֲוָה. [i]temp conj דִּי *that*. [j]Gp sc 3mp מרט hapax *be plucked*. [k]K גַּף noun mp, Q גַּפָּה noun ms, both w/ 3fs gen sx *wing*. [l]Gp sc 3fs נטל *be lifted*. [m]noun fs emph אֲרַע *earth, land*. [n]noun fdu רְגַל *foot*. [o]Hp sc 3fs קום. [p]noun ms cstr לְבַב *heart*. [q]Gp sc 3ms יהב.

5 [a]interj אֲרוּ *behold!* [b]noun fs abs חֵיוָה *beast*. [c]noun fs abs אָחֳרִי *another*. [d]adj fs abs תִנְיָן hapax *second*. [e]G ptcp fs abs דמה *resemble*. [f]noun ms abs דֹּב hapax *bear*. [g]noun ms abs שְׂטַר hapax *side*. [h]card w/ m noun חַד *one*. [i]Hp sc 3fs קום. [j]card w/ f noun תְּלָת *three*.

[k]noun fp abs עִלַע hapax *rib*. [l]noun ms פֻּם w/ 3fs gen sx *mouth*. [m]prep בֵּין *between*. [n]K שִׁנַּיַה noun fdu, Q שִׁנֵּה noun fs, both w/ 3fs gen sx *tooth*. [o]adv כֵּן *thus*. [p]G ptcp mp abs אֲמַר. [q]prep לְ w/ 3fs gen sx. [r]G imv 2fs קום. [s]G imv 2fs אכל *eat*. [t]noun ms abs בְּשַׂר *flesh*. [u]adj fp abs שַׂגִּיא *much*.

6 [a]prep בָּאתַר *after*. [b]prox dem pron ms דְּנָה *this*. [c]G ptcp ms abs חֲזֵה. [d]G sc 1cs הֲוָה. [e]interj אֲרוּ *behold!* [f]adj fs abs אָחֳרִי *another*. [g]noun ms abs נְמַר hapax *leopard*. [h]prep לְ w/ 3fs gen sx. [i]noun fp abs גַּף *wing*. [j]card w/ f noun אַרְבַּע *four*. [k]gen part דִּי *of*. [l]noun ms abs עוֹף *bird*. [m]K גַּבַּיַה p, Q גַּבַּה s, both noun m גַּב w/ 3fs gen sx hapax *side* (HALOT), *back* (NRSV, NJPS). [n]card w/ m noun אַרְבַּע *four*. [o]noun mp abs רֵאשׁ *head*. [p]noun fs emph חֵיוָה *animal, beast*. [q]noun ms abs שָׁלְטָן *empire; dominion*. [r]Gp sc 3ms יהב.

7 [a]prep בָּאתַר *after*. [b]prox dem pron ms דְּנָה *this*. [c]G ptcp ms abs חֲזֵה. [d]G sc 1cs הֲוָה. [e]noun mp cstr חֱזוּ *vision*. [f]noun ms emph לֵילִי *night*. [g]interj אֲרוּ *behold!* [h]noun fs abs חֵיוָה *animal, beast*. [i]K רְבִיעָיַה, Q רְבִיעָאָה [Ed רְבִיעִי], both adj fs abs *fourth*. [j]Gp ptcp fs abs דחל *feared, fearful*. [k]adj fs abs אֵימְתָן hapax *terrible*. [l]adj fs abs תַּקִּיף *powerful, mighty*.

יַתִּירָאᵐ וְשִׁנַּיִ֣ן דִּי־פַרְזֶל֩ᵖ לַהּˢ רַבְרְבָ֨ן אָכְלָ֤הˢ וּמַדֱּקָ֙ה וּשְׁאָרָ֔אᵘ
בְּרַגְלַיהּᵛ רָפְסָ֑הʷ וְהִ֣יאˣ מְשַׁנְּיָ֗הʸ מִן־כָּל־חֵיוָתָא֙ᵃᵃ דִּ֣יᵇᵇ קָֽדָמַ֔יהּᶜᶜ
וְקַרְנַ֖יִןᵈᵈ עֲשַֽׂרᵉᵉ לַֽהּ׃ᶠᶠ ⁸ מִשְׂתַּכַּ֨לᵃ הֲוֵ֜ יתᵇ בְּקַרְנַיָּ֗א וַאֲל֤וּᵈ קֶ֣רֶן אָֽחֳרִי֙ᵉ
זְעֵירָ֜הᵍ סִלְקָ֣ת֙ʰ בֵּֽינֵיהֵ֔ן וּתְלָ֗תᶦ מִן־קַרְנַיָּא֙ קַדְמָֽיָתָ֔אʲ אֶתְעֲקַ֖רוּᵏ מִן־
קָֽדָמַ֑יהּᵐ וַאֲל֗וּⁿ עַיְנִ֞ין כְּעַיְנֵ֤יᵖ אֲנָשָׁא֙ᵠ בְּקַרְנָא־דָ֔אʳ וּפֻ֖םˢ מְמַלִּ֥ל רַבְרְבָֽן׃ᵗ

⁹ חָזֵ֣הᵃ הֲוֵ֗ יתᵇ עַ֣ד דִּ֤יᶜ כָרְסָוָן֙ᵈ רְמִ֔יוᵉ וְעַתִּ֥יקᶠ יוֹמִ֖יןᵍ יְתִ֑בʰ
לְבוּשֵׁ֣הּᶦ ׀ כִּתְלַ֣גᵏ חִוָּ֗רᵏ וּשְׂעַ֤רˡ רֵאשֵׁהּ֙ᵐ כַּעֲמַ֣רⁿ נְקֵ֔אᵒ
כָּרְסְיֵהּᵖ שְׁבִיבִ֣יןᵠ דִּי־נ֔וּרˢ גַּלְגִּלּ֖וֹהִיᵗ נ֥וּר דָּלִֽקˢᵘ׃

¹⁰ נְהַ֣רᵃ דִּֽי־נ֗וּרᶜ נָגֵ֤דᵈ וְנָפֵק֙ᵉ מִן־קָֽדָמ֔וֹהִיᶠ
אֶ֤לֶףᵍ אַלְפִים֙ʰ יְשַׁמְּשׁוּנֵּ֔הֿᶦ וְרִבּ֥וֹᵏ רִבְבָ֖ן קָֽדָמ֣וֹהִי יְקוּמ֑וּןᵐˡ
דִּינָ֣אⁿ יְתִ֔בᵒ וְסִפְרִ֖יןᵖ פְּתִֽיחוּ׃ᵠ

---

7 ᵐadv יַתִּיר *excessively.* ⁿS73d שֵׁן *two teeth* or *two rows of teeth.* ᵒgen part דִּי *of.* ᵖnoun ms abs פַּרְזֶל *iron.* ᵠprep לְ w/ 3fs gen sx. ʳadj fp abs רַב *great.* ˢG sc 3fs אכל *eat.* ᵗH ptcp fs abs דקק *pulverize.* ᵘnoun ms emph שְׁאָר *rest, remainder.* ᵛK בְּרַגְלַיהּ noun fp, Q בְּרַגְלַהּ noun fs, both w/ 3ms gen sx *foot.* ʷG ptcp fs abs רפס *trample.* ˣindep pers pron 3fs הִיא *she, it.* ʸDp ptcp fp abs שׁנה *be different.* ᶻnoun ms cstr כֹּל. ᵃᵃnoun fp emph חֵיוָה *animal, beast.* ᵇᵇrel pron דִּי *which, that.* ᶜᶜK קָֽדָמַיה, Q קָֽדָמַהּ [so Ed; L, *BHS* ״קׄ״], both prep קֳדָם w/ 3fs gen sx. ᵈᵈnoun fp abs (noun fdu in form) קֶרֶן *horn.* ᵉᵉcard w/ f noun עֲשַׂר *ten.* ᶠᶠprep לְ w/ 3fs gen sx.

8 ᵃtD ptcp ms abs שׂכל hapax *contemplate.* ᵇG sc 1cs הוה. ᶜnoun fp emph קֶרֶן *horn.* ᵈinterj אֲלוּ *behold!* ᵉnoun fs abs קֶרֶן *horn.* ᶠadj fs abs אָחֳרִי *another.* ᵍadj fs abs זְעֵיר hapax *little.* ʰG sc 3fs סלק *come up.* ᶦK בֵּֽינֵיהֵן prep בֵּין w/ 3mp gen sx, Q בֵּֽינֵיהֵן prep בֵּין w/ 3fp gen sx, both *between.* ʲcard w/ f noun תְּלָת *three.* ᵏadj fp emph קַדְמָי *earlier, first.* ᵏtG sc 3mp, אֶתְעֲקַרוּ Q אֶתְעֲקַרָה tG sc 3fp, both עקר hapax *be ripped out.* ᵐK קָֽדָמַיה, Q קָֽדָמֵהּ, both prep קֳדָם w/ 3fs gen sx. ⁿinterj אֲלוּ *behold!* ᵒnoun fp abs, ᵖnoun fp cstr עַיִן *eye.* ᵠ73e קֶרֶן *horn.* ʳprox dem adj fs דָּא *this.* ˢnoun ms abs פֻּם *mouth.* ᵗD ptcp ms abs מלל *speak.*

ᵘadj fp abs רַב *big things.*

9 ᵃG ptcp ms abs חזה. ᵇG sc 1cs הוה. ᶜtemp conj דִּי *that.* ᵈnoun mp abs כָּרְסֵא *throne.* ᵉGp sc 3mp רמה *be placed.* ᶠnoun ms cstr עַתִּיק *ancient.* ᵍnoun mp abs יוֹם *day.* ʰG sc 3ms יתב *sit.* ᶦnoun ms לְבוּשׁ w/ 3ms gen sx *clothing.* ʲnoun ms abs תְּלַג hapax *snow.* ᵏadj ms abs חִוָּר hapax *white.* ˡnoun ms cstr שְׂעַר *hair.* ᵐnoun ms רֵאשׁ w/ 3ms gen sx *head.* ⁿnoun ms abs עֲמַר hapax *wool.* ᵒadj ms abs נְקֵא hapax *pure.* ᵖnoun ms כָּרְסֵא w/ 3ms gen sx *throne.* ᵠnoun mp abs שְׁבִיב *flame.* ʳgen part דִּי *of.* ˢnoun ms abs נוּר *fire.* ᵗnoun mp גַּלְגַּל w/ 3ms gen sx hapax *wheel.* ᵘG ptcp ms abs דלק hapax *be on fire, burning, flaming.*

10 ᵃnoun ms cstr נְהַר *river.* ᵇgen part דִּי *of.* ᶜnoun ms abs נוּר *fire.* ᵈG ptcp ms abs נגד hapax *flow.* ᵉG ptcp ms abs נפק *go out.* ᶠprep קֳדָם w/ 3ms gen sx. ᵍcard, m, s, cs אֲלַף *thousand.* ʰK אַלְפִים Heb ending, Q אַלְפִין, both card mp abs אֲלַף *thousand.* ᶦD pc 3mp שׁמשׁ w/ 3ms acc sx hapax *minister, attend, serve.* ʲcard ms cs רִבּוֹ *myriad, 10,000.* ᵏK רִבְבָן, Q רִבְבָן, both card fp abs רִבּוֹ *myriad, 10,000.* ˡprep קֳדָם w/ 3ms gen sx [so Ed; L, *BHS* ״קׄ״]. ᵐG pc 3mp קום. ⁿnoun ms emph דִּין *court.* ᵒG sc 3ms יתב *sit.* ᵖnoun mp abs סְפַר *book.* ᵠGp sc 3mp פתח *be opened.*

11 חָזֵ֣הⁱ הֲוֵ֣יתᵇ בֵּאדַ֔יִןᶜ מִן־קָ֕לᵈ מִלַּיָּ֥אᵉ רַבְרְבָתָ֖אᶠ דִּ֣יᵍ קַרְנָ֣אʰ מְמַלֱּלָ֑הⁱ חָזֵ֣הᵃ הֲוֵ֣יתᵇ עַ֣דᵏ דִּ֣יʲ קְטִילַ֣תᵏ חֵֽיוְתָ֗אˡ וְהוּבַ֤דᵐ גִּשְׁמַהּⁿ וִיהִיבַ֖תᵒ לִיקֵדַ֥תᵖ

12 אֶשָּֽׁאᵍ׃ וּשְׁאָרᵃ חֵיוָתָ֔אᵇ הֶעְדִּ֖יוᶜ שָׁלְטָנְה֑וֹןᵈ וְאַרְכָ֧הᵉ בְחַיִּ֛יןᶠ יְהִ֥יבַתᵍ לְה֖וֹןʰ עַד־זְמַ֥ןⁱ וְעִדָּֽןʲ׃ 13 חָזֵ֤הᵃ הֲוֵיתᵇ בְּחֶזְוֵ֣יᶜ לֵֽילְיָ֔אᵈ

וַאֲר֗וּᵉ עִם־עֲנָנֵ֤יᶠ שְׁמַיָּאᵍ כְּבַ֥רʰ אֱנָ֖שׁⁱ אָתֵ֣הᵏ הֲוָ֑הˡ וְעַד־עַתִּ֤יקᵐ יֽוֹמַיָּאⁿ מְטָ֔הᵒ וּקְדָמ֖וֹהִיᵖ הַקְרְבֽוּהִיᵍ׃

14 וְלֵ֨הּᵃ יְהִ֤יבᵇ שָׁלְטָןᶜ וִיקָ֣רᵈ וּמַלְכ֔וּᵉ וְכֹ֣לᶠ עַֽמְמַיָּ֗אᵍ אֻמַיָּ֤אʰ וְלִשָּֽׁנַיָּאⁱ לֵ֣הּᵃ יִפְלְח֑וּןʲ שָׁלְטָנֵ֗הּᵏ שָׁלְטָ֤ןˡ עָלַם֙ᵐ דִּֽי־לָ֣אⁿ יֶעְדֵּ֔הᵒ וּמַלְכוּתֵ֖הּᵖ דִּֽי־לָ֥אⁿ תִתְחַבַּֽלᵍ׃ פ

15 אֶתְכְּרִיַּ֣תᵃ רוּחִ֗יᵇ אֲנָ֤הᶜ דָנִיֵּאל֙ בְּג֣וֹאᵈ נִדְנֶ֔הᵉ וְחֶזְוֵ֥יᶠ רֵאשִׁ֖יᵍ יְבַהֲלֻנַּֽנִיʰ׃

---

11 ᵃG ptcp ms abs חזה. ᵇG sc 1cs הוה. ᶜtemp adv אֱדַיִן (w/ בְּ) *immediately; then.* ᵈnoun ms cstr קָל *sound, voice.* ᵉnoun fp emph מִלָּה *word.* ᶠadj fp emph רַב *great.* ᵍrel pron דִּי *which, that.* ʰnoun fs emph קֶרֶן *horn.* ⁱD ptcp fs abs מלל *speak.* ʲtemp conj דִּי *that.* ᵏGp sc 3fs קטל *be killed.* ˡnoun fs emph חֵיוָה *animal, beast.* ᵐHp sc 3ms אבד *be destroyed.* ⁿnoun ms גְּשֵׁם w/ 3fs gen sx *body.* ᵒGp sc 3fs יהב. ᵖnoun fs cstr יְקֵדָה hapax *burning.* ᵍnoun fs abs אֶשָּׁא hapax *fire.*

12 ᵃnoun ms cstr שְׁאָר *rest, remainder.* ᵇnoun fp emph חֵיוָה *animal, beast.* ᵃ⁻ᵇ form a casus pendens, *as for the rest of the beasts.* ᶜH sc 3mp עדה *remove.* Unexpressed plural subject = a passive. ᵈnoun ms שָׁלְטָן w/ 3mp gen sx *empire; dominion.* ᵉnoun fs abs אַרְכָה *lengthening, extension.* ᶠnoun mp abs חַיִּין *life.* ᵍGp sc 3fs יהב. ʰprep לְ w/ 3mp gen sx. ⁱnoun ms abs זְמַן indicates a point in time, a *moment,* or a set or fixed time such as the *date* of a recurring feast, or even the *time* of an appointment, e.g., the third hour. ʲnoun ms abs עִדָּן indicates time in general or a length of time such as a year *season, time.*

13 ᵃG ptcp ms abs חזה. ᵇG sc 1cs הוה. ᶜnoun mp cstr חֱזוּ *vision.* ᵈnoun ms emph לֵילִי *night.* ᵉinterj אֲרוּ *behold!* ᶠnoun mp

cstr עֲנָן hapax *cloud.* ᵍnoun mp emph שְׁמַיִן. ʰnoun ms cstr II בַּר *son.* ⁱnoun ms abs אֱנָשׁ *humanity.* ʲ⁻ⁱ*human being.* ᵏG ptcp ms abs אתה *come.* ˡG sc 3ms הוה. ᵐnoun ms cstr עַתִּיק *ancient.* ⁿnoun mp emph יוֹם *day.* ᵒG sc 3ms מטא *reach.* ᵖprep קֳדָם w/ 3ms gen sx. ᵍH sc 3mp קרב w/ 3ms acc sx *bring near, present.* Unexpressed plural subject = a passive.

14 ᵃprep לְ w/ 3ms gen sx. ᵇGp sc 3ms יהב. ᶜnoun ms abs שָׁלְטָן *empire; dominion.* ᵈnoun ms abs יְקָר *honor.* ᵉnoun fs abs מַלְכוּ *kingship, sovereignty.* ᶠnoun ms cstr כֹּל. ᵍnoun mp emph עַם *people.* ʰnoun fp emph אֻמָּה *nation.* ⁱnoun mp emph לִשָּׁן *tongue.* ʲG pc 3mp פלח *serve.* ᵏnoun ms שָׁלְטָן w/ 3ms gen sx *empire; dominion.* ˡnoun ms cstr שָׁלְטָן *empire; dominion.* ᵐnoun ms abs עָלַם *eternity.* ⁿrel pron דִּי *that which, one which.* ᵒG pc 3ms עדה *pass away.* ᵖnoun fs מַלְכוּ w/ 3ms gen sx *kingship, sovereignty.* ᵍtD pc 3fs חבל *be destroyed.*

15 ᵃtG sc 3fs כרה hapax *be distressed, troubled, disturbed.* ᵇnoun fs רוּחַ w/ 1cs gen sx *spirit.* ᶜindep pers pron 1cs אֲנָה *I.* ᵈnoun ms cstr גַּו *midst.* ᵉnoun ms abs נְדַן hapax, Pers lw *sheath = body.* ᶠnoun mp cstr חֱזוּ *vision.* ᵍnoun ms רֵאשׁ w/ 1cs gen sx *head.* ʰD pc 3mp בהל w/ 1cs acc sx *terrify.*

16 קִרְבֵת֙ᵃ עַל־חַד֙ᵇ מִן־קָאֲמַיָּ֔אᶜ וְיַצִּיבָ֥אᵈ אֶבְעֵֽא־מִנֵּ֖הּᵉ עַל־כָּל־דְּנָ֑הᵍ
וַאֲמַר־לִ֕יⁱ וּפְשַׁ֥ר מִלַּיָּ֖אᵏ יְהוֹדְעִנַּֽנִיˡ: 17 אִלֵּין֙ᵃ חֵיוָתָ֣אᵇ רַבְרְבָתָ֔אᶜ דִּ֥י אִנִּ֖יןᵈ
אַרְבַּֽעᵉ אַרְבְּעָ֣הᶠ מַלְכִ֔ין יְקוּמ֖וּןᵍ מִן־אַרְעָֽאʰ: 18 וִֽיקַבְּלוּן֙ᵃ מַלְכוּתָ֔אᵇ
קַדִּישֵׁ֖יᶜ עֶלְיוֹנִ֑יןᵈ וְיַחְסְנ֤וּןᵉ מַלְכוּתָא֙ᶠ עַד־עָ֣לְמָ֔אᵍ וְעַ֖ד עָלַ֥ם עָלְמַיָּֽאʰ: 19 אֱדַ֗יִן צְבִית֙ᵃ לְיַצָּבָ֔אᵇ עַל־חֵֽיוְתָא֙ᶜ רְבִיעָ֣יְתָ֔אᵈ דִּֽי־הֲוָ֥תᵉ שָֽׁנְיָ֖הᵍ
מִן־כָּלְּהֵ֑ןʰ דְּחִילָ֥הⁱ יַתִּ֨ירָה֙ʲ שִׁנַּ֣יַּֽהּᵏ דִּֽי־פַרְזֶל֙ˡ וְטִפְרַ֣יַּֽהּʳ דִּֽי־נְחָ֔שׁᵒ
אָֽכְלָ֣הᵖ מַדֱּקָ֔הᵍ וּשְׁאָרָ֖אˢ בְּרַגְלַ֥יַּֽהּᵗ רָֽפְסָֽהᵘ: 20 וְעַל־קַרְנַיָּ֣אᵃ עֲשַׂר֮ᵇ דִּ֣יᶜ
בְרֵאשַׁהּ֒ᵈ וְאָחֳרִ֗יᵉ דִּ֤יᶠ סִלְקַת֙ᵍ וּנְפַ֣לוּʰ מִן־קֳדָמַ֔יַּֽהּⁱ תְּלָ֑תʲ וְקַרְנָ֨אᵏ דִכֵּ֜ןˡ
וְעַיְנִ֣יןᵐ לַ֗הּⁿ וּפֻם֙ᵒ מְמַלִּ֣לᵖ רַבְרְבָ֔ןᵍ וְחֶזְוַהּ֙ʳ רַ֣בˢ מִן־חַבְרָתַֽהּᵗ: 21 חָזֵ֣הᵃ
הֲוֵ֔יתᵇ וְקַרְנָ֣אᶜ דִכֵּ֗ןᵈ עָֽבְדָ֥הᵉ קְרָ֖בᶠ עִם־קַדִּישִׁ֑יןᵍ וְיָכְלָ֖הʰ לְהֽוֹןⁱ: 22 עַ֣ד

---

16 ᵃG sc 1cs קרב *approach.* ᵇcard w/ m noun חַד *one.* ᶜG ptcp mp emph קום. ᵈadj fs abs יַצִּיב what is *certain; correct.* ᵉG pc 1cs בעה *seek.* ᶠprep מִן w/ 3ms gen sx. ᵍnoun ms cstr כֹּל. ʰprox dem pron ms דְּנָה *this.* ⁱG sc 3ms אמר. ʲprep לְ w/ 1cs gen sx. ᵏnoun fs emph מִלָּה prophetic *word.* ˡH pc 3ms ידע w/ 1cs acc sx.

17 ᵃprox dem adj cp אִלֵּין *these.* ᵇnoun fp emph חֵיוָה *animal, beast.* ᶜadj fp emph רַב *great.* ᵈprox dem pron 3fp אִנִּין hapax, as copula *are.* ᵉcard w/ f noun, ᶠcard w/ m noun אַרְבַּע *four.* ᵍG pc 3mp קום. ʰnoun fs emph אֲרַע *earth, land.*

18 ᵃD pc 3mp קבל *receive.* ᵇnoun fs emph מַלְכוּ *kingdom.* ᶜadj mp cstr קַדִּישׁ *holy.* ᵈnoun mp abs עֶלְיוֹן Heb lw, *pl. tan., most high.* ᵉH pc 3mp חסן *possess.* ᶠnoun ms emph, ᵍnoun ms cstr, ʰnoun mp emph עָלַם *eternity.*

19 ᵃG sc 1cs צבה *desire, wish.* ᵇD inf יצב hapax *ascertain, make certain of.* ᶜnoun fs emph חֵיוָה *animal, beast.* ᵈnoun fs emph רְבִיעָי *fourth.* ᵉrel pron דִּי *which, that.* ᶠG sc 3fs הוה. ᵍG ptcp fs abs שׁנה *be different.* ʰK כָּלְּהוֹן noun ms w/ 3mp gen sx, Q כָּלְּהֵין noun ms כֹּל w/ 3fp gen sx. ⁱGp ptcp fs abs דחל *feared.* ʲadv יַתִּיר *excessively.* ᵏK שִׁנַּיַּה noun fdu, Q שִׁנַּהּ noun fs, both שֵׁן w/ 3fs gen sx *tooth.* ˡgen part דִּי *of* [So

BHS, Ed; L, *BHL** דִּי (no ־)]. ᵐnoun ms abs פַּרְזֶל *iron.* ⁿK וְטִפְרַיַּה noun fp, Q וְטִפְרַהּ noun fs, both טְפַר w/ 3fs gen sx *claw.* ᵒgen part דִּי *of.* ᵖnoun ms abs נְחָשׁ *bronze.* ᵍG sc 3fs אכל *eat.* ʳH ptcp fs abs דקק *pulverize.* ˢnoun ms emph שְׁאָר *rest, remainder.* ᵗK בְּרַגְלַיַּה noun fp, Q בְּרַגְלַהּ noun fs, both רְגַל w/ 3fs gen sx *foot.* ᵘG ptcp fs abs רפס *trample.*

20 ᵃnoun fp emph קֶרֶן *horn.* ᵇcard w/ f noun עֲשַׂר *ten.* ᶜrel pron דִּי *which, that.* ᵈnoun ms abs רֵאשׁ w/ 3fs gen sx *head.* ᵉadj fs abs אָחֳרִי *another.* ᶠrel pron דִּי *which, that.* ᵍG sc 3fs סלק *come up.* ʰK וּנְפַלוּ G sc 3mp, Q וּנְפַלָה G sc 3fp, both נפל *fall.* ⁱK קֳדָמַיַּה Q קֳדָמַהּ, both prep קֳדָם w/ 3fs gen sx. ʲcard w/ f noun תְּלָת *three.* ᵏnoun fs emph קֶרֶן *horn.* ˡdist dem adj c, s דִּכֵּן *that.* ᵐnoun fp abs עַיִן *eye.* ⁿprep לְ w/ 3fs gen sx. ᵒnoun ms abs פֻּם *mouth* [So Ed; L, *BHL**; *BHS* מ"]. ᵖD ptcp ms abs מלל *speak.* ᵍadj fp abs רַב *great things.* ʳnoun ms חֱזוּ w/ 3fs gen sx *appearance.* ˢadj ms abs רַב *great.* ᵗnoun fs חַבְרָה w/ 3fs gen sx *companion.*

21 ᵃG ptcp ms abs חזה. ᵇG sc 1cs הוה. ᶜnoun fs emph קֶרֶן *horn.* ᵈdist dem adj c s דִּכֵּן *that.* ᵉG ptcp fs abs עבד. ᶠnoun ms abs קְרָב hapax Akk lw *war.* ᵍadj mp abs קַדִּישׁ *holy.* ʰG ptcp fs abs יכל *be more able, overpower.* ⁱprep לְ w/ 3mp gen sx.

דִּי־אֲתָהᵇ עַתִּיקᶜ יֽוֹמַיָּאᵈ וְדִינָאᵉ יְהִבᶠ לְקַדִּישֵׁיᵍ עֶלְיוֹנִיןʰ וְזִמְנָאⁱ מְטָהʲ
וּמַלְכוּתָאᵏ הֶחֱסִנוּˡ קַדִּישִֽׁיןᵐ׃

23 ᵃ כֵּן אֲמַר ᵇ   חֵיוְתָאᶜ רְבִיעָיְתָאᵈ
מַלְכוּ רְבִיעָיאᵉ תֶּהֱוֵאᶠ בְּאַרְעָאᵍʰ
דִּיⁱ תִשְׁנֵאʲ מִן־כָּל־ᵏמַלְכְוָתָאˡ
וְתֵאכֻלᵐ כָּל־ᵏ־אַרְעָאʰ
וּתְדוּשִׁנַּהⁿ וְתַדְּקִנַּהᵒ׃

24 ᵃ וְקַרְנַיָּא עֲשַׂר ᵇ   מִנַּהᶜ מַלְכוּתָהᵈ
עַשְׂרָהᵉ מַלְכִין יְקֻמֻוןᶠ
וְהוּאʲ יִשְׁנֵאᵏ מִן־קַדְמָיֵאˡ   וְאָחֳרָןᵍ יְקוּםʰ אַחֲרֵיהוֹןⁱ
וּתְלָתָהᵐ מַלְכִין יְהַשְׁפִּלʰ׃

25 ᵃ וּמִלִּין לְצַדᵇ עִלָּיאᶜ יְמַלִּלᵈ
וְיִסַבַּרʰ לְהַשְׁנָיָהⁱ זִמְנִיןʲ וְדָתᵏ   וּלְקַדִּישֵׁיᵉ עֶלְיוֹנִיןᶠ יְבַלֵּאᵍ
וְיִתְיַהֲבוּןˡ בִּידֵהᵐ׃   עַד־עִדָּןⁿ וְעִדָּנִיןᵒ וּפְלַגᵖ עִדָּןⁿ׃

---

22 ᵃtemp conj דִּי *that.* ᵇG sc 3ms אתה *come.* ᶜnoun ms cstr עַתִּיק *ancient.* ᵈnoun mp emph יוֹם *day.* ᵉnoun ms emph דִּין *judgment, justice.* ᶠGp sc 3ms יהב. ᵍadj mp cstr קַדִּישׁ *holy.* ʰnoun mp abs עֶלְיוֹן Heb lw, *pl. tan., most high.* ⁱnoun ms emph זְמַן indicates a point in time, a *moment,* or a set or fixed time such as the *date* of a recurring feast, or even the *time* of an appointment, e.g., the third hour; *holiday.* ʲG sc 3ms מטא *arrive.* ᵏnoun fs emph מַלְכוּ *kingdom.* ˡH sc 3mp חסן *possess.* ᵐadj mp abs קַדִּישׁ *holy.*

23 ᵃadv כֵּן *thus.* ᵇG sc 3ms אמר. ᶜnoun fs emph חֵיוָה *animal, beast.* ᵈnoun fs emph רְבִיעָי *fourth.* ᵉnoun fs abs מַלְכוּ *kingdom.* ᶠK רְבִיעָיָא, Q רְבִיעָאָה [Ed רְבִי״], both noun fs emph רְבִיעָי *fourth.* ᵍG pc 3fs הוה *be.* ʰnoun fs emph אֲרַע *earth, land.* ⁱrel pron דִּי *which, that.* ʲG pc 3fs שׁנה *be different.* ᵏnoun ms cstr כֹּל. ˡnoun fp emph מַלְכוּ *kingdom.* ᵐG pc 3fs אכל *eat.* ⁿG pc 3fs דושׁ w/ 3fs acc sx hapax *trample.* ᵒH pc 3fs דקק w/ 3fs acc sx *pulverize.*

24 ᵃnoun fp emph קֶרֶן *horn.* ᵇcard w/ f noun עֲשַׂר *ten.* ᶜprep מִן w/ 3fs gen sx. Perhaps a demonstrative suffix *-hā* rather than a pronominal suffix, *from (this) kingdom.*

ᵈnoun fs emph מַלְכוּ *kingship, sovereignty; kingdom.* ᵉcard w/ m noun עֲשַׂר *ten.* ᶠG pc 3mp קום. ᵍadj ms abs אָחֳרָן *another.* ʰG pc 3ms קום. ⁱprep אַחֲרֵי [אַחַר HALOT] w/ 3mp gen sx *after.* ʲindep pers pron 3ms הוּא *he.* ᵏG pc 3ms שׁנה *be different.* ˡnoun mp emph קַדְמָי *earlier.* ᵐcard w/ m noun תְּלָת *three.* ⁿH pc 3ms שׁפל *humble, subdue.*

25 ᵃnoun fp abs מִלָּה *word.* ᵇnoun ms cstr צַד *side;* w/ לְ *against* or *toward.* ᶜK עִלָּיָא, Q עִלָּאָה, both noun ms emph עִלָּי *most high.* ᵈD pc 3ms מלל *speak.* ᵉadj mp cstr קַדִּישׁ *holy.* ᶠnoun mp abs עֶלְיוֹן Heb lw, *pl. tan, most high* [so BHS, Ed; L, BHL* עֶלְיוֹנִין]. ᵍD pc 3ms בלה hapax *harass, wear out.* ʰG pc 3ms סבר hapax *intend.* ⁱH inf שׁנה trans *change.* ʲnoun mp abs זְמַן indicates a point in time, a *moment,* or a set or fixed time such as the *date* of a recurring feast, or even the *time* of an appointment, e.g., the third hour; *holiday.* ᵏnoun fs abs דָּת Pers lw *law.* ˡtG pc 3mp יהב. ᵐnoun fs יַד w/ 3ms gen sx *hand.* ⁿnoun ms abs, ᵒnoun mp abs עִדָּן indicates time in general or a length of time such as a year *season, time.* ᵖnoun ms cstr פְּלַג hapax *half.*

²⁶ וְדִינָ֖אᵃ יִתִּ֑בᵇ וְשָׁלְטָנֵהּᶜ יְהַעְדּ֔וֹןᵈ

לְהַשְׁמָדָ֥ה וּלְהוֹבָדָ֖הᶠ עַד־סוֹפָֽאᵍ׃

²⁷ וּמַלְכוּתָ֨הᵃ וְשָׁלְטָנָ֜אᵇ וּרְבוּתָ֗אᶜ

דִּיᵈ מַלְכְוָת֙ᵉ תְּח֣וֹתᶠ כָּל־שְׁמַיָּ֔אʰᵍ

יְהִיבַ֕תⁱ לְעַ֖םʲ קַדִּישֵׁ֣יᵏ עֶלְיוֹנִ֑יןˡ

מַלְכוּתֵהּᵐ מַלְכ֣וּתᵒ עָלַ֔ם וְכֹלᵍ שָׁלְטָנַיָּ֔אᵖ

לֵהּᵠ יִפְלְח֖וּן וְיִֽשְׁתַּמְּעֽוּןˢ׃

²⁸ עַד־כָּ֖הᵃ סוֹפָ֣אᵇ דִֽי־מִלְּתָ֑אᶜ אֲנָ֨הᵉ דָֽנִיֵּ֜אלᵈ רַעְיוֹנַ֣יᵍ שַׂגִּ֣יאᶠ ׀ יְבַהֲלֻנַּ֗נִיʰ

וְזִיוַיⁱ יִשְׁתַּנּ֣וֹןʲ עֲלַ֔יᵏ וּמִלְּתָ֖אᶜ בְּלִבִּ֥יˡ נִטְרֵֽתᵐ׃

פ

---

²⁶ ᵃnoun ms emph דִּין *court*. ᵇD pc 3ms יתב *sit*. ᶜnoun ms שָׁלְטָן w/ 3ms gen sx *empire; dominion*. ᵈH pc 3mp עדה *remove*. ᵉH inf שמד hapax *annihilate*. ᶠH inf אבד *destroy*. ᵍnoun ms emph סוֹף *end*.

²⁷ ᵃnoun fs emph מַלְכוּ *kingship, sovereignty*. ᵇnoun ms emph שָׁלְטָן *empire; dominion*. ᶜnoun fs emph רְבוּ *greatness*. ᵈgen part דִּי *of*. ᵉnoun fp cstr מַלְכוּ *kingdom*. ᶠprep תְּחוֹת *under*. ᵍnoun ms cstr כֹּל. ʰnoun mp emph שְׁמַיִן. ⁱGp sc 3fs יהב. ʲnoun ms cstr עַם *people*. ᵏadj mp cstr קַדִּישׁ *holy*. ˡnoun mp abs עֶלְיוֹן Heb lw, *pl. tan, most high*. ᵐnoun fs מַלְכוּ w/ 3ms gen sx *kingdom*. ⁿnoun fs cstr

מַלְכוּ *kingdom*. ᵒnoun ms abs עָלַם *eternity*. ᵖnoun mp emph שָׁלְטָן *empire; dominion*. ᵠprep לְ w/ 3ms gen sx. ʳG pc 3mp פלח *serve*. ˢtD pc 3mp שמע *hear, heed*.

²⁸ ᵃadv כָּה hapax *here*. ᵇnoun ms emph סוֹף *end*. ᶜgen part דִּי *of*. ᵈnoun fs emph מִלָּה prophetic *word*. ᵉindep pers pron 1cs אֲנָה *I*. ᶠadj ms abs שַׂגִּיא as adv *greatly*. ᵍnoun mp רַעְיוֹן w/ 1cs gen sx *thought*. ʰD pc 3mp בהל w/ 1cs acc sx *terrify*. ⁱnoun mp זִיו w/ 1cs gen sx *splendor, radiance*. ʲtD pc 3mp שנה *be changed*. ᵏprep עַל־ w/ 1cs gen sx. ˡnoun ms לֵב w/ 1cs gen sx hapax *heart*. ᵐG sc 1cs נטר hapax *keep*.

EZRA עזרא

4 ⁸ רְחוּם ᵃבְּעֵל־טְעֵם ᵇᵈᶜ וְשִׁמְשַׁי ᵉ סָפְרָא ᶠ כְּתַבוּ ᵍ אִגְּרָה ʰ חֲדָה ⁱ עַל־ יְרוּשְׁלֶם לְאַרְתַּחְשַׁשְׂתְּא ʲ מַלְכָּא כְּנֵמָא ᵏ: ⁹ אֱדַיִן רְחוּם ᵃᵈᶜ בְּעֵל־טְעֵם ᵇ וְשִׁמְשַׁי ᵉ סָפְרָא ᶠ וּשְׁאָר ᵍ כְּנָוָתְהוֹן ʰ דִּינָיֵא ⁱ וַאֲפַרְסַתְכָיֵא ʲ טַרְפְּלָיֵא ᵏ אֲפָרְסָיֵא ˡ אַרְכְוָי ᵐ בָּבְלָיֵא ⁿ שׁוּשַׁנְכָיֵא ᵒ דֶּהוּא ᴾ עֵלְמָיֵא ᵠ: ¹⁰ וּשְׁאָר ᵃ אֻמַּיָּא ᵇ דִּי ᶜ הַגְלִי ᵈ אָסְנַפַּר ᵉ רַבָּא ᶠ וְיַקִּירָא ᵍ וְהוֹתֵב ʰ הִמּוֹ ⁱ בְּקִרְיָה ʲ דִּי ᵏ שָׁמְרָיִן ˡ וּשְׁאָר ᵐ עֲבַר־נַהֲרָה ᵐ וּכְעֶנֶת ⁿ: ¹¹ דְּנָה ᵃ פַּרְשֶׁגֶן ᵇ אִגַּרְתָּא ᶜ דִּי ᵈ שְׁלַחוּ ᵉ עֲלוֹהִי ᶠ עַל־אַרְתַּחְשַׁשְׂתְּא ᵍ מַלְכָּא עַבְדָיִךְ ʰ אֱנָשׁ ⁱ עֲבַר־נַהֲרָה ⁱ וּכְעֶנֶת:
פ

Ezra 4:8–6:18

8 ᵃPN *Rehum*. ᵇnoun ms cstr בְּעֵל *lord, master*. ᶜnoun ms abs טְעֵם *statement*. ᵈ⁻ᵈ= Akk calque *chancellor, chief government official*. ᵉPN *Shimshai*. ᶠnoun ms emph סָפַר *scribe*. ᵍG sc 3mp כתב *write*. ʰnoun fs abs אִגְּרָה Akk lw (?) *letter*. ⁱcard w/ f noun חַד *one, a*. ʲPN *Artaxerxes*. ᵏadv כְּנֵמָא *thus*.

9 ᵃPN *Rehum*. ᵇnoun ms cstr בְּעֵל *lord, master*. ᶜnoun ms abs טְעֵם *statement*. ᵈ⁻ᵈ= Akk calque *chancellor, chief government official*. ᵉPN *Shimshai*. ᶠnoun ms emph סָפַר *scribe*. ᵍnoun ms cstr שְׁאָר *rest, remainder*. ʰnoun mp כְּנָת w/ 3mp gen sx Akk lw *associate, colleague*. The following list of terms is problematic; cf. *BHS* for suggested emendations. ⁱnoun mp emph דִּינָיֵא hapax *Dinaite*. ʲnoun mp emph אֲפַרְסַתְכָי hapax 1) *Apharsatechite* or Pers lw [three possible Pers words]; 2) *ambassador*; 3) *top official*; 4) *royal ambassador*. ᵏnoun mp emph טַרְפְּלָי hapax 1) *Tripolisite*; 2) *an official of the Persian chancellery of Across the River in Tripolis*; 3) a general term *class of official*. ˡnoun mp emph אֲפָרְסָי hapax *Apharsite* unknown GN. ᵐK אַרְכְוָי [so Ed, no K/Q], Q אַרְכְוָיֵא [so L; *BHS* ʺאַרְכְּ], both noun mp emph

ᵃᵣₖₑᵥᵢ hapax *Urukite*. ⁿnoun mp emph בָּבְלָי hapax *Babylonians* [Ed ʺבְּבָ]. ᵒnoun mp emph שׁוּשַׁנְכָי hapax, Pers lw (?) *Susaite*. ᴾK דְּהוּא [read w/ some הוּא ?] rel pron דְּ (< דִּי) + indep pers pron 3ms הוּא hapax = *that is*; Q דְּהָיֵא [Ed דְּʺ] PN *Dehaye*. ᵠnoun mp emph עֵלְמָי hapax *Elamite*.

10 ᵃnoun ms cstr שְׁאָר *rest, remainder*. ᵇnoun fp emph אֻמָּה *nation*. ᶜrel pron דִּי *who, which, that*. ᵈH sc 3ms גלה *deport, exile*. ᵉPN *Osnappar* unidentified Ass king. ᶠadj ms emph רַב *great*. ᵍnoun ms emph יַקִּיר *noble*. ʰH sc 3ms יתב *make dwell, settle*. ⁱindep pers pron 3mp הִמּוֹ as dir obj *them*. ʲnoun fp emph קִרְיָה *city*. ᵏgen part דִּי *of*. ˡGN *Samaria*. ᵐ⁻ᵐGN *Beyond the River*. ⁿadv כְּעֶנֶת introduces body of a letter *and now*.

11 ᵃprox dem pron ms דְּנָה *this*. ᵇnoun ms cstr פַּרְשֶׁגֶן Pers lw *copy*. ᶜnoun fs emph אִגְּרָה Akk lw (?) *letter*. ᵈrel pron דִּי *who, which, that*. ᵉG sc 3mp שלח *send*. ᶠprep עַל w/ 3ms gen sx. ᵍPN *Artaxerxes*. ʰK עַבְדָיִךְ [so L, no K/Q] noun mp, Q עַבְדָךְ [Ed דָּ́ʺ] noun ms, both עֲבַד w/ 2ms gen sx *slave*. ⁱ⁻ⁱGN *Beyond the River*. ʲadv כְּעֶנֶת introduces body of a letter *and now*.

יְדִיעַᵃ לֶהֱוֵאᵇ לְמַלְכָּאᵇ דִּיᵈ יְהוּדָיֵאᵈ דִּיᵉ סְלִקוּᶠ מִן־לְוָתָךְᵍ עֲלֶינָאʰ 12

אֲתוֹᶦ לִירוּשְׁלֶם קִרְיְתָאʲ מָרָדְתָּאᵏ וּבִאישְׁתָּאˡ בָּנַיִןᵐ וְשׁוּרַיᵑ אשׁכללוᵒ

וְאֻשַּׁיָּאᵖ יַחִיטוּᵠ׃ 13 כְּעַןᵃ יְדִיעַᵇ לֶהֱוֵאᶜ לְמַלְכָּא דִּיᵈ הֵןᵉ קִרְיְתָאᶠ דָךְᵍ

תִּתְבְּנֵאʰ וְשׁוּרַיָּהᶦ יִשְׁתַּכְלְלוּןʲ מִנְדָּה־בְלוֹᵏ וַהֲלָךְˡ לָא יִנְתְּנוּןᵐ וְאַפְּתֹםᵑ

מַלְכִיםᵖ תְּהַנְזִק׃ᵠ 14 כְּעַן כָּל־קֳבֵלᵈ דִּי־מְלַחᵉ הֵיכְלָאᶠ מְלַחְנָאᵍʰ

וְעַרְוַתˡ מַלְכָּא לָא אֲרִיךְʲ־לַנָאᵏ לְמֶחֱזֵאˡ עַל־דְּנָהᵐ שְׁלַחְנָאᵒ

וְהוֹדַעְנָאᵖ לְמַלְכָּא׃ 15 דִּיᵃ יְבַקַּרᵇ בִּסְפַר־דָּכְרָנַיָּאᵈ דִּי אֲבָהָתָךְᶠ

וּתְהַשְׁכַּחᵍ בִּסְפַר דָּכְרָנַיָּאᵈ וְתִנְדַּעᶦ דִּי קִרְיְתָאʰ דָךְᵏ קִרְיָאˡ מָרָדָאᵐ

וּמְהַנְזְקַתᵑ מַלְכִין וּמְדִנָןᵒ וְאֶשְׁתַּדּוּרᵖ עָבְדִיןᵠ בְּגַוַּהʳ מִן־יוֹמָתˢ עָלְמָאᵗ

12 ᵃGp ptcp ms abs ידע. ᵇG juss 3ms הוה. ᶜepex conj דִּי *that*. ᵈnoun mp emph יְהוּדִי *Jew; Judean*. ᵉrel pron דִּי *who, that*. ᶠG sc 3mp סלק *come up*. ᵍprep לְוָת w/ 2ms gen sx, hapax *with*. ʰprep עַל w/ 1cp gen sx. ᶦG sc 3mp אתה *come*. ʲnoun fs emph קִרְיָה *city*. ᵏnoun fs emph מָרָד *rebellious* [L unclear; BHS "מָרֵד; Ed "מָרָ"]. ˡnoun fs emph בְּאִישׁ hapax *bad, evil* [BHS, K וּבְאִישְׁתָּא, Q וּבִישְׁתָּא, both noun fs emph בְּאִישׁ]. ᵐG ptcp mp abs בנה *(re)build*. ᵑK וְשׁוּרַי [Ed "וְשׁ", no K/Q], Q וְשׁוּרַיָּא, both noun mp emph שׁוּר *wall*. ᵒK אֶשְׁכְּלִלוּ H sc 3mp שׁכלל *finish*; Q שַׁכְלִילוּ [Ed שַׁכְלִלוּ] Š sc 3mp כלל *finish*. ᵖnoun mp emph אֹשׁ Sum lw *foundation*. ᵠG/H pc 3mp חוט hapax *sew*. With אֹשׁ as object, either an idiom is present meaning *repair foundations* (all modern translations) or some such, or חוט is to be connected to Akkadian *ḫāṭu inspect foundations*, or an emendation is needed (see HALOT s.v. for suggestions).

13 ᵃtransitional conj כְּעַן introduces new idea *now*. ᵇGp ptcp ms abs ידע. ᶜG juss 3ms הוה. ᵈepex conj דִּי *that*. ᵉhypoth conj הֵן *if*. ᶠnoun fs emph קִרְיָה *city*. ᵍdist dem adj fs דָךְ *that*. ʰtG pc 3fs בנה *be rebuilt*. ᶦnoun mp emph שׁוּר *wall*. ʲŠt25 כלל *be finished*. ᵏnoun fs abs מִדָּה Akk lw *tribute, tax*. ˡnoun ms abs בְּלוֹ Akk lw *tax* paid in kind, *produce tax*. ᵐnoun ms abs הֲלָךְ Akk lw *field* or *produce tax*. ᵑG pc 3mp נתן *give*. ᵒadv (?) אַפְּתֹם hapax either Akk lw *surely, certainly* or Pers lw *finally*. ᵖnoun mp abs מֶלֶךְ Heb ending. ᵠH pc 3fs נזק *damage*.

14 ᵃtransitional conj כְּעַן introduces new idea *now*. ᵇ= כְּ + לְ *according to*. ᶜconj דִּי *that*. ᵈ⁻ᵈ= *because, since*. ᵉnoun ms cstr מְלַח *salt*. ᶠnoun ms emph הֵיכַל *palace*. ᵍG sc 1cp מלח hapax *salt*. ʰ⁻ʰ= *be loyal to the throne* or *be under a covenantal obligation of loyalty to the throne* or *be on the throne's payroll*. ᶦnoun fs cstr עֶרְוָה hapax *nakedness*, by extension *shame*. ʲadj ms abs אֲרִיךְ hapax Pers lw *worthy of an Aryan*, i.e., *proper, fitting*. ᵏprep לְ w/ 1cp gen sx. ˡG inf חזה. ᵐprox dem pron ms דְּנָה *this*. ᵑ⁻ᵑ= *on this basis, for this reason*. ᵒG sc 1cp שׁלח *send*. ᵖH sc 1cp ידע.

15 ᵃpurp conj דִּי *so that*. ᵇD pc 3ms בקר *search*. ᶜnoun ms cstr סְפַר *book*. ᵈnoun mp emph דָּכְרָן *records*. ᵉgen part דִּי *of*. ᶠnoun mp אָב w/ 2ms gen sx *father*. ᵍH pc 2ms שׁכח *find*. ʰG pc 2ms ידע. ᶦepex conj דִּי *that*. ʲnoun fs emph קִרְיָה *city*. ᵏdist dem adj fs דָךְ *that*. ˡnoun fs abs קִרְיָה *city*. ᵐadj fs abs מָרָד *rebellious*. ᵑH ptcp fs cstr נזק *damager*. ᵒnoun fp abs מְדִינָה *district, province*. ᵖnoun ms abs אֶשְׁתַּדּוּר *insurrection*. ᵠG ptcp mp abs עבד. ʳnoun ms גַּו w/ 3fs gen sx *midst = within it*. ˢnoun mp cstr יוֹם *day*. ᵗnoun ms emph עָלַם *antiquity*.

עַל־דְּנָהˢᵘ קִרְיְתָאˢ דָּךְˣ הָחָרְבַתᵞ: 16 מְהוֹדְעִיןᵃ אֲנַחְנָהᵇ לְמַלְכָּא דִּי הֵן קִרְיְתָא דָךְᵉ תִּתְבְּנֵאᵍ וְשׁוּרַיָּהʰ יִשְׁתַּכְלְלוּןⁱ לָקֳבֵל דְּנָהᵏ חֲלָקᵐ בַּעֲבַר נַהֲרָהⁿ לָא אִיתַיᵒ לָךְᵖ פ

17 פִּתְגָמָאᵃ שְׁלַחᵇ מַלְכָּא עַל־רְחוּםᶜ בְּעֵל־טְעֵםᵈᵉ וְשִׁמְשַׁיᵍ סָפְרָאʰ וּשְׁאָרⁱ כְּנָוָתְהוֹןʲ דִּי יָתְבִיןˡ בְּשָׁמְרָיִןᵐ וּשְׁאָר עֲבַר־ נַהֲרָהⁿ שְׁלָםᵒ וּכְעֶתᵖ: ס 18 נִשְׁתְּוָנָאᵃ דִּי שְׁלַחְתּוּןᶜ עֲלֶינָאᵈ מְפָרַשᵉ קֱרִיʰ קָדָמָיᵍ: 19 וּמִנִּיᵃ שִׂים טְעֵםᶜ וּבַקַּרוּᵈ וְהַשְׁכַּחוּ דִּי קִרְיְתָאᵍ דָךְʰ מִן־יוֹמָתⁱ עָלְמָאʲ עַל־מַלְכִיןᵏ מִתְנַשְּׂאָה וּמְרַדˡ וְאֶשְׁתַּדּוּרᵐ מִתְעֲבֶד־בַּהⁿ: ס 20 וּמַלְכִין תַּקִּיפִיןᵃ הֲווֹᵇ עַל־יְרוּשְׁלֶם וְשַׁלִּיטִיןᶜ בְּכֹלᵈ עֲבַר נַהֲרָהᵉ וּמִדָּהᶠ בְלוֹᵍ וַהֲלָךְʰ מִתְיְהֵבⁱ לְהוֹןʲ: 21 כְּעַןᵃ שִׂימוּᵇ טְעֵםᶜ לְבַטָּלָאᵈ גֻּבְרַיָּאᵉ אִלֵּךְᶠ וְקִרְיְתָא דָךְᵍ לָאʰ

---

15 ᵘprox dem pron ms דְּנָה *this.* ᵛ⁻ᵛ= *on this basis, for this reason.* ʷnoun fs emph קִרְיָה *city.* ˣdist dem adj fs דָּךְ *that.* ᵞHp sc 3fs חרב hapax *be laid waste.*

16 ᵃH ptcp mp abs ידע *we hereby inform.* ᵇindep pers pron 1cp אֲנַחְנָה *we.* ᶜepex conj דִּי *that.* ᵈhypoth conj הֵן *if.* ᵉnoun fs emph קִרְיָה *city.* ᶠdist dem adj fs דָךְ *that.* ᵍtG PC 3fs בנה *be rebuilt.* ʰnoun mp emph שׁוּר *wall.* ⁱŠt25 כלל *be finished.* ˡלְ + noun ms cstr קֳבֵל *to what is in front of.* ᵏprox dem pron ms דְּנָה *this.* ˡ⁻ˡ= *because of this, then.* ᵐnoun ms abs חֲלָק *portion, share.* ⁿ⁻ⁿGN *Beyond the River.* ᵒpart. of existence אִיתַי *there is.* ᵖprep לְ w/ 2ms gen sx.

17 ᵃnoun ms emph פִּתְגָם Pers lw *word, answer.* ᵇG sc 3ms שׁלח *send.* ᶜPN Rehum. ᵈnoun ms cstr בְּעֵל *lord, master.* ᵉnoun ms abs טְעֵם *statement.* ᶠ⁻ᶠ= Akk calque *chancellor, chief government official.* ᵍPN Shimshai. ʰnoun ms emph סָפַר *scribe.* ⁱnoun ms cstr שְׁאָר *rest, remainder.* ʲnoun mp כְּנָת w/ 3mp gen sx Akk lw *associate, colleague.* ᵏrel pron דִּי *who, that.* ˡG ptcp mp abs יתב *dwell.* ᵐGN *Samaria.* ⁿ⁻ⁿGN *Beyond the River.* ᵒnoun ms abs שְׁלָם *peace.* ᵖadv כְּעֶנֶת introduces body of a letter *and now.*

18 ᵃnoun ms emph נִשְׁתְּוָן Pers lw *letter.* ᵇrel pron דִּי *which, that.* ᶜG sc 2mp שלח *send.* ᵈprep־עַל w/ 1cp gen sx. ᵉDp ptcp ms

abs פרש hapax *separated, made distinct; translated; explained.* ᶠGp sc 3ms קרא *be read.* ᵍprep קֳדָם w/ 1cs gen sx.

19 ᵃprep מִן w/ 1cs gen sx. ᵇGp sc 3ms שִׂים. ᶜnoun ms abs טְעֵם *statement.* ᵈD sc 3mp בקר *search.* ᵉH sc 3mp שכח *find.* Unexpressed subject in ᵈˎᵉ = passive. ᶠepex conj דִּי *that.* ᵍnoun fs emph קִרְיָה *city.* ʰdist dem adj fs דָךְ *that.* ⁱnoun mp cstr יוֹם *day.* ʲnoun ms emph עָלַם *antiquity* [so Ed; L, *BHS* ″עָ]. ᵏtD ptcp fs abs נשא *rise up against.* Participle here and in ᵒ indicates continuous and habitual action. ˡnoun ms abs מְרַד hapax *rebellion.* ᵐnoun ms abs אֶשְׁתַּדּוּר *insurrection.* ⁿtG ptcp ms abs עבד. ᵒprep בְּ w/ 3fs gen sx.

20 ᵃadj mp abs תַּקִּיף *powerful, mighty.* ᵇG sc 3mp הוה. ᶜadj mp abs שַׁלִּיט *ruler; powerful, mighty.* ᵈnoun ms cstr כֹּל. ᵉ⁻ᵉGN *Beyond the River.* ᶠnoun fs abs מִדָּה Akk lw *tribute, tax.* ᵍnoun ms abs בְּלוֹ Akk lw *tax paid in kind, produce tax.* ʰnoun ms abs הֲלָךְ Akk lw *field* or *produce tax.* ⁱtG ptcp ms abs יהב. ʲprep לְ w/ 3mp gen sx.

21 ᵃtransitional conj כְּעַן introduces new idea *now.* ᵇG imv 2mp שִׂים. ᶜnoun ms abs טְעֵם *statement.* ᵈD inf בטל trans *stop.* ᵉnoun mp emph גְּבַר *man, person.* ᶠdist dem adj cp אִלֵּךְ *those.* ᵍnoun fs emph קִרְיָה *city.* ʰdist dem adj fs דָךְ *that.*

תִתְבְּנֵא֮ עַד־מִנִּ֣יᵏ טַעְמָ֣א יִתְּשָֽׂם׃ 22 וּזְהִירִ֣ין הֱו֧וּᵇ שָׁל֛וּᶜ לְמֶעְבַּ֖דᵉᵈ

עַל־דְּנָ֑הᶠ לְמָ֣הᵍ יִשְׂגֵּ֥א חֲבָלָ֖אʰ לְהַנְזָקַ֥ת מַלְכִֽיןʲ׃ ס 23 אֱדַ֗יִן

מִן־דִּ֣יᵇᵃ פַּרְשֶׁ֤גֶן נִשְׁתְּוָנָא֙ᵈ דִּ֚י אַרְתַּחְשַׁשְׂתְּאᶠ מַלְכָּ֔א קֱרִ֣י קֳדָם־ᵍ

רְח֣וּםʰ וְשִׁמְשַׁ֣י סָֽפְרָ֑אʲ וּכְנָוָתְה֖וֹןᵏ אֲזַ֣לוּ בִבְהִיל֣וּˡ לִירוּשְׁלֶ֔ם עַל־ᵐ

יְהוּדָיֵאⁿ וּבַטִּ֥לוּᵒ הִמּ֖וֹᵖ בְּאֶדְרָ֥עᑫ וְחָֽיִלʳ׃ ס 24 בֵּאדַ֗יִןᵃ בְּטֵלַת֮ᵇ

עֲבִידַת֒ᶜ בֵּית־אֱלָהָ֣אᵈ דִּ֣יᵉ בִּירוּשְׁלֶ֑ם וַהֲוָת֙ᵉ בָּֽטְלָ֔אᶠ עַ֚ד שְׁנַ֣תᵍ תַּרְתֵּ֔יןʰ

לְמַלְכ֖וּתʲ דָּרְיָ֥וֶשׁ מֶֽלֶךְ־פָּרָֽסᵏ׃
פ

5 1 וְהִתְנַבִּ֞יᵇᵃ חַגַּ֣יᶜ נְבִיאָ֗ה וּזְכַרְיָ֤ה בַר־עִדּוֹא֙ᵉᵈ נְבִיאַיָּ֔אᶠ עַל־יְהוּדָיֵ֕אʰ

דִּ֥י בִיהוּדʲ וּבִירוּשְׁלֶ֑ם בְּשֻׁ֛ם אֱלָ֥הּ יִשְׂרָאֵ֖ל עֲלֵיהֽוֹןᵏˡ׃ ס 2 בֵּאדַ֣יִןᵃ

קָ֡מוּ זְרֻבָּבֶ֣לᶜ בַּר־שְׁאַלְתִּיאֵל֩ᵉᵈ וְיֵשׁ֨וּעᶠ בַּר־יֽוֹצָדָ֜קᵍ וְשָׁרִ֣יוʰ לְמִבְנֵ֗אⁱ

בֵּ֤ית אֱלָהָא֙ʲ דִּ֣י בִּירֽוּשְׁלֶ֔ם וְעִמְּה֛וֹןˡ נְבִיַּאיָּ֥אᵏ דִֽי־אֱלָהָ֖אᵐ מְסָעֲדִ֥יןⁿ

לְהֽוֹןᵒ׃
פ

---

21 ⁱtG pc 3fs בנה *be rebuilt.* ʲprep מִן w/ 1cs gen sx. ᵏnoun ms emph טְעֵם *statement.* ˡtG pc 3ms שׂים.

22 ᵃadj mp abs זְהִיר hapax *careful.* ᵇG imv 2mp הוה. ᶜnoun fs abs שָׁלוּ *negligence.* ᵈG inf עבד. ᵉ⁻ᵉ= *take care not to fail to act.* ᶠprox dem pron ms דְּנָה *this.* ᵍimpers interr pron מָה *what;* w/ לְ *why? for what purpose?* ʰG pc 3ms שׂגא *become big, grow.* ⁱnoun ms emph חֲבָל *harm.* ʲnoun fs cstr הַנְזָקָה hapax *injury* or H inf נזק *injure.*

23 ᵃtemp conj דִּי *that.* ᵇ⁻ᵇ= *after, as soon as.* ᶜnoun ms cstr פַּרְשֶׁגֶן Pers lw *copy.* ᵈnoun ms emph נִשְׁתְּוָן Pers lw *letter.* ᵉgen part דִּי *of.* ᶠK אַרְתַּחְשַׁשְׂתְּ, Q אַרְתַּחְשַׁשְׂתְּא [Ed שַׂשְׂתְּא״, no K/Q], both PN *Artaxerxes.* ᵍGp sc 3ms קרא *be read.* ʰPN *Rehum.* ⁱPN *Shimshai.* ʲnoun ms emph סְפַר *scribe.* ᵏnoun mp כְּנָת w/ 3mp gen sx Akk lw *associate, colleague.* ˡG sc 3mp אזל *go.* ᵐnoun fs abs בְּהִילוּ hapax *haste.* ⁿnoun mp emph יְהוּדָי *Jew; Judean.* ᵒD sc 3mp בטל trans *stop.* ᵖindep pers pron 3mp הִמּוֹ as dir obj *them.* ᑫnoun fs abs אֶדְרָע hapax *arm = by force.* ʳnoun ms abs חַיִל *power.*

24 ᵃtemp adv אֱדַיִן (w/ בְּ) *immediately; then.* ᵇG sc 3fs בטל intrans *cease, be idle.*

ᶜnoun fs cstr עֲבִידָה *work.* ᵈrel pron דִּי *which, that.* ᵉG sc 3fs הוה. ᶠG ptcp fs abs בטל intrans *cease, be idle.* Participle with הוה expresses continuous action, *work... was idle until....* ᵍnoun fs cstr I שְׁנָה *year.* ʰcard w/ f noun תְּרֵין *two.* ⁱnoun fs cstr מַלְכוּ *reign.* ʲPN *Darius.* ᵏGN *Persia.*

5

1 ᵃtD sc 3ms נבא hapax *prophesy.* ᵇPN *Haggai.* ᶜK נְבִיאָה, Q נְבִיָּא, both noun ms emph נְבִיא *prophet.* ᵈPN *Zechariah.* ᵉnoun ms cstr II בַּר *son.* ᶠPN *Iddo.* ᵍK נְבִיַּאיָא, Q נְבִיַּיָּא, both noun mp emph נְבִיא *prophet.* ʰnoun mp emph יְהוּדָי *Jew; Judean.* ⁱrel pron דִּי *who, that.* ʲGN *Judah.* ᵏnoun ms cstr שֵׁם *name.* ˡprep עַל w/ 3mp gen sx.

2 ᵃtemp adv אֱדַיִן (w/ בְּ) *immediately; then.* ᵇG sc 3mp קום. ᶜPN *Zerubbabel.* ᵈnoun ms cstr II בַּר *son.* ᵉPN *Shealtiel.* ᶠPN *Jeshua.* ᵍPN *Jozadak.* ʰD sc 3mp שרה *begin.* ⁱG inf בנה *rebuild.* ʲrel pron דִּי *which, that.* ᵏprep עִם w/ 3mp gen sx. ˡK נְבִיַּאיָא [Ed נְבִיאָה, no K/Q], Q נְבִיַּיָּא, both noun mp emph נְבִיא *prophet.* ᵐgen part דִּי *of.* ⁿD ptcp mp abs סעד hapax *support* [Ed מְסָ״]. ᵒprep לְ w/ 3mp gen sx.

3 בֵּהּ־זִמְנָאᵇ אֲתָאᶜ עֲלֵיהוֹןᵈ תַּתְּנַיᵉ פַּחַתᶠ עֲבַר־נַהֲרָהᵍ וּשְׁתַר בּוֹזְנַיʰ
וּכְנָוָתְהוֹןⁱ וְכֵןʲ אָמְרִיןᵏ לְהֹםˡ מַן־שָׂםᵐ לְכֹםᵒ טְעֵםᵖ בַּיְתָא דְנָהᵠ לִבְּנֵאʳ
וְאֻשַּׁרְנָאˢ דְנָה לְשַׁכְלָלָהᵗ ۠ 4 אֱדַיִן כְּנֵמָאᵃ אֲמַרְנָאᵇ לְהֹםᶜ
מַן־אִנּוּןᵈ שְׁמָהָתᵉ גֻּבְרַיָּאᶠ דִּי־דְנָה בִּנְיָנָאⁱ בָּנַיִןʲ ۠ 5 וְעֵיןᵃ אֱלָהֲהֹםᵇ
הֲוָתᶜ עַל־שָׂבֵיᵈ יְהוּדָיֵאᵉ וְלָא־בַטִּלוּᶠ הִמּוֹᵍ עַד־טַעְמָאʰ לְדָרְיָוֶשׁ יְהָךʲ
וֶאֱדַיִן יְתִיבוּןᵏ נִשְׁתְּוָנָאˡ עַל־דְּנָהᵐ ۠ פ

6 פַּרְשֶׁגֶןᵃ אִגַּרְתָּאᵇ דִּי־שְׁלַחᵈ תַּתְּנַי פַּחַתᶠ עֲבַר־נַהֲרָהᵍ וּשְׁתַר
בּוֹזְנַיʰ וּכְנָוָתֵהּ אֲפַרְסְכָיֵאʲ דִּי בַּעֲבַר נַהֲרָהˡ עַל־דָּרְיָוֶשׁ מַלְכָּאᵐ ۠
7 פִּתְגָמָאᵃ שְׁלַחוּᵇ עֲלוֹהִיᶜ וְכִדְנָהᵈ כְּתִיבᵉ בְּגַוֵּהᶠ לְדָרְיָוֶשׁᵍ מַלְכָּא
שְׁלָמָאʰ כֹּלָּא ۠ 8 יְדִיעַᵃ לֶהֱוֵאᵇ לְמַלְכָּא דִּי־אֲזַלְנָאᵈ לִיהוּדᵉ

---

3 ᵃprep בְּ w/ 3ms gen sx. ᵇnoun ms emph זְמַן *time.* ᶜG sc 3ms אתה *come.* ᵈprep עַל־ w/ 3mp gen sx. ᵉPN *Tattenai.* ᶠnoun ms cstr פֶּחָה *governor.* ᵍ⁻ᵍGN *Beyond the River.* ʰ⁻ʰPN *Shethar-bozenai.* ⁱnoun mp כְּנָת w/ 3mp gen sx, Akk lw *associate, colleague.* ʲadv כֵּן *thus.* ᵏG ptcp mp abs אמר. ˡprep לְ w/ 3mp gen sx. ᵐpers interr pron מַן *who?* ⁿG sc 3ms שׂים. ᵒprep לְ w/ 2mp gen sx. ᵖnoun ms abs טְעֵם *statement.* ᵠprox dem adj ms דְּנָה *this.* ʳG inf בנה *rebuild.* Old form of the infinitive. ˢnoun ms emph אֻשַּׁרְנָא Pers or Akk lw *shrine* (?), *structure* (?), *furnishings* (?). ᵗŠ inf כלל *finish, compete.*

4 ᵃadv כְּנֵמָא *thus.* ᵇG sc 1cp אמר. ᶜprep לְ w/ 3mp gen sx. ᵈpers interr pron מַן *who?* = *what?* ᵉindep pers pron 3mp אִנּוּן as copula *are.* ᶠnoun mp cstr שֻׁם *name.* ᵍnoun mp emph גְּבַר *man, person.* ʰrel pron דִּי *who, that.* ⁱprox dem adj ms דְּנָה *this.* Sometimes the dem adj precedes the noun. ʲnoun ms emph בִּנְיָן hapax *building.* ᵏG ptcp mp abs בנה *rebuild.*

5 ᵃnoun fs cstr עַיִן *eye.* ᵇnoun ms אֱלָה w/ 3mp gen sx. ᶜG sc 3fs הוה. ᵈadj mp cstr שָׂב *gray headed* = *elders.* ᵉnoun mp emph יְהוּדִי *Jew; Judean.* ᶠD sc 3mp בטל trans *stop.* ᵍindep pers pron 3mp הִמּוֹ as dir obj

them. ʰnoun ms emph טְעֵם *statement.* ⁱPN *Darius.* ʲG pc 3ms הך (or הוך; BDB הלך) *go, reach.* ᵏH pc 3mp תוב trans *return.* Treat ʲ and ᵏ as subjunctives, *should reach...should return,* and not as past tense. ˡnoun ms emph נִשְׁתְּוָן Pers lw *letter.* ᵐprox dem pron ms דְּנָה *this.*

6 ᵃnoun ms cstr פַּרְשֶׁגֶן Pers lw *copy.* ᵇnoun fs emph אִגְּרָה Akk lw (?) *letter.* ᶜrel pron דִּי *which, that.* ᵈG sc 3ms שלח *send.* ᵉPN *Tattenai.* ᶠnoun ms cstr פֶּחָה *governor.* ᵍ⁻ᵍGN *Beyond the River.* ʰ⁻ʰPN *Shethar-bozenai.* ⁱnoun fp כְּנָת w/ 3ms gen sx Akk lw *associate, colleague.* ʲnoun mp emph אֲפַרְסְכָי Akk or Pers lw, official title, *apharsechai-official;* or a people, *Apharsechite.* ᵏrel pron דִּי *who, that.* ˡ⁻ˡGN *Beyond the River.* ᵐPN *Darius.*

7 ᵃnoun ms emph פִּתְגָם Pers lw *word, report.* ᵇG sc 3mp שלח *send.* ᶜprep עַל־ w/ 3ms gen sx. ᵈprox dem pron ms דְּנָה w/ prep כְּ *like this, thus.* ᵉGp sc 3ms כתב *be written.* ᶠnoun ms גּוּ w/ 3ms gen sx *midst* = *within it.* ᵍPN *Darius.* ʰnoun ms emph שְׁלָם *peace.* ⁱnoun ms emph כֹּל.

8 ᵃGp ptcp ms abs ידע. ᵇG juss 3ms הוה. ᶜepex conj דִּי *that.* ᵈG sc 1cp אזל *go.* ᵉGN *Judah.*

מְדִינְתָּאᶠ לְבֵית אֱלָהָא רַבָּאᵍ וְהוּאʰ מִתְבְּנֵאⁱ אֶבֶן גְּלָלᵏ וְאָעˡ
מִתְּשָׂםᵐ בְּכֻתְלַיָּאⁿ וַעֲבִידְתָּאᵒ דָךᵖ אָסְפַּרְנָא�q מִתְעַבְדָאʳ וּמַצְלַחˢ
בְּיֶדְהֹם:ᵗ ס 9 אֱדַיִן שְׁאֵלְנָאª לְשָׂבַיָּאᵇ אִלֵּךְᶜ כְּנֵמָאᵈ אֲמַרְנָאᵉ
לְהֹםᶠ מַן־שָׂםᵍ לְכֹם טְעֵםʰ בַּיְתָאⁱ דְנָהʲ לְמִבְנְיֵהᵏ וְאֻשַּׁרְנָאᵐ דְנָה
לְשַׁכְלָלָה: 10 וְאַףª שְׁמָהָתְהֹםᵇ שְׁאֵלְנָאᶜ לְהֹםᵈ לְהוֹדָעוּתָךְᵉ דִּיᶠ
נִכְתֻּבᵍ שֻׁם־גֻּבְרַיָּאʰ דִּיⁱ בְרָאשֵׁיהֹם:ᵏ ס 11 וּכְנֵמָאª פִתְגָמָאᵇ
הֲתִיבוּנָאᶜ לְמֵמַרᵈ אֲנַחְנָאᵉ הִמּוֹᶠ עַבְדוֹהִיᵍ דִּי־אֱלָהᵸⁱ שְׁמַיָּאⁱ וְאַרְעָאʲ
וּבָנַיִן בַּיְתָאᵏ דִּי־הֲוָאᵐ בְנֵהⁿ מִקַּדְמַתᵒ דְּנָהᵖ שְׁנִיןq שַׂגִּיאָןˢʳ וּמֶלֶךְᵘ
לְיִשְׂרָאֵל רַבᵗ בְּנָהᵛ וְשַׁכְלְלֵה:ʷ 12 לָהֵןᵃ מִן־דִּיᶜ הַרְגִּזוּᵈ אֲבָהָתַנָאᵉ
לֶאֱלָהּ שְׁמַיָּאᶠ יְהַבᵍ הִמּוֹʰ בְּיַדⁱ נְבוּכַדְנֶצַּר מֶלֶךְ־בָּבֶל כַּסְדָּיאʲ וּבַיְתֵהᵏ

---

8 ᶠnoun fs emph מְדִינָה *district, province.* ᵍadj ms emph רַב *great.* ʰindep pers pron 3ms הוּא *he, it.* ⁱtG ptcp ms abs בנה *being rebuilt.* ʲnoun fs cstr אֶבֶן *stone.* ᵏadj ms abs גְּלָל *huge; hewn.* ˡnoun ms abs אָע *timber.* ᵐtG ptcp ms abs שׂים. ⁿnoun mp emph כְּתַל *wall.* ᵒnoun fs emph עֲבִידָה *work.* ᵖdist dem adj fs דָּךְ *that.* qadv אָסְפַּרְנָא Pers lw *diligently, exactly.* ʳtD ptcp fs abs עבד. ˢH ptcp ms abs צלח *prosper, succeed.* ᵗnoun fs יַד w/ 3mp gen sx *hand.*

9 ªG sc 1cp שׁאל *ask.* ᵇadj mp emph שָׂב *gray headed = elders.* ᶜdist dem adj cp אִלֵּךְ *those.* ᵈadv כְּנֵמָא *thus.* ᵉG sc 1cp אמר. ᶠprep לְ w/ 3mp gen sx. ᵍpers interr pron מַן *who?* ʰG sc 3ms שׂים. ⁱprep לְ w/ 2mp gen sx. ʲnoun ms abs טְעֵם *statement.* ᵏprox dem adj ms דְּנָה *this.* ˡG inf בנה *rebuild.* The form is in the emphatic state. ᵐnoun ms emph אֻשַּׁרְנָא Pers or Akk lw *shrine (?), structure (?), furnishings (?).* ⁿŠ inf כלל *finish, compete.*

10 ªconj אַף *also.* ᵇnoun mp שֻׁם w/ 3mp gen sx *name.* ᶜG sc 1cp שׁאל *ask.* ᵈprep לְ w/ 3mp gen sx. ᵉH inf ידע w/ 2ms acc sx. ᶠpurp conj דִּי *so that.* ᵍG pc 1cp כתב *write.* ʰnoun ms cstr שֻׁם *name.* ⁱnoun mp emph גְּבַר *man, person.* ʲrel pron דִּי *who, that.*

ᵏnoun mp רֵאשׁ w/ 3mp gen sx *head.*

11 ªadv כְּנֵמָא *thus.* ᵇnoun ms emph פִּתְגָם Pers lw *word, answer.* ᶜH sc 3mp תוב w/ 1cp acc sx trans *return (w/ sx) to.* ᵈG inf אמר. ᵉindep pers pron 1cp אֲנַחְנָה *we.* ᶠindep pers pron 3mp הִמּוֹ as copula *are.* ᵍnoun mp עֲבֵד w/ 3ms gen sx *slave, servant.* ʰgen part דִּי *of.* ⁱnoun mp emph שְׁמַיִן. ʲnoun fs emph אֲרַע *earth, land.* ᵏG ptcp mp abs בנה *rebuild.* ˡrel pron דִּי *which, that.* ᵐG sc 3ms הוה. ⁿGp ptcp ms abs בנה *built.* ᵒnoun fp abs קַדְמָה *earlier time.* ᵖprox dem pron ms דְּנָה *this.* qnoun fp abs ı שְׁנָה *year.* ʳadj fp abs שַׂגִּיא *many.* ˢ⁻ˢ= *many years ago.* ᵗadj ms abs רַב *great.* ᵘ⁻ᵘ= *a great king of Israel.* ᵛG sc 3ms בנה w/ 3ms acc sx *build.* ʷŠ sc 3ms כלל w/ 3ms acc sx *finish.*

12 ªdisj ıı לָהֵן *but.* ᵇtemp conj דִּי *that.* ᶜ⁻ᶜ= *after, as soon as.* ᵈH sc 3mp רגז hapax *enrage.* ᵉnoun mp אַב w/ 1cp gen sx *father* [L, *BHL**, *BHS* אֲבָהָת; Ed אֲבָהָת]. ᶠnoun mp emph שְׁמַיִן. ᵍG sc 3ms יהב. ʰindep pers pron 3mp הִמּוֹ as dir obj *them.* ⁱnoun fs cstr יַד *hand.* ʲK כַּסְדָּיא, Q כַּסְדָּאֵה, both noun mp emph כַּסְדָּי = *Chaldean.* ᵏnoun ms emph בַּיִת.

דְנָהˡ סַתְרֵהᵐ וְעַמָּהⁿ הַגְלִיᵒ לְבָבֶל: ס   13 בְּרַםᵃ בִּשְׁנַתᵇ חֲדָהᶜ

לְכוֹרֶשׁᵈ מַלְכָּא דִּיᵉ בָבֶל כּוֹרֶשׁᵈ מַלְכָּא שָׂםᶠ טְעֵםᵍ בֵּית־אֱלָהָאʰ דְנָה

לִבְּנֵא: 14 וְ֠אַףᵃ מָאנַיָּאᵇ דִי־בֵית־אֱלָהָאᶜ דִּי דַהֲבָהᵈ וְכַסְפָּאᵉ דִּיᶠ

נְבוּכַדְנֶצַּר הַנְפֵּקᵍ מִן־הֵיכְלָאʰ דִּי בִירוּשְׁלֶםⁱ וְהֵיבֵל הִמּוֹ לְהֵיכְלָאʲ

דִּי בָבֶל הַנְפֵּקᵍ הִמּוֹ כּוֹרֶשׁᵏ מַלְכָּא מִן־הֵיכְלָאʰ דִּי בָבֶל וִיהִיבוּ

לְשֵׁשְׁבַּצַּרˡ שְׁמֵהᵐ דִּי פֶחָהⁿ שָׂמֵהᵒ: 15 וַאֲמַר־לֵהᵃ| אֵלֶּהᶜ מָאנַיָּאᵈ

שֵׂאᵉ אֵזֵלᶠ אֲחֵת־הִמּוֹᵍ בְּהֵיכְלָאʰ דִּי בִירוּשְׁלֶםⁱ וּבֵית אֱלָהָא יִתְבְּנֵאᵏ

עַל־אַתְרֵהˡ: ס 16 אֱדַיִןᵃ שֵׁשְׁבַּצַּר דֵּךְᵇ אֲתָאᶜ יְהַבᵈ אֻשַּׁיָּאᵉ

דִּי־בֵית אֱלָהָא דִּיᵍ בִירוּשְׁלֶם וּמִן־אֱדַיִן וְעַד־כְּעַןʰ מִתְבְּנֵאⁱ וְלָא

שְׁלִםʲ: 17 וּכְעַןᵃ הֵןᵇ עַל־מַלְכָּא טָבᶜ יִתְבַּקַּרᵈ בְּבֵית גִּנְזַיָּאᵉ דִּי־מַלְכָּא

תַמָּהᵍ דִּיʰ בְּבָבֶל הֵן אִיתַיⁱ דִּי־מִן־כּוֹרֶשׁˡ מַלְכָּא שִׂיםᵐ טְעֵםⁿ

לְמִבְנֵאᵒ בֵּית־אֱלָהָא דֵךְᵖ בִּירוּשְׁלֶם וּרְעוּתᵠ מַלְכָּא עַל־דְּנָה יִשְׁלַחˢ

---

12 ˡprox dem adj ms דְּנָה *this.* ᵐG sc 3ms סתר II w/ 3ms acc sx hapax *destroy.* ⁿnoun ms emph עַם *people.* ᵒH sc 3ms גלה *deport, exile.* The direct object may precede the verb (and be refered to by a resumptive accusative suffix on the verb).

13 ᵃdisj בְּרַם *but, however.* ᵇnoun fs cstr I שָׁנָה *year.* ᶜcard w/ f noun חַד *one.* ᵈPN *Cyrus.* ᵉgen part דִּי *of.* ᶠG sc 3ms שִׂים. ᵍnoun ms abs טְעֵם *statement.* ʰprox dem adj ms דְּנָה *this.* ⁱG inf בנה *rebuild.* Old form of the infinitive.

14 ᵃconj אַף *also.* ᵇnoun mp emph מָאן *vessel.* ᶜgen part דִּי *of.* ᵈnoun ms emph דְּהַב *gold.* ᵉnoun ms emph כְּסַף *silver.* The emphatic state is used here for general designation. ᶠrel pron דִּי *who, which, that.* ᵍH sc 3ms נפק *bring out.* ʰnoun ms emph הֵיכַל *temple, palace.* ⁱH sc 3ms יבל *bring.* ʲindep pers pron 3mp הִמּוֹ as dir obj *them.* ᵏPN *Cyrus.* ˡGp25 יהב. ᵐPN *Sheshbazzar.* ⁿnoun ms שֵׁם w/ 3ms gen sx *name.* ᵒnoun ms abs פֶּחָה *governor.* ᵖG sc 3ms שִׂים w/ 3ms acc sx.

15 ᵃG sc 3ms אמר. ᵇprep לְ w/ 3ms gen sx. ᶜK אֵלֶּה prox dem adj cp *these;* Q אֵל prox dem adj cp hapax אֵל *these.* The demonstrative adjective sometimes pre-

cedes the noun. ᵈnoun mp emph מָאן *vessel.* ᶜ⁻ᵈ form a casus pendens, *as for these vessels.* ᵉG imv 2ms נשא *carry, take.* ᶠG imv 2ms אזל *go.* ᵍH imv 2ms נחת *deposit.* ʰindep pers pron 3mp הִמּוֹ as dir obj *them.* ⁱnoun ms emph הֵיכַל *temple.* ʲrel pron דִּי *which, that.* ᵏtG juss 3ms בנה *be rebuilt.* ˡnoun ms אֲתַר w/ 3ms gen sx *place.*

16 ᵃPN *Sheshbazzar.* ᵇdist dem adj ms דֵּךְ *that.* ᶜG sc 3ms אתה *come.* ᵈG sc 3ms יהב. ᵉnoun mp emph אֻשׁ Sum lw *foundation.* ᶠgen part דִּי *of.* ᵍrel pron דִּי *which, that.* ʰtemp adv כְּעַן *now.* ⁱtG ptcp ms abs בנה *being rebuilt.* ʲGp ptcp ms abs שלם *be finished.*

17 ᵃtransitional conj כְּעַן introduces new idea *now.* ᵇhypoth conj הֵן *if, whether.* ᶜadj ms abs טָב *good.* ᵈtD juss 3ms בקר *be searched.* ᵉnoun mp emph גְּנַז *storage.* ᶠgen part דִּי *of.* ᵍloc adv תַּמָּה *there.* ʰrel pron דִּי *which, that.* ⁱpart. of existence אִיתַי *there is.* ʲepex conj דִּי *that.* ᵏ⁻ᵏ= *it is (a fact) that.* ˡPN *Cyrus.* ᵐGp sc 3ms שִׂים. ⁿnoun ms abs טְעֵם *statement.* ᵒG inf בנה *rebuild.* ᵖdist dem adj ms דֵּךְ *that.* ᵠnoun fs cstr רְעוּ *will, pleasure.* ʳprox dem pron ms דְּנָה *this.* ˢG PC 3ms שלח *send.*

עֲלֵֽינָאᵗ‪|‬ ס   6 ¹ בֵּאדַ֣יִןᵃ דָּרְיָ֣וֶשׁᵇ מַלְכָּ֗א שָׂ֣םᶜ טְעֵ֑םᵈ וּבַקַּ֣רוּ‪|‬ᵉ
בְּבֵ֣ית סִפְרַיָּ֗אᵍᶠ דִּ֧י גִנְזַיָּ֛אⁱ מְהַחֲתִ֥יןʲ תַּמָּ֖הᵏ בְּבָבֶֽלlk׃ ² וְהִשְׁתְּכַ֣חᵃ
בְּאַחְמְתָ֣אᵇ בְּבִֽירְתָ֗אᶜ דִּ֛יᵈ בְּמָדַ֥יᵉ מְדִינְתָּ֖הᶠ מְגִלָּ֣הᵍ חֲדָ֑הʰ וְכֵן־כְּתִ֥יבʲ
בְּגַוַּ֖הּᵏ דִּכְרוֹנָֽה׃l
פ

³ בִּשְׁנַ֣תᵃ חֲדָ֗הᵇ לְכ֣וֹרֶשׁᶜ מַלְכָּ֔א כּ֣וֹרֶשׁ מַלְכָּ֗א שָׂ֣םᵈ טְעֵ֑םᵉ בֵּית־
אֱלָהָ֣א בִֽירוּשְׁלֶ֗ם בַּיְתָ֤א יִתְבְּנֵאᶠ אֲתַרᵍ דִּֽי־דָבְחִ֣ין דִּבְחִ֔יןʰ וְאֻשּׁ֖וֹהִיⁱ
מְסֽוֹבְלִ֑ין רוּמֵהּᵐ אַמִּ֣יןⁿ שִׁתִּ֗יןᵒ פְּתָיֵ֖הᵖ אַמִּ֥ין שִׁתִּֽין׃ ⁴ נִדְבָּכִ֞יןᵃ
דִּֽי־אֶ֤בֶןᵇ גְּלָלᵈ תְּלָתָ֙אᵉ וְנִדְבָּ֖ךᶠ דִּֽי־אָ֣עᵍ חֲדַ֑תʰ וְנִ֨פְקְתָ֔אⁱ מִן־בֵּ֥ית
מַלְכָּ֖א תִּתְיְהִֽבʲ׃ ⁵ וְ֠אַףᵃ מָאנֵ֣יᵇ בֵית־אֱלָהָא֮ᶜ דִּ֣י דַהֲבָ֣הᵈ וְכַסְפָּ֒אᵉ
דִּ֣יᶠ נְבֽוּכַדְנֶצַּ֗ר הַנְפֵּ֛קᵍ מִן־הֵיכְלָאʰ דִּֽי־בִירוּשְׁלֶ֖ם וְהֵיבֵ֣לⁱ לְבָבֶ֑ל
יַהֲתִיב֗וּןʲ וִ֠יהָךᵏ לְהֵיכְלָ֤א דִּֽי־בִירוּשְׁלֶם֙ לְאַתְרֵ֔הּˡ וְתַחֵ֖תᵐ בְּבֵ֥ית
אֱלָהָֽאᵉ׃ ס   ⁶ כְּעַ֡ןᵃ תַּ֠תְּנַיᵇ פַּחַ֨תᶜ עֲבַֽר־נַהֲרָ֜הᵈ שְׁתַ֤ר בּוֹזְנַ֨יᵉ

---

¹⁷ ᵗprep עַל־ w/ 1cp gen sx.

6

1 ᵃtemp adv אֱדַיִן (w/ בְּ) *immediately; then.* ᵇPN *Darius.* ᶜG sc 3ms שׂים. ᵈnoun ms abs טְעֵם *statement.* ᵉD sc 3mp בקר *search.* ᶠnoun mp emph סְפַר *book.* ᵍ⁻ᵍ= *archive.* ʰrel pron דִּי *which, that.* ⁱnoun mp emph גְּנַז *treasure.* ʲHp ptcp mp abs נחת *be deposited.* ᵏloc adv תַּמָּה *there.* ˡ⁻ˡ= *in the archives where the treasures are deposited.*

2 ᵃtG sc 3ms שׁכח *be found.* ᵇGN hapax *Ecbatana.* ᶜnoun fs emph בִּירָה hapax *citadel.* ᵈrel pron דִּי *which, that.* ᵉGN *Media.* ᶠnoun fs emph מְדִינָה *district, province.* ᵍnoun fs abs מְגִלָּה hapax *scroll.* ʰcard w/ f noun חַד *one, a.* ⁱadv כֵּן *thus* [so BHS (Ed ״וְכְ״); L, BHL* (?) וְ]. ʲGp sc 3ms כתב *be written.* ᵏnoun ms גַּו w/ 3fs gen sx *midst* = *within it.* ˡnoun ms emph דִּכְרוֹן hapax *record, memorandum.*

3 ᵃnoun fs cstr שְׁנָה *year.* ᵇcard w/ f noun חַד *one.* ᶜPN *Cyrus.* ᵈG sc 3ms שׂים. ᵉnoun ms abs טְעֵם *statement.* ᶠtG juss 3ms בנה *be rebuilt.* ᵍnoun ms abs אֲתַר *place.* ʰrel pron דִּי *which, that* = *where.* ⁱG ptcp mp abs דבח hapax *sacrifice.* *Unexpressed subject may express passive.* ʲnoun mp abs דְּבַח hapax *sacrifice.* ᵏnoun mp אֻשׁ w/ 3ms gen

sx Sum lw *foundation.* ˡDp ptcp mp abs סבל hapax, *maintained* (HALOT), *erected;* or Š ptcp mp abs ובל *sacrificing, offering,* which requires emending ᵏ to אֻשּׁוֹהִי *its burnt offereings,* see NRSV. ᵐnoun ms רוּם w/ 3ms gen sx *height.* ⁿnoun fp abs אַמָּה *cubit.* ᵒcard שִׁתִּין *sixty.* ᵖnoun ms פְּתַי w/ 3ms gen sx *width.*

4 ᵃnoun mp abs נִדְבָּךְ *course, layer.* ᵇgen part דִּי *of.* ᶜnoun fs cstr אֶבֶן *stone.* ᵈadj ms abs גְּלָל *huge; hewn.* ᵉcard w/ m noun תְּלָת *three.* ᶠnoun ms abs נִדְבָּךְ *course.* ᵍnoun ms abs אָע *timber.* ʰadj fs cstr חֲדַת hapax *new.* Some emend to חַד *one.* ⁱnoun fs emph נִפְקָה *expenses.* ʲtG juss 3fs יהב.

5 ᵃconj אַף *also.* ᵇnoun mp cstr מָאן *vessel.* ᶜgen part דִּי *of.* ᵈnoun ms emph דְּהַב *gold.* ᵉnoun ms emph כְּסַף *silver.* ᶠrel pron דִּי *which, that.* ᵍH sc 3ms נפק *bring out.* ʰnoun ms emph הֵיכַל *temple.* ⁱH sc 3ms יבל *bring.* ʲH juss 3mp תוב trans *return.* ᵏG juss 3ms הך (or הוך; BDB הלך) *go, reach.* ˡnoun ms אֲתַר w/ 3ms gen sx *place.* ᵐH pc 2ms נחת *deposit.*

6 ᵃtransitional conj כְּעַן introduces new idea *now.* ᵇPN *Tattenai.* ᶜnoun ms cstr פֶּחָה *governor.* ᵈ⁻ᵈGN *Beyond the River.* ᵉ⁻ᵉPN *Shethar-bozenai.*

וּכְנָוָתְהוֹןᶠ אֲפַרְסְכָיֵאᵍ דִּיʰ בַּעֲבַרⁱ נַהֲרָהʲ רַחִיקִיןᵏ הֲווֹˡ מִן־
תַּמָּהᵐᴸ: 7 שְׁבֻקוּᵃ לַעֲבִידַתᵇ בֵּית־אֱלָהָא דֵךְᶜ פַּחַתᵈ יְהוּדָיֵאᵉ וּלְשָׂבֵיᶠ
יְהוּדָיֵאᵉ בֵּית־אֱלָהָא דֵךְᵍ יִבְנוֹן עַל־אַתְרֵהʰ: 8 וּמִנִּיᵃ שִׂים טְעֵםᶜ
לְמָאᶠ דִּי־תַעַבְדוּןᶠᵉ עִם־שָׂבֵיᵍ יְהוּדָיֵאⁱ אִלֵּךְʲ לְמִבְנֵאᵏ בֵּית־אֱלָהָא
דֵךְˡ וּמִנִּכְסֵיᵐ מַלְכָּא דִּיⁿ מִדַּתᵒ עֲבַר נַהֲרָהᵖ אָסְפַּרְנָא נִפְקְתָאᵠ
תֶּהֱוֵאʳ מִתְיַהֲבָאˢ לְגֻבְרַיָּאᵗ אִלֵּךְ דִּי־לָא לְבַטָּלָאᵘ: 9 וּמָהᵃ
חַשְׁחָןᵇ וּבְנֵי תוֹרִיןᵈ וְדִכְרִיןᵉ וְאִמְּרִיןᶠ לַעֲלָוָןᵍ לֶאֱלָהּ שְׁמַיָּאʰ
חִנְטִיןⁱ מְלַחʲ חֲמַרᵏ וּמְשַׁחˡ כְּמֵאמַרᵐ כָּהֲנַיָּאⁿ דִּי־בִירוּשְׁלֶם
לֶהֱוֵאᵖ מִתְיַהֵבᵠ לְהֹםʳ יוֹם|ˢ בְּיוֹםᵗ דִּי־לָאᵘ שָׁלוּᵛ: 10 דִּי־ᵃ
לֶהֱוֹןᵇ מְהַקְרְבִיןᶜ נִיחוֹחִיןᵈ לֶאֱלָהּ שְׁמַיָּאᵉ וּמְצַלַּיִןᵉ לְחַיֵּיᵍ מַלְכָּא
וּבְנוֹהִיʰ: 11 וּמִנִּיᵃ שִׂים טְעֵםᵇ דִּיᶜ כָל־אֱנָשᵈ דִּיᵉ יְהַשְׁנֵאᵍ פִּתְגָמָאʰ

6 ᶠnoun mp כְּנָת w/ 3mp gen sx Akk lw *associate, colleague.* ᵍnoun mp emph אֲפַרְסְכָי Akk or Pers lw, official title, *apharsechai-official*; or a people, *Apharsechite.* ʰrel pron דִּי *who, that.* ⁱ⁻ⁱGN *Beyond the River.* ʲadj mp abs רַחִיק hapax *far away.* ᵏG imv 2mp הוה. ˡloc adv תַּמָּה *there.* ᵐ⁻ᵐ= *stay far away from there.*

7 ᵃG imv 2mp שבק *leave (w/ לְ) smthg alone, unencumbered.* ᵇnoun fs cstr עֲבִידָה *work.* ᶜdist dem adj ms דֵךְ *that.* ᵈnoun ms cstr פֶּחָה *governor.* ᵉnoun mp emph יְהוּדָי *Jew; Judean.* ᶠadj mp cstr שָׂב *gray headed = elders.* ᵍG juss 3mp בנה *rebuild.* ʰnoun ms אֲתַר w/ 3ms gen sx *place.*

8 ᵃprep מִן w/ 1cs gen sx. ᵇGp sc 3ms שִׂים. ᶜnoun ms abs טְעֵם *statement.* ᵈimpers correl pron מָה (alt spelling) *what.* ᵉrel pron דִּי *which, that.* ᶠ⁻ᶠ= w/ לְ *concerning that which.* ᵍG pc 2mp עבד [so Ed; L, BHS "תְּ]. ʰadj mp cstr שָׂב *gray headed = elders.* ⁱnoun mp emph יְהוּדָי *Jew; Judean.* ʲdist dem adj cp אִלֵּךְ *those.* ᵏG inf בנה *rebuild.* ˡdist dem adj ms דֵךְ *that.* ᵐnoun mp cstr נְכַס Sum lw *property, wealth.* ⁿnoun fs cstr מִדָּה Akk lw *tribute, tax.* ᵒ⁻ᵒGN *Beyond the River.* ᵖadv אָסְפַּרְנָא Pers lw *competely, exactly.* ᵠnoun fs emph נִפְקָה *expenses.* ʳG pc 3fs הוה. ˢtG ptcp fs abs יהב. ᵗnoun mp

emph גְּבַר *man, person.* ᵘD inf בטל *trans stop.*

9 ᵃimpers correl pron מָה *that which, whatever.* ᵇadj fp abs חַשְׁחָה hapax *needed, necessity.* ᶜnoun mp cstr II בַּר *son.* ᵈnoun mp abs תּוֹר *bull.* ᵉnoun mp abs דְּכַר *ram.* ᶠnoun mp abs אִמַּר *lamb.* ᵍnoun fp abs עֲלָוָה hapax *burnt offering.* ʰnoun mp emph שְׁמַיִן. ⁱnoun fp abs חִנְטָה *wheat.* ʲnoun ms abs מְלַח *salt.* ᵏnoun ms abs חֲמַר *wine.* ˡnoun ms abs I מְשַׁח *anointing oil.* ᵐnoun ms cstr מֵאמַר *word, command.* ⁿnoun mp emph כָּהֵן *priest.* ᵒrel pron דִּי *who, which, that.* ᵖG juss 3ms הוה. ᵠtG ptcp ms abs יהב. ʳprep לְ w/ 3mp gen sx. ˢnoun ms abs יוֹם *day.* ᵗSo BHS, Ed; L, BHL* יוֹם (no |). ᵘ⁻ᵘ= *without.* ᵛnoun fs abs שָׁלוּ *negligence.* ʷ⁻ʷ= *without fail.*

10 ᵃpurp conj דִּי *so that.* ᵇG pc 3mp הוה. ᶜH ptcp mp abs קרב *offer.* ᵈnoun mp abs נִיחוֹחַ *soothing sacrifice; incense offering.* ᵉnoun mp emph שְׁמַיִן. ᶠD ptcp mp abs צלה *pray.* ᵍnoun mp cstr חַיִּין *life.* ʰnoun mp II בַּר w/ 3ms gen sx *son.*

11 ᵃprep מִן w/ 1cs gen sx. ᵇGp sc 3ms שִׂים. ᶜnoun ms abs טְעֵם *statement.* ᵈepex conj דִּי *that.* ᵉnoun ms cstr כֹּל *who, that.* ᶠrel pron דִּי *who, that.* ᵍH pc 3ms שנה *trans change.* ʰnoun ms emph פִּתְגָם Pers lw *word, edict.*

דְּנָֽהⁱ יִתְנְסַ֤חʲ אָעᵏ מִן־בַּיְתֵהּˡ וּזְקִ֖יף יִתְמְחֵ֣אⁿ עֲלֹ֑הִי וּבַיְתֵ֛הּˡ
נְו֖לוּᵖ יִתְעֲבֵ֥דᵍ עַל־דְּנָֽהʳ: ¹² וֵֽאלָהָ֞אˢ ⁱⁿ דִּ֣י שַׁכִּ֧ןᵇ שְׁמֵ֣הᶜ תַּמָּ֗הᵈ יְמַגַּ֞רᵉ
כָּל־מֶ֤לֶךְᶠ וְעַםᵍ | דִּ֣יⁱ יִשְׁלַ֤חʰ יְדֵהּⁱ לְהַשְׁנָיָ֔הʲ לְחַבָּלָ֛הᵏ בֵּית־אֱלָהָ֥א דֵ֖ךְˡ
דִּ֣י בִירֽוּשְׁלֶ֑ם אֲנָ֤הᵐ דָרְיָ֨וֶשׁⁿ שָׂ֣מֶתᵒ טְעֵ֔םᵖ אָסְפַּ֖רְנָאᵍ יִתְעֲבִֽדʳ: פ

¹³ אֱדַ֡יִן תַּתְּנַ֞יᵃ פַּחַ֧תᵇ עֲבַֽר־נַהֲרָ֛הᶜ שְׁתַ֥ר בּוֹזְנַ֖יᵈ וּכְנָוָתְה֑וֹןᵉ לָקֳבֵ֗לᶠ דִּי־
שְׁלַ֞חᵍ דָּרְיָ֧וֶשׁⁱ מַלְכָּ֛א כְּנֵ֖מָאʲ אָסְפַּ֥רְנָאᵏ עֲבַֽדוּˡ: ¹⁴ וְשָׂבֵ֤יᵃ יְהוּדָיֵא֙ᵇ בָּנַ֣יִןᶜ
וּמַצְלְחִ֔יןᵈ בִּנְבוּאַת֙ᵉ חַגַּ֣יᶠ נְבִיָּ֔הᵍ וּזְכַרְיָ֖הʰ בַּר־עִדּ֑וֹאⁱ וּבְנ֣וֹʲ וְשַׁכְלִ֗לוּᵏ
מִן־טַ֨עַם֙ᵐ אֱלָ֣הּ יִשְׂרָאֵ֔ל וּמִטְּעֵם֙ᵐ כּ֣וֹרֶשׁⁿ וְדָרְיָ֔וֶשׁ וְאַרְתַּחְשַׁ֖שְׂתְּאᵖ
מֶ֥לֶךְ פָּרָֽסᵍ: ¹⁵ וְשֵׁיצִ֗יאᵃ בַּיְתָ֤הᵇ דְנָה֙ᶜ עַ֣ד י֣וֹםᵈ תְּלָתָ֗הᵉ לִירַ֣חᶠ אֲדָ֔רᵍ
דִּי־הִ֥יאⁱ שְׁנַת־שֵׁ֖תʲ לְמַלְכ֥וּתˡ דָּרְיָ֖וֶשׁ מַלְכָּֽאᵐ: פ
¹⁶ וַעֲבַ֣דוּᵃ בְנֵֽי־יִ֠שְׂרָאֵל כָּהֲנַיָּ֨אᶜ וְלֵוָיֵ֜אᵈ וּשְׁאָ֣רᵉ בְּנֵי־גָלוּתָ֗אᶠ חֲנֻכַּת֙ᵍ

---

11 ⁱprox dem adj ms דְּנָה *this.* ʲtG PC 3ms נסח hapax *be pulled out.* ᵏnoun ms abs אָע *timber.* ˡnoun ms בַּיִת w/ 3ms gen sx. ᵐGp ptcp ms abs זקף hapax *raised.* ⁿtG PC 3ms מחא *be impaled.* ᵒprep עַל w/ 3ms gen sx. ᵖnoun fs abs נְוָלוּ Akk lw (?) *dunghill; latrine pit.* ᵍtG PC 3ms עבד. ʳprox dem pron ms דְּנָה *this.* ˢ⁻ˢ= *on this basis, for this reason.*

12 ᵃrel pron דִּי *who, which, that.* ᵇD sc 3ms שכן *cause to dwell, settle.* ᶜnoun ms שֵׁם w/ 3ms gen sx *name.* ᵈloc adv תַּמָּה *there.* ᵉD juss 3ms מגר hapax *overthrow.* ᶠnoun ms cstr כֹּל. ᵍnoun ms abs עַם *people.* ʰG PC 3ms שלח *send.* ⁱnoun fs יַד w/ 3ms gen sx *hand.* ʲH inf שנה trans *change.* ᵏD inf חבל *destroy.* ˡdist dem adj ms דֵּךְ *that.* ᵐindep pers pron 1cs אֲנָה *I.* ⁿPN *Darius.* ᵒG sc 1cs שׂים. ᵖnoun ms abs טְעֵם *statement.* ᵍadv אָסְפַּרְנָא Pers lw *diligently, exactly.* ʳtG juss 3ms עבד.

13 ᵃPN *Tattenai.* ᵇnoun ms cstr פֶּחָה *governor.* ᶜ⁻ᶜGN *Beyond the River.* ᵈ⁻ᵈPN *Shethar-bozenai.* ᵉnoun mp כְּנָת w/ 3mp gen sx Akk lw *associate, colleague.* ᶠˡ + noun ms abs קֳבֵל *to what is in front = according to.* ᵍrel pron דִּי *that which.* ʰG sc 3ms שלח *send.* ⁱPN *Darius.* ʲadv כְּנֵמָא *thus.* ᵏadv אָסְפַּרְנָא Pers lw *diligently, exactly.* ˡG sc

3mp עבד.

14 ᵃadj mp cstr שָׂב *gray headed = elders.* ᵇnoun mp emph יְהוּדִי *Jew; Judean.* ᶜG ptcp mp abs בנה *rebuild.* ᵈH ptcp mp abs צלח *prosper.* ᵉnoun fs cstr נְבוּאָה hapax *prophesying.* ᶠPN *Haggai.* ᵍK נְבִיָּה, Q נְבִיא [so L; *BHS,* Ed אְיָּ"], both noun ms emph נְבִיא *prophet.* ʰPN *Zechariah.* ⁱnoun ms cstr II בַּר *son.* ʲPN *Iddo.* ᵏG sc 3mp בנה *rebuild.* ˡŠ sc 3mp כלל *finish.* ᵐnoun ms cstr טְעֵם *statement.* Vocalization of first is a Hebraism or a Massoretic construction. ⁿPN *Cyrus.* ᵒPN *Darius.* ᵖPN *Artaxerxes.* ᵍGN *Persia.*

15 ᵃŠ sc 3ms שיצא hapax, Akk lw *compete.* ᵇnoun ms emph בַּיִת. ᶜprox dem adj ms דְּנָה *this.* ᵈnoun ms abs יוֹם *day.* ᵉcard w/ m noun תְּלָת *three.* ᶠnoun ms cstr יְרַח *month.* ᵍMonth Name *Adar.* Here and ʲ⁻ᵏ are standard date formulæ. ʰrel pron דִּי *which, that.* ⁱindep pers pron 3fs הִיא as copula *is.* ʲnoun fs cstr I שְׁנָה *year.* ᵏcard w/ f noun שֵׁת *six.* ˡnoun fs מַלְכוּ *reign.* ᵐPN *Darius.*

16 ᵃG sc 3mp עבד. ᵇnoun mp cstr II בַּר *son.* ᶜnoun mp emph כָּהֵן *priest.* ᵈnoun mp emph לֵוִי *Levite.* ᵉnoun ms cstr שְׁאָר *rest, remainder.* ᶠnoun fs emph גָּלוּ *exile.* ᵍnoun fs cstr חֲנֻכָּה *dedication.*

בֵּית־אֱלָהָ֥א דְנָ֖ה בְּחֶדְוָֽה׃ 17 וְהַקְרִ֗בוּᵃ לַחֲנֻכַּת֮ᵇ בֵּית־אֱלָהָ֣א דְנָה֒ᶜ
תּוֹרִ֣יןᵈ מְאָ֔ה דִּכְרִ֥ין מָאתַ֖יןᵍ אִמְּרִ֣יןᵍ אַרְבַּ֣עᵢ מְאָ֑הⁱ וּצְפִירֵ֨יⁱ עִזִּ֜יןᵏ
לְחַטָּיָ֣אᵐ עַל־כָּל־יִשְׂרָאֵ֗לⁿ תְּרֵֽי־עֲשַׂר֙ᵒ לְמִנְיָ֖ןᵖ שִׁבְטֵ֥יᵠ יִשְׂרָאֵֽל׃
18 וַהֲקִ֣ימוּᵃ כָהֲנַיָּ֣אᵇ בִּפְלֻגָּתְה֗וֹןᶜ וְלֵוָיֵא֙ᵈ בְּמַחְלְקָתְה֔וֹןᵉ עַל־עֲבִידַ֥תᶠ
אֱלָהָ֖אᵍ דִּ֣יᵍ בִּירוּשְׁלֶ֑ם כִּכְתָ֖בᵸ סְפַ֥רⁱ מֹשֶֽׁהʲ׃
פ

16 ᵸprox dem adj ms דְּנָה *this.* ⁱnoun fs abs
חֶדְוָה hapax *joy.*

17 ᵃH sc 3mp קרב *offer.* ᵇnoun fs cstr חֲנֻכָּה
dedication. ᶜprox dem adj ms דְּנָה *this.*
ᵈnoun mp abs תּוֹר *bull.* ᵉcard מְאָה *hundred.* ᶠnoun mp abs דְּכַר *ram.* ᵍcard du מְאָה
two hundred. ᵸnoun mp abs אִמַּר *lamb.*
ⁱcard w/ f noun אַרְבַּע *four.* ʲnoun mp cstr
צְפִיר hapax *he goat.* ᵏnoun fp abs עֵז hapax *she goat.* ˡ⁻ˡ= *billy goat.* ᵐK לְחַטָּיָא, Q
לְחַטָּאָה, both D inf חטא *make a sin offering.* ⁿnoun ms cstr כֹּל. ᵒ⁻ᵒcard w/ f noun

תְּרֵי־עֲשַׂר *twelve.* ᵖnoun ms cstr מִנְיָן hapax
number. ᵠnoun mp cstr שְׁבַט hapax *tribe.*

18 ᵃH sc 3mp קוּם. Unexpressed plural subject is equivalent of passive. ᵇnoun mp
emph כָּהֵן *priest.* ᶜnoun fp פְּלֻגָּה w/ 3mp
gen sx hapax *division.* ᵈnoun mp emph
לֵוִי *Levite.* ᵉnoun fp מַחְלְקָה w/ 3mp gen sx
hapax *section, course, division.* ᶠnoun fs
cstr עֲבִידָה *work.* ᵍrel pron דִּי *which, that.*
ᵸnoun ms cstr כְּתָב *writing, instruction.*
ⁱnoun ms cstr סְפַר *book.* ʲPN *Moses.*

Ezra עֶזְרָא

7 ¹² אַרְתַּחְשַׁסְתְּא^a מֶ֫לֶךְ^b מַלְכַיָּא^c לְעֶזְרָא^c כָהֲנָא^d סָפַר^e דָּתָא^f דִּי־^g אֱלָהּ שְׁמַיָּא^h גְּמִירⁱ וּכְעֶ֫נֶת^j: ¹³ מִנִּי^a שִׂים^b טְעֵם^c דִּי^d כָל־מִתְנַדַּב^f בְּמַלְכוּתִי^g מִן־עַמָּה^h יִשְׂרָאֵל וְכָהֲנ֫וֹהִיⁱ וְלֵוָיֵא^j לִמְהָךְ^k לִירוּשְׁלֶם עִמָּךְ^l יְהָךְ^m: ¹⁴ כָּל־קֳבֵל^a דִּי^{cb} מִן־קֳדָם מַלְכָּא וְשִׁבְעַת^d יָעֲטֹ֫הִי^e שְׁלִיחַ^f לְבַקָּרָא^g עַל־יְהוּד^h וְלִירוּשְׁלֶם בְּדָתⁱ אֱלָהָךְ^j דִּי בִידָךְ^k: ¹⁵ וּלְהֵיבָלָה^a כְּסַף^b וּדְהַב^c דִּי־מַלְכָּא וְיָעֲטֹ֫הִי^e הִתְנַדַּ֫בוּ^f לֶאֱלָהּ יִשְׂרָאֵל דִּי בִירוּשְׁלֶם מִשְׁכְּנֵהּ^g: ¹⁶ וְכֹל^a כְּסַף^b וּדְהַב^c דִּי^d תְהַשְׁכַּח^e בְּכֹל מְדִינַת^f בָּבֶל עִם הִתְנַדָּבוּת^g עַמָּא^h וְכָהֲנַיָּאⁱ מִתְנַדְּבִין^j לְבֵית אֱלָהֲהֹם^k דִּי בִירוּשְׁלֶם^l: ¹⁷ כָּל־קֳבֵל^{cb} דְּנָה^a אָסְפַּ֫רְנָא^d תִקְנֵא^e בְּכַסְפָּא^f דְנָה^g

Ezra 7:12–26

¹² ^aPN *Artaxerxes*. ^bnoun mp emph מֶ֫לֶךְ. ^cPN *Ezra*. ^dnoun ms emph כָּהֵן *priest*. ^enoun ms cstr סָפַר *scribe*. ^fnoun fs emph דָּת Pers lw *law*. ^ggen part דִּי *of*. ^hnoun mp emph שְׁמַיִן. ⁱGp ptcp ms abs גמר hapax *perfect, completed*; as adv *completely = and so on*, that is, with all the proper greetings to be supplied (?); abbreviated greeting, assume שְׁלָם *perfect peace* (?). ^jadv כְּעֶ֫נֶת introduces body of a letter *and now*.

¹³ ^aprep מִן w/ 1cs gen sx. ^bGp sc 3ms שׂים. ^cnoun ms abs טְעֵם *statement*. ^depex conj דִּי *that*. ^enoun ms cstr כֹּל. ^ftD ptcp ms abs נדב *volunteer*. ^gnoun fs מַלְכוּ w/ 1cs gen sx *kingdom*. ^hnoun ms emph עַם *people*. ⁱnoun mp כָּהֵן w/ 3ms gen sx *priest*. ^jnoun mp emph לֵוִי *Levite*. ^kG inf הך (or הוך; BDB הלך) *go*. ^lprep עִם w/ 2ms gen sx. ^mG PC 3ms הך (or הוך; BDB הלך) *go*.

¹⁴ ^a= כְּ + לְ *according to*. ^bconj דִּי *that*. ^{c–c}= *for, since*. ^dcard cstr w/ m noun שְׁבַע *seven*. ^eG ptcp mp יעט w/ 3ms gen sx *adviser*. ^fGp ptcp ms abs שלח *sent*. ^gD inf בקר *search*. ^hGN *Judah*. ⁱnoun fs cstr דָּת Pers lw *law*.

^jnoun ms אֱלָהּ w/ 2ms gen sx. ^krel pron דִּי *which, that*. ^lnoun fs יַד w/ 2ms gen sx *hand*.

¹⁵ ^aH inf יבל *bring*. ^bnoun ms abs כְּסַף *silver*. ^cnoun ms abs דְּהַב *gold*. ^drel pron דִּי *who, which, that*. ^eG ptcp mp יעט w/ 3ms gen sx *adviser*. ^ftD sc 3mp נדב *volunteer*. ^gnoun ms מִשְׁכַּן w/ 3ms gen sx hapax *dwelling*.

¹⁶ ^anoun ms cstr כֹּל. ^bnoun ms abs כְּסַף *silver*. ^cnoun ms abs דְּהַב *gold*. ^drel pron דִּי *who, which, that*. ^eH PC 2ms שכח *find*. ^fnoun fs cstr מְדִינָה *district, province*. ^gnoun fs cstr הִתְנַדָּבוּ (= tD60 נדב) *gift, donation; contributing*. ^hnoun ms emph עַם *people*. ⁱnoun mp emph כָּהֵן *priest*. ^jtD ptcp mp abs נדב *volunteer*. ^knoun ms אֱלָהּ w/ 3mp gen sx.

¹⁷ ^a= כְּ + לְ *according to*. ^bprox dem pron ms דְּנָה *this*. ^{c–c}= *because of this, therefore*. ^dadv אָסְפַּ֫רְנָא Pers lw *competely, exactly*. ^eG PC 2ms קנה hapax *buy*. ^fnoun ms emph כְּסַף *silver*. ^gprox dem adj ms דְּנָה *this*.

תוֹרִיןʰ| דִּכְרִיןⁱ אִמְּרִיןʲ וּמִנְחָתְהוֹןᵏ וְנִסְכֵּיהוֹןˡ וּתְקָרֵבᵐ הִמּוֹⁿ עַל־
מַדְבְּחָהᵒ דִּי בֵּית אֱלָהֲכֹםᵖ דִּי בִירוּשְׁלֶם�۹: 18 וּמָהᵃ דִיᶜᵇ עֲלָיִךְᵈ וְעַל־
אֶחָיִךְᵉ יֵיטַבᶠ בִּשְׁאָרᵍ כַּסְפָּאʰ וְדַהֲבָהⁱ לְמֶעְבַּדʲ כִּרְעוּתᵏ אֱלָהֲכֹםˡ
תַּעַבְדוּןᵐ: 19 וּמָאנַיָּאᵃ דִּי־מִתְיַהֲבִיןᵇ לָךְᵈ לְפָלְחָןᵉ בֵּית אֱלָהָךְᶠ הַשְׁלֵםᵍ
קֳדָם אֱלָהּ יְרוּשְׁלֶם: 20 וּשְׁאָרᵃ חַשְׁחוּתᵇ בֵּית אֱלָהָךְᶜ דִּיᵈ יִפֶּל־לָךְᵉ⁻ᶠ
לְמִנְתַּןᵍ תִּנְתֵּןᵍ מִן־בֵּית גִּנְזֵיⁱ מַלְכָּא: 21 וּמִנִּיᵃ אֲנָהᵇ אַרְתַּחְשַׁסְתְּאᶜ
מַלְכָּא שִׂיםᵈ טְעֵםᵉ לְכֹלᶠ גִּזַּבְרַיָּאᵍ דִּיʰ בַּעֲבַר נַהֲרָהⁱ דִּי כָל־דִּי
יִשְׁאֲלֶנְכוֹןᵏ עֶזְרָאˡ כָהֲנָהᵐ סָפַרⁿ דָּתָאᵒ דִּי־אֱלָהּ שְׁמַיָּאᵖ אָסְפַּרְנָא۹
יִתְעֲבֵדʳ: 22 עַד־כְּסַףᵃ כַּכְּרִיןᵇ מְאָהᶜ וְעַד־חִנְטִיןᵈ כֹּרִיןᵉ מְאָהᶠ וְעַד־
חֲמַרᵍ בַּתִּיןᶠ מְאָהᶜ וְעַד־בַּתִּיןᵍ מְשַׁחʰ מְאָהᶜ וּמְלַחⁱ דִּי־לָאʲ⁻ᵏᵐ

17ʰnoun mp abs תּוֹר *bull.* ⁱnoun mp abs דְּכַר *ram.* ʲnoun mp abs אִמַּר *lamb.* ᵏnoun fp abs מִנְחָה w/ 3mp gen sx *grain offering.* ˡnoun mp נְסַךְ w/ 3mp gen sx hapax *libation.* ᵐD pc 2ms קרב *offer.* ⁿindep pers pron 3mp הִמּוֹ as dir obj *them.* ᵒnoun ms emph מַדְבַּח hapax *altar.* ᵖgen part דִּי *of.* ۹noun ms אֱלָהּ w/ 2mp gen sx. ʳrel pron דִּי *which, that.*

18ᵃimpers correl pron מָה *that which, whatever.* ᵇrel pron דִּי *who, which, that.* ᶜ⁻ᶜ= *whatever.* ᵈK עֲלַיִךְ, Q עֲלָךְ, both prep עַל־ w/ 2ms gen sx. ᵉK אֶחָיִךְ or אַחָיִךְ, both noun mp; Q אֲחָךְ noun ms, all w/ 2ms gen sx *brother.* ᶠG pc 3ms יטב *be good* (w/ עַל־) *to.* ᵍnoun ms cstr שְׁאָר *rest, remainder.* ʰnoun ms emph כְּסַף *silver.* ⁱnoun ms emph דְּהַב *gold.* ʲG inf עבד. ᵏnoun fs cstr רְעוּ *will, pleasure.* ˡnoun ms אֱלָהּ w/ 2mp gen sx. ᵐG pc 2mp עבד.

19ᵃnoun mp emph מָאן *vessel.* ᵇrel pron דִּי *which, that.* ᶜtG ptcp mp abs יהב. ᵈprep לְ w/ 2ms gen sx. ᵉnoun ms cstr פָּלְחָן hapax *service, ritual observance.* ᶠnoun ms אֱלָהּ w/ 2ms gen sx. ᵍH imv 2ms שלם *fully deliver.*

20ᵃnoun ms cstr שְׁאָר *rest, remainder.*

ᵇnoun fs cstr חַשְׁחוּ hapax *needs.* ᶜnoun ms אֱלָהּ w/ 2ms gen sx. ᵈrel pron דִּי *who, which, that.* ᵉG pc 3ms נפל *fall* [so BHS, Ed; L, BHL* (?) יִפֵּל]. ᶠprep לְ w/ 2ms gen sx. ᵍG inf, ʰG pc 2ms נתן *give.* ⁱnoun mp cstr גְּנַז *treasury.*

21ᵃprep מִן w/ 1cs gen sx. ᵇindep pers pron 1cs אֲנָה *I.* ᶜPN *Artaxerxes.* ᵈGp sc 3ms שׂים. ᵉnoun ms abs טְעֵם *statement.* ᶠnoun ms cstr כֹּל. ᵍnoun mp emph גְּזַבְר hapax *treasurer.* ʰrel pron דִּי *who, that.* ⁱ⁻ⁱGN *Beyond the River.* ʲepex conj דִּי *that.* ᵏG pc 3ms שאל w/ 2mp acc sx *ask.* ˡPN *Ezra.* ᵐnoun ms emph כָּהֵן *priest.* ⁿnoun ms cstr סָפַר *scribe.* ᵒnoun fs emph דָּת Pers lw *law.* ᵖgen part דִּי *of.* ۹noun mp emph שְׁמַיִן. ʳadv אָסְפַּרְנָא Pers lw *competely, exactly.* ˢtG pc 3ms עבד.

22ᵃnoun ms abs כְּסַף *silver.* ᵇnoun fp abs כַּכָּר hapax, *weight measure talent.* ᶜcard מְאָה *hundred.* ᵈnoun fp abs חִנְטָה *wheat.* ᵉnoun mp abs כֹּר hapax, *volume measure kor.* ᶠnoun ms abs חֲמַר *wine.* ᵍnoun mp abs בַּת *volume measure bath.* ʰnoun ms abs I מְשַׁח *anointing oil.* ⁱnoun ms abs מְלַח *salt.* ʲrel pron דִּי *which, that.* ᵏ⁻ᵏ= *without.*

כְּתָב^{ml}: 23 כָּל־דִּי^{a-b} מִן־טַעַם^c אֱלָהּ שְׁמַיָּא^d יִתְעֲבֵד^e אַדְרַזְדָּא^d לְבֵית
אֱלָהּ שְׁמַיָּא^d דִּי־לְמָה^{g-h} לֶהֱוֵאⁱ קְצַף^j עַל־מַלְכוּת^k מַלְכָּא וּבְנוֹהִי:
24 וּלְכֹם^a מְהוֹדְעִין^b דִּי^c כָל־^dכָּהֲנַיָּא^e וְלֵוָיֵא^f זַמָּרַיָּא^g תָרָעַיָּא^h נְתִינַיָּאⁱ
וּפָלְחֵי^j בֵּית אֱלָהָא דְנָה^k מִנְדָּה^l בְלוֹ^m וַהֲלָךְⁿ לָא שַׁלִּיט^o לְמִרְמֵא^p
עֲלֵיהֹם^q: 25 וְאַנְתְּ^a עֶזְרָא^b כְּחָכְמַת^c אֱלָהָךְ^d דִּי־בִידָךְ^f מֶנִּי^g שָׁפְטִין^h
וְדַיָּנִיןⁱ דִּי־לֶהֱוֹן^k דָּאניִן^l לְכָל־עַמָּה^m דִּיⁿ בַּעֲבַר נַהֲרָה^o לְכָל־יָדְעֵי^p
דָּתֵי^q אֱלָהָךְ^r וְדִי^r לָא יָדַע^s תְּהוֹדְעוּן^t: 26 וְכָל־דִּי־^{a-b}לָא לֶהֱוֵא^c עָבֵד^d
דָּתָא^e דִּי־אֱלָהָךְ^f וְדָתָא^g דִּי מַלְכָּא אָסְפַּרְנָא^h דִּינָהⁱ לֶהֱוֵא^j מִתְעֲבֵד^k
מִנֵּהּ^l הֵן^m לְמוֹתⁿ הֵן^m לִשְׁרֹשׁוּ^o הֵן־לַעֲנָשׁ^p נִכְסִין^q וְלֶאֱסוּרִין^r: פ

---

22 ^lnoun ms abs כְּתָב *writing, instruction*. ^{m-m}= *without limit*.

23 ^anoun ms cstr כֹּל. ^brel pron דִּי *who, which, that*. ^cnoun ms cstr טְעֵם *statement*. ^dnoun mp emph שְׁמַיִן. ^etG PC 3ms עבד. ^fadv אַדְרַזְדָּא hapax *competely, exactly*. ^gcaus conj דִּי *for*. ^himpers interr pron מָה *what*; w/ לְ *why?* ⁱG PC 3ms הוה. ^jnoun ms abs קְצַף hapax *fury, wrath*. ^knoun fs cstr מַלְכוּ *kingship, sovereignty; kingdom*. ^lnoun mp II בַּר w/ 3ms gen sx *son*.

24 ^aprep לְ w/ 2mp gen sx. ^bH ptcp mp abs ידע. ^cepex conj דִּי *that*. ^dnoun ms cstr כֹּל. ^enoun mp emph כָּהֵן *priest*. ^fnoun mp emph לֵוִי *Levite*. ^gnoun mp emph זַמָּר hapax *singer*. ^hnoun mp emph תָּרָע hapax *gatekeeper, doorkeeper*. ⁱnoun mp emph נָתִין hapax *temple slave*. ^jG ptcp mp cstr פלח *servant*. ^kprox dem adj ms דְּנָה *this*. ^lnoun fs abs מִדָּה Akk lw *tribute, tax*. ^mnoun ms abs בְּלוֹ Akk lw *tax paid in kind, produce tax*. ⁿnoun ms abs הֲלָךְ Akk lw *field or produce tax*. ^oadj ms abs שַׁלִּיט (w/ לְ + inf) *lawful, permitted*. ^pG inf רמה *throw = impose*. ^qprep עַל w/ 3mp gen sx.

25 ^aindep pers pron 2ms אַנְתְּ *you*. ^bPN *Ezra*. ^cnoun fs cstr חָכְמָה *wisdom*. ^dnoun ms אֱלָהּ w/ 2ms gen sx. ^erel pron דִּי *who, which, that*. ^fnoun fs יַד w/ 2ms gen sx *hand*. ^gD imv 2ms מנה *appoint*. ^hG ptcp mp abs שפט hapax *magistrate, judge*. ⁱnoun mp abs דִּין hapax *judge*. ^jrel pron דִּי *who, which, that*. ^kG PC 3mp הוה. ^lK דָּאנִין, Q דָּאיְנִין [Ed דָּיְנִין], both G ptcp mp abs דין hapax *make a judgement, judge*. ^mnoun ms cstr כֹּל. ⁿnoun ms emph עַם *people*. ^{o-o}GN *Beyond the River*. ^pG ptcp mp cstr ידע. ^qnoun fp cstr דָּת Pers lw *law*. ^rnoun ms אֱלָהּ w/ 2ms gen sx. ^sG ptcp ms abs ידע, ^tH PC 2mp ידע.

26 ^anoun ms cstr כֹּל. ^brel pron דִּי *who, which, that*. ^cG PC 3ms הוה. ^dG ptcp ms abs עבד. ^enoun fs emph דָּת Pers lw *law*. ^fgen part דִּי *of*. ^gnoun ms אֱלָהּ w/ 2ms gen sx. ^hadv אָסְפַּרְנָא Pers lw *competely, exactly*. ⁱnoun ms emph דִּין *judgment*. ^jG juss 3ms הוה. ^ktG ptcp ms abs עבד. ^lprep מִן w/ 3ms gen sx. ^mhypoth conj הֵן *if, whether*. ⁿnoun ms abs מוֹת hapax *death*. ^oK לִשְׁרֹשׁוּ noun ms abs, Q שְׁרֹשִׁי noun fs abs hapax *rooting out = banishment*. ^pnoun ms cstr עֲנָשׁ hapax *confiscation*. ^qnoun mp abs נְכַס Sum lw *property, wealth*. ^rnoun mp abs אֱסוּר *fetters = imprisonment*.

Vocabulary and Morphology Lists

FREQUENCY LISTS

LIST #1: VOCABULARY OCCURING TWO TIMES OR MORE

	WORD	GLOSS(ES)	NOTES	POS	FREQ.
1	וְ	*and, but*		conj	731
		and, but		disj	
2	לְ	*to, for, belonging to*		prep	378
3	דִּי	*who, which, that*		pron	162 (332)
		that, so that; for, because; when		conj	101 (332)
		of		part	69 (332)
4	בְּ	*in, into; by, through, with*		prep	226
5	מֶלֶךְ	*king*		noun	180
6	מִן־	*from, away from, out of, some of, because of; than*		prep	119
		from, away from, out of, some of, because of; than		adv	
7	עַל־	*on, upon, over, concerning, about, against; to, toward*		prep	104
8	אֱלָהּ	*God; god, deity*		noun	95
9	לָא	*no, not*		part	82
10	כֹּל	*all, each, every, the whole, the entirety*		noun	80
11	אמר	(G) *say; order*		verb	71
12	הוה	(G) *be, become, exist; occur, happen*		verb	71
13	כְּ	*like, as; about, approximately; according to, corresponding with;* conj (w/ inf) *as soon as*		prep	63
14	דְּנָה	*this*		pron	35 (58)
		this		adj	23 (58)
15	אֱדַיִן	*then*		conj	57
		then		adv	
16	מַלְכוּ	*kingship, sovereignty; reign; kingdom, realm*		noun	56
17	דָּנִיֵּאל	*Daniel*		PN	52
18	ידע	(G) *know, learn; understand;* (H) *make known, communicate*		verb	47
19	בַּיִת	*house; palace; temple*		noun	45

	WORD	GLOSS(ES)	NOTES	POS	FREQ.
20	קֳדָם	before, in the presence of		prep	42
21	שְׁמַיִן	sky, heaven		noun	37
22	עַד־	as far as, until, up to; during, within		prep	35
		until		conj	
23	קום	(G) arise, get up; be established, endure; (H) raise, erect; found, establish; appoint; (Hp) be set up, erected; (D) set up, erect		verb	35
24	פְּשַׁר	interpretation		noun	33
25	קֳבֵל	that which is in front		noun	32
		facing, opposite, corresponding to		prep	
		because		conj	
26	חזה	(G) see, perceive; (Gp ptcp) proper, customary		verb	31
27	נְבוּכַדְנֶצַּר	Nebuchadnezzar		PN	31
28	טְעֵם	good taste, sophistication, tact; statement; command; advice, report		noun	30
29	ענה I	(G) answer, reply; begin to speak		verb	30
30	יהב	(G) give; (tG) be given		verb	28
31	עבד	(G) do, make; (tG) be done; be turned into		verb	28
32	יְרוּשְׁלֶם	Jerusalem		GN	26
33	שׂים	(G) put, place, lay; (tG) be put; be turned into		verb	26
34	אֱנָשׁ	individual *person, human being*; coll *people, humanity*		noun	25
35	בָּבֶל	Babylon		GN	25
36	מִלָּה	word [15x]; prophetic *word* [4x]; *thing* [3x]; *matter* [2x]		noun	24
37	דְּהַב	gold		noun	23
38	רַב	great [19x]; *chief* [3x]; *many* [1x]		adj	23
39	בנה	(G) rebuild [10x]; *(re)build* [5x]; (tG) *be rebuilt* [5x]; (tG ptcp) *being rebuilt* [2x]		verb	22
40	כְּל־ (כְּ + לְ =)	according to		comp prep	22
41	עִם	with		prep	22
42	אֲרַע	earth, land [20x]; prep *beneath, inferior* [1x]	Always emphatic singular (אַרְעָא).	noun	21
43	גְּבַר	man, person		noun	21
44	חֵלֶם	dream		noun	21

	WORD	GLOSS(ES)	NOTES	POS	FREQ.
45	שְׁנָה	(H) trans *change* [6x]; (G) *be different* [4x]; intrans *change* [2x]; (w/ 3ms suffix) intrans *changed on him* [1x]; (G ptcp) intrans *changed* [1x]; (tD) intrans *change* [2x]; *be changed* [2x]; (D) trans *change* [1x]; trans *change = violate* [1x]; (Dp) *be different* [1x]		verb	21
46	חֵיוָה	*animal, beast*		noun	20
47	עָלַם	*eternity* [18x]; *antiquity* [2x]		noun	20
48	II בַּר	*son*		noun	19
49	פַּרְזֶל	*iron*		noun	19
50	נוּר	*fire*		noun	18
51	אִיתַי	*there is* [11x]; (w/ 2mp suffix) *you are?* [2x]; (w/ 2ms suffix) *are you?* [1x]; (w/ 1cp suffix) *we are* [1x]; *it is* [1x]; *there are* [1x]		part	17
52	יַד	*hand*		noun	17
53	צְלֵם	*statue* [16x]; *image* [1x]		noun	17
54	שְׁכַח	(tG) *be found* [9x]; (H) *find* [8x]		verb	17
55	אֲנָה	*I*		pron	16
56	אתה	(G) *come* [7x]; (H) *bring* [7x]; (Hp) *be brought* [2x]		verb	16
57	הֵן	*if, whether*		conj	16
58	יוֹם	*day*		noun	16
59	אַנְתְּ	*you*		pron	15
60	דָּרְיָוֶשׁ	*Darius*		PN	15
61	הוּא	*he* [8x]; as copula *are* [3x]; as copula *is* [2x]; *he, it* [1x]		pron	14 (15)
		that		adj	1 (15)
62	חוה	(H) *show, make known, declare* [11x]; (D) *show, make known, declare* [4x]		verb	15
63	עַם	*people*		noun	15
64	אִלֵּךְ	*those*		adj	14
65	דָּת	*law* [11x]; *decree* [2x]; *verdict* [1x]		noun	14
66	חַד	*one* [7x]; *one, a* [5x]; *one, as multiplicative times* [1x]; *one, (w/ כְּ) as one, together* [1x]		num	14
67	חַכִּים	*wise*	Always plural.	adj	14
68	מֵישַׁךְ	*Meshach*		PN	14
69	עֲבֵד נְגוֹ	*Abednego*		PN	14
70	עֲבַר נַהֲרָה	*Beyond the River*		GN	14
71	II עלל	(G) *enter* [7x]; (H) *bring* [5x]; (Hp) *be brought* [2x]		verb	14

	WORD	GLOSS(ES)	NOTES	POS	FREQ.
72	קֶרֶן	*horn*		noun	14
73	רֵאשׁ	*head*		noun	14
74	שַׁדְרַךְ	*Shadrach*		PN	14
75	שלח	(G) *send* [12x]; (Gp) *sent* [2x]		verb	14
76	שָׁלְטָן	*empire; dominion*		noun	14
77	גּוֹ	*midst*		noun	13
78	כְּסַף	*silver*		noun	13
79	כְּעַן	introduces new idea *now*		conj	10 (13)
		now [2x]; introduces new idea *now* [1x]		adv	3 (13)
80	עִדָּן	indicates time in general or a length of time such as a year *season, time* [9x]; *time* [4x]		noun	13
81	קַדִּישׁ	*holy*		adj	13
82	שַׂגִּיא	*great* [3x]; *very* [2x]; *abundant* [2x]; *much* [1x]; *many* [1x]		adj	9 (13)
		greatly [2x]; *very* [2x]		adv	4 (13)
83	בעה	(G) *seek, request* [11x]; (D) *seek* [1x]		verb	12
84	הֵיכַל	*palace* [6x]; *temple* [5x]; *temple, sanctuary* [1x]		noun	12
85	חֱזוּ	*vision* [11x]; *appearance* [1x]		noun	12
86	יכל	(G) *be able* [11x]; *be more able, overpower* [1x]		verb	12
87	כְּתָב	*writing, instruction*		noun	12
88	מָה	*that which, what* [8x]; (w/ לְ) *why? for what purpose?* [2x]; *whatever* [1x]; (w/ לְ) *concerning what* [1x]		pron	12
89	רמה	(tG) *be thrown* [5x]; (G) *throw* [4x]; *throw = impose* [1x]; (Gp) *be thrown* [1x]; *be placed* [1x]		verb	12
90	שְׁאָר	*rest, remainder*		noun	12
91	שֵׁם	*name*		noun	12
92	זְמַן	*time, set time, appointment, moment, date, holiday*		noun	11
93	מְדִינָה	*district, province*		noun	11
94	נפל	(G) *fall*		verb	11
95	נפק	(H) *bring out* [5x]; (G) *go out* [4x]; *go out = be issued* [1x]; *come out* [1x]		verb	11
96	סגד	(G) *prostrate oneself, bow down to the ground*		verb	11
97	קרא	(G) *read* [5x]; *be read* [2x]; *cry out, shout* [3x]; (tD) *be called* [1x]		verb	11
98	רוּחַ	*spirit* [8x]; *wind* [3x]		noun	11
99	תְּלָת	*three*		num	11

	WORD	GLOSS(ES)	NOTES	POS	FREQ.
100	אַרְיֵה	lion	Emphatic plural 9 times out of 10 (אַרְיָוָתָא).	noun	10
101	אַתּוּן	furnace		noun	10
102	גֹּב	den		noun	10
103	דקק	(H) pulverize [9x]; (G) break [1x]		verb	10
104	יְהוּדִי	Jew; Judean	Emphatic plural 9 times out of 10 (יְהוּדָיֵא).	noun	10
105	מַן	whoever [6x]; who? [4x]		pron	10
106	עֶלְי	most high	Always emphatic singular (עִלָּאָה).	noun	10
107	פֶּחָה	governor		noun	10
108	פלח	(G) serve [9x]; (G ptcp) servant [1x]		verb	10
109	צבה	(G) desire, wish		verb	10
110	שַׁלִּיט	sovereign, powerful, mighty [6x]; ruler [1x]; lawful, permitted [1x]		adj	8 (10)
		official [1x]; sovereign [1x]		noun	2 (10)
111	אַב	father		noun	9
112	אֲחַשְׁדַּרְפַּן	satrap	Always emphatic plural (אֲחַשְׁדַּרְפְּנַיָּא).	noun	9
113	גלה	(G) reveal [3x]; (G ptcp) revealer [2x]; (Gp) be revealed [2x]; (H) deport, exile [2x]		verb	9
114	הִמּוֹ	as dir obj them [8x]; as copula are [1x]		pron	9
115	חֲסַף	clay		noun	9
116	נְחָשׁ	bronze		noun	9
117	עדה	(H) remove, depose [4x]; (G) pass away, be annulled [3x]; touch (w/ בְּ) [1x]; pass (w/ מִן) out of [1x]		verb	9
118	קרב	(G) approach [5x]; (H) offer [2x]; present [1x]; (D) offer [1x]		verb	9
119	רָזָה	secret, mystery		noun	9
120	שׁיזב	(Š) rescue		verb	9
121	שׁמע	(G) hear [8x]; (tD) hear, heed [1x]		verb	9
122	אֶבֶן	stone		noun	8

	WORD	GLOSS(ES)	NOTES	POS	FREQ.
123	אֻמָּה	nation	Emphatic plural 7 times out of 8 (אֻמַיָּא).	noun	8
124	אַרְבַּע	four		num	8
125	בהל	(D) terrify [7x]; (tD) be terrified [1x]		verb	8
126	חָכְמָה	wisdom		noun	8
127	יקד	(G) burn		verb	8
128	יִשְׂרָאֵל	Israel		GN	8
129	יַתִּיר	extraordinary, excessive		adj	5 (8)
		excessively		adv	3 (8)
130	כָּהֵן	priest		noun	8
131	כּוֹרֶשׁ	Cyrus		PN	8
132	כֵּן	thus		adv	8
133	כַּשְׂדָּי	Babylonian astrologer or sage [7x]; Chaldean [1x]		noun	8
134	כתב	(G) write [6x]; (Gp) be written [2x]		verb	8
135	מְאָה	hundred		num	8
136	מטא	(G) reach [7x]; arrive [1x]		verb	8
137	סלק	(G) come up [5x]; (H) bring up [2x]; (Hp) be brought up [1x]		verb	8
138	קִרְיָה	city		noun	8
139	רַבְרְבָנִין	lord		noun	8
140	תוב	(G) intrans return [3x]; (H) trans return [3x]; trans return (w/ suffix) to [1x]; trans give a reply (w/ suffix) to [1x]		verb	8
141	אבד	(H) kill [4x]; destroy [1x]; (G) perish [1x]; (Hp) be destroyed [1x]		verb	7
142	אזל	(G) go		verb	7
143	אכל	(G) eat		verb	7
144	אָסְפַּרְנָא	diligently		adv	7
145	אֱסָר	prohibition		noun	7
146	בֵּלְטְשַׁאצַּר	Belteshazzar		PN	7
147	בֵּלְשַׁאצַּר	Belshazzar		PN	7
148	בַּר I	field	Always emphatic singular (בָּרָא).	noun	7
149	דור	(G) dwell		verb	7
150	הִיא	she [1x]; she, it [3x]; as copula is [2x]; as copula are [1x]		pron	7

	WORD	GLOSS(ES)	NOTES	POS	FREQ.
151	חַיִל	power [4x]; power, army [3x]		noun	7
152	יְקָר	honor		noun	7
153	כלל	(Š) finish, complete [4x + 1x Qere]; (Št) be finished [2x]; (H) finish [1x, Ketiv]		verb	7
154	כְּנָת	associate, colleague	Plural and with 3mp gen sx 6 times out of 7 (כְּנָוָתְהוֹן).	noun	7
155	לְבַב	heart		noun	7
156	II לָהֵן	except		prep	4 (7)
		but [2x], unless [1x]		disj	3 (7)
157	לִשָּׁן	tongue	Emphatic plural 6 times out of 7 (לִשָּׁנַיָּא).	noun	7
158	מָאן	vessel		noun	7
159	נתן	(G) give		verb	7
160	עֲבֵד	slave, servant		noun	7
161	לָקֳבֵל	to the front of = before [4x]; to what is in front of [1x]; to what is in front = according to [1x]; in the face of = because [1x]		prep phrase	7
162	קטל	(Gp, tG, tD) be killed [4x]; (G, D) kill [3x]		verb	7
163	קָל	sound, voice		noun	7
164	רְגַל	foot		noun	7
165	רשם	(G) write [4x]; (Gp) be written [3x]		verb	7
166	שלט	(G) rule [4x]; have power (w/ בְּ) over [1x]; (H) make rule [2x]		verb	7
167	I שְׁנָה	year		noun	7
168	תּוֹר	bull	Always absolute plural (תּוֹרִין).	noun	7
169	אָחֳרִי	another		adj	5 (6)
		another		noun	1 (6)
170	אִילָן	tree	Emphatic singular 5 times out of 6 (אִילָנָא).	noun	6
171	אַרְתַּחְשַׁשְׁתְּא	Artaxerxes		PN	6
172	אָשַׁף	conjurer; exorcist		noun	6
173	בטל	(D) trans stop [4x]; (G) intrans cease(d) [2x]		verb	6

	WORD	GLOSS(ES)	NOTES	POS	FREQ.
174	גְזַר	(G ptcp) *diviner* [4x]; (tG) *cut out* [1x]; *be cut out* [1x]		verb	6
175	דָּא	*this*		pron	5 (6)
		this		adj	1 (6)
176	דחל	(Gp ptcp) *feared* [3x]; (G) *fear* [2x]; (D) *frighten* [1x]		verb	6
177	דֵּךְ	*that*		adj	6
178	דֵּךְ	*that*		adj	6
179	הֲ		3 times with *hatef patach* (הֲ), 3 times with *patach* (הַ).	part	6
180	זִיו	*splendor, brightness, radiance*		noun	6
181	חבל	(D) *destroy* [3x]; (tD) *be destroyed* [3x]		verb	6
182	חיה	(G) *live* [5x]; (H) *let live* [1x]		verb	6
183	חֲמַר	*wine*		noun	6
184	יְהוּד	*Judah*		GN	6
185	מִשְׁכַּב	*bed*		noun	6
186	נחת	(G) *descend* [2x]; (H) *deposit* [2x]; (Hp) *be brought down, deposed* [1x]; *deposited* [1x]		verb	6
187	סָפַר	*scribe*		noun	6
188	עֲבִידָה	*work* [4x]; *administration* [2x]		noun	6
189	פֻּם	*mouth*		noun	6
190	פָּרַס	*Persia*		GN	6
191	פִּתְגָם	*word, answer* [3x]; *sentence* [1x]; *report* [1x]; *edict* [1x]	Emphatic singular 5 times out of 6 (פִּתְגָמָא).	noun	6
192	צלח	(H) *prosper* [3x]; *promote* [1x]; (D) *pray* [2x]		verb	6
193	רבה	(G) *grow* [3x]; *grow, become great* [2x]; (D) *make great, promote* [1x]		verb	6
194	רְבִיעָי	*fourth*		adj	3 (6)
		fourth		noun	3 (6)
195	רַעְיוֹן	*thought*		noun	6
196	שׁאל	(G) *ask*		verb	6
197	שְׁבַע	*seven*		num	6
198	שרה	(G) *loosen* [1x]; (D) *loosen* [1x]; *begin* [1x]; (Gp) *dwell* [1x]; *untied* [1x]; (tD) *giving away* [1x]		verb	6
199	אָחֳרָן	*another*		adj	5

	WORD	GLOSS(ES)	NOTES	POS	FREQ.
200	אֲלוּ	*behold!*		interj	5
201	אִלֵּין	*these*		adj	4 (5)
		these		pron	1 (5)
202	אָע	*timber*		noun	5
203	אֲרוּ	*behold!*		interj	5
204	אַרְיוֹךְ	*Arioch*		PN	5
205	אֲתַר	*place*		noun	5
206	בקר	(D) *search* [4x]; (tD) *be searched* [1x]		verb	5
207	בְּרַם	*but* [1x]; *but, however* [4x]		disj	5
208	גְּשֵׁם	*body*		noun	5
209	דִּין	*judgment, justice* [3x]; *court* [2x]		noun	5
210	חַי I	*living*		adj	3 (5)
		living		noun	2 (5)
211	חַרְטֹם	*magician*		noun	5
212	טַל	*dew*		noun	5
213	יַצִּיב	*certain, firm* [2x]; what is *certain, correct* [1x]		adj	3 (5)
		(w/ מִן) adv *certainly*		noun	1 (5)
		certainly		adv	1 (5)
214	יתב	(G) *sit* [2x]; *dwell* [1x]; (D) *sit* [1x]; (H) *make dwell, settle* [1x]		verb	5
215	כְּדִי (כְּ + דִי)	*when*		conj	5
216	כְּנֵמָא	*thus*		adv	5
217	לֵילִי	*night*	Always emphatic singular (לֵילְיָא).	noun	5
218	מָדַי	*Media*		GN	5
219	מלל	(D) *speak*		verb	5
220	מנה	(D) *appoint* [4x]; (G) *count* [1x]		verb	5
221	סְגַן	*prefect*	Emphatic plural 4 times out of 5 (סְגְנַיָּא).	noun	5
222	סוֹף	*end*		noun	5
223	סְפַר	*book*		noun	5
224	סְרַךְ	high official *president*		noun	5
225	עַיִן	*eye*		noun	5

	WORD	GLOSS(ES)	NOTES	POS	FREQ.
226	עֲשַׂב	vegetation, plants	Emphatic singular 4 times out of 5 (עִשְׂבָּא).	noun	5
227	צבע	(tD) be drenched [3x]; be soaked [1x]; (D) drench [1x]		verb	5
228	רוּם	height	Always with 3ms gen sx (רוּמֵהּ).	noun	5
229	שָׂב	gray headed = elders		adj	5
230	שבח	(D) praise		verb	5
231	שבק	(G) leave [3x]; leave (w/ לְ) smthg alone, unencumbered [1x]; (tG) be left (w/ לְ) to [1x]		verb	5
232	שָׁעָה	hour = moment		noun	5
233	שתה	(G) drink [2x]; drink (w/ בְּ) from [3x]		verb	5
234	תְּחוֹת	under		prep	5
235	תַּקִּיף	powerful, mighty [3x]; strong [2x]		adj	5
236	תקף	(G) become strong [4x]; (D) make strong; enforce [1x]		verb	5
237	אֲלַף	thousand		num	4
238	אַמָּה	cubit	Always absolute plural (אַמִּין).	noun	4
239	אֲנַחְנָה	we		pron	4
240	אַף	also		conj	4
241	II ברך	(G, D) bless [2x]; (Gp, Dp) blessed [2x]		verb	4
242	גָּלוּ	exile	Always emphatic singular (גָּלוּתָא).	noun	4
243	דָּר	generation		noun	4
244	הַדָּבַר	companion		noun	4
245	הך	(G) go [3x]; reach [1x]		verb	4
246	זְמָר	musical instrument	Always emphatic singular (זְמָרָא).	noun	4
247	זַן	type, kind	Always construct plural (זְנֵי).	noun	4
248	חלף	(G) pass over		verb	4
249	חֲנֻכָּה	dedication	Always construct singular (חֲנֻכַּת).	noun	4
250	טרד	(G) drive away [2x]; (Gp) be driven away [2x]		verb	4
251	כהל	(G) be able		verb	4
252	כְּעֶנֶת	introduces body of a letter and now		adv	4

	WORD	GLOSS(ES)	NOTES	POS	FREQ.
253	כְּפַת	(Gp) *be tied up* [1x]; (D) *tie up* [1x]; (Dp ptcp) *tied up* [2x]		verb	4
254	לֵוִי	*Levite*	Always emphatic plural (לֵוָיֵא).	noun	4
255	מִדָּה	*tribute, tax*		noun	4
256	מְדוֹר	*dwelling*		noun	4
257	מְחָא	(G, D) *strike* [3x]; (tG) *be impaled* [1x]		verb	4
258	מִנְדַּע	*knowledge*		noun	4
259	מָרֵא	*lord*		noun	4
260	מַשְׁרוֹקִי	*pipe*	Always emphatic singular (מַשְׁרוֹקִיתָא).	noun	4
261	נְבִיא	*prophet*		noun	4
262	עֶלְיוֹן	*most high*	Always absolute plural (עֶלְיוֹנִין).	noun	4
263	עֲנַף	*bough, branches*	Always with 3ms gen sx (עַנְפּוֹהִי).	noun	4
264	עֲרַב	(Dp) *mixed* [2x]; (tD) *intermingle* [2x]		verb	4
265	עֲשַׂר	*ten*		num	4
266	פְּסַנְתֵּרִין	*psalterion*		noun	4
267	צִפַּר	*bird*	Always plural.	noun	4
268	קִיתָרֹס	*kitharos, zither*	Always absolute singular (קַתְרוֹס).	noun	4
269	רְבוּ	*greatness*		noun	4
270	רוּם	(G) *be high* [1x]; (D) *praise* [1x]; (H) *exalt* [1x]; (tD) *exalt oneself* [1x]		verb	4
271	רְחוּם	*Rehum*		PN	4
272	שְׁתַר בּוֹזְנַי	*Shethar-bozenai*		PN	4
273	שָׁלוּ	*negligence* [3x]; *negligence = blasphemy* [1x]		noun	4
274	שְׁלָם	*peace*		noun	4
275	שִׁמְשַׁי	*Shimshai*		PN	4
276	שְׁפַל	(H) *humble* [2x], *humiliate* [1x], *bring low* [1x]		verb	4
277	שִׁתִּין	*sixty*		num	4
278	תַּמָּה	*there*		adv	4
279	תַּתְּנַי	*Tattenai*		PN	4
280	אִגְּרָה	*letter*		noun	3

	WORD	GLOSS(ES)	NOTES	POS	FREQ.
281	אָזֵה	(G) *heat, stoke*		verb	3
282	אַחֲרֵי	*after*		prep	3
283	אַל	*not*		part	3
284	אמן	(H) *trust* [1x]; (Hp ptcp) *trustworthy* [2x]		verb	3
285	אִמַּר	*lamb*	Always absolute plural (אִמְּרִין).	noun	3
286	אֵנֵב	*fruit*	Always with 3ms gen sx (אִנְבֵּה).	noun	3
287	אִנּוּן	*they* [1x]; as copula *are* [1x]		pron	2 (3)
		those		adj	1 (3)
288	אֱסוּר	*band* [2x]; *fetters = imprisonment* [1x]		noun	3
289	אֶצְבַּע	*toe* [2x]; *finger* [1x]	Always plural.	noun	3
290	אַרְגְּוָן	*purple*	Always emphatic singular (אַרְגְּוָנָא).	noun	3
291	אֹשׁ	*foundation*	Always plural.	noun	3
292	אָת	*sign*	Always plural.	noun	3
293	בָּאתַר	*after*		prep	3
294	בְּלוֹ	*tax* paid in kind, *produce tax*		noun	3
295	בְּעֵל	*lord, master*		noun	3
296	בְּשַׁר	*flesh*		noun	3
297	גְּנַז	*storage* [1x]; *treasure* [1x]; *treasury* [1x]	Always plural.	noun	3
298	גַּף	*wing*	Always plural.	noun	3
299	דִּכֵּן	*that*		adj	3
300	דְּכַר	*ram*	Always absolute plural (דִּכְרִין).	noun	3
301	הדר	(D) *glorify*		verb	3
302	הֲדַר	*majesty*		noun	3
303	הלך	(D, H) *walk* [3x]		verb	3
304	הֲלָךְ	*field* or *produce tax*		noun	3
305	הִמּוֹן	as dir obj *them*		pron	3
306	המונך	*necklace, chain*	Always emphatic singular (הַמְנִיכָא).	noun	3
307	הִתְבְּהָלָה	*haste*		noun	3
308	חֲבָל	*harm*		noun	3

	WORD	GLOSS(ES)	NOTES	POS	FREQ.
309	חֲבַר	*friend, companion*	Always plural and with 3ms gen sx (חַבְרוֹהִי).	noun	3
310	חֲלָק	*portion, lot* [1x]; *portion, share* [1x]		noun	3
311	טעם	(D) *feed*		verb	3
312	יבל	(H) *bring*		verb	3
313	יעט	(G ptcp) *adviser* [2x]; (tD) *consult together* [1x]		verb	3
314	כנש	(G, tD) *assemble*		verb	3
315	כָּרְסֵא	*throne*		noun	3
316	לבש	(G) *wear* [2x]; (H) *clothe* [1x]		verb	3
317	לָהֵן I	*therefore*		conj	3
318	לְחֵנָה	*consort, concubine, prostitute*	Always plural and with suffix.	noun	3
319	מְלַח	*salt*		noun	3
320	מַתְּנָה	*gift*	Always plural.	noun	3
321	נדב	(tD) *volunteer*		verb	3
322	נְוָלוּ	*dunghill; latrine pit*	Twice as נְוָלִי.	noun	3
323	נזק	(G) *come to grief* (HALOT); *be damaged* [1x]; (H) *damage* [1x]; (H ptcp) *damager* [1x]		verb	3
324	נצל	(H) *deliver*		verb	3
325	נשׂא	(G) *carry, lift* [1x]; *carry, take* [1x]; (tD) *rise up against* [1x]		verb	3
326	נִשְׁתְּוָן	*letter*	Always emphatic singular (נִשְׁתְּוָנָא).	noun	3
327	סַבְּכָא	*trigon*	Twice as שַׂבְּכָא.	noun	3
328	סוּמְפֹּנְיָה	*symphonia*		noun	3
329	עֶזְרָא	*Ezra*		PN	3
330	עִיר	*watcher*		noun	3
331	עֳפִי	*leaves* [2x]; *foliage* [1x]	Always with 3ms gen sx (עָפְיֵה).	noun	3
332	עִקַּר	*stump*		noun	3
333	עַתִּיק	*ancient*		noun	3
334	פַּרְשֶׁגֶן	*copy*		noun	3
335	צַוַּאר	*neck*		noun	3
336	קבל	(D) *receive*		verb	3

	WORD	GLOSS(ES)	NOTES	POS	FREQ.
337	קַדְמָי	*earlier* [1x]; *earliest, first* [1x]		noun	2 (3)
		earlier		adj	1 (3)
338	קְטַר	*knot* [2x]; *knot = joint* [1x]	Always plural.	noun	3
339	קְצָת	*end*		noun	3
340	רגשׁ	(H) *throng* [= *conspire* (?)]		verb	3
341	שׂגא	(G) *become great, grow* [2x]; *become big, grow* [1x]		verb	3
342	שָׂכְלְתָנוּ	*prudence, insight* [2x]; *insight* [1x]		noun	3
343	שְׂעַר	*hair*		noun	3
344	שֵׁגַל	*second-tier wife; concubine*	Always plural and with suffix.	noun	3
345	שׁוּר	*wall*	Always emphatic plural (שׁוּרַיָּא/שׁוּרַיָּה).	noun	3
346	שׁחת	(Gp ptcp) *corrupted, bad*		verb	3
347	שׁלם	(H) *complete, finish off* [1x]; *fully deliver* [1x]; (Gp) *be finished* [1x]		verb	3
348	שֵׁן	*tooth*		noun	3
349	שׁפר	(G) *be pleasant, pleasing*		verb	3
350	שְׁרֹשׁ	*root*	Always plural and with 3ms gen sx (שָׁרְשׁוֹהִי).	noun	3
351	תַּלְתָּא	*triumvir* (official of the third rank), *rank third*		noun	3
352	תְּמַהּ	*wonder*	Always plural.	noun	3
353	אֲדַרְגָּזַר	*counselor*	Always emphatic plural (אֲדַרְגָּזְרַיָּא).	noun	2
354	אַזְדָּא	*publicly known* thus *irrevocable*		adj	2
355	אֵלֶּה	*these*		pron	2
356	אֲנַף	*face*	Always plural and with 3ms gen sx (אַנְפּוֹהִי).	noun	2
357	אֲפַרְסְכָי	*official title, apharsechai-official;* or *a people, Apharsechite*	Always emphatic plural (אֲפַרְסְכָיֵא).	noun	2
358	אֲרַח	*path*	Always plural and with suffix.	noun	2
359	אַרְכָה	*lengthening, extension*		noun	2
360	אֲשַׁרְנָא	*shrine* (?), *structure* (?), *furnishings* (?)		noun	2

	WORD	GLOSS(ES)	NOTES	POS	FREQ.
361	אֶשְׁתַּדּוּר	*insurrection*		noun	2
362	בֵּין	*between*		prep	2
363	בָּעוּ	*request, prayer*		noun	2
364	בַּת	volume measure *bath*	Always absolute plural (בַּתִּין).	noun	2
365	גְּבוּרָה	*might*	Always emphatic singular (גְּבוּרְתָא).	noun	2
366	גִּדְבַר	*treasurer*	Always emphatic plural (גִּדְבְרַיָּא).	noun	2
367	גדד	(G) *chop down*		verb	2
368	גְּזֵרָה	*decree*	Always construct singular (גְּזֵרַת).	noun	2
369	גְּלָל	*huge; hewn*		adj	2
370	דִּבְרָה	*matter*	Always construct singular (דִּבְרַת).	noun	2
371	דִּכְרָן	*records*	Always emphatic plural (דִּכְרָנַיָּא).	noun	2
372	דמה	(G) *resemble*		verb	2
373	דֶּתֶא	*grass*	Always emphatic singular (דִּתְאָא).	noun	2
374	דְּתָבַר	*judge*	Always emphatic plural (דְּתָבְרַיָּא).	noun	2
375	הַדָּם	*limb*	Always absolute plural (הַדָּמִין).	noun	2
376	זוע	(G) *tremble*		verb	2
377	זְכַרְיָה	*Zechariah*		PN	2
378	חַגַּי	*Haggai*		PN	2
379	חַיִּין	*life*	Always plural.	noun	2
380	חֲזוֹת	*visibleness, ability to be seen* (?); *branches, canopy of a tree* (?)	Always with 3ms gen sx (חֲזוֹתֵהּ).	noun	2
381	חֱמָה	*fury*		noun	2
382	חִנְטָה	*wheat*	Always absolute plural (חִנְטִין).	noun	2
383	חנן	(G) *show mercy, grace* [1x]; (tD) *seek mercy, grace* [1x]		verb	2
384	חסן	(H) *possess*		verb	2
385	חֵסֶן	*power, might*		noun	2

	WORD	GLOSS(ES)	NOTES	POS	FREQ.
386	חֲצַף	(H) *be harsh*		verb	2
387	טָב	*good*		adj	2
388	טוּר	*mountain*		noun	2
389	טִין	*unfired pottery*	Always emphatic singular (טִינָא).	noun	2
390	טְפַר	*nail* [1x]; *claw* [1x]		noun	2
391	ידה	(H) *give thanks*		verb	2
392	יַם	*sea*	Always emphatic singular (יַמָּא).	noun	2
393	יַקִּיר	*difficult*		adj	1 (2)
		noble		noun	1 (2)
394	יְרַח	*month*		noun	2
395	כְּתַל	*wall*		noun	2
396	לְבוּשׁ	*clothing*		noun	2
397	מֵאמַר	*word, command*		noun	2
398	מָזוֹן	*food*		noun	2
399	מלא	(G) *fill* [1x]; (tG) *be filled* [1x]		verb	2
400	מַלְאַךְ	*angel*	Always singular with 3ms gen sx (מַלְאֲכֵה).	noun	2
401	מַלְכָּה	*queen*	Always emphatic singular (מַלְכְּתָא).	noun	2
402	מְנֵא	Sum. lw, weight measure *mina*, or Gp ptcp ms מנה *counted*; *MENE*		noun	2
403	מִנְחָה	*grain offering*		noun	2
404	מָרַד	*rebellious*		noun	2
405	מְשַׁח I	*anointing oil*		noun	2
406	נִבְזְבָּה	*present, reward*		noun	2
407	נִדְבָּךְ	*course, layer*		noun	2
408	נַהִירוּ	*enlightenment*		noun	2
409	נטל	(G) *lift* [1x]; (Gp) *be lifted* [1x]		verb	2
410	נִיחוֹחַ	*soothing sacrifice; incense offering*	Always absolute plural (נִיחוֹחִין).	noun	2
411	נְכַס	*property, wealth*	Always plural.	noun	2
412	נְשַׁר	*eagle*		noun	2

	WORD	GLOSS(ES)	NOTES	POS	FREQ.
413	נִפְקָה	*expenses*	Always emphatic singular (נִפְקְתָא).	noun	2
414	סוּף	(G) *be fulfilled* [1x]; (H) *bring to an end, annihilate* [1x]		verb	2
415	סַרְבָּל	*trousers* (?); *coat* (?)	Always plural and with 3mp gen sx (סַרְבָּלֵיהוֹן).	noun	2
416	עִדּוֹא	*Iddo*		PN	2
417	עוֹף	*bird*		noun	2
418	עִזְקָה	*signet ring*		noun	2
419	עִלָּה	*cause, pretext*		noun	2
420	פַּס	*palm*		noun	2
421	פְּרֵס	*volume measure peres, weight measure one-half a mina; one-half shekel*		noun	2
422	פשׁר	(G, D) *interpret*		verb	2
423	פתח	(Gp) *be opened*		verb	2
424	פְּתָי	*width*	Always singular with 3ms gen sx (פְּתָיֵהּ).	noun	2
425	צַד	*concerning*		noun	2
426	קַדְמָה	*earlier time*		noun	2
427	קְיָם	*statute*		noun	2
428	קַיָּם	*enduring, established*		adj	2
429	קְרַץ	*bits*	Always plural and with suffix.	noun	2
430	קְשֹׁט	*truth*		noun	2
431	רִבּוֹ	*myriad, 10,000*	Once as רִבּוֹ (ms), once as רִבְבָן (fp).	num	2
432	רֵו	*appearance*	Always singular with 3ms gen sx (רֵוֵהּ).	noun	2
433	רְעוּ	*will, pleasure*	Always construct singular (רְעוּת).	noun	2
434	רעע	(G, D) *crush*		verb	2
435	רפס	(G) *trample*		verb	2
436	שְׁבִיב	*flame*		noun	2
437	שׁוה	(Gp) *become like* [1x, Ketiv]; (D) *make the same as* [1x, Qere]; (tD) *be turned into* [1x]		verb	2

	WORD	GLOSS(ES)	NOTES	POS	FREQ.
438	שְׁכַן	(G) *dwell* [1x]; (D) *cause to dwell, settle* [1x]		verb	2
439	שִׁלְטוֹן	*official*	Always construct plural (שִׁלְטֹנֵי).	noun	2
440	שָׁמְרָיִן	*Samaria*		GN	2
441	שַׁפִּיר	*beautiful*		adj	2
442	שֵׁשְׁבַּצַּר	*Sheshbazzar*		PN	2
443	שֵׁת	*six*		num	2
444	תְּדִיר	as adv *continually*	Always emphatic singular (תְּדִירָא).	noun	2
445	תְּלָתִין	*thirty*		num	2
446	תְּקֵל	weight measure *shekel*, or pun on תקל Gp ptcp ms תְּקִיל *weighed*		noun	2
447	תְּרֵין	*two*	Always תַּרְתֵּין.	num	2
448	תְּרֵי־עֲשַׂר	*twelve*		num	2
449	תְּרַע	*door, gate* [1x]; *door, opening* [1x]		noun	2
450	תִּפְתָּי	*magistrate*	Always emphatic plural (תִּפְתָּיֵא).	noun	2

LIST #2: *HAPAX LEGOMENA*

	LEX. FORM	GLOSS(ES)	ATT. FORM	PARSING	VERSE
1	אִדַּר	*threshing floor*	אִדְּרֵי־	noun mp cstr	Dan 2:35
2	אַדְרַזְדָּא	*diligently*	אַדְרַזְדָּא	adv	Ezra 7:23
3	אֶדְרָע	*arm* = *by force*	בְּאֶדְרָע	noun fs abs	Ezra 4:23
4	אַח	*brother*	אֶחָךְ	noun ms w/ 2ms gen sx	Ezra 7:18
5	אֲחִידָה	*riddle*	אֲחִידָן	noun fp abs	Dan 5:12
6	אַחְמְתָא	*Ecbatana*	בְּאַחְמְתָא	GN	Ezra 6:2
7	אַחֲרִי	*end*	בְּאַחֲרִית	noun fs cstr	Dan 2:28
8	אָחֳרֵין	*at last*	אָחֳרֵין	adv	Dan 4:5
9	אֵימְתָן	*terrible*	וְאֵימְתָנִי	adj fs abs	Dan 7:7
10	אֵל	*these*	אֵל	prox dem adj cp	Ezra 5:15

	LEX. FORM	GLOSS(ES)	ATT. FORM	PARSING	VERSE
11	אִנִּין	as copula *are*	אִנִּין	prox dem pron 3fp	Dan 7:17
12	אנס	*oppress, bother*	אָנֵס	G ptcp ms abs	Dan 4:6
13	אַנְתּוּן	*you*	אַנְתּוּן	indep pers pron 2mp	Dan 2:8
14	אָסְנַפַּר	*Osnappar* unidentified Assyrian king	אָסְנַפַּר	PN	Ezra 4:10
15	אֲפָרְסָי	*Apharsite* unknown GN	אֲפָרְסָיֵא	noun mp emph	Ezra 4:9
16	אֲפַרְסַתְכָי	(1) *Apharsatechite* or Pers. lw [three possible Pers. words]; (2) *ambassador*; (3) *top official*; (4) *royal ambassador*	וַאֲפַרְסַתְכָיֵא	noun mp emph	Ezra 4:9
17	אַפְּתֹם	*surely* (?), *certainly* (?), *finally* (?)	וְאַפְּתֹם	adv	Ezra 4:13
18	אֲרִיךְ	*worthy of an Aryan,* i.e., *proper, fitting*	אֲרִיךְ	adj ms abs	Ezra 4:14
19	אַרְכֻבָּא	*knee*	וְאַרְכֻבָּתֵהּ	noun fp w/ 3ms gen sx	Dan 5:6
20	אַרְכְּוָי	*Urukite*	אַרְכְּוָיֵא	noun mp emph	Ezra 4:9
21	אֲרָמִי	*Aramaic*	אֲרָמִית	adj fs abs	Dan 2:4
22	אֲרְעִי	*bottom*	לְאַרְעִית	noun fs cstr	Dan 6:25
23	אֲרַק	*earth, land*	וְאַרְקָא	noun fs emph	Jer 10:11
24	אֶשָּׁא	*fire*	אֶשָּׁא	noun fs abs	Dan 7:11
25	בְּאִישׁ	*bad, evil*	וּבְאִישְׁתָּא	noun fs emph	Ezra 4:12
26	באש	*be bad, evil to* (w/ עַל־)	בְּאֵשׁ	G sc 3ms	Dan 6:15
27	בַּבְלָי	*Babylonians*	בָּבְלָיֵא	noun mp emph	Ezra 4:9
28	בדר	*scatter*	וּבַדַּרוּ	D imv 2mp	Dan 4:11
29	בְּהִילוּ	*haste*	בִּבְהִילוּ	noun fs abs	Ezra 4:23
30	בִּינָה	*understanding*	בִּינָה	noun fs abs	Dan 2:21
31	בִּירָה	*citadel*	בְּבִירְתָא	noun fs emph	Ezra 6:2
32	בית	*spend the night*	וּבָת	G sc 3ms	Dan 6:19
33	בָּל	*mind*	בָּל	noun ms abs	Dan 6:15
34	בלה	*harass, wear out*	יְבַלֵּא	D pc 3ms	Dan 7:25
35	בִּנְיָן	*building, structure*	בִּנְיָנָא	noun ms emph	Ezra 5:4
36	בנס	*be enraged*	בְּנַס	G sc 3ms	Dan 2:12
37	בִּקְעָה	*plain*	בְּבִקְעַת	noun fs cstr	Dan 3:1

	LEX. FORM	GLOSS(ES)	ATT. FORM	PARSING	VERSE
38	בְּרַךְ I	*kneel*	בָּרֵךְ	G ptcp ms abs	Dan 6:11
39	בְּרַךְ	*knee*	בִּרְכוֹהִי	noun fp w/ 3ms gen sx	Dan 6:11
40	גַּב	*side* (*HALOT*), *back* (NRSV, NJPS)	גַּבַּהּ	noun ms w/ 3fs gen sx	Dan 7:6
41	גְּבַר	*hero, warrior, strong man*	גִּבָּרֵי־	noun mp cstr	Dan 3:20
42	גֵּוָה	*pride*	בְּגֵוָה	noun fs abs	Dan 4:34
43	גוּח	*stir up*	מְגִיחָן	H ptcp fp abs	Dan 7:2
44	גִּזְבַּר	*treasurer*	גִּזַּבְרַיָּא	noun mp emph	Ezra 7:21
45	גִּיר	*plaster*	גִּירָא	noun ms emph	Dan 5:5
46	גַּלְגַּל	*wheel*	גַּלְגִּלּוֹהִי	noun mp w/ 3ms gen sx	Dan 7:9
47	גמר	*perfect, completed;* as adv *completely* (?)	גְּמִיר	Gp ptcp ms abs	Ezra 7:12
48	גְּרַם	*bone*	גַּרְמֵיהוֹן	noun mp w/ 3mp gen sx	Dan 6:25
49	דֹּב	*bear*	לְדֹב	noun ms abs	Dan 7:5
50	דבח	*sacrifice*	דָּבְחִין	G ptcp mp abs	Ezra 6:3
51	דְּבַח	*sacrifice*	דִּבְחִין	noun mp abs	Ezra 6:3
52	דבק	*adhere, stick together*	דָּבְקִין	G ptcp mp abs	Dan 2:43
53	דֶּהָיֵא	(Ketiv) *that is;* (Qere) *Dehaye*	דֶּהָיֵא	(K) rel pron דְּ (< דִּי) + indep pers pron 3ms; (Q) PN	Ezra 4:9
54	דּוּרָא	*Dura*	דּוּרָא	GN	Dan 3:1
55	דוּשׁ	*trample*	וּתְדוּשִׁנַּהּ	G PC 3fs w/ 3fs acc sx	Dan 7:23
56	דַּחֲוָה	*food* (?), *table* (?); *concubine* (?), *dancing girl* (?); *diversion* (?)	וְדַחֲוָן	noun fp abs	Dan 6:19
57	דִּין	*judge*	דָּאיְנִין	G ptcp mp abs	Ezra 7:25
58	דַּיָּן	*judge*	וְדַיָּנִין	noun mp abs	Ezra 7:25
59	דִּינָיֵא	*Dinaite*	דִּינָיֵא	noun mp emph	Ezra 4:9
60	דִּכְרוֹן	*record, memorandum*	דִּכְרוֹנָה	noun ms emph	Ezra 6:2
61	דלק	*be on fire*	דָּלִק	G ptcp ms abs	Dan 7:9
62	דְּרָע	*arm*	וּדְרָעוֹהִי	noun fp w/ 3ms gen sx	Dan 2:32

	LEX. FORM	GLOSS(ES)	ATT. FORM	PARSING	VERSE
63	הָא	behold! look!	הָא־	dem part	Dan 3:25
64	הָא	behold!	הָא־	dem part	Dan 2:43
65	הַנְזָקָה	injury	לְהַנְזָקַת	noun fs cstr	Ezra 4:22
66	הַרְהֹר	imaginations, fantasies	וְהַרְהֹרִין	noun mp abs	Dan 4:2
67	הִתְנַדָּבוּ	gift, donation	הִתְנַדָּבוּת	noun fs cstr	Ezra 7:16
68	זְבַן	buy	זָבְנִין	G ptcp mp abs	Dan 2:8
69	זְהִיר	careful	וּזְהִירִין	adj mp abs	Ezra 4:22
70	זוּד	be arrogant; act presumptuously	לַהֲזָדָה	H inf	Dan 5:20
71	זוּן	be fed	יִתְּזִין	tG PC 3ms	Dan 4:9
72	זָכוּ	innocence	זָכוּ	noun fs abs	Dan 6:23
73	זְמַן	conspire	הִזְדְּמִנְתּוּן	tG SC 2mp	Dan 2:9
74	זַמָּר	singer	זַמָּרַיָּא	noun mp emph	Ezra 7:24
75	זְעֵיר	little	זְעֵירָה	adj fs abs	Dan 7:8
76	זְעִק	yell	זְעִק	G SC 3ms	Dan 6:21
77	זְקַף	raised	וּזְקִיף	Gp ptcp ms abs	Ezra 6:11
78	זְרֻבָּבֶל	Zerubbabel	זְרֻבָּבֶל	PN	Ezra 5:2
79	זְרַע	seed	בִּזְרַע	noun ms abs	Dan 2:43
80	חֲבוּלָה	wrong, harm, crime	חֲבוּלָה	noun fs abs	Dan 6:23
81	חַבְרָה	companion	חַבְרָתַהּ	noun fs w/ 3fs gen sx	Dan 7:20
82	חֲדֶה	chest	חֲדוֹהִי	noun ms w/ 3ms gen sx	Dan 2:32
83	חֶדְוָה	joy	בְּחֶדְוָה	noun fs abs	Ezra 6:16
84	חֲדַת	new	חֲדַת	adj fs cstr	Ezra 6:4
85	חוּט	repair	יַחִיטוּ	G/H PC 3mp	Ezra 4:12
86	חִוָּר	white	חִוָּר	adj ms abs	Dan 7:9
87	חֲטָא	sin, make a sin offering	לְחַטָּאָה	D inf	Ezra 6:17
88	חֲטִי	sin	וַחֲטָאָךְ	noun ms w/ 2ms gen sx	Dan 4:24
89	חֲנַנְיָה	Hananiah	וְלַחֲנַנְיָה	PN	Dan 2:17
90	חַסִּיר	lacking	חַסִּיר	adj ms abs	Dan 5:27
91	חֲרַב	be laid waste	הָחָרְבַת	Hp SC 3fs	Ezra 4:15
92	חֲרַךְ	be singed	הִתְחָרַךְ	tD SC 3ms	Dan 3:27

	LEX. FORM	GLOSS(ES)	ATT. FORM	PARSING	VERSE
93	חֲרַץ	*hip*	חַרְצֵהּ	noun ms w/ 3ms gen sx	Dan 5:6
94	חשב	*be thought of*	חֲשִׁיבִין	Gp ptcp mp abs	Dan 4:32
95	חֲשׁוֹךְ	*darkness*	בַחֲשׁוֹכָא	noun ms emph	Dan 2:22
96	חשׁח	*need*	חַשְׁחִין	G ptcp mp abs	Dan 3:16
97	חַשְׁחָה	*needed*	חַשְׁחָן	adj fp abs	Ezra 6:9
98	חַשְׁחוּ	*needs*	חַשְׁחוּת	noun fs cstr	Ezra 7:20
99	חשׁל	*smash*	וְחָשֵׁל	G ptcp ms abs	Dan 2:40
100	חתם	*seal*	וְחַתְמַהּ	G sc 3ms w/ 3fs acc sx	Dan 6:18
101	טאב	*be good to* (w/ עַל־) X = X *was glad*	טְאֵב	G sc 3ms	Dan 6:24
102	טַבָּח	*executioners, bodyguard*	טַבָּחַיָּא	noun mp emph	Dan 2:14
103	טְוָת	*fasting*	טְוָת	noun fs abs	Dan 6:19
104	טלל	*find shade*	תַּטְלֵל	H pc 3fs	Dan 4:9
105	טַרְפְּלָי	(1) *Tripolisite*; (2) *an official of the Persian chancellery of Across the River in Tripolis*; (3) a general term *class of official*	טַרְפְּלָיֵא	noun mp emph	Ezra 4:9
106	יַבֶּשָׁה	*dry land, earth*	יַבֶּשְׁתָּא	noun fs emph	Dan 2:10
107	יְגַר	*heap*	יְגַר	noun ms cstr	Gen 31:47
108	יְגַר שָׂהֲדוּתָא	*Jegar-sahadutha*	יְגַר שָׂהֲדוּתָא	GN	Gen 31:47
109	יטב	*be good* (w/ עַל־) *to*	יֵיטַב	G pc 3ms	Ezra 7:18
110	יוֹצָדָק	*Jozadak*	יוֹצָדָק	PN	Ezra 5:2
111	יסף	*be added*	הוּסְפַת	Hp sc 3fs	Dan 4:33
112	יצב	*ascertain, make certain of*	לְיַצָּבָא	D inf	Dan 7:19
113	יְקֵדָה	*burning*	לִיקֵדַת	noun fs cstr	Dan 7:11
114	יַרְכָה	*thigh*	וְיַרְכָתֵהּ	noun fp w/ 3ms gen sx	Dan 2:32
115	יֵשׁוּעַ	*Jeshua*	וְיֵשׁוּעַ	PN	Ezra 5:2
116	יָת	*whom*	יָתְהוֹן	sign def dir obj w/ 3mp gen sx	Dan 3:12
117	כִּדְבָה	*lie, false*	כִדְבָה	noun fs abs	Dan 2:9
118	כָּה	*here*	כָּה	adv	Dan 7:28
119	כַּוָּה	*window*	וְכַוִּין	noun fp abs	Dan 6:11
120	כַּכַּר	*weight measure talent*	כַּכְּרִין	noun fp abs	Ezra 7:22

	LEX. FORM	GLOSS(ES)	ATT. FORM	PARSING	VERSE
121	כַּשְׂדָּי (כַּשְׂדָּי =)	Chaldean	כַּשְׂדָּאָה	noun mp emph	Ezra 5:12
122	כֹּר	volume measure *kor*	כֹּרִין	noun mp abs	Ezra 7:22
123	כַּרְבְּלָה	cap, hat	וְכַרְבְּלָתְהוֹן	noun fp w/ 3mp gen sx	Dan 3:21
124	כרה	be distressed, troubled, disturbed	אֶתְכְּרִיַּת	tG sc 3fs	Dan 7:15
125	כָּרוֹז	herald	וְכָרוֹזָא	noun fs emph	Dan 3:4
126	כרז	herald, proclaim	וְהַכְרִזוּ	H sc 3mp	Dan 5:29
127	לֵב	heart	בְּלִבִּי	noun ms w/ 1cs gen sx	Dan 7:28
128	לְוָת	with	לְוָתָךְ	prep w/ 2ms gen sx	Ezra 4:12
129	לְחֶם	feast	לְחֶם	noun ms abs	Dan 5:1
130	מֹאזְנֵא	balance	בְמֹאזַנְיָא	noun mp emph	Dan 5:27
131	מְגִלָּה	scroll	מְגִלָּה	noun fs abs	Ezra 6:2
132	מגר	overthrow	יְמַגַּר	D juss 3ms	Ezra 6:12
133	מוֹת	death	לְמוֹת	noun ms abs	Ezra 7:26
134	מַדְבַּח	altar	מַדְבְּחָה	noun ms emph	Ezra 7:17
135	מָדַי	Mede	מָדָאָה	noun ms emph	Dan 6:1
136	מַחְלְקָה	section, course, division	בְמַחְלְקָתְהוֹן	noun fp w/ 3mp gen sx	Ezra 6:18
137	מִישָׁאֵל	Mishael	מִישָׁאֵל	PN	Dan 2:17
138	מלח	salt	מְלַחְנָא	G sc 1cp	Ezra 4:14
139	מְלַךְ	advice	מִלְכִּי	noun ms w/ 1cs gen sx	Dan 4:24
140	מִנְיָן	number	לְמִנְיָן	noun ms cstr	Ezra 6:17
141	מַעֲבָד	work, deed	מַעֲבָדוֹהִי	noun mp w/ 3ms gen sx	Dan 4:34
142	מְעֵה	belly	מְעוֹהִי	noun mp w/ 3ms gen sx	Dan 2:32
143	מֵעָל	entering = setting	מֶעָלֵי	adj mp cstr	Dan 6:15
144	מְרַד	rebellion	וּמְרַד	noun ms abs	Ezra 4:19
145	מרט	be plucked	מְרִיטוּ	Gp sc 3mp	Dan 7:4
146	מֹשֶׁה	Moses	מֹשֶׁה	PN	Ezra 6:18

	LEX. FORM	GLOSS(ES)	ATT. FORM	PARSING	VERSE
147	מִשְׁכַּן	dwelling	מִשְׁכְּנֵהּ	noun ms w/ 3ms gen sx	Ezra 7:15
148	מִשְׁתֵּא	banquet	מִשְׁתְּיָא	noun ms emph	Dan 5:10
149	נבא	prophesy	וְהִתְנַבִּי	tD sc 3ms	Ezra 5:1
150	נְבוּאָה	prophesying	בִּנְבוּאַת	noun fs cstr	Ezra 6:14
151	נגד	flow	נָגֵד	G ptcp ms abs	Dan 7:10
152	נֶבְרְשָׁה	lampstand	נֶבְרַשְׁתָּא	noun fs emph	Dan 5:5
153	נֶגֶד	toward	נֶגֶד	prep	Dan 6:11
154	נֹגַהּ	first light	בְּנָגְהָא	noun ms emph	Dan 6:20
155	נדד	flee	נַדַּת	G sc 3fs	Dan 6:19
156	נְדַן	sheath = body	נִדְנֶה	noun ms abs	Dan 7:15
157	נְהַר	river	נְהַר	noun ms cstr	Dan 7:10
158	נְהוֹר	light	וּנְהוֹרָא	noun ms emph	Dan 2:22
159	נוד	flee	תְּנֻד	G juss 3fs	Dan 4:11
160	נטר	keep	נִטְרֵת	G sc 1cs	Dan 7:28
161	נְמַר	leopard	כִּנְמַר	noun ms abs	Dan 7:6
162	נסח	be pulled out	יִתְנְסַח	tG pc 3ms	Ezra 6:11
163	נסך	pour out = offer	לְנַסָּכָה	D inf	Dan 2:46
164	נְסַךְ	libation	וְנִסְכֵּיהוֹן	noun mp w/ 3mp gen sx	Ezra 7:17
165	נִצְבָּה	hardness, strength	נִצְבְּתָא	noun fs emph	Dan 2:41
166	נצח	distinguish oneself, surpass	מִתְנַצַּח	tD ptcp ms abs	Dan 6:4
167	נְקֵא	pure	נְקֵא	adj ms abs	Dan 7:9
168	נקש	knock	נָקְשָׁן	G ptcp fp abs	Dan 5:6
169	נְשִׁין	wives	וּנְשֵׁיהוֹן	noun fp w/ 3mp gen sx	Dan 6:25
170	נִשְׁמָה	breath	נִשְׁמְתָךְ	noun fs w/ 2ms gen sx	Dan 5:23
171	נְתִין	temple slave	נְתִינַיָּא	noun mp emph	Ezra 7:24
172	נתר	strip off	אַתַּרוּ	H imv 2mp	Dan 4:11
173	סבל	maintained (?)	מְסוֹבְלִין	Dp ptcp mp abs	Ezra 6:3
174	סבר	intend	וְיִסְבַּר	G pc 3ms	Dan 7:25
175	סגר	close, shut	וּסֲגַר	G sc 3ms	Dan 6:23
176	סעד	support	מְסָעֲדִין	D ptcp mp abs	Ezra 5:2

	LEX. FORM	GLOSS(ES)	ATT. FORM	PARSING	VERSE
177	I סְתַר	hidden	וּמְסַתְּרָתָא	Dp ptcp fp emph	Dan 2:22
178	II סְתַר	destroy	סַתְרֵהּ	G sc 3ms w/ 3ms acc sx	Ezra 5:12
179	עוֹד	still	עוֹד	adv	Dan 4:28
180	עֲוָיָה	iniquity	וַעֲוָיָתָךְ	noun fp w/ 2ms gen sx	Dan 4:24
181	עוּר	chaff	כְּעוּר	noun ms abs	Dan 2:35
182	עֵז	she goat	עִזִּין	noun fp abs	Ezra 6:17
183	עֲזַרְיָה	Azariah	וַעֲזַרְיָה	PN	Dan 2:17
184	עֵטָה	counsel	עֵטָא	noun fs abs	Dan 2:14
185	עֵלָּא	over	וְעֵלָּא	prep	Dan 6:3
186	עֲלָוָה	burnt offering	לַעֲלָוָן	noun fp abs	Ezra 6:9
187	עִלִּי	upstairs room	בְּעִלִּיתֵהּ	noun fs w/ 3ms gen sx	Dan 6:11
188	עֵלְמָי	Elamites	עֵלְמָיֵא	noun mp emph	Ezra 4:9
189	עֲלַע	rib	עִלְעִין	noun fp abs	Dan 7:5
190	עַמִּיק	deep	עַמִּיקָתָא	adj fp emph	Dan 2:22
191	עֲמַר	wool	כַּעֲמַר	noun ms abs	Dan 7:9
192	עֲנֵה	poor, miserable	עָנֵיִן	adj mp abs	Dan 4:24
193	עֲנָן	cloud	עֲנָנֵי	noun mp cstr	Dan 7:13
194	עֲנָשׁ	confiscation	לַעֲנָשׁ	noun ms cstr	Ezra 7:26
195	עֲצִיב	anxious (?), sad (?)	עֲצִיב	adj ms abs	Dan 6:21
196	עקר	be ripped out	אֶתְעֲקַרָה	tG sc 3fp	Dan 7:8
197	עָר	adversary	לְעָרָךְ	noun ms w/ 2ms gen sx	Dan 4:16
198	עֲרָד	wild donkey	עֲרָדַיָּא	noun mp emph	Dan 5:21
199	עַרְוָה	nakedness	וְעַרְוַת	noun fs cstr	Ezra 4:14
200	עֶשְׂרִין	twenty	וְעֶשְׂרִין	num	Dan 6:2
201	עשׁת	intend active sense	עֲשִׁית	Gp ptcp ms abs	Dan 6:4
202	עֲתִיד	ready	עֲתִידִין	adj mp abs	Dan 3:15
203	פֶּחָר	potter	פֶּחָר	noun ms abs	Dan 2:41
204	פטישׁ	garment; shirt (?); trousers (?)	פַּטְּשֵׁיהוֹן	noun mp w/ 3mp gen sx	Dan 3:21
205	פלג	divided	פְּלִיגָה	Gp ptcp fs abs	Dan 2:41

	LEX. FORM	GLOSS(ES)	ATT. FORM	PARSING	VERSE
206	פְּלַג	*half*	וּפְלַג	noun ms cstr	Dan 7:25
207	פְּלֻגָּה	*division*	בִּפְלֻגָּתְהוֹן	noun fp w/ 3mp gen sx	Ezra 6:18
208	פֻּלְחָן	*service, ritual observance*	לְפָלְחָן	noun ms cstr	Ezra 7:19
209	פרס	*be divided*	פְּרִיסַת	Gp sc 3fs	Dan 5:28
210	פַּרְסִי	*Persian*	פָּרְסָאָה	noun ms emph	Dan 6:29
211	פרק	*wipe away; ransom*	פְּרֻק	G imv 2ms	Dan 4:24
212	פרש	*separated, made distinct; translated; explained*	מְפָרַשׁ	Dp ptcp ms abs	Ezra 4:18
213	צְבוּ	*thing, matter*	צְבוּ	noun fs abs	Dan 6:18
214	צְדָא	*truth; true*	הַצְדָא	adv w/ interr ה	Dan 3:14
215	צִדְקָה	*righteousness, charity*	בְּצִדְקָה	noun fs abs	Dan 4:24
216	צְפִיר	*he goat*	וּצְפִירֵי	noun mp cstr	Ezra 6:17
217	קַיְט	*summer*	קַיְט	noun ms abs	Dan 2:35
218	קנה	*buy*	תִקְנֵא	G pc 2ms	Ezra 7:17
219	קצף	*be furious*	וּקְצַף	G sc 3ms	Dan 2:12
220	קְצַף	*fury, wrath*	קְצַף	noun ms abs	Ezra 7:23
221	קצץ	*cut off, lop off*	וְקַצִּצוּ	D imv 2mp	Dan 4:11
222	קְרָב	*war*	קְרָב	noun ms abs	Dan 7:21
223	רְבוּ	*greatness*	וּרְבוּתָא	noun fs emph	Dan 7:27
224	רגז	*enrage*	הַרְגִּזוּ	H sc 3mp	Ezra 5:12
225	רְגַז	*rage*	בִּרְגַז	noun ms abs	Dan 3:13
226	רַחִיק	*far away*	רַחִיקִין	adj mp abs	Ezra 6:6
227	רַחֲמִין	*compassion*	וְרַחֲמִין	noun mp abs	Dan 2:18
228	רחץ	*trust (w/ עַל־) in*	הִתְרְחִצוּ	tG sc 3mp	Dan 3:28
229	רֵיחַ	*smell, odor*	וְרֵיחַ	noun ms cstr	Dan 3:27
230	רַעֲנַן	*flourishing, happy*	וְרַעֲנַן	adj ms abs	Dan 4:1
231	שַׂבְּכָא	*trigon*	שַׂבְּכָא	noun fs abs	Dan 3:7
232	שָׂהֲדוּ	*witness, testimony*	שָׂהֲדוּתָא	noun fs emph	Gen 31:47
233	שְׂטַר	*side*	וְלִשְׂטַר־	noun ms abs	Dan 7:5
234	שׂכל	*contemplate*	מִשְׂתַּכַּל	tD ptcp ms abs	Dan 7:8
235	שׂנא	*hater, enemy*	לְשָׂנְאָךְ	G ptcp ms w/ 2ms acc sx	Dan 4:16
236	שְׁאֵלָה	*decision*	שְׁאֵלְתָא	noun fs emph	Dan 4:14
237	שְׁאַלְתִּיאֵל	*Shealtiel*	שְׁאַלְתִּיאֵל	PN	Ezra 5:2

	LEX. FORM	GLOSS(ES)	ATT. FORM	PARSING	VERSE
238	שְׁבַט	tribe	שִׁבְטֵי	noun mp cstr	Ezra 6:17
239	שבש	be perplexed	מִשְׁתַּבְּשִׁין	tD ptcp mp abs	Dan 5:9
240	שדר	exert, make every effort	מִשְׁתַּדַּר	tD ptcp ms abs	Dan 6:15
241	שׁוּשַׁנְכִי	Susaite	שׁוּשַׁנְכָיֵא	noun mp emph	Ezra 4:9
242	שׁיצִיא	complete	וְשֵׁיצִיא	Š sc 3ms	Ezra 6:15
243	שְׁלֵא	carefree	שְׁלֵה	adj ms abs	Dan 4:1
244	שְׁלֵוָה	ease, serenity	לִשְׁלֵוְתָךְ	noun fs w/ 2ms gen sx	Dan 4:24
245	שמד	annihilate	לְהַשְׁמָדָה	H inf	Dan 7:26
246	שמם	be appalled	אֶשְׁתּוֹמַם	tD PC 1cs	Dan 4:16
247	שמש	minister, attend, serve	יְשַׁמְּשׁוּנֵּה	D PC 3mp w/ 3ms acc sx	Dan 7:10
248	שְׁמַשׁ	sun	שִׁמְשָׁא	noun ms emph	Dan 6:15
249	שנה	change	לְהַשְׁנָיָה	H inf	Dan 7:25
250	II שְׁנָה	sleep	וְשִׁנְתֵּהּ	noun fs w/ 3ms gen sx	Dan 6:19
251	שפט	judge	שָׁפְטִין	G ptcp mp abs	Ezra 7:25
252	שְׁפַל	low, lowest	וּשְׁפַל	noun ms cstr	Dan 4:14
253	שְׁפַרְפָּר	dawn	בִּשְׁפַרְפָּרָא	noun ms emph	Dan 6:20
254	שָׁק	shin, leg	שָׁקוֹהִי	noun fp w/ 3ms gen sx	Dan 2:33
255	שְׁרֹשׁוּ	rooting out = banishment	לִשְׁרֹשִׁי	noun fs abs	Ezra 7:26
256	תבר	fragile, brittle	תְּבִירָה	Gp ptcp fs abs	Dan 2:42
257	תוה	be astonished, startled, horrified	תְּוַהּ	G sc 3ms	Dan 3:24
258	תְּלַג	snow	כִּתְלַג	noun ms abs	Dan 7:9
259	תְּלִיתָי	third	תְּלִיתָאָה	adj fs abs	Dan 2:39
260	תִּנְיָן	second	תִּנְיָנָה	adj fs abs	Dan 7:5
261	תִּנְיָנוּת	second time, again	תִּנְיָנוּת	adv	Dan 2:7
262	תקל	be weighed	תְּקִילְתָּה	Gp sc 2ms	Dan 5:27
263	תקן	be reestablished	הָתְקְנַת	Hp sc 3fs	Dan 4:33
264	תְּקָף	strength, might	בִּתְקָף	noun ms cstr	Dan 4:27
265	תְּקֹף	strength	וְתָקְפָּא	noun ms emph	Dan 2:37
266	תָּרָע	gatekeeper, doorkeeper	תָּרָעַיָּא	noun mp emph	Ezra 7:24

PARTS OF SPEECH

LIST #3: VERBS

	ROOT	GLOSS(ES)	FREQ.
1	אמר	(G) *say; order*	71
2	הוה	(G) *be, become, exist; occur, happen*	71
3	ידע	(G) *know, learn; understand;* (H) *make known, communicate*	47
4	קום	(G) *arise, get up; be established, endure;* (H) *raise, erect; found, establish; appoint;* (Hp) *be set up, erected;* (D) *set up, erect*	35
5	חזה	(G) *see, perceive;* (Gp ptcp) *proper, customary*	31
6	I ענה	(G) *answer, reply; begin to speak*	30
7	יהב	(G) *give;* (tG) *be given*	28
8	עבד	(G) *do, make;* (tG) *be done; be turned into*	28
9	שים	(G) *put, place, lay;* (tG) *be put; be turned into*	26
10	בנה	(G) *rebuild* [10x]; *(re)build* [5x]; (tG) *be rebuilt* [5x]; (tG ptcp) *being rebuilt* [2x]	22
11	שנה	(H) trans *change* [6x]; (G) *be different* [4x]; intrans *change* [2x]; (w/ 3ms suffix) intrans *changed on him* [1x]; (G ptcp) intrans *changed* [1x]; (tD) intrans *change* [2x]; *be changed* [2x]; (D) trans *change* [1x]; trans *change = violate* [1x]; (Dp) *be different* [1x]	21
12	שכח	(tG) *be found* [9x]; (H) *find* [8x]	17
13	אתה	(G) *come* [7x]; (H) *bring* [7x]; (Hp) *be brought* [2x]	16
14	חוה	(H) *show, make known, declare* [11x]; (D) *show, make known, declare* [4x]	15
15	II עלל	(G) *enter* [7x]; (H) *bring* [5x]; (Hp) *be brought* [2x]	14
16	שלח	(G) *send* [12x]; (Gp) *sent* [2x]	14
17	בעה	(G) *seek, request* [11x]; (D) *seek* [1x]	12
18	יכל	(G) *be able* [11x]; *be more able, overpower* [1x]	12
19	רמה	(tG) *be thrown* [5x]; (G) *throw* [4x]; *throw = impose* [1x]; (Gp) *be thrown* [1x]; *be placed* [1x]	12
20	נפל	(G) *fall*	11

	ROOT	GLOSS(ES)	FREQ.
21	נפק	(H) *bring out* [5x]; (G) *go out* [4x]; *go out = be issued* [1x]; *come out* [1x]	11
22	סגד	(G) *prostrate oneself, bow down to the ground*	11
23	קרא	(G) *read* [5x]; *be read* [2x]; *cry out, shout* [3x]; (tD) *be called* [1x]	11
24	דקק	(H) *pulverize* [9x]; (G) *break* [1x]	10
25	פלח	(G) *serve* [9x]; (G ptcp) *servant* [1x]	10
26	צבה	(G) *desire, wish*	10
27	גלה	(G) *reveal* [3x]; (G ptcp) *revealer* [2x]; (Gp) *be revealed* [2x]; (H) *deport, exile* [2x]	9
28	עדה	(H) *remove, depose* [4x]; (G) *pass away, be annulled* [3x]; *touch* (w/ בְּ) [1x]; *pass* (w/ מִן) *out of* [1x]	9
29	קרב	(G) *approach* [5x]; (H) *offer* [2x]; *present* [1x]; (D) *offer* [1x]	9
30	שׁיזב	(Š) *rescue*	9
31	שׁמע	(G) *hear* [8x]; (tD) *hear, heed* [1x]	9
32	בהל	(D) *terrify* [7x]; (tD) *be terrified* [1x]	8
33	יקד	(G) *burn*	8
34	כתב	(G) *write* [6x]; (Gp) *be written* [2x]	8
35	מטא	(G) *reach* [7x]; *arrive* [1x]	8
36	סלק	(G) *come up* [5x]; (H) *bring up* [2x]; (Hp) *be brought up* [1x]	8
37	תוב	(G) intrans *return* [3x]; (H) trans *return* [3x]; trans *return* (w/ suffix) *to* [1x]; trans *give a reply* (w/ suffix) *to* [1x]	8
38	אבד	(H) *kill* [4x]; *destroy* [1x]; (G) *perish* [1x]; (Hp) *be destroyed* [1x]	7
39	אזל	(G) *go*	7
40	אכל	(G) *eat*	7
41	דור	(G) *dwell*	7
42	כלל	(Š) *finish, complete* [4x + 1x Qere]; (Št) *be finished* [2x]; (H) *finish* [1x, Ketiv]	7
43	נתן	(G) *give*	7
44	קטל	(Gp, tG, tD) *be killed* [4x]; (G, D) *kill* [3x]	7
45	רשׁם	(G) *write* [4x]; (Gp) *be written* [3x]	7
46	שׁלט	(G) *rule* [4x]; *have power* (w/ בְּ) *over* [1x]; (H) *make rule* [2x]	7
47	בטל	(D) trans *stop* [4x]; (G) intrans *cease(d)* [2x]	6
48	גזר	(G ptcp) *diviner* [4x]; (tG) *cut out* [1x]; *be cut out* [1x]	6
49	דחל	(Gp ptcp) *feared* [3x]; (G) *fear* [2x]; (D) *frighten* [1x]	6
50	חבל	(D) *destroy* [3x]; (tD) *be destroyed* [3x]	6
51	חיה	(G) *live* [5x]; (H) *let live* [1x]	6

	ROOT	GLOSS(ES)	FREQ.
52	נחת	(G) *descend* [2x]; (H) *deposit* [2x]; (Hp) *be brought down, deposed* [1x]; *deposited* [1x]	6
53	צלח	(H) *prosper* [3x]; *promote* [1x]; (D) *pray* [2x]	6
54	רבה	(G) *grow* [3x]; *grow, become great* [2x]; (D) *make great, promote* [1x]	6
55	שאל	(G) *ask*	6
56	שרה	(G) *loosen* [1x]; (D) *loosen* [1x]; *begin* [1x]; (Gp) *dwell* [1x]; *untied* [1x]; (tD) *giving away* [1x]	6
57	בקר	(D) *search* [4x]; (tD) *be searched* [1x]	5
58	יתב	(G) *sit* [2x]; *dwell* [1x]; (D) *sit* [1x]; (H) *make dwell, settle* [1x]	5
59	מלל	(D) *speak*	5
60	מנה	(D) *appoint* [4x]; (G) *count* [1x]	5
61	צבע	(tD) *be drenched* [3x]; *be soaked* [1x]; (D) *drench* [1x]	5
62	שבח	(D) *praise*	5
63	שבק	(G) *leave* [3x]; *leave* (w/ לְ) *smthg alone, unencumbered* [1x]; (tG) *be left* (w/ לְ) *to* [1x]	5
64	שתה	(G) *drink* [2x]; *drink* (w/ בְּ) *from* [3x]	5
65	תקף	(G) *become strong* [4x]; (D) *make strong; enforce* [1x]	5
66	II ברך	(G, D) *bless* [2x]; (Gp, Dp) *blessed* [2x]	4
67	הך	(G) *go* [3x]; *reach* [1x]	4
68	חלף	(G) *pass over*	4
69	טרד	(G) *drive away* [2x]; (Gp) *be driven away* [2x]	4
70	כהל	(G) *be able*	4
71	כפת	(Gp) *be tied up* [1x]; (D) *tie up* [1x]; (Dp ptcp) *tied up* [2x]	4
72	מחא	(G, D) *strike* [3x]; (tG) *be impaled* [1x]	4
73	ערב	(Dp) *mixed* [2x]; (tD) *intermingle* [2x]	4
74	רום	(G) *be high* [1x]; (D) *praise* [1x]; (H) *exalt* [1x]; (tD) *exalt oneself* [1x]	4
75	שפל	(H) *humble* [2x]; *humiliate* [1x]; *bring low* [1x]	4
76	אזה	(G) *heat, stoke*	3
77	אמן	(H) *trust* [1x]; (Hp ptcp) *trustworthy* [2x]	3
78	הדר	(D) *glorify*	3
79	הלך	(D, H) *walk*	3
80	טעם	(D) *feed*	3
81	יבל	(H) *bring*	3
82	יעט	(G ptcp) *adviser* [2x]; (tD) *consult together* [1x]	3

	ROOT	GLOSS(ES)	FREQ.
83	כנש	(G, tD) *assemble*	3
84	לבש	(G) *wear* [2x]; (H) *clothe* [1x]	3
85	נדב	(tD) *volunteer*	3
86	נזק	(G) *come to grief* (HALOT); *be damaged* [1x]; (H) *damage* [1x]; (H ptcp) *damager* [1x]	3
87	נצל	(H) *deliver*	3
88	נשׂא	(G) *carry, lift* [1x]; *carry, take* [1x]; (tD) *rise up against* [1x]	3
89	קבל	(D) *receive*	3
90	רגש	(H) *throng* [= *conspire* (?)]	3
91	שׂגא	(G) *become great, grow* [2x]; *become big, grow* [1x]	3
92	שחת	(Gp ptcp) *corrupted, bad*	3
93	שלם	(H) *complete, finish off* [1x]; *fully deliver* [1x]; (Gp) *be finished* [1x]	3
94	שפר	(G) *be pleasant, pleasing*	3
95	גדד	(G) *chop down*	2
96	דמה	(G) *resemble*	2
97	זוע	(G) *tremble*	2
98	חנן	(G) *show mercy, grace* [1x]; (tD) *seek mercy, grace* [1x]	2
99	חסן	(H) *possess*	2
100	חצף	(H) *be harsh*	2
101	ידה	(H) *give thanks*	2
102	מלא	(G) *fill* [1x]; (tG) *be filled* [1x]	2
103	נטל	(G) *lift* [1x]; (Gp) *be lifted* [1x]	2
104	סוף	(G) *be fulfilled* [1x]; (H) *bring to an end, annihilate* [1x]	2
105	פשר	(G, D) *interpret*	2
106	פתח	(Gp) *be opened*	2
107	רעע	(G, D) *crush*	2
108	רפס	(G) *trample*	2
109	שׁוה	(Gp) *become like* [1x, Ketiv]; (D) *make the same as* [1x, Qere]; (tD) *be turned into* [1x]	2
110	שׁכן	(G) *dwell* [1x]; (D) *cause to dwell, settle* [1x]	2
111	אנס	(G) *oppress, bother*	1
112	באש	(G) *be bad, evil to* (w/ עַל־)	1
113	בדר	(D) *scatter*	1
114	בית	(G) *spend the night*	1

	ROOT	GLOSS(ES)	FREQ.
115	בלה	(D) *harass, wear out*	1
116	בנס	(G) *be enraged*	1
117	ברך I	(G) *kneel*	1
118	גוח	(H) *stir up*	1
119	גמר	(Gp ptcp) *perfect, completed*; as adv *completely* (?)	1
120	דבח	(G) *sacrifice*	1
121	דבק	(G) *adhere, stick together*	1
122	דוש	(G) *trample*	1
123	דין	(G) *judge*	1
124	דלק	(G) *be on fire*	1
125	זבן	(G) *buy*	1
126	זוד	(H) *be arrogant; act presumptuously*	1
127	זון	(tG) *be fed*	1
128	זמן	(tG) *conspire*	1
129	זעק	(G) *yell*	1
130	זקף	(Gp ptcp) *raised*	1
131	חוט	(G/H) *repair*	1
132	חטא	(D) *sin, make a sin offering*	1
133	חרב	(Hp) *be laid waste*	1
134	חרך	(tD) *be singed*	1
135	חשב	(Gp) *be thought of*	1
136	חשח	(G) *need*	1
137	חשל	(G) *smash*	1
138	חתם	(G) *seal*	1
139	טאב	(G) *be good to* (w/ עַל-) *X = X was glad*	1
140	טלל	(H) *find shade*	1
141	יטב	(G) *be good* (w/ עַל-) *to*	1
142	יסף	(Hp) *be added*	1
143	יצב	(D) *ascertain, make certain of*	1
144	כרה	(tG) *be distressed, troubled, disturbed*	1
145	כרז	(H) *herald, proclaim*	1
146	מגר	(D) *overthrow*	1
147	מלח	(G) *salt*	1
148	מרט	(Gp) *be plucked*	1

	ROOT	GLOSS(ES)	FREQ.
149	נבא	(tD) *prophesy*	1
150	נגד	(G) *flow*	1
151	נדד	(G) *flee*	1
152	נוד	(G) *flee*	1
153	נטר	(G) *keep*	1
154	נסח	(tG) *be pulled out*	1
155	נסך	(D) *pour out = offer*	1
156	נצח	(tD) *distinguish oneself, surpass*	1
157	נקשׁ	(G) *knock*	1
158	נתר	(H) *strip off*	1
159	סבל	(Dp) *maintained* (?)	1
160	סבר	(G) *intend*	1
161	סגר	(G) *close, shut*	1
162	סעד	(D) *support*	1
163	סתר I	(Dp ptcp) *hidden*	1
164	סתר II	(G) *destroy*	1
165	עקר	(tG) *be ripped out*	1
166	עשׁת	(Gp) *intend* active sense	1
167	פלג	(Gp ptcp) *divided*	1
168	פרס	(Gp) *be divided*	1
169	פרק	(G) *wipe away; ransom*	1
170	פרשׁ	(Dp ptcp) *separated, made distinct; translated; explained*	1
171	קנה	(G) *buy*	1
172	קצף	(G) *be furious*	1
173	קצץ	(D) *cut off, lop off*	1
174	רגז	(H) *enrage*	1
175	רחץ	(tG) *trust* (w/ עַל־) *in*	1
176	שׂכל	(tD) *contemplate*	1
177	שׂנא	(G ptcp) *hater, enemy*	1
178	שׁבשׁ	(tD) *be perplexed*	1
179	שׁדר	(tD) *exert, make every effort*	1
180	שׁיציא	(Š) *complete*	1
181	שׁמד	(H) *annihilate*	1

	ROOT	GLOSS(ES)	FREQ.
182	שמם	(tD) *be appalled*	1
183	שמש	(D) *minister, attend, serve*	1
184	שנה	(H) *change*	1
185	שפט	(G) *judge*	1
186	תבר	(Gp ptcp) *fragile, brittle*	1
187	תוה	(G) *be astonished, startled, horrified*	1
188	תקל	(Gp) *be weighed*	1
189	תקן	(Hp) *be reestablished*	1

LIST #4: COMMON NOUNS

	WORD	GLOSS(ES)	ATT. FORM	FREQ.
1	מֶלֶךְ	*king*		180
2	אֱלָה	*God; god, deity*		95
3	כֹּל	*all, each, every, the whole, the entirety*		80
4	מַלְכוּ	*kingship, sovereignty; reign; kingdom, realm*		56
5	בַּיִת	*house; palace; temple*		45
6	שְׁמַיִן	*sky, heaven*		37
7	פְּשַׁר	*interpretation*		33
8	קֳבֵל	*that which is in front*		32
9	טְעֵם	*good taste, sophistication, tact; statement; command; advice, report*		30
10	אֱנָשׁ	*individual person, human being;* coll *people, humanity*		25
11	מִלָּה	*word* [15x]; prophetic *word* [4x]; *thing* [3x]; *matter* [2x]		24
12	דְּהַב	*gold*		23
13	אֲרַע	*earth, land* [20x]; prep *beneath, inferior* [1x]	Always emphatic singular (אַרְעָא).	21
14	גְּבַר	*man, person*		21
15	חֵלֶם	*dream*		21
16	חֵיוָה	*animal, beast*		20

	WORD	GLOSS(ES)	ATT. FORM	FREQ.
17	עָלַם	eternity [18x]; antiquity [2x]		20
18	II בַּר	son		19
19	פַּרְזֶל	iron		19
20	נוּר	fire		18
21	יַד	hand		17
22	צְלֵם	statue [16x]; image [1x]		17
23	יוֹם	day		16
24	עַם	people		15
25	דָּת	law [11x]; decree [2x]; verdict [1x]		14
26	קֶרֶן	horn		14
27	רֵאשׁ	head		14
28	שָׁלְטָן	empire; dominion		14
29	גּו	midst		13
30	כְּסַף	silver		13
31	עִדָּן	season, time [9x]; time [4x]		13
32	הֵיכַל	palace [6x]; temple [5x]; temple, sanctuary [1x]		12
33	חֶזְו	vision [11x]; appearance [1x]		12
34	כְּתָב	writing, instruction		12
35	שְׁאָר	rest, remainder		12
36	שֻׁם	name		12
37	זְמַן	time, set time, appointment, moment, date, holiday		11
38	מְדִינָה	district, province		11
39	רוּחַ	spirit [8x]; wind [3x]		11
40	אַרְיֵה	lion	Emphatic plural 9 times out of 10 (אַרְיָוָתָא).	10
41	אַתּוּן	furnace		10
42	גֹּב	den		10
43	יְהוּדִי	Jew; Judean	Emphatic plural 9 times out of 10 (יְהוּדָיֵא).	10
44	עֶלִּי	most high	Always emphatic singular (עֶלָּאָה).	10
45	פֶּחָה	governor		10
46	אַב	father		9

	WORD	GLOSS(ES)	ATT. FORM	FREQ.
47	אֲחַשְׁדַּרְפַּן	satrap	Always emphatic plural (אֲחַשְׁדַּרְפְּנַיָּא).	9
48	חֲסַף	clay		9
49	נְחָשׁ	bronze		9
50	רָזָה	secret, mystery		9
51	אֶבֶן	stone		8
52	אֻמָּה	nation	Emphatic plural 7 times out of 8 (אֻמַּיָּא).	8
53	חָכְמָה	wisdom		8
54	כָּהֵן	priest		8
55	כַּשְׂדָּי	Babylonian astrologer or sage [7x]; Chaldean [1x]		8
56	קִרְיָה	city		8
57	רַבְרְבָנִין	lord		8
58	אֱסָר	prohibition		7
59	I בַּר	field	Always emphatic singular (בְּרָא).	7
60	חַיִל	power [4x]; power, army [3x]		7
61	יְקָר	honor		7
62	כְּנָת	associate, colleague	Plural and with 3mp gen sx 6 times out of 7 (כְּנָוָתְהוֹן).	7
63	לְבַב	heart		7
64	לִשָּׁן	tongue	Emphatic plural 6 times out of 7 (לִשָּׁנַיָּא).	7
65	מָאן	vessel		7
66	עֲבֵד	slave, servant		7
67	קָל	sound, voice		7
68	רְגַל	foot		7
69	I שְׁנָה	year		7
70	תּוֹר	bull	Always absolute plural (תּוֹרִין).	7
71	אִילָן	tree	Emphatic singular 5 times out of 6 (אִילָנָא).	6
72	אָשַׁף	conjurer; exorcist		6
73	זִיו	splendor, brightness, radiance		6

	WORD	GLOSS(ES)	ATT. FORM	FREQ.
74	חֲמַר	wine		6
75	מִשְׁכַּב	bed		6
76	סָפַר	scribe		6
77	עֲבִידָה	work [4x]; administration [2x]		6
78	פֻּם	mouth		6
79	פִּתְגָם	word, answer [3x]; sentence [1x]; report [1x]; edict [1x]	Emphatic singular 5 times out of 6 (פִּתְגָמָא).	6
80	רַעְיוֹן	thought		6
81	אָע	timber		5
82	אֲתַר	place		5
83	גְּשֵׁם	body		5
84	דִּין	judgment, justice [3x]; court [2x]		5
85	חַרְטֹם	magician		5
86	טַל	dew		5
87	לֵילֵי	night	Always emphatic singular (לֵילְיָא).	5
88	סְגַן	prefect	Emphatic plural 4 times out of 5 (סְגְנַיָּא).	5
89	סוֹף	end		5
90	סְפַר	book		5
91	סְרַךְ	high official president		5
92	עַיִן	eye		5
93	עֲשַׂב	vegetation, plants	Emphatic singular 4 times out of 5 (עִשְׂבָּא).	5
94	רוּם	height	Always with 3ms gen sx (רוּמֵהּ).	5
95	שָׁעָה	hour = moment		5
96	אַמָּה	cubit	Always absolute plural (אַמִּין).	4
97	גָּלוּ	exile	Always emphatic singular (גָּלוּתָא).	4
98	דָּר	generation		4
99	הַדָּבַר	companion		4
100	זְמָר	musical instrument	Always emphatic singular (זְמָרָא).	4

	WORD	GLOSS(ES)	ATT. FORM	FREQ.
101	זַן	*type, kind*	Always construct plural (זְנֵי).	4
102	חֲנֻכָּה	*dedication*	Always construct singular (חֲנֻכַּת).	4
103	לֵוִי	*Levite*	Always emphatic plural (לֵוָיֵא).	4
104	מִדָּה	*tribute, tax*		4
105	מְדוֹר	*dwelling*		4
106	מַנְדַּע	*knowledge*		4
107	מָרֵא	*lord*		4
108	מַשְׁרוֹקִי	*pipe*	Always emphatic singular (מַשְׁרוֹקִיתָא).	4
109	נְבִיא	*prophet*		4
110	עֶלְיוֹן	*most high*	Always absolute plural (עֶלְיוֹנִין).	4
111	עֲנַף	*bough, branches*	Always with 3ms gen sx (עַנְפּוֹהִי).	4
112	פְּסַנְתֵּרִין	*psalterion*		4
113	צִפַּר	*bird*	Always plural.	4
114	קִיתרס	*kitharos, zither*	Always absolute singular (קַתְרוֹס).	4
115	רְבוּ	*greatness*		4
116	שָׁלוּ	*negligence* [3x]; *negligence = blasphemy* [1x]		4
117	שְׁלָם	*peace*		4
118	אִגְּרָה	*letter*		3
119	אִמַּר	*lamb*	Always absolute plural (אִמְּרִין).	3
120	אֵנֶב	*fruit*	Always with 3ms gen sx (אִנְבֵּהּ).	3
121	אֱסוּר	*band* [2x]; *fetters = imprisonment* [1x]		3
122	אֶצְבַּע	*toe* [2x]; *finger* [1x]	Always plural.	3
123	אַרְגְּוָן	*purple*	Always emphatic singular (אַרְגְּוָנָא).	3
124	אֹשׁ	*foundation*	Always plural.	3
125	אָת	*sign*	Always plural.	3

	WORD	GLOSS(ES)	ATT. FORM	FREQ.
126	בְּלוֹ	tax paid in kind, *produce tax*		3
127	בְּעֵל	lord, *master*		3
128	בְּשַׂר	flesh		3
129	גְּנַז	storage [1x]; *treasure* [1x]; *treasury* [1x]	Always plural.	3
130	גַּף	wing	Always plural.	3
131	דְּכַר	ram	Always absolute plural (דִּכְרִין).	3
132	הֲדַר	majesty		3
133	הֲלָךְ	*field* or *produce tax*		3
134	המונך	necklace, *chain*	Always emphatic singular (הַמְנִיכָא).	3
135	הִתְבְּהָלָה	haste		3
136	חֲבָל	harm		3
137	חֲבַר	friend, *companion*	Always plural and with 3ms gen sx (חַבְרוֹהִי).	3
138	חֲלָק	portion, *lot* [1x]; *portion, share* [1x]		3
139	כָּרְסֵא	throne		3
140	לְחֵנָה	consort, *concubine, prostitute*	Always plural and with suffix.	3
141	מְלַח	salt		3
142	מַתְּנָה	gift	Always plural.	3
143	נְוָלוּ	dunghill; *latrine pit*	Twice as נְוָלִי.	3
144	נִשְׁתְּוָן	letter	Always emphatic singular (נִשְׁתְּוָנָא).	3
145	סַבְּכָא	trigon	Twice as שַׂבְּכָא.	3
146	סוּמְפֹּנְיָה	symphonia		3
147	עִיר	watcher		3
148	עֳפִי	leaves [2x]; *foliage* [1x]	Always with 3ms gen sx (עָפְיֵהּ).	3
149	עִקַּר	stump		3
150	עַתִּיק	ancient		3
151	פַּרְשֶׁגֶן	copy		3
152	צַוַּאר	neck		3
153	קְטַר	knot [2x]; *knot = joint* [1x]	Always plural.	3
154	קְצָת	end		3

	WORD	GLOSS(ES)	ATT. FORM	FREQ.
155	רְבִיעִי	*fourth*		3 (6)
156	שָׂכְלְתָנוּ	*prudence, insight* [2x]; *insight* [1x]		3
157	שְׂעַר	*hair*		3
158	שֵׁגַל	*second-tier wife; concubine*	Always plural and with suffix.	3
159	שׁוּר	*wall*	Always emphatic plural (שׁוּרַיָּא/שׁוּרַיֵּהּ).	3
160	שֵׁן	*tooth*		3
161	שְׁרֹשׁ	*root*	Always plural and with 3ms gen sx (שָׁרְשׁוֹהִי).	3
162	תַּלְתָּא	*triumvir* (official of the third rank), *rank third*		3
163	תְּמַהּ	*wonder*	Always plural.	3
164	אֲדַרְגָּזַר	*counselor*	Always emphatic plural (אֲדַרְגָּזְרַיָּא).	2
165	אֲנַף	*face*	Always plural and with 3ms gen sx (אַנְפּוֹהִי).	2
166	אֲפַרְסְכָי	official title, *apharsechai-official*; or a people, *Apharsechite*	Always emphatic plural (אֲפַרְסְכָיֵא).	2
167	אֲרַח	*path*	Always plural and with suffix.	2
168	אַרְכָה	*lengthening, extension*		2
169	אֲשַׁרְנָא	*shrine* (?), *structure* (?), *furnishings* (?)		2
170	אֶשְׁתַּדּוּר	*insurrection*		2
171	בָּעוּ	*request* [1x]; *request, prayer* [1x]		2
172	בַּת	volume measure *bath*	Always absolute plural (בַּתִּין).	2
173	גְּבוּרָה	*might*	Always emphatic singular (גְּבוּרְתָא).	2
174	גְּדָבַר	*treasurer*	Always emphatic plural (גְּדָבְרַיָּא).	2
175	גְּזֵרָה	*decree*	Always construct singular (גְּזֵרַת).	2
176	דִּבְרָה	*matter*	Always construct singular (דִּבְרַת).	2
177	דִּכְרָן	*records*	Always emphatic plural (דִּכְרָנַיָּא).	2

	WORD	GLOSS(ES)	ATT. FORM	FREQ.
178	דְּתֶא	grass	Always emphatic singular (דִּתְאָא).	2
179	דְּתָבַר	judge	Always emphatic plural (דְּתָבְרַיָּא).	2
180	הַדָּם	limb	Always absolute plural (הַדָּמִין).	2
181	חַיִּין	life	Always plural.	2
182	חֲזוֹת	visibleness, ability to be seen (?); branches, canopy of a tree (?)	Always with 3ms gen sx (חֲזוֹתֵהּ).	2
183	חַי I	living		2 (5)
184	חֵמָה	fury		2
185	חִנְטָה	wheat	Always absolute plural (חִנְטִין).	2
186	חֶסֶן	power, might		2
187	טוּר	mountain		2
188	טִין	unfired pottery	Always emphatic singular (טִינָא).	2
189	טְפַר	nail [1x]; claw [1x]		2
190	יַם	sea	Always emphatic singular (יַמָּא).	2
191	יְרַח	month		2
192	כְּתַל	wall		2
193	לְבוּשׁ	clothing		2
194	מֵאמַר	word, command		2
195	מָזוֹן	food		2
196	מַלְאַךְ	angel	Always singular with 3ms gen sx (מַלְאֲכֵהּ).	2
197	מַלְכָּה	queen	Always emphatic singular (מַלְכְּתָא).	2
198	מְנֵא	Sum. lw, weight measure mina, or Gp ptcp ms מנה counted; MENE		2
199	מִנְחָה	grain offering		2
200	מָרָד	rebellious		2
201	מְשַׁח I	anointing oil		2
202	נִבְזְבָּה	present, reward		2

	WORD	GLOSS(ES)	ATT. FORM	FREQ.
203	נִדְבָּךְ	course, layer		2
204	נַהִירוּ	enlightenment		2
205	נִיחֹחַ	soothing sacrifice; incense offering	Always absolute plural (נִיחֹחִין).	2
206	נְכַס	property, wealth	Always plural.	2
207	נְשַׁר	eagle		2
208	נִפְקָה	expenses	Always emphatic singular (נִפְקְתָא).	2
209	סַרְבָּל	trousers (?); coat (?)	Always plural and with 3mp gen sx (סַרְבָּלֵיהוֹן).	2
210	עוֹף	bird		2
211	עִזְקָה	signet ring		2
212	עִלָּה	cause, pretext		2
213	פַּס	palm		2
214	פְּרֵס	volume measure *peres*, weight measure one-half a mina; one-half shekel		2
215	פְּתָי	width	Always singular with 3ms gen sx (פְּתָיֵהּ).	2
216	צַד	concerning		2
217	קַדְמָה	earlier time		2
218	קַדְמָי	earlier [1x]; earliest, first [1x]		2 (3)
219	קְיָם	statute		2
220	קְרַץ	bits	Always plural and with suffix.	2
221	קְשֹׁט	truth		2
222	רֵו	appearance	Always singular with 3ms gen sx (רֵוֵהּ).	2
223	רְעוּ	will, pleasure	Always construct singular (רְעוּת).	2
224	שְׁבִיב	flame		2
225	שִׁלְטוֹן	official	Always construct plural (שִׁלְטֹנֵי).	2
226	שַׁלִּיט	official [1x]; sovereign [1x]		2 (10)
227	תְּדִיר	as adv *continually*	Always emphatic singular (תְּדִירָא).	2

	WORD	GLOSS(ES)	ATT. FORM	FREQ.
228	תְּקֵל	weight measure *shekel*, or pun on תְּקִיל Gp ptcp ms תקל *weighed*		2
229	תְּרַע	*door, gate* [1x]; *door, opening* [1x]		2
230	תִּפְתָּי	*magistrate*	Always emphatic plural (תִּפְתָּיֵא).	2
231	אִדַּר	*threshing floor*	אִדְּרֵי־	1
232	אֶדְרָע	*arm = by force*	בְּאֶדְרָע	1
233	אַח	*brother*	אֶחָךְ	1
234	אֲחִידָה	*riddle*	אֲחִידָן	1
235	אַחֲרִי	*end*	בְּאַחֲרִית	1
236	אָחֳרִי	*another*	אָחֳרִי	1 (6)
237	אֲפָרְסִי	*Apharsite* unknown GN	אֲפָרְסָיֵא	1
238	אֲפַרְסַתְכָי	(1) *Apharsatechite* or Pers. lw [three possible Pers. words]; (2) *ambassador*; (3) *top official*; (4) *royal ambassador*	וַאֲפַרְסַתְכָיֵא	1
239	אַרְכֻבָּא	*knee*	וְאַרְכֻבָּתֵהּ	1
240	אַרְכְּוָי	*Urukite*	אַרְכְּוָיֵא	1
241	אַרְעִי	*bottom*	לְאַרְעִית	1
242	אֲרַק	*earth, land*	וְאַרְקָא	1
243	אֶשָּׁא	*fire*	אֶשָּׁא	1
244	בְּאִישׁ	*bad, evil*	וּבְאִישְׁתָּא	1
245	בַּבְלִי	*Babylonians*	בָּבְלָיֵא	1
246	בְּהִילוּ	*haste*	בִּבְהִילוּ	1
247	בִּינָה	*understanding*	בִינָה	1
248	בִּירָה	*citadel*	בְּבִירְתָא	1
249	בַּל	*mind*	בָּל	1
250	בִּנְיָן	*building, structure*	בִּנְיָנָא	1
251	בִּקְעָה	*plain*	בְּבִקְעַת	1
252	בֶּרֶךְ	*knee*	בִּרְכוֹהִי	1
253	גַּב	*side* (HALOT), *back* (NRSV, NJPS)	גַּבַּהּ	1
254	גִּבָּר	*hero, warrior, strong man*	גִּבָּרֵי־	1
255	גֵּוָה	*pride*	בְּגֵוָה	1
256	גִּזְבַּר	*treasurer*	גִזַבְרַיָּא	1
257	גִּיר	*plaster*	גִּירָא	1
258	גַּלְגַּל	*wheel*	גַּלְגִּלּוֹהִי	1

	WORD	GLOSS(ES)	ATT. FORM	FREQ.
259	גְּרֶם	bone	גַּרְמֵיהוֹן	1
260	דֹּב	bear	לְדֹב	1
261	דְּבַח	sacrifice	דִּבְחִין	1
262	דַּחֲוָה	food (?), table (?); concubine (?), dancing girl (?); diversion (?)	וְדַחֲוָן	1
263	דַּיָּן	judge	וְדַיָּנִין	1
264	דִּינָיֵא	Dinaite	דִּינָיֵא	1
265	דִּכְרוֹן	record, memorandum	דִּכְרוֹנָה	1
266	דְּרַע	arm	וּדְרָעוֹהִי	1
267	הַנְזָקָה	injury	לְהַנְזָקַת	1
268	הַרְהֹר	imaginations, fantasies	וְהַרְהֹרִין	1
269	הִתְנַדָּבוּ	gift, donation	הִתְנַדָּבוּת	1
270	זָכוּ	innocence	זָכוּ	1
271	זַמָּר	singer	זַמָּרַיָּא	1
272	זְרַע	seed	בִּזְרַע	1
273	חֲבוּלָה	wrong, harm, crime	חֲבוּלָה	1
274	חַבְרָה	companion	חַבְרָתַהּ	1
275	חֲדֶה	chest	חֲדוֹהִי	1
276	חֶדְוָה	joy	בְּחֶדְוָה	1
277	חֲטִי	sin	וַחֲטָאָךְ	1
278	חֲרַץ	hip	חַרְצֵהּ	1
279	חֲשׁוֹךְ	darkness	בַּחֲשׁוֹכָא	1
280	חַשְׁחוּ	needs	חַשְׁחוּת	1
281	טַבָּח	executioners, bodyguard	טַבָּחַיָּא	1
282	טְוָת	fasting	טְוָת	1
283	טַרְפְּלָי	(1) Tripolisite; (2) an official of the Persian chancellery of Across the River in Tripolis; (3) a general term class of official	טַרְפְּלָיֵא	1
284	יַבֶּשָׁה	dry land, earth	יַבֶּשְׁתָּא	1
285	יְגַר	heap	יְגַר	1
286	יַצִּיב	(w/ מִן) adv certainly	יַצִּיב	1 (5)
287	יְקֵדָה	burning	לִיקֵדַת	1
288	יַקִּיר	noble	וִיקִּירָא	1 (2)
289	יַרְכָה	thigh	וְיַרְכָתֵהּ	1

	WORD	GLOSS(ES)	ATT. FORM	FREQ.
290	כִּדְבָה	*lie, false*	כִדְבָה	1
291	כַּוָּה	*window*	וְכַוִּין	1
292	כַּכַּר	weight measure *talent*	כַּכְּרִין	1
293	כַּסְדָּי (= כַּשְׂדָּי)	*Chaldean*	כַּסְדָּאָה	1
294	כֹּר	volume measure *kor*	כֹּרִין	1
295	כַּרְבְּלָה	*cap, hat*	וְכַרְבְּלָתְהוֹן	1
296	כָּרוֹז	*herald*	וְכָרוֹזָא	1
297	לֵב	*heart*	בְּלִבִּי	1
298	לְחֶם	*feast*	לְחֶם	1
299	מֹאזְנֵא	*balance*	בְמֹאזַנְיָא	1
300	מְגִלָּה	*scroll*	מְגִלָּה	1
301	מוֹת	*death*	לְמוֹת	1
302	מַדְבַּח	*altar*	מַדְבְּחָה	1
303	מָדַי	*Mede*	מָדָאָה	1
304	מַחְלְקָה	*section, course, division*	בְּמַחְלְקָתְהוֹן	1
305	מְלַךְ	*advice*	מִלְכִּי	1
306	מִנְיָן	*number*	לְמִנְיָן	1
307	מַעֲבָד	*work, deed*	מַעֲבָדוֹהִי	1
308	מְעֵה	*belly*	מְעוֹהִי	1
309	מְרַד	*rebellion*	וּמְרַד	1
310	מִשְׁכַּן	*dwelling*	מִשְׁכְּנֵהּ	1
311	מִשְׁתֵּא	*banquet*	מִשְׁתְּיָא	1
312	נְבוּאָה	*prophesying*	בִּנְבוּאַת	1
313	נֶבְרְשָׁה	*lampstand*	נֶבְרַשְׁתָּא	1
314	נְגַהּ	*first light*	בְּנָגְהָא	1
315	נְדַן	*sheath = body*	נִדְנֶה	1
316	נְהַר	*river*	נְהַר	1
317	נְהוֹר	*light*	וּנְהוֹרָא	1
318	נְמַר	*leopard*	כִּנְמַר	1
319	נְסַךְ	*libation*	וְנִסְכֵּיהוֹן	1
320	נִצְבָּה	*hardness, strength*	נִצְבְּתָא	1
321	נָשִׁין	*wives*	וּנְשֵׁיהוֹן	1
322	נִשְׁמָה	*breath*	נִשְׁמְתָךְ	1

	WORD	GLOSS(ES)	ATT. FORM	FREQ.
323	נְתִין	temple slave	נְתִינַיָּא	1
324	עֲוָיָה	iniquity	וַעֲוָיָתָךְ	1
325	עוּר	chaff	כְּעוּר	1
326	עֵז	she goat	עִזִּין	1
327	עֵטָה	counsel	עֵטָא	1
328	עֲלָוָה	burnt offering	לַעֲלָוָן	1
329	עִלִּי	upstairs room	בְּעִלִּיתֵהּ	1
330	עֵלְמָי	Elamites	עֵלְמָיֵא	1
331	עֲלַע	rib	עִלְעִין	1
332	עֲמַר	wool	כַּעֲמַר	1
333	עֲנָן	cloud	עֲנָנֵי	1
334	עֲנָשׁ	confiscation	לַעֲנָשׁ	1
335	עַר	adversary	לְעָרָךְ	1
336	עֲרָד	wild donkey	עֲרָדַיָּא	1
337	עַרְוָה	nakedness	וְעַרְוַת	1
338	פֶּחָר	potter	פֶּחָר	1
339	פטיש	garment; shirt (?); trousers (?)	פַּטְּשֵׁיהוֹן	1
340	פְּלַג	half	וּפְלַג	1
341	פְּלֻגָּה	division	בִּפְלֻגָּתְהוֹן	1
342	פָּלְחָן	service, ritual observance	לְפָלְחָן	1
343	פָּרְסִי	Persian	פָּרְסָאָה	1
344	צְבוּ	thing, matter	צְבוּ	1
345	צִדְקָה	righteousness, charity	בְּצִדְקָה	1
346	צְפִיר	he goat	וּצְפִירֵי	1
347	קַיְט	summer	קַיְט	1
348	קְצַף	fury, wrath	קְצַף	1
349	קְרָב	war	קְרָב	1
350	רְבוּ	greatness	וּרְבוּתָא	1
351	רְגַז	rage	בִּרְגַז	1
352	רַחֲמִין	compassion	וְרַחֲמִין	1
353	רֵיחַ	smell, odor	וְרֵיחַ	1
354	שַׂבְּכָא	trigon	שַׂבְּכָא	1
355	שָׂהֲדוּ	witness, testimony	שָׂהֲדוּתָא	1
356	שְׂטַר	side	וְלִשְׂטַר־	1

	WORD	GLOSS(ES)	ATT. FORM	FREQ.
357	שְׁאֵלָה	*decision*	שְׁאֵלְתָּא	1
358	שְׁבַט	*tribe*	שִׁבְטֵי	1
359	שׁוּשַׁנְכִי	*Susaite*	שׁוּשַׁנְכָיֵא	1
360	שְׁלֵוָה	*ease, serenity*	לִשְׁלֵוְתָךְ	1
361	שְׁמַשׁ	*sun*	שִׁמְשָׁא	1
362	שְׁנָה II	*sleep*	וְשִׁנְתֵּהּ	1
363	שְׁפַל	*low, lowest*	וּשְׁפַל	1
364	שְׁפַרְפָּר	*dawn*	בִּשְׁפַרְפָּרָא	1
365	שָׁק	*shin, leg*	שָׁקוֹהִי	1
366	שְׁרֹשׁוּ	*rooting out = banishment*	לִשְׁרֹשִׁי	1
367	תְּלַג	*snow*	כִּתְלַג	1
368	תְּקָף	*strength, might*	בִּתְקָף	1
369	תְּקֹף	*strength*	וְתָקְפָּא	1
370	תָּרָע	*gatekeeper, doorkeeper*	תָּרָעַיָּא	1

LIST #5: PROPER NOUNS

WORD	GLOSS	FREQ.

PERSONAL NAMES

	WORD	GLOSS	FREQ.
1	דָּנִיֵּאל	*Daniel*	52
2	נְבוּכַדְנֶצַּר	*Nebuchadnezzar*	31
3	דָּרְיָוֶשׁ	*Darius*	15
4	מֵישַׁךְ	*Meshach*	14
5	עֲבֵד נְגוֹ	*Abednego*	14
6	שַׁדְרַךְ	*Shadrach*	14
7	כּוֹרֶשׁ	*Cyrus*	8
8	בֵּלְטְשַׁאצַּר	*Belteshazzar*	7
9	בֵּלְשַׁאצַּר	*Belshazzar*	7
10	אַרְתַּחְשַׁשְׂתְּא	*Artaxerxes*	6
11	אַרְיוֹךְ	*Arioch*	5
12	רְחוּם	*Rehum*	4

	WORD	GLOSS	FREQ.
13	שִׁמְשַׁי	*Shimshai*	4
14	שְׁתַר בּוֹזְנַי	*Shethar-bozenai*	4
15	תַּתְּנַי	*Tattenai*	4
16	עֶזְרָא	*Ezra*	3
17	זְכַרְיָה	*Zechariah*	2
18	חַגַּי	*Haggai*	2
19	עִדּוֹא	*Iddo*	2
20	שֵׁשְׁבַּצַּר	*Sheshbazzar*	2
21	אָסְנַפַּר	*Osnappar* unidentified Assyrian king	1
22	דֶּהָיֵא	*Dehaye* (Qere only)	1
23	זְרֻבָּבֶל	*Zerubbabel*	1
24	חֲנַנְיָה	*Hananiah*	1
25	יוֹצָדָק	*Jozadak*	1
26	יֵשׁוּעַ	*Jeshua*	1
27	מִישָׁאֵל	*Mishael*	1
28	מֹשֶׁה	*Moses*	1
29	עֲזַרְיָה	*Azariah*	1
30	שְׁאַלְתִּיאֵל	*Shealtiel*	1

GEOGRAPHICAL NAMES

1	יְרוּשְׁלֶם	*Jerusalem*	26
2	בָּבֶל	*Babylon*	25
3	עֲבַר נַהֲרָה	*Beyond the River*	14
4	יִשְׂרָאֵל	*Israel*	8
5	יְהוּד	*Judah*	6
6	פָּרַס	*Persia*	6
7	מָדַי	*Media*	5
8	שָׁמְרָיִן	*Samaria*	2
9	אַחְמְתָא	*Ecbatana*	1
10	דּוּרָא	*Dura*	1
11	יְגַר שָׂהֲדוּתָא	*Jegar-sahadutha*	1

MONTH NAME

1	אֲדָר	*Adar*	1

LIST #6: ADJECTIVES

	WORD	GLOSS(ES)	FREQ.
1	דְּנָה	*this*	23 (58)
2	רַב	*great* [19x]; *chief* [3x]; *many* [1x]	23
3	אִלֵּךְ	*those*	14
4	חַכִּים	*wise*	14
5	קַדִּישׁ	*holy*	13
6	שַׂגִּיא	*great* [3x]; *very* [2x]; *abundant* [2x]; *much* [1x]; *many* [1x]	9 (13)
7	שַׁלִּיט	*sovereign, powerful, mighty* [6x]; *ruler* [1x]; *lawful, permitted* [1x]	8 (10)
8	דֵּךְ	*that*	6
9	דֵּךְ	*that*	6
10	אָחֳרִי	*another*	5 (6)
11	אָחֳרָן	*another*	5
12	יַתִּיר	*extraordinary, excessive*	5 (8)
13	שָׂב	*gray headed = elders*	5
14	תַּקִּיף	*powerful, mighty* [3x]; *strong* [2x]	5
15	אִלֵּין	*these*	4 (5)
16	חַי I	*living*	3 (5)
17	יַצִּיב	*certain, firm* [2x]; *what is certain, correct* [1x]	3 (5)
18	רְבִיעִי	*fourth*	3 (6)
19	דִּכֵּן	*that*	3
20	אַזְדָּא	*publicly known* thus *irrevocable*	2
21	גְּלָל	*huge; hewn*	2
22	טָב	*good*	2
23	קַיָּם	*enduring, established*	2
24	שַׁפִּיר	*beautiful*	2
25	אֵימְתָן	*terrible*	1
26	אֵל	*these*	1 (Q)
27	אִנּוּן	*those*	1 (3)
28	אֲרִיךְ	*worthy of an Aryan, i.e., proper, fitting*	1
29	אֲרָמִי	*Aramaic*	1
30	דָּא	*this*	1 (6)
31	הוּא	*that*	1 (15)

	WORD	GLOSS(ES)	FREQ.
32	זְהִיר	*careful*	1
33	זְעֵיר	*little*	1
34	חֲדַת	*new*	1
35	חִוָּר	*white*	1
36	חַסִּיר	*lacking*	1
37	חַשְׁחָה	*needed*	1
38	יַקִּיר	*difficult*	1 (2)
39	מֶעָל	*entering = setting*	1
40	נְקֵא	*pure*	1
41	עַמִּיק	*deep*	1
42	עֲנֵה	*poor, miserable*	1
43	עֲצִיב	*anxious* (?), *sad* (?)	1
44	עֲתִיד	*ready*	1
45	קַדְמָי	*earlier*	1 (3)
46	רַחִיק	*far away*	1
47	רַעֲנַן	*flourishing, happy*	1
48	שְׁלֵא	*carefree*	1
49	תְּלִיתָי	*third*	1
50	תִּנְיָן	*second*	1

LIST #7: PRONOUNS

	WORD	PARSING	GLOSS(ES)	FREQ.
RELATIVE PRONOUN				
1	דִּי		*who, which, that*	162 (332)
INDEPENDENT PERSONAL PRONOUNS				
1	אֲנָה	1cs	*I*	16
2	אַנְתְּ	2ms	*you*	15
3	הוּא	3ms	*he* [8x]; as copula *are* [3x]; as copula *is* [2x]; *he, it* [1x]	14 (15)
4	הִמּוֹ	3mp	as dir obj *them* [8x]; as copula *are* [1x]	9

	WORD	PARSING	GLOSS(ES)	FREQ.
5	הִיא	3fs	*she* [1x]; *she, it* [3x]; as copula *is* [2x]; as copula *are* [1x]	7
6	אֲנַ֫חְנָה	1cp	*we*	4
7	הִמּוֹן	3mp	as dir obj *them*	3
8	אִנּוּן	3mp	*they* [1x]; as copula *are* [1x]	2 (3)
9	אַנְתּוּן	2mp	*you*	1

DEMONSTRATIVE PRONOUNS (ALL PROXIMATE)

1	דְּנָה	ms	*this*	35 (58)
2	דָּא	fs	*this*	5 (6)
3	אֵ֫לֶּה	mp	*these*	2
4	אִלֵּין	cp	*these*	1 (5)
5	אִנִּין	3fp	as copula *are*	1

INDEFINITE, CORRELATIVE, AND INTERROGATIVE PRONOUNS

1	מָה	impers correl pron	*that which, what* [8x]; (w/ לְ) *why?* *for what purpose?* [2x]; *whatever* [1x]; (w/ לְ) *concerning what* [1x]	12
		impers interr pron	*what?* [2x]; *what*; (w/ לְ) *why? for what purpose?* [2x]	
2	מַן	pers indef pron	*whoever* [6x]	10
		pers interr pron	*who?* [4x]	

COMPOUND PRONOUN

1	דְּהִיא	rel pron דְּ (< דִּי) + indep pers pron 3ms	*that is* (Ketiv only)	1 (K)

LIST #8: PREPOSITIONS

	WORD	GLOSS(ES)	FREQ.
1	לְ	*to, for, belonging to*	378
2	בְּ	*in, into; by, through, with*	226
3	מִן־	*from, away from, out of, some of, because of; than*	119

	WORD	GLOSS(ES)	FREQ.
4	עַל־	on, upon, over, concerning, about, against; to, toward	104
5	כְּ	like, as; about, approximately; according to, corresponding with; conj (w/ inf) as soon as	63
6	קֳדָם	before, in the presence of	42
7	עַד־	as far as, until, up to; during, within	35
8	קֳבֵל	facing, opposite, corresponding to	32
9	עִם	with	22
10	תְּחוֹת	under	5
11	II לָהֵן	except	4 (7)
12	אַחֲרֵי	after	3
13	בָּאתַר	after	3
14	בֵּין	between	2
15	לְוָת	with	1
16	נֶגֶד	toward	1
17	עֵלָּא	over	1

COMPOUND PREPOSITION

	WORD	GLOSS(ES)	FREQ.
1	(כְּ + לְ =) כְּל־	according to	22

PREPOSITIONAL PHRASE

	WORD	GLOSS(ES)	FREQ.
1	לָקֳבֵל	to the front of = before [4x]; to what is in front of [1x]; to what is in front = according to [1x]; in the face of = because [1x]	7

LIST #9: NUMBERS

	WORD	GLOSS(ES)	FREQ.
1	חַד	one [7x]; one, a [5x]; one, as multiplicative times [1x]; one, (w/ בְּ) as one, together [1x]	14
2	תְּלָת	three	11
3	אַרְבַּע	four	8
4	מְאָה	hundred	8
5	שְׁבַע	seven	6

	WORD	GLOSS(ES)	FREQ.
6	אֲלַף	*thousand*	4
7	עֲשַׂר	*ten*	4
8	שִׁתִּין	*sixty*	4
9	רִבּוֹ	*myriad, 10,000*	2
10	שֵׁת	*six*	2
11	תְּלָתִין	*thirty*	2
12	תְּרֵין	*two*	2
13	תְּרֵי־עֲשַׂר	*twelve*	2
14	עֶשְׂרִין	*twenty*	1

LIST #10: ADVERBS

	WORD	GLOSS(ES)	FREQ.
1	מִן־	*from, away from, out of, some of, because of; than*	119
2	אֱדַיִן	*then*	57
3	כֵּן	*thus*	8
4	אָסְפַּרְנָא	*diligently*	7
5	כְּנֵמָא	*thus*	5
6	כְּעֶנֶת	introduces body of a letter *and now*	4
7	שַׂגִּיא	*greatly* [2x]; *very* [2x]	4 (13)
8	תַּמָּה	*there*	4
9	יַתִּיר	*excessively*	3 (8)
10	כְּעַן	*now* [2x]; introduces new idea *now* [1x]	3 (13)
11	אַדְרַזְדָּא	*diligently*	1
12	אָחֲרֵין	*at last*	1
13	אַפְּתֹם	*surely* (?), *certainly* (?), *finally* (?)	1
14	יַצִּיב	*certainly*	1 (5)
15	כָּה	*here*	1
16	עוֹד	*still*	1
17	צְדָא	*truth; true*	1
18	תִּנְיָנוּת	*second time, again*	1

LIST #11: CONJUNCTIONS

	WORD	GLOSS(ES)	FREQ.
1	וְ	and, but	731
2	דִּי	that, so that; for, because; when	101 (332)
3	אֱדַיִן	then	57
4	עַד־	until	35
5	קֳבֵל	because	32
6	הֵן	if, whether	16
7	כְּעַן	introduces new idea now	10 (13)
8	כְּדִי (= כְּ + דִּי)	when	5
9	אַף	also	4
10	I לָהֵן	therefore	3

LIST #12: DISJUNCTIVES

	WORD	GLOSS(ES)	FREQ.
1	וְ	and, but	731
2	בְּרַם	but [1x]; but, however [4x]	5
3	II לָהֵן	but [2x]; unless [1x]	3 (7)

LIST #13: INTERJECTIONS

	WORD	GLOSS	FREQ.
1	אֲלוּ	behold!	5
2	אֲרוּ	behold!	5

LIST #14: PARTICLES

	WORD	GLOSS(ES)	FREQ.
1	לָא	*no, not*	82
2	דִּי	*of*	69 (332)
3	אִיתַי	*there is* [11x]; (w/ 2mp suffix) *you are?* [2x]; (w/ 2ms suffix) *are you?* [1x]; (w/ 1cp suffix) *we are* [1x]; *it is* [1x]; *there are* [1x]	17
4	הֲ	marks a question	6
5	אַל	*not*	3
6	הָא	*behold! look!*	1
7	הֵא	*behold!*	1
8	יָת	sign of def dir obj	1

LIST #15: COLLOCATIONS

	COLLOCATION	GLOSS(ES)	VERSE(S)

COLLOCATIONS OCCURRING MORE THAN ONCE

1	כָּל־קֳבֵל דִּי	*because, since*	Dan 2:8, 41, 45; 4:15; 5:12; 6:4, 5, 11, 23; Ezra 4:14
		because	Dan 2:10, 40; 3:29
		though, although	Dan 5:22
		for, since	Ezra 7:14
2	כָּל־קֳבֵל דְּנָה	*because of this, therefore*	Dan 2:12, 24; 3:7; 6:10; 7:17
		because of this	Dan 3:8
		therefore	Dan 3:22
3	חֵיוַת בָּרָא	*wild animal*	Dan 2:38; 4:9, 18, 20, 22, 29
4	מַן־דִּי	*whoever*	Dan 3:6, 11; 4:14, 22, 29; 5:21

	COLLOCATION	GLOSS(ES)	VERSE(S)
5	מָה דִי	that which; whatever	Dan 2:28, 29 (*bis*), 45
		whatever	Ezra 7:18
6	דִּי־לָא	without	Ezra 6:9; 7:22
		(w/ בְּ) not by means of, without	Dan 2:34
		(w/ בְּ) not through, without	Dan 2:45
7	מִן־דִּי	because	Dan 3:22
		after, as soon as	Dan 4:23; Ezra 4:23; 5:12
8	בְּעֵל־טְעֵם	chancellor, chief government official	Ezra 4:8, 9, 17
9	בַּר אֱנָשׁ	human being	Dan 7:13
	בְּנֵי אֲנָשָׁא	human beings	Dan 2:38; 5:21
10	עַל־דְּנָה	on this basis, for this reason	Ezra 4:14, 15
11	אֲכַלוּ קַרְצֵיהוֹן	slander (w/ דִּי) smn; *accuse*	Dan 3:8
	אֲכַלוּ קַרְצוֹהִי		Dan 6:25
12	יִבְעֵה בָעוּ	pray	Dan 6:8
	בְּעָא בָּעוּתֵהּ		Dan 6:14
13	הַדָּמִין תִּתְעַבְדוּן	torn limb from limb	Dan 2:5
	הַדָּמִין יִתְעֲבֵד		Dan 3:29
14	כְּמָה	how!	Dan 3:33 (*bis*)
15	מְשָׁרֵא קִטְרִין	solve problems	Dan 5:12
	קִטְרִין לְמִשְׁרֵא		Dan 5:16
16	עִם־דָּר וְדָר	from generation to generation	Dan 3:33; 4:31

COLLOCATION	GLOSS(ES)	VERSE(S)

COLLOCATIONS OCCURRING ONLY ONCE

	COLLOCATION	GLOSS(ES)	VERSE(S)
17	אִיתַי דִּי־	*it is (a fact) that*	Ezra 5:17
18	בֵּהּ בְּלֵילְיָא	*in this very night*	Dan 5:30
19	בֵּית סִפְרַיָּא	*archive*	Ezra 6:1
20	בְּבֵית סִפְרַיָּא דִּי גִנְזַיָּא מְהַחֲתִין תַּמָּה	*in the archives where the treasures are deposited*	Ezra 6:1
21	דִּי־לָא כְתָב	*without limit*	Ezra 7:22
22	דִּי־לָא שָׁלוּ	*without fail*	Ezra 6:9
23	דִּי לֵהּ־	*his*	Dan 2:20
24	הֵא־כְדִי	*behold! as that = just as*	Dan 2:43
25	הֲוָא עָבֵד מִן־קַדְמַת דְּנָה	*he was doing from before this = he had always done so*	Dan 6:11
26	זְהִירִין הֱווֹ שָׁלוּ לְמֶעְבַּד	*take care not to fail to act*	Ezra 4:22
27	חַד־שִׁבְעָה	*seven times*	Dan 3:19
28	כְּבַר שְׁנִין שִׁתִּין וְתַרְתֵּין	*being about sixty-two years old*	Dan 6:1
29	כְּלָה־	*as nothing*	Dan 4:32
30	לְמָא דִי־	*concerning that which*	Ezra 6:8
31	לָקֳבֵל דְּנָה	*because of this, then*	Ezra 4:16
32	מְלַח הֵיכְלָא מְלַחְנָא	*be loyal to the throne*	Ezra 4:14
33	מֶלֶךְ לְיִשְׂרָאֵל רַב	*a great king of Israel*	Ezra 5:11
34	מִן־קְשֹׁט דִּי	*truly*	Dan 2:47
35	מִקַּדְמַת דְּנָה שְׁנִין שַׂגִּיאָן	*many years ago*	Ezra 5:11
36	עַד אָחֳרֵין	*finally*	Dan 4:5
37	עַד־דִּבְרַת דִּי	*in order that*	Dan 4:14
38	עַד דִּי	*until*	Dan 4:20
39	עַל־דִּבְרַת	*in order that*	Dan 2:30
40	עַל־מָה	*why? for what purpose?*	Dan 2:15
41	צְפִירֵי עִזִּין	*billy goats*	Ezra 6:17
42	רַחִיקִין הֱווֹ מִן־תַּמָּה	*stay far away from there*	Ezra 6:6

VERBS BY STEM

LIST #16: G STEM

- Attested conjugations: sc, pc, juss, impv, ptcp, inf.
- 341 unique attested forms.

PGN	WORD	ROOT	GLOSS(ES)	VERSE(S)

SUFFIX CONJUGATION

PGN	WORD	ROOT	GLOSS(ES)	VERSE(S)
3ms	כְּתַב	כתב	*write*	Dan 6:26; 7:1
	בְּנַס	בנס	*be enraged*	Dan 2:12
	וּקְצַף	קצף	*be furious*	Dan 2:12
	שְׁפַר	שפר	*be pleasant, pleasing*	Dan 3:32; 6:2
	רְשַׁם	רשם	*write*	Dan 6:10
	וּסֲגַר	סגר	*close, shut*	Dan 6:23
	סְגִד	סגד	*prostrate oneself, bow down to the ground*	Dan 2:46
	וּתְקֵף	תקף	*become strong*	Dan 4:8, 17
	זְעִק	זעק	*yell*	Dan 6:21
	שְׁלֵט	שלט	*have power (w/ בְּ) over*	Dan 3:27
	קְרֵב	קרב	*approach*	Dan 3:26
	שְׁאֵל	שאל	*ask*	Dan 2:10
	טְאֵב	טאב	*be good to (w/ עַל-) X = X was glad*	Dan 6:24
	בְּאֵשׁ	באש	*be bad, evil to (w/ עַל-)*	Dan 6:15
	שְׁמַע	שמע	*hear*	Dan 6:15
	שְׁלַח	שלח	*send*	Dan 3:2, 28; 6:23; Ezra 4:17; 5:6; 6:13
	עֲבַד	עבד	*do, make*	Dan 3:1, 32; 5:1
	אֲזַל	אזל	*go*	Dan 2:17, 24; 6:19, 20

PGN	WORD	ROOT	GLOSS(ES)	VERSE(S)
	אֲמַר־	אמר	*say; order*	Dan 2:24, 25, 46; 3:13, 20; 5:2, 29; 6:17, 24; 7:1, 23
	וַאֲמַר	אמר	*say; order*	Dan 2:12; 6:25; 7:16; Ezra 5:15
	יְדַע	ידע	*know; learn; understand*	Dan 5:21; 6:11
	יְהַב־	יהב	*give*	Dan 2:37, 38, 48; 5:18, 19; Ezra 5:12, 16
	יְתִב	יתב	*sit*	Dan 7:9, 10
	נְפַל	נפל	*fall*	Dan 2:46; 4:28
	נְפַק	נפק	*go out*	Dan 2:14
	וּנְשָׂא	נשא	*carry, lift*	Dan 2:35
	מְטָא	מטא	*reach*	Dan 4:25
	מְטָה	מטא	*reach*	Dan 7:13, 22
	רְבָה	רבה	*grow*	Dan 4:8, 17, 30
	אֲתָה	אתה	*come*	Dan 7:22
	אֲתָא	אתה	*come*	Ezra 5:3, 16
	וּבְעָה	בעה	*seek, request*	Dan 2:16
	מְנָה־	מנה	*count*	Dan 5:26
	חֲזָה	חזה	*see; perceive*	Dan 4:20; 7:1
	הֲוָה	הוה	*be, become, exist; occur, happen*	Dan 4:26; 5:19 (8x); 7:13
	הֲוָא	הוה	*be, become, exist; occur, happen*	Dan 6:4, 11, 15; Ezra 5:11
	בְּעָא	בעה	*seek, request*	Dan 2:49
	תְּוַהּ	תוה	*be astonished, startled, horrified*	Dan 3:24
	וְקָם	קום	*arise, get up; be established, endure*	Dan 3:24
	וּבָת	בית	*spend the night*	Dan 6:19
	רָם	רום	*be high*	Dan 5:20
	שָׂם	שׂים	*put, place, lay*	Dan 5:12; 6:14, 15; Ezra 5:3, 9, 13; 6:1, 3
	עַל	II עלל	*enter*	Dan 2:16, 24; 4:5; 6:11
	סַתְרֵהּ	II סתר	*destroy* (w/ 3ms acc sx)	Ezra 5:12
	שָׂמֵהּ	שׂים	*put, place, lay* (w/ 3ms acc sx)	Ezra 5:14
	בְּנָהִי	בנה	*(re)build* (w/ 3ms acc sx)	Ezra 5:11
	וְחַתְמַהּ	חתם	*seal* (w/ 3fs acc sx)	Dan 6:18

PGN	WORD	ROOT	GLOSS(ES)	VERSE(S)
3fs	תְּקִפַת	תקף	become strong	Dan 5:20
	סְלִקַת	סלק	come up	Dan 7:20
	סִלְקַת	סלק	come up	Dan 7:8
	בְּטֵלַת	בטל	intrans cease(d)	Ezra 4:24
	אָכְלָה	אכל	eat	Dan 7:7, 19
	וַאֲמֶרֶת	אמר	say; order	Dan 5:10
	נֶפְקַת	נפק	go out = be issued	Dan 2:13
	רְבָת	רבה	grow, become great	Dan 4:19
	עֲדָת	עדה	touch (w/ בְּ); pass (w/ מִן) out of	Dan 3:27; 4:28
	עֲנָת	ענה I	answer, reply; begin to speak	Dan 5:10
	הֲוָת	הוה	be, become, exist; occur, happen	Dan 2:35; 7:19; Ezra 5:5
	וַהֲוָת	הוה	be, become, exist; occur, happen	Ezra 4:24
	עַלַּת	עלל II	enter	Dan 5:10
	נַדַּת	נדד	flee	Dan 6:19
	סָפַת	סוף	be fulfilled	Dan 4:30
	מְחָת	מחא	strike	Dan 2:35
	וּמְחָת	מחא	strike	Dan 2:34
	מְטָת	מטא	reach	Dan 4:21
	וּמְטָת	מטא	reach	Dan 4:19
	וּמְלָת	מלא	fill	Dan 2:35
3mp	כְּתַבוּ	כתב	write	Ezra 4:8
	קְרִיבוּ	קרב	approach	Dan 6:13
	קְרִבוּ	קרב	approach	Dan 3:8
	סְלִקוּ	סלק	come up	Dan 2:29; Ezra 4:12
	שְׁלֵטוּ	שלט	rule	Dan 6:25
	שְׁלַחוּ	שלח	send	Ezra 4:11; 5:7
	עֲבַדוּ	עבד	do, make	Jer 10:11; Ezra 6:13
	וַעֲבַדוּ	עבד	do, make	Ezra 6:16
	אֲמַרוּ	אמר	say; order	Dan 4:23
	אֲכַלוּ	אכל	eat	Dan 6:25
	וַאֲכַלוּ	אכל	eat	Dan 3:8
	אֲזַלוּ	אזל	go	Ezra 4:23

PGN	WORD	ROOT	GLOSS(ES)	VERSE(S)
	נְפַלוּ	נפל	*fall*	Dan 3:23
	וִיהַבוּ	יהב	*give*	Dan 3:28
	אֲתוֹ	אתה	*come*	Ezra 4:12
	וּבְנוֹ	בנה	*rebuild*	Ezra 6:14
	וּבְעוֹ	בעה	*seek*	Dan 2:13
	רְמוֹ	רמה	*throw*	Dan 6:25
	וּרְמוֹ	רמה	*throw*	Dan 6:17
	עֲנוֹ	I ענה	*answer, reply; begin to speak*	Dan 2:7, 10; 3:9, 16; 6:14
	שְׁנוֹ	שנה	intrans *change*	Dan 3:27
	הֲווֹ	הוה	*be, become, exist; occur, happen*	Dan 5:19; 6:5; Ezra 4:20
	וַהֲווֹ	הוה	*be, become, exist; occur, happen*	Dan 2:35
	אִשְׁתִּיו	שתה	*drink*	Dan 5:4
	וְאִשְׁתִּיו	שתה	*drink* (w/ בְּ) *from*	Dan 5:3
	מְטוֹ	מטא	*reach*	Dan 6:25
	קָמוּ	קום	*arise, get up; be established, endure*	Ezra 5:2
	שָׂמוּ	שים	*put, place, lay*	Dan 3:12
	דָּקוּ	דקק	*break*	Dan 2:35
	שְׁנוֹהִי	שנה	intrans *changed on him* (w/ 3ms acc sx)	Dan 5:6
3fp	נְפַקָה	נפק	*come out*	Dan 5:5
	וּנְפַלָה	נפל	*fall*	Dan 7:20
2ms	רְשַׁמְתָּ	רשם	*write*	Dan 6:13, 14
	וּתְקֵפְתְּ	תקף	*become strong*	Dan 4:19
	עֲבַדְתְּ	עבד	*do, make*	Dan 4:32
	יְדַעְתָּ	ידע	*know; learn; understand*	Dan 5:22
	יְהַבְתְּ	יהב	*give*	Dan 2:23
	יְכֵלְתָּ	יכל	*be able*	Dan 2:47
	הֲוַיְתָ	הוה	*be, become, exist; occur, happen*	Dan 2:31, 34
	חֲזַיְתָ	חזה	*see; perceive*	Dan 2:43, 45; 4:17
	חֲזַיְתָה	חזה	*be, become, exist; occur, happen*	Dan 2:41 (*bis*)
	רְבַת	רבה	*grow, become great*	Dan 4:19
	שָׂמְתָּ	שים	*put, place, lay*	Dan 3:10

PGN	WORD	ROOT	GLOSS(ES)	VERSE(S)
2mp	שְׁלַחְתּוּן	שלח	send	Ezra 4:18
	חֲזֵיתוֹן	חזה	see; perceive	Dan 2:8
1cs	קִרְבֵת	קרב	approach	Dan 7:16
	שִׁמְעֵת	שמע	hear	Dan 5:16
	וְשִׁמְעֵת	שמע	hear	Dan 5:14
	נִטְלֵת	נטל	lift	Dan 4:31
	נִטְרֵת	נטר	keep	Dan 7:28
	יִדְעֵת	ידע	know; learn; understand	Dan 4:6
	אַמְרֵת	אמר	say; order	Dan 4:5
	עַבְדֵת	עבד	do, make	Dan 3:15; 6:23
	צְבִית	צבה	desire, wish	Dan 7:19
	הֲוֵית	הוה	be, become, exist; occur, happen	Dan 4:1, 7, 10; 7:2, 4, 6, 7, 8, 9, 11 (*bis*), 13, 21
	חֲזֵית	חזה	see; perceive	Dan 2:26; 4:2, 6, 15
	שָׂמֵת	שים	put, place, lay	Ezra 6:12
	בֱּנַיְתַהּ	בנה	(re)build (w/ 3fs acc sx)	Dan 4:27
1cp	שְׁלַחְנָא	שלח	send	Ezra 4:14
	מְלַחְנָא	מלח	salt	Ezra 4:14
	אֲמַרְנָא	אמר	say; order	Ezra 5:4, 9
	אֲזַלְנָא	אזל	go	Ezra 5:8
	שְׁאֵלְנָא	שאל	ask	Ezra 5:9, 10
	רְמֵינָא	רמה	throw	Dan 3:24
	בְּעֵינָא	בעה	seek	Dan 2:23

PREFIX CONJUGATION

PGN	WORD	ROOT	GLOSS(ES)	VERSE(S)
3ms	יִלְבַּשׁ	לבש	wear	Dan 5:7
	וְיִסְבַּר	סבר	intend	Dan 7:25
	יִשְׁלַט	שלט	rule	Dan 5:7
	וְיִסְגֻּד	סגד	prostrate oneself, bow down to the ground	Dan 3:6, 10, 11
	יִשְׁלַח	שלח	send	Ezra 5:17; 6:12

PGN	WORD	ROOT	GLOSS(ES)	VERSE(S)
	יִשְׁמַע	שמע	*hear*	Dan 3:10
	יִמְטֵא	מטא	*reach*	Dan 4:8, 17
	יֵאכֻל	אכל	*eat*	Dan 4:30
	יֵאמַר	אמר	*say; order*	Dan 3:29
	וְיֵאמַר	אמר	*say; order*	Dan 4:32
	יִשְׂגֵּא	שגא	*become big, grow*	Ezra 4:22
	יִקְרֵה	קרא	*read*	Dan 5:7
	יִבְעֵה	בעה	*request; seek*	Dan 6:8, 13
	יֶעְדֵּה	עדה	*pass away*	Dan 7:14
	יִשְׁנֵא	שנה	*be different*	Dan 7:24
	יִצְבֵּא	צבה	*desire, wish*	Dan 4:14, 22, 29; 5:21
	לֶהֱוֵה	הוה	*be, become, exist; occur, happen*	Dan 4:22
	לֶהֱוֵא	הוה	*be, become, exist; occur, happen*	Dan 2:28, 29 (*bis*), 41, 45; 5:29; 6:3; 7:23, 26
	יְקוּם	קום	*arise, get up; be established, endure*	Dan 6:20; 7:24
	יְתוּב	תוב	intrans *return*	Dan 4:31, 33 (*bis*)
	יֵיטַב	יטב	*be good* (w/ עַל־) *to*	Ezra 7:18
	יוּכַל	יכל	*be able*	Dan 2:10
	יִכֻּל	יכל	*be able*	Dan 3:29
	יְהָךְ	הך	*reach*	Ezra 5:5; 7:13
	יִנְתֵּן־	נתן	*give*	Dan 2:16
	יִפֵּל	נפל	*fall*	Dan 3:6, 10, 11
	יִפֵּל־	נפל	*fall*	Ezra 7:20
	יִתְּנִנַּהּ	נתן	*give* (w/ 3fs acc sx)	Dan 4:14, 22, 29
	יִשְׁאֶלֶנְכוֹן	שאל	*ask* (w/ 2mp acc sx)	Ezra 7:21
	הַיִכֻל	יכל	*be able* (w/ interr ה)	Dan 6:21
3fs	תִּשְׁלַט	שלט	*rule*	Dan 2:39
	וְתֵאכֻל	אכל	*eat*	Dan 7:23
	תְּקוּם	קום	*arise, get up; be established, endure*	Dan 2:39, 44
	תְּדוּר	דור	*dwell*	Dan 4:18
	תִּשְׁנֵא	שנה	intrans *change; be different*	Dan 6:18; 7:23
	תֶּהֱוֵה	הוה	*be, become, exist; occur, happen*	Dan 2:41, 42 (*bis*)

PGN	WORD	ROOT	GLOSS(ES)	VERSE(S)
	תֶּהֱוֵא	הוה	*be, become, exist; occur, happen*	Dan 2:40; 4:24; 7:23; Ezra 6:8
	תֶעְדֵּא	עדה	*be annulled; pass away*	Dan 6:9, 13
	וְתֵרֹעַ	רעע	*crush*	Dan 2:40
	וּתְדוּשִׁנַּהּ	דושׁ	*trample* (w/ 3fs acc sx)	Dan 7:23
3mp	יִסְגְּדוּן	סגד	*prostrate oneself, bow down to the ground*	Dan 3:28
	יִפְלְחוּן	פלח	*serve*	Dan 3:28; 7:14, 27
	יַחְלְפוּן	חלף	*pass over*	Dan 4:20, 22, 29
	יִנְתְּנוּן	נתן	*give*	Ezra 4:13
	יִנְדְּעוּן	ידע	*know; learn; understand*	Dan 4:14
	יְקוּמוּן	קום	*arise, get up; be established, endure*	Dan 7:10, 17
	יְקֻמוּן	קום	*arise, get up; be established, endure*	Dan 7:24
	יְדוּרָן	דור	*dwell*	Dan 4:9
	יַחִיטוּ	חוט	[possibly H stem] *repair*	Ezra 4:12
	וְיִשְׁתּוֹן	שתה	*drink* (w/ בְּ) *from*	Dan 5:2
	לֶהֱוֹן	הוה	*be, become, exist; occur, happen*	Dan 2:43 (*bis*); 6:2, 3, 27; Ezra 6:10; 7:25
	יִקְרוֹן	קרא	*read*	Dan 5:15
3fp	יִשְׁכְּנָן	שכן	*dwell*	Dan 4:18
2ms	תִּשְׁלַט	שלט	*rule*	Dan 5:16
	תִלְבַּשׁ	לבשׁ	*wear*	Dan 5:16
	וְתִרְשֻׁם	רשם	*write*	Dan 6:9
	תִּנְתֵּן	נתן	*give*	Ezra 7:20
	תִּנְדַּע	ידע	*know; learn; understand*	Dan 2:30; 4:22, 23, 29
	וְתִנְדַּע	ידע	*know; learn; understand*	Ezra 4:15
	תִקְנֵא	קנה	*buy*	Ezra 7:17
	תִּיכּוּל	יכל	*be able*	Dan 5:16
	תִּכוּל	יכל	*be able*	Dan 5:16
2mp	וְתִסְגְּדוּן	סגד	*prostrate oneself, bow down to the ground*	Dan 3:5, 15

PGN	WORD	ROOT	GLOSS(ES)	VERSE(S)
	תִּשְׁמְעוּן	שמע	hear	Dan 3:5, 15
	תַּעַבְדוּן	עבד	do, make	Ezra 6:8; 7:18
	תֵּאמְרוּן	אמר	say; order	Jer 10:11
	תִּפְּלוּן	נפל	fall	Dan 3:5, 15
1cs	אֶבְעֵא־	בעה	seek	Dan 7:16
	אֶקְרֵא	קרא	read	Dan 5:17
	וְאִנְדַּע	ידע	know; learn; understand	Dan 2:9
1cp	נִכְתֻּב	כתב	write	Ezra 5:10
	נִסְגֻּד	סגד	prostrate oneself, bow down to the ground	Dan 3:18
	נֵאמַר	אמר	say; order	Dan 2:36

JUSSIVE

PGN	WORD	ROOT	GLOSS(ES)	VERSE(S)
3ms	יִשְׁפַּר	שפר	be pleasant, pleasing	Dan 4:24
	יֵאמַר	אמר	say; order	Dan 2:7
	יִשְׂגֵּא	שגא	become great, grow	Dan 3:31; 6:26
	לֶהֱוֵא	הוה	be, become, exist; occur, happen	Dan 2:20; 3:18; 4:12, 13; Ezra 5:8; 6:9; 7:26
	וִיהָךְ	הך	go	Ezra 6:5
3fs	תְּנֻד	נוד	flee	Dan 4:11
3mp	יַחְלְפוּן	חלף	pass over	Dan 4:13
	יֵאבַדוּ	אבד	perish	Jer 10:11
	יִבְנוֹן	בנה	rebuild	Ezra 6:7
3fp	לֶהֶוְיָן	הוה	be, become, exist; occur, happen	Dan 5:17

IMPERATIVE

PGN	WORD	ROOT	GLOSS(ES)	VERSE(S)
2ms	פְּרֻק	פרק	wipe away; ransom	Dan 4:24
	אֱמַר	אמר	say; order	Dan 2:4; 4:6, 15
	אֱזֶל־	אזל	go	Ezra 5:15

PGN	WORD	ROOT	GLOSS(ES)	VERSE(S)
	חֱיִי	חיה	*live*	Dan 2:4; 3:9; 5:10; 6:7, 22
	דַּע	ידע	*know; learn; understand*	Dan 6:16
	הַב	יהב	*give*	Dan 5:17
	שֵׂא	נשׂא	*carry, take*	Ezra 5:15
2fs	אֲכֻלִי	אכל	*eat*	Dan 7:5
	קוּמִי	קום	*arise, get up; be established, endure*	Dan 7:5
2mp	שְׁבֻקוּ	שבק	*leave; (w/ לְ) leave smthg alone, unencumbered*	Dan 4:12, 20; Ezra 6:7
	אֱמַרוּ	אמר	*say; order*	Dan 2:9
	שִׂימוּ	שׂים	*put, place, lay*	Ezra 4:21
	גֹּדּוּ	גדד	*chop down*	Dan 4:11, 20
	וֶאֱתוֹ	אתה	*come*	Dan 3:26
	הֱווֹ	הוה	*be, become, exist; occur, happen*	Ezra 4:22
	הֱווֹ	הוה	*be, become, exist; occur, happen*	Ezra 6:6
	פֻּקוּ	נפק	*go out*	Dan 3:26

PARTICIPLE

ms	קָטֵל	קטל	*kill*	Dan 5:19
	פָּלַח־	פלח	*serve*	Dan 6:17, 21
	בָּרֵךְ	ברך I	*kneel*	Dan 6:11
	דָּלִק	דלק	*be on fire*	Dan 7:9
	כָּהֵל	כהל	*be able*	Dan 2:26; 4:15
	וְחָשֵׁל	חשל	*smash*	Dan 2:40
	שָׁאֵל	שאל	*ask*	Dan 2:11, 27
	נָגֵד	נגד	*flow*	Dan 7:10
	וְנָפֵק	נפק	*go out*	Dan 7:10
	נָזִק	נזק	*come to grief (HALOT); be damaged*	Dan 6:3
	נָחֵת	נחת	*descend*	Dan 4:10, 20
	עָבֵד	עבד	*do, make*	Dan 4:32; 6:11; Ezra 7:26
	וְעָבֵד	עבד	*do, make*	Dan 6:28
	אָמַר	אמר	*say; order*	Dan 4:4, 11

PGN	WORD	ROOT	GLOSS(ES)	VERSE(S)
	וַאֲמַר	אמר	*say; order*	Dan 2:5, 8, 15, 20, 26, 27, 47; 3:14, 19, 24, 25, 26, 28; 4:16, 20, 27; 5:7, 13, 17; 6:13, 17, 21; 7:2
	אֲנַס	אנס	*oppress, bother*	Dan 4:6
	קְרָא	קרא	*cry out, shout*	Dan 3:4; 4:11; 5:7
	יְדַע	ידע	*know; learn; understand*	Dan 2:8, 22; Ezra 7:25
	יְהַב	יהב	*give*	Dan 2:21
	יְכֵל	יכל	*be able*	Dan 3:17; 4:34
	צְבֵא	צבה	*desire, wish*	Dan 5:19 (4x)
	שְׁתֵה	שתה	*drink*	Dan 5:1
	גְּלֵא	גלה	*reveal*	Dan 2:22, 28
	וְגָלֵא	גלה	*revealer*	Dan 2:29
	וְגַלֵּה	גלה	*reveal*	Dan 2:47
	דָּמֵה	דמה	*resemble*	Dan 3:25
	בְּעֵא	בעה	*seek*	Dan 6:12, 14
	חֲזֵה	חזה	*see; perceive*	Dan 2:31, 34, 25; 4:7, 10; 5:5; 7:2, 4, 6, 7, 9, 11 (*bis*), 13, 21
	עֲנֵה	I ענה	*answer, reply; begin to speak*	Dan 2:5, 8, 15, 20, 26, 27, 47; 3:14, 19, 24, 25, 26, 28; 4:16 (*bis*), 27; Dan 5:7, 13, 17; 6:13, 17, 21; 7:2
	אֲתֵה	אתה	*come*	Dan 7:13
	קָאֵם	קום	*arise, get up; be established, endure*	Dan 2:31
	לְשָׂנְאָךְ	שנא	*hater, enemy* (w/ 2ms acc sx)	Dan 4:16
fs	כְּתְבָה	כתב	*write*	Dan 5:5
	עֲבְדָה	עבד	*do, make*	Dan 7:21
	בְּטֵלָא	בטל	intrans *cease(d)*	Ezra 4:24
	רָפְסָה	רפס	*trample*	Dan 7:7, 19
	דָּמְיָה	דמה	*resemble*	Dan 7:5
	שָׁנְיָה	שנה	*be different*	Dan 7:19
	וְיָכְלָה	יכל	*be more able, overpower*	Dan 7:21
	יָקֵדְתָּא	יקד	[emphatic form] *burn*	Dan 3:6, 11, 15, 17, 20, 21, 23, 26

PGN	WORD	ROOT	GLOSS(ES)	VERSE(S)
mp	סָגְדִין	סגד	*prostrate oneself, bow down to the ground*	Dan 3:7, 12, 14
	שָׁפְטִין	שפט	*judge*	Ezra 7:25
	דָּבְקִין	דבק	*adhere, stick together*	Dan 2:43
	גָּזְרִין	גזר	*diviner*	Dan 2:27; 5:11
	וְגָזְרַיָּא	גזר	*[emphatic form]* diviner	Dan 4:4; 5:7
	טָרְדִין	טרד	*drive away*	Dan 4:22, 29
	זָבְנִין	זבן	*buy*	Dan 2:8
	נָפְקִין	נפק	*go out*	Dan 3:26
	עָבְדִין	עבד	*do, make*	Ezra 4:15
	שָׁמְעִין	שמע	*hear*	Dan 3:7; 5:23
	דָּבְחִין	דבח	*sacrifice*	Ezra 6:3
	פָּלְחִין	פלח	*serve*	Dan 3:12, 14, 17, 18
	וּפָלְחֵי	פלח	*servant*	Ezra 7:24
	אָמְרִין	אמר	*say; order*	Dan 3:4; 4:28; 6:6, 7; 7:5; Ezra 5:3
	וְאָמְרִין	אמר	*say; order*	Dan 2:7, 10; 3:9, 16, 24; 6:13, 14, 16
	חַשְׁחִין	חשח	*need*	Dan 3:16
	וְדָחֲלִין	דחל	*fear*	Dan 5:19; 6:27
	כָּהֲלִין	כהל	*be able*	Dan 5:8, 15
	נָפְלִין	נפל	*fall*	Dan 3:7
	יָדְעִין	ידע	*know; learn; understand*	Dan 5:23
	יָדְעֵי	ידע	*know; learn; understand*	Dan 2:21; Ezra 7:25
	יָכְלִין	יכל	*be able*	Dan 2:27; 4:15; 6:5
	יָתְבִין	יתב	*dwell*	Ezra 4:17
	יָהֲבִין	יהב	*give*	Dan 6:3
	בָּנַיִן	בנה	*(re)build*	Ezra 4:12; 5:4; 6:14
	וּבְנַיִן	בנה	*(re)build*	Ezra 5:11
	חָזַיִן	חזה	*see; perceive*	Dan 3:27; 5:23
	שָׁתַיִן	שתה	*drink (w/ בְּ) from*	Dan 5:23
	שָׁנַיִן	שנה	*intrans changed*	Dan 5:9
	בָּעַיִן	בעה	*seek*	Dan 6:5
	עָנַיִן	ענה I	*answer, reply; begin to speak*	Dan 3:24

PGN	WORD	ROOT	GLOSS(ES)	VERSE(S)
	וְקָיְמִין	קום	*arise, get up; be established, endure*	Dan 3:3
	קָאֲמַיָּא	קום	[emphatic form] *arise, get up; be established, endure*	Dan 7:16
	זָיְעִין	זוע	*tremble*	Dan 5:19; 6:27
	דָיְרִין	דור	*dwell*	Dan 2:38; 3:31; 6:26
	דָיְרֵי	דור	*dwell*	Dan 4:32
	וְדָיְרֵי	דור	*dwell*	Dan 4:32
	דָאיְנִין	דין	*judge*	Ezra 7:25
	עָלִין	עלל II	*enter*	Dan 4:4; 5:8
	וְיָעֲטוֹהִי	יעט	*adviser* (w/ 3ms gen sx)	Ezra 7:15
	יָעֲטוֹהִי	יעט	*adviser* (w/ 3ms gen sx)	Ezra 7:14
fp	סָלְקָן	סלק	*come up*	Dan 7:3
	וְכָתְבָן	כתב	*write*	Dan 5:5
	נָקְשָׁן	נקש	*knock*	Dan 5:6
	שָׁנְיָן	שנה	*be different*	Dan 7:3

INFINITIVE

	WORD	ROOT	GLOSS(ES)	VERSE(S)
	לְמִפְשַׁר	פשר	*interpret*	Dan 5:16
	לְמִכְנַשׁ	כנשׁ	*assemble*	Dan 3:2
	לְמִשְׁבַּק	שבק	*leave*	Dan 4:23
	לְמֶעְבַּד	עבד	*do, make*	Ezra 4:22; 7:18
	לְמִנְתַּן	נתן	*give*	Ezra 7:20
	לְמִקְרֵא	קרא	*read*	Dan 5:8, 16
	לְמֵאמַר	אמר	*say; order*	Dan 2:9
	לְמֵמַר	אמר	*say; order*	Ezra 5:11
	לְמִגְלֵא	גלה	*reveal*	Dan 2:47
	לְמִבְעֵא	בעה	*seek*	Dan 2:18
	לְמֶחֱזֵא	חזה	*see; perceive*	Ezra 4:14
	לְמִבְנֵא	בנה	*rebuild*	Ezra 5:2, 17; 6:8
	לִבְּנֵא	בנה	*rebuild*	Ezra 5:3, 13
	לְמִבְנְיָה	בנה	*rebuild*	Ezra 5:9
	לְמִשְׁרֵא	שרה	*loosen*	Dan 5:16
	לְמִרְמֵא	רמה	*throw*	Dan 3:20; Ezra 7:24

PGN	WORD	ROOT	GLOSS(ES)	VERSE(S)
	לְמֵזֵא	אזה	*heat, stoke*	Dan 3:19
	לְמֵתֵא	אתה	*come*	Dan 3:2
	בְּמִחַן	חנן	*show mercy, grace*	Dan 4:24
	לִמְהָךְ	הך	*go*	Ezra 7:13
	לְמֵזְיֵהּ	אזה	*heat, stoke* (w/ 3ms acc sx)	Dan 3:19
	וּכְמִצְבְּיֵהּ	צבה	*desire, wish* (w/ 3ms gen sx)	Dan 4:32
	וּכְמִקְרְבֵהּ	קרב	*approach* (w/ 3ms gen sx)	Dan 6:21

LIST #17: Gp STEM

- Attested conjugations: SC, ptcp.
- 44 unique attested forms.

PGN	WORD	ROOT	GLOSS(ES)	VERSE(S)

SUFFIX CONJUGATION

PGN	WORD	ROOT	GLOSS(ES)	VERSE(S)
3ms	קְטִיל	קטל	*be killed*	Dan 5:30
	כְּתִיב	כתב	*be written*	Ezra 5:7; 6:2
	רְשִׁים	רשם	*be written*	Dan 5:24, 25; 6:11
	טְרִיד	טרד	*be driven away*	Dan 4:30; 5:21
	יְהִיב	יהב	*be given*	Dan 7:4, 6, 14
	יְהֵב	יהב	*be given*	Dan 7:22
	שְׁלִיחַ	שלח	*sent*	Dan 5:24
	שְׁוִי	שוה	*become like*	Dan 5:21 (K)
	קְרִי	קרא	*be read*	Ezra 4:18, 23
	גְּלִי	גלה	*be revealed*	Dan 2:19
	גֱּלִי	גלה	*be revealed*	Dan 2:30
	שִׂים	שים	*be put, placed, laid*	Dan 3:29; 4:3; 6:27; Ezra 5:17; 6:8, 11; 7:13, 21
3fs	קְטִילַת	קטל	*be killed*	Dan 7:11
	פְּרִיסַת	פרס	*be divided*	Dan 5:28
	יְהִיבַת	יהב	*be given*	Dan 7:12, 27

PGN	WORD	ROOT	GLOSS(ES)	VERSE(S)
	וִיהִיבַת	יהב	be given	Dan 5:28; 7:11
	וּנְטִילַת	נטל	be lifted	Dan 7:4
	וְשֻׂמַת	שׂים	be put, placed, laid	Dan 6:18
3mp	מְרִיטוּ	מרט	be plucked	Dan 7:4
	פְּתִיחוּ	פתח	be opened	Dan 7:10
	כְּפִתוּ	כפת	be tied up	Dan 3:21
	וִיהִיבוּ	יהב	be given	Ezra 5:14
	רְמִיו	רמה	be placed	Dan 7:9
	וּרְמִיו	רמה	be thrown	Dan 3:21
2ms	תְּקִילְתָּה	תקל	be weighed	Dan 5:27

PARTICIPLE

PGN	WORD	ROOT	GLOSS(ES)	VERSE(S)
ms	דְּחִיל	דחל	feared	Dan 2:31
	בְּרִיךְ	II ברך	blessed	Dan 3:28
	גְּמִיר	גמר	perfect, completed; as adv completely (?)	Ezra 7:12
	וּזְקִיף	זקף	raised	Ezra 6:11
	שְׁלִם	שלם	be finished	Ezra 5:16
	יְדִיעַ	ידע	be known; be learned; be understood	Dan 3:18; Ezra 4:12, 13; 5:8
	שְׁלִיחַ	שלח	sent	Ezra 7:14
	עֲשִׂית	עשׂת	intend active sense	Dan 6:4
	חֲזֵה	חזה	seen = normal	Dan 3:19
	בְּנֵה	בנה	(re)build	Ezra 5:11
	אֲזֵה	אזה	heat, stoke	Dan 3:22
	שָׁרֵא	שרה	dwell	Dan 2:22
fs	פְּלִיגָה	פלג	divided	Dan 2:41
	תְּבִירָה	תבר	fragile, brittle	Dan 2:42
	דְּחִילָה	דחל	feared	Dan 7:7, 19
	וּשְׁחִיתָה	שחת	corrupted, bad	Dan 2:9; 6:5 (bis)

PGN	WORD	ROOT	GLOSS(ES)	VERSE(S)
mp	חֲשִׁיבִין	חשׁב	*be thought of*	Dan 4:32
	שְׁרַיִן	שׁרה	*untied*	Dan 3:25
fp	פְּתִיחָן	פתח	*be opened*	Dan 6:11

LIST #18: tG STEM

• Attested conjugations: SC, PC, juss, ptcp, inf.
• 36 unique attested forms.

PGN	WORD	ROOT	GLOSS(ES)	VERSE(S)

SUFFIX CONJUGATION

PGN	WORD	ROOT	GLOSS(ES)	VERSE(S)
3ms	הִשְׁתְּכַח	שׁכח	*be found*	Dan 2:35; 6:24
	וְהִשְׁתְּכַח	שׁכח	*be found*	Ezra 6:2
	הִתְמְלִי	מלא	*be filled*	Dan 3:19
3fs	הִתְגְּזֶרֶת	גזר	*be cut out*	Dan 2:34
	אִתְגְּזֶרֶת	גזר	*cut out*	Dan 2:45
	הִשְׁתְּכַחַת	שׁכח	*be found*	Dan 5:11, 12, 14; 6:5, 23
	אֶתְכְּרִיַּת	כרה	*be distressed, troubled, disturbed*	Dan 7:15
3mp	הִתְרְחִצוּ	רחץ	*trust (w/ עַל-) in*	Dan 3:28
3fp	אֶתְעֲקַרָה	עקר	*be ripped out*	Dan 7:8
2ms	וְהִשְׁתְּכַחַתְּ	שׁכח	*be found*	Dan 5:27
2mp	הִזְדְּמִנְתּוּן	זמן	*conspire*	Dan 2:9

PGN	WORD	ROOT	GLOSS(ES)	VERSE(S)

PREFIX CONJUGATION

PGN	WORD	ROOT	GLOSS(ES)	VERSE(S)
3ms	יִתְעֲבֵד	עבד	*be done; be turned into*	Dan 3:29; Ezra 6:11; 7:23
	יִתְעֲבֵד	עבד	*be done; be turned into*	Ezra 7:21
	יִתְּנְסַח	נסח	*be pulled out*	Ezra 6:11
	יִתְרְמֵא	רמה	*be thrown*	Dan 3:6, 11; 6:8, 13
	יִתְמְחֵא	מחא	*be impaled*	Ezra 6:11
	יִתְּשָׂם	שׂים	*be put; be turned into*	Ezra 4:21
	יִתְּזִין	זון	*be fed*	Dan 4:9
3fs	תִּתְבְּנֵא	בנה	*be rebuilt*	Ezra 4:13, 16, 21
	תִּשְׁתְּבִק	שבק	*be left (w/ לְ) to*	Dan 2:44
3mp	וְיִתְיַהֲבוּן	יהב	*be given*	Dan 7:25
	יִתְּשָׂמוּן	שׂים	*be put; be turned into*	Dan 2:5
2mp	תִּתְעַבְדוּן	עבד	*be done; be turned into*	Dan 2:5
	תִּתְרְמוֹן	רמה	*be thrown*	Dan 3:15

JUSSIVE

PGN	WORD	ROOT	GLOSS(ES)	VERSE(S)
3ms	יִתְיְהִב	יהב	*be given*	Dan 4:13
	יִתְעֲבֵד	עבד	*be done; be turned into*	Ezra 6:12
	יִתְבְּנֵא	בנה	*be rebuilt*	Ezra 5:15; 6:3
3fs	תִּתְיְהִב	יהב	*be given*	Ezra 6:4

PARTICIPLE

PGN	WORD	ROOT	GLOSS(ES)	VERSE(S)
ms	מִתְיְהֵב	יהב	*be given*	Ezra 4:20; 6:9
	מִתְבְּנֵא	בנה	*being rebuilt*	Ezra 5:8, 16
	מִתְעֲבֵד	עבד	*be done; be turned into*	Ezra 7:26
	מִתְעֲבֶד־	עבד	*be done; be turned into*	Ezra 4:19
	מִתְּשָׂם	שׂים	*be put; be turned into*	Ezra 5:8
fs	מִתְיַהֲבָא	יהב	*be given*	Ezra 6:8

PGN	WORD	ROOT	GLOSS(ES)	VERSE(S)
mp	מִתְיְהַבִין	יהב	*be given*	Ezra 7:19

INFINITIVE

	לְהִתְקְטָלָה	קטל	*be killed*	Dan 2:13

LIST #19: D STEM

- Attested conjugations: SC, PC, juss, impv, ptcp, inf.
- 73 unique attested forms.

PGN	WORD	ROOT	GLOSS(ES)	VERSE(S)

SUFFIX CONJUGATION

PGN	WORD	ROOT	GLOSS(ES)	VERSE(S)
3ms	קַטֵּל	קטל	*kill*	Dan 3:22
	קַבֵּל	קבל	*receive*	Dan 6:1
	שַׁכֵּן	שכן	*cause to dwell, settle*	Ezra 6:12
	מַלֵּל	מלל	*speak*	Dan 6:22
	בָּרֵךְ	II ברך	*bless*	Dan 2:19
	מַנִּי	מנה	*appoint*	Dan 2:24
	וּמַנִּי	מנה	*appoint*	Dan 2:49
	רַבִּי	רבה	*make great, promote*	Dan 2:48
2ms	שַׁבַּחְתָּ	שבח	*praise*	Dan 5:23
	הַדַּרְתָּ	הדר	*glorify*	Dan 5:23
	מַנִּיתָ	מנה	*appoint*	Dan 3:12
1cs	שַׁבְּחֵת	שבח	*praise*	Dan 4:31
	וְהַדְּרֵת	הדר	*glorify*	Dan 4:31
	בָּרְכֵת	II ברך	*bless*	Dan 4:31
3mp	בַּטִּלוּ	בטל	trans *stop*	Ezra 5:5
	וּבַטִּלוּ	בטל	trans *stop*	Ezra 4:23

PGN	WORD	ROOT	GLOSS(ES)	VERSE(S)
	וּבַקַּרוּ	בקר	*search*	Ezra 4:19; 6:1
	וְשַׁבַּחוּ	שבח	*praise*	Dan 5:4
	וְשָׁרִיו	שרה	*begin*	Ezra 5:2
	שַׁנִּיו	שנה	trans *change* = *violate*	Dan 3:28
	שַׁוִּיו	שוה	*make the same as*	Dan 5:21
	חַבְּלוּנִי	חבל	*destroy* (w/ 1cs acc sx)	Dan 6:23

PREFIX CONJUGATION

PGN	WORD	ROOT	GLOSS(ES)	VERSE(S)
3ms	יְבַקַּר	בקר	*search*	Ezra 4:15
	יְמַלִּל	מלל	*speak*	Dan 7:25
	יִמְחֵא	מחא	*strike*	Dan 4:32
	יְבַלֵּא	בלה	*harass, wear out*	Dan 7:25
	יִתְּב	יתב	*sit*	Dan 7:26
	יְחַוִּנַּה	חוה	*show, make known, declare* (w/ 3fs acc sx)	Dan 2:11
	יְחַוִּנַּנִי	חוה	*make known* (w/ 1cs acc sx)	Dan 5:7
	וִידַחֲלַנִּי	דחל	*frighten* (w/ 1cs acc sx)	Dan 4:2
2ms	וּתְקָרֵב	קרב	*offer*	Ezra 7:17
1cs	אֲחַוֵּא	חוה	*show, make known, declare*	Dan 2:24
3mp	וִיקַבְּלוּן	קבל	*receive*	Dan 7:18
	יְטַעֲמוּן	טעם	*feed*	Dan 4:22, 29
	יִבְעוֹן	בעה	*seek*	Dan 4:33
	יְבַהֲלֻנֵּהּ	בהל	*terrify* (w/ 3ms acc sx)	Dan 4:16
	יְבַהֲלוּנֵּהּ	בהל	*terrify* (w/ 3ms acc sx)	Dan 5:6
	יְטַעֲמוּנֵּהּ	טעם	*feed* (w/ 3ms acc sx)	Dan 5:21
	יְשַׁמְּשׁוּנֵּהּ	שמש	*minister, attend, serve* (w/ 3ms acc sx)	Dan 7:10
	יְבַהֲלַנִּי	בהל	*terrify* (w/ 1cs acc sx)	Dan 4:2; 7:15, 28
2mp	תְּקַבְּלוּן	קבל	*receive*	Dan 2:6
1cp	נְחַוֵּא	חוה	*show, make known, declare*	Dan 2:4

PGN	WORD	ROOT	GLOSS(ES)	VERSE(S)
JUSSIVE				
3ms	יְמַגַּר	מגר	*overthrow*	Ezra 6:12
	יְבַהֲלָךְ	בהל	*terrify* (w/ 2ms acc sx)	Dan 4:16
3mp	יְשַׁנּוֹן	שנה	trans *change*	Dan 4:13
	יְבַהֲלוּךְ	בהל	*terrify* (w/ 2ms acc sx)	Dan 5:10
IMPERATIVE				
2ms	מֶנִּי	מנה	*appoint*	Ezra 7:25
2mp	וּבַדַּרוּ	בדר	*scatter*	Dan 4:11
	וְקַצִּצוּ	קצץ	*cut off, lop off*	Dan 4:11
	וְחַבְּלוּהִי	חבל	*destroy* (w/ 3ms acc sx)	Dan 4:20
PARTICIPLE				
ms	מְפַשַּׁר	פשר	*interpret*	Dan 5:12
	וּמְהַדַּר	הדר	*glorify*	Dan 4:34
	מְהַלֵּךְ	הלך	*walk*	Dan 4:26
	מְמַלִּל	מלל	*speak*	Dan 7:8, 20
	מְשַׁבַּח	שבח	*praise*	Dan 4:34
	וּמְשַׁבַּח	שבח	*praise*	Dan 2:23
	וּמְצַלֵּא	צלה	*pray*	Dan 6:11
	וּמְשָׁרֵא	שרה	*loosen*	Dan 5:12
	מְרָעַע	רעע	*crush*	Dan 2:40
	וּמְרוֹמֵם	רום	*praise*	Dan 4:34
fs	מְמַלְלָה	מלל	*speak*	Dan 7:11
mp	מְצַבְּעִין	צבע	*drench*	Dan 4:22
	מְסָעֲדִין	סעד	*support*	Ezra 5:2
	וּמְצַלַּיִן	צלה	*pray*	Ezra 6:10

PGN	WORD	ROOT	GLOSS(ES)	VERSE(S)

INFINITIVE

	לְקַטְלָה	קטל	kill	Dan 2:14
	לְבַטָּלָא	בטל	trans stop	Ezra 4:21; 6:8
	לְבַקָּרָא	בקר	search	Ezra 7:14
	לְכַפָּתָה	כפת	tie up	Dan 3:20
	וּלְתַקָּפָה	תקף	make strong; enforce	Dan 6:8
	לְחַבָּלָה	חבל	destroy	Ezra 6:12
	לְנַסָּכָה	נסך	pour out = offer	Dan 2:46
	לְחַטָּאָה	חטא	sin, make a sin offering	Ezra 6:17
	לְיַצָּבָא	יצב	ascertain, make certain of	Dan 7:19
	לְקַיָּמָה	קום	set up, erect	Dan 6:8

LIST #20: Dp STEM

- Attested conjugation: ptcp.
- 7 unique attested forms.

PGN	WORD	ROOT	GLOSS(ES)	VERSE(S)

PARTICIPLE

ms	מְפָרַשׁ	פרשׁ	separated, made distinct; translated; explained	Ezra 4:18
	מְבָרַךְ	ברך II	blessed	Dan 2:20
	מְעָרַב	ערב	mixed	Dan 2:41, 43
mp	מְכַפְּתִין	כפת	tied up	Dan 3:23, 24
	מְסוֹבְלִין	סבל	maintained (?)	Ezra 6:3
fp	מְשַׁנְיָה	שנה	be different	Dan 7:7
	וּמְסַתְּרָתָא	סתר I	[emphatic form] hidden	Dan 2:22

LIST #21: tD STEM

- Attested conjugations: SC, PC, juss, ptcp.
- 33 unique attested forms.

PGN	WORD	ROOT	GLOSS(ES)	VERSE(S)
SUFFIX CONJUGATION				
3ms	הִתְחָרַךְ	חרך	be singed	Dan 3:27
	אֶשְׁתַּנִּי	שנה	intrans *change*	Dan 3:19
	וְהִתְנַבִּי	נבא	*prophesy*	Ezra 5:1
3mp	הִתְנַדַּבוּ	נדב	*volunteer*	Ezra 7:15
	אִתְיָעַטוּ	יעט	*consult together*	Dan 6:8
2ms	הִתְרוֹמַמְתָּ	רום	*exalt oneself*	Dan 5:23
PREFIX CONJUGATION				
3ms	יִצְטַבַּע	צבע	*be soaked*	Dan 4:30
	יִשְׁתַּוֵּה	שוה	*be turned into*	Dan 3:29
	יִשְׁתַּנֵּא	שנה	intrans *change*	Dan 2:9
3fs	תִּתְחַבַּל	חבל	*be destroyed*	Dan 2:44; 6:27; 7:14
3mp	וְיִשְׁתַּמְּעוּן	שמע	*hear, heed*	Dan 7:27
	יִשְׁתַּנּוֹן	שנה	*be changed*	Dan 7:28
1cs	אֶשְׁתּוֹמַם	שמם	*be appalled*	Dan 4:16
JUSSIVE				
3ms	יִתְבַּקַּר	בקר	*be searched*	Ezra 5:17
	יִצְטַבַּע	צבע	*be drenched*	Dan 4:12, 20; 5:21
	יִתְקְרֵי	קרא	*be called*	Dan 5:12
3mp	יִשְׁתַּנּוֹ	שנה	*be changed*	Dan 5:10

PGN	WORD	ROOT	GLOSS(ES)	VERSE(S)

PARTICIPLE

PGN	WORD	ROOT	GLOSS(ES)	VERSE(S)
ms	מִתְנַדַּב	נדב	*volunteer*	Ezra 7:13
	מִתְנַצַּח	נצח	*distinguish oneself, surpass*	Dan 6:4
	וּמִתְחַנַּן	חנן	*seek mercy, grace*	Dan 6:12
	מִתְבְּהַל	בהל	*be terrified*	Dan 5:9
	מִתְעָרַב	ערב	*intermingle*	Dan 2:43
	מִשְׂתַּכַּל	שׂכל	*contemplate*	Dan 7:8
	מִשְׁתַּדַּר	שׂדר	*exert, make every effort*	Dan 6:15
fs	מִתְעַבְדָא	עבד	*be done; be turned into*	Ezra 5:8
	מִתְנַשְּׂאָה	נשׂא	*rise up against*	Ezra 4:19
mp	מִתְקַטְּלִין	קטל	*be killed*	Dan 2:13
	מִתְנַדְּבִין	נדב	*volunteer*	Ezra 7:16
	מִתְכַּנְּשִׁין	כנש	*assemble*	Dan 3:3
	וּמִתְכַּנְּשִׁין	כנש	*assemble*	Dan 3:27
	מִתְעָרְבִין	ערב	*intermingle*	Dan 2:43
	מִשְׁתָּרַיִן	שׂרה	*giving way*	Dan 5:6
	מִשְׁתַּבְּשִׁין	שׂבשׂ	*be perplexed*	Dan 5:9

LIST #22: H STEM

- Attested conjugations: SC, PC, juss, impv, ptcp, inf.
- 126 unique attested forms.

PGN	WORD	ROOT	GLOSS(ES)	VERSE(S)

SUFFIX CONJUGATION

PGN	WORD	ROOT	GLOSS(ES)	VERSE(S)
3ms	הַצְלַח	צלח	*promote*	Dan 3:30; 6:29
	הַנְפֵּק	נפק	*bring out*	Dan 5:2, 14 (*bis*); 6:5
	וְהוֹתֵב	יתב	*make dwell, settle*	Ezra 4:10
	וְהֵיבֵל	יבל	*bring*	Ezra 5:14; 6:5

PGN	WORD	ROOT	GLOSS(ES)	VERSE(S)
	הוֹדַע	ידע	*make known, communicate*	Dan 2:15, 17, 45
	וְהוֹדַע	ידע	*make known, communicate*	Dan 2:28
	הֲקֵים	קום	*raise, erect; found, establish; appoint*	Dan 3:2, 3 (*bis*), 5, 7
	וַהֲקֵים	קום	*raise, erect; found, establish; appoint*	Dan 6:2
	הֵימִן	אמן	*trust*	Dan 6:24
	הַיְתִי	אתה	*bring*	Dan 5:13
	הַגְלִי	גלה	*deport, exile*	Ezra 4:10; 5:12
	הֲתִיב	תוב	trans *return*	Dan 2:14
	הַדִּקוּ	דקק	*pulverize*	Dan 6:25
	הַנְעֵל	עלל II	*bring*	Dan 2:25; 6:19
	וְהַשְׁלְטֵהּ	שלט	*make rule* (w/ 3ms acc sx)	Dan 2:48
	הֲקִימֵהּ	קום	*raise, erect; found, establish; appoint* (w/ 3ms acc sx)	Dan 5:11
	אֲקִימֵהּ	קום	*raise, erect; found, establish; appoint* (w/ 3ms acc sx)	Dan 3:1
	וְהַשְׁלְמַהּ	שלם	*complete, finish off* (w/ 3fs acc sx)	Dan 5:26
	וְהַשְׁלְטָךְ	שלט	*make rule* (w/ 2ms acc sx)	Dan 2:38
	הוֹדְעָךְ	ידע	*make known, communicate* (w/ 2ms acc sx)	Dan 2:29
3fs	וְהַדֵּקֶת	דקק	*pulverize*	Dan 2:34, 35
3mp	וְהַלְבִּישׁוּ	לבש	*clothe*	Dan 5:29
	וְהַקְרִבוּ	קרב	*offer*	Ezra 6:17
	וְהַכְרִזוּ	כרז	*herald, proclaim*	Dan 5:29
	הַרְגִּזוּ	רגז	*enrage*	Ezra 5:12
	הַרְגִּשׁוּ	רגש	*throng* [= *conspire* (?)]	Dan 6:7, 12, 16
	וְהַשְׁכַּחוּ	שכח	*find*	Dan 6:12; Ezra 4:19
	הַנְפִּקוּ	נפק	*bring out*	Dan 5:3
	הֶחֱסִנוּ	חסן	*possess*	Dan 7:22
	וַהֲקִימוּ	קום	*raise, erect; found, establish; appoint*	Ezra 6:18
	הֶעְדִּיו	עדה	*remove*	Dan 5:20
	הֶעְדִּיו	עדה	*remove*	Dan 7:12
	הַיְתִיו	אתה	*bring*	Dan 5:3, 23
	וְהַיְתִיו	אתה	*bring*	Dan 6:17, 25

PGN	WORD	ROOT	GLOSS(ES)	VERSE(S)
	הַסִּקוּ	סלק	*bring up*	Dan 3:22
	אֲשַׁכְלִלוּ	שכלל	*finish*	Ezra 4:12 (K)
	הַקְרְבוּהִי	קרב	*present* (w/ 3ms acc sx)	Dan 7:13
	הֲתִיבוּנָא	תוב	trans *return* (w/ suffix) *to* (w/ 1cp acc sx)	Ezra 5:11
2ms	הַשְׁפֵּלְתְּ	שפל	*humble*	Dan 5:22
	הֲקֵימְתָּ	קום	*raise, erect; found, establish; appoint*	Dan 3:12, 18
	הוֹדַעְתַּנִי	ידע	*make known, communicate* (w/ 1cs acc sx)	Dan 2:23
	הוֹדַעְתֶּנָא	ידע	*make known, communicate* (w/ 1cp acc sx)	Dan 2:23
1cs	הַשְׁכַּחַת	שכח	*find*	Dan 2:25
	הֲקֵימֶת	קום	*raise, erect; found, establish; appoint*	Dan 3:14
1cp	הַשְׁכַּחְנָה	שכח	*find*	Dan 6:6
	וְהוֹדַעְנָא	ידע	*make known, communicate*	Ezra 4:14

PREFIX CONJUGATION

PGN	WORD	ROOT	GLOSS(ES)	VERSE(S)
3ms	יְהַשְׁפֵּל	שפל	*humble*	Dan 7:24
	יְהוֹדַע	ידע	*make known, communicate*	Dan 2:25
	יְהַחֲוֵה	חוה	*make known*	Dan 5:12
	יְהַשְׁנֵא	שנה	trans *change*	Ezra 6:11
	יְקִים	קום	*raise, erect; found, establish; appoint*	Dan 2:44; 4:14
	יְהָקֵים	קום	*raise, erect; found, establish; appoint*	Dan 5:21; 6:16
	יְהוֹדְעִנַּנִי	ידע	*make known, communicate* (w/ 1cs acc sx)	Dan 7:16
3fs	תְּהַנְזִק	נזק	*damage*	Ezra 4:13
	תַּטְלֵל	טלל	*find shade*	Dan 4:9
	תַּדִּק	דקק	*pulverize*	Dan 2:40, 44
	וְתָסֵיף	סוף	*bring to an end, annihilate*	Dan 2:44
	וְתַדְּקִנַּהּ	דקק	*pulverize* (w/ 3fs acc sx)	Dan 7:23

PGN	WORD	ROOT	GLOSS(ES)	VERSE(S)
3mp	וְיַחְסְנוּן	חסן	*possess*	Dan 7:18
	יְהַעְדּוֹן	עדה	*remove*	Dan 7:26
	יְהוֹדְעוּן	ידע	*make known, communicate*	Dan 2:30
	יְהֹבְדוּן	אבד	*kill*	Dan 2:18
	יְתִיבוּן	תוב	trans *return*	Ezra 5:5
	יַחִיטוּ	חוט	*repair*	Ezra 4:12
	יְהוֹדְעַנַּנִי	ידע	*make known, communicate* (w/ 1cs acc sx)	Dan 4:3
2ms	תְהַשְׁכַּח	שכח	*find*	Ezra 7:16
	וּתְהַשְׁכַּח	שכח	*find*	Ezra 4:15
	תְּקִים	קום	*raise, erect; found, establish; appoint*	Dan 6:9
	וְתַחֵת	נחת	*deposit*	Ezra 6:5
2mp	תְּהוֹדְעוּן	ידע	*make known, communicate*	Ezra 7:25
	תְּהַחֲוֹן	חוה	*show, make known, declare*	Dan 2:6
	תְהוֹדְעוּנַּנִי	ידע	*make known, communicate* (w/ 1cs acc sx)	Dan 2:5
	תְהוֹדְעֻנַּנִי	ידע	*make known, communicate* (w/ 1cs acc sx)	Dan 2:9
	תְּהַחֲוֻנַּנִי	חוה	*show, make known, declare* (w/ 1cs acc sx)	Dan 2:9
1cs	אֲהוֹדְעִנֵּהּ	ידע	*make known, communicate* (w/ 3ms acc sx)	Dan 5:17
1cp	נְהַשְׁכַּח	שכח	*find*	Dan 6:6
	נְהַחֲוֵה	חוה	*show, make known, declare*	Dan 2:7

JUSSIVE

PGN	WORD	ROOT	GLOSS(ES)	VERSE(S)
3mp	יְהָתִיבוּן	תוב	trans *return*	Ezra 6:5
2mp	תְּהוֹבֵד	אבד	*kill*	Dan 2:24

PGN	WORD	ROOT	GLOSS(ES)	VERSE(S)

IMPERATIVE

PGN	WORD	ROOT	GLOSS(ES)	VERSE(S)
2ms	הַשְׁלֵם	שלם	*fully deliver*	Ezra 7:19
	אֲחֵת	נחת	*deposit*	Ezra 5:15
	הַעֶלְנִי	עלל II	*bring* (w/ 1cs acc sx)	Dan 2:24
2mp	אַתַּרוּ	נתר	*strip off*	Dan 4:11
	הַחֲוֻנִי	חוה	*show, make known, declare* (w/ 1cs acc sx)	Dan 2:6

PARTICIPLE

PGN	WORD	ROOT	GLOSS(ES)	VERSE(S)
ms	מַשְׁפִּיל	שפל	*bring low*	Dan 5:19
	וּמַצְלַח	צלח	*prosper*	Ezra 5:8
	מְהַדֵּק	דקק	*pulverize*	Dan 2:40
	וּמַצֵּל	נצל	*deliver*	Dan 6:28
	מְהַעְדֵּה	עדה	*remove, depose*	Dan 2:21
	מְהַשְׁנֵא	שנה	trans *change*	Dan 2:21
	מַחֵא	חיה	*let live*	Dan 5:19
	מָרִים	רום	*exalt*	Dan 5:19
	וּמְהָקֵים	קום	*raise, erect; found, establish; appoint*	Dan 2:21
	מְהוֹדֵא	ידה	*give thanks*	Dan 2:23
	וּמוֹדֵא	ידה	*give thanks*	Dan 6:11
fs	וּמְהַנְזְקַת	נזק	*damager*	Ezra 4:15
	מְהַחְצְפָה	חצף	*be harsh*	Dan 2:15
	מַחְצְפָה	חצף	*be harsh*	Dan 3:22
	מַדְּקָה	דקק	*pulverize*	Dan 7:19
	וּמַדֱּקָה	דקק	*pulverize*	Dan 7:7
mp	מְהַקְרְבִין	קרב	*offer*	Ezra 6:10
	וּמַצְלְחִין	צלח	*prosper*	Ezra 6:14
	מַהְלְכִין	הלך	*walk*	Dan 3:25; 4:34
	מְהוֹדְעִין	ידע	*make known, communicate*	Dan 4:4, 16; 7:24
fp	מְגִיחָן	גוח	*stir up*	Dan 7:2

PGN	WORD	ROOT	GLOSS(ES)	VERSE(S)

INFINITIVE

	לְהַשְׁפָּלָה	שפל	*humiliate*	Dan 4:34
	לְהַשְׁמָדָה	שמד	*annihilate*	Dan 7:26
	לְהַשְׁכָּחָה	שכח	*find*	Dan 6:5
	לְהוֹדָעָה	ידע	*make known, communicate*	Dan 5:8
	לְהוֹבָדָה	אבד	*kill*	Dan 2:12, 24
	וּלְהוֹבָדָה	אבד	*destroy*	Dan 7:26
	לְהַשְׁנָיָה	שנה	trans *change*	Dan 6:9, 16; 7:25; Ezra 6:12
	לְהַיְתָיָה	אתה	*bring*	Dan 3:13; 5:12
	לְהַחֲוָיָה	חוה	*show, make known, declare*	Dan 2:10, 16, 27; 3:32; 5:15
	וַאַחֲוָיַת	חוה	*make known*	Dan 5:12
	לְהֶעָלָה	II עלל	*bring*	Dan 5:7
	לְהַנְעָלָה	II עלל	*bring*	Dan 4:3
	לְהַצָּלָה	נצל	*deliver*	Dan 3:29
	וּלְהֵיבָלָה	יבל	*bring*	Ezra 7:15
	לַהֲזָדָה	זוד	*be arrogant; act presumptuously*	Dan 5:20
	לְהַנְסָקָה	סלק	*bring up*	Dan 6:24
	לְהוֹדָעֻתַנִי	ידע	*make known, communicate* (w/ 1cs acc sx)	Dan 2:26; 4:15; 5:15, 16
	לְהוֹדָעוּתָךְ	ידע	*make known, communicate* (w/ 2ms acc sx)	Ezra 5:10
	לְהַצָּלוּתֵהּ	נצל	*deliver* (w/ 3ms acc sx)	Dan 6:15
	לַהֲקָמוּתֵהּ	קום	*raise, erect; found, establish; appoint* (w/ 3ms acc sx)	Dan 6:4
	לַהֲתָבוּתָךְ	תוב	trans *give a reply* (w/ suffix) *to* (w/ 2ms acc sx)	Dan 3:16

LIST #23: Hp STEM

- Attested conjugations: sc, ptcp.
- 15 unique attested forms.

PGN	WORD	ROOT	GLOSS(ES)	VERSE
SUFFIX CONJUGATION				
3ms	וְהוּבַד	אבד	*be destroyed*	Dan 7:11
	הָנְחַת	נחת	*be brought down, deposed*	Dan 5:20
	הֻעַל	II עלל	*be brought*	Dan 5:13
	וְהֻסַּק	סלק	*be brought up*	Dan 6:24
3fs	הָתְקְנַת	תקן	*be reestablished*	Dan 4:33
	הָחָרְבַת	חרב	*be laid waste*	Ezra 4:15
	הֲקִימַת	קום	*be set up, erected*	Dan 7:4
	הֲקֵמַת	קום	*be set up, erected*	Dan 7:5
	הוּסְפַּת	יסף	*be added*	Dan 4:33
	וְהֵיתָיִת	אתה	*be brought*	Dan 6:18
3mp	הֻעַלּוּ	II עלל	*be brought*	Dan 5:15
	הֵיתָיוּ	אתה	*be brought*	Dan 3:13
PARTICIPLE				
ms	מְהֵימַן	אמן	*trustworthy*	Dan 6:5
	וּמְהֵימַן	אמן	*trustworthy*	Dan 2:45
mp	מְהַחֲתִין	נחת	*deposited*	Ezra 6:1

LIST #24: Š STEM

- Attested conjugations: SC, PC, ptcp, inf.
- 14 unique attested forms.

PGN	WORD	ROOT	GLOSS(ES)	VERSE(S)
SUFFIX CONJUGATION				
3ms	שֵׁיזִיב	שיזב	*rescue*	Dan 6:28
	וְשֵׁיזִב	שיזב	*rescue*	Dan 3:28
	וְשֵׁיצִיא	שיציא	*complete*	Ezra 6:15
	וְשַׁכְלְלֵהּ	כלל	*finish* (w/ 3ms acc sx)	Ezra 5:11
3mp	שַׁכְלִלוּ	כלל	*finish*	Ezra 4:12
	וְשַׁכְלִלוּ	כלל	*finish*	Ezra 6:14
PREFIX CONJUGATION				
3ms	יְשֵׁיזִב	שיזב	*rescue*	Dan 3:17
	יְשֵׁיזְבִנָּךְ	שיזב	*rescue* (w/ 2ms acc sx)	Dan 6:17
	יְשֵׁיזְבִנְכוֹן	שיזב	*rescue* (w/ 2mp acc sx)	Dan 3:15
PARTICIPLE				
ms	מְשֵׁיזִב	שיזב	*rescue*	Dan 6:28
INFINITIVE				
	לְשַׁכְלָלָה	כלל	*finish, complete*	Ezra 5:3, 9
	לְשֵׁיזָבוּתֵהּ	שיזב	*rescue* (w/ 3ms acc sx)	Dan 6:15
	לְשֵׁיזָבוּתָךְ	שיזב	*rescue* (w/ 2ms acc sx)	Dan 6:21
	לְשֵׁיזָבוּתַנָא	שיזב	*rescue* (w/ 1cp acc sx)	Dan 3:17

LIST #25: Št STEM

- Attested conjugation: PC.
- 1 unique attested form.

PGN	WORD	ROOT	GLOSS	VERSES

PREFIX CONJUGATION

3mp   יִשְׁתַּכְלְלוּן   כלל   *be finished*   Ezra 4:13, 16

VERBS BY ROOT TYPE

LIST #26: STRONG VERBS

STEM/CONJ.	PGN	WORD	ROOT	GLOSS(ES)	VERSE(S)
G SC	3ms	כְּתַב	כתב	write	Dan 6:26; 7:1
		בְּנַס	בנס	be enraged	Dan 2:12
		וּקְצַף	קצף	be furious	Dan 2:12
		שְׁפַר	שפר	be pleasant, pleasing	Dan 3:32; 6:2
		רְשַׁם	רשם	write	Dan 6:10
		וּסֲגַר	סגר	close, shut	Dan 6:23
		סְגִד	סגד	prostrate oneself, bow down to the ground	Dan 2:46
		וּתְקֵף	תקף	become strong	Dan 4:8, 17
		שְׁלֵט	שלט	have power (w/ בְּ) over	Dan 3:27
		קְרֵב	קרב	approach	Dan 3:26
		סַתְרֵהּ	סתר II	destroy (w/ 3ms acc sx)	Ezra 5:12
	3fs	תְּקְפַת	תקף	become strong	Dan 5:20
		בְּטֵלַת	בטל	intrans cease(d)	Ezra 4:24
	3mp	כְּתַבוּ	כתב	write	Ezra 4:8
		קָרִיבוּ	קרב	approach	Dan 6:13
		קְרִבוּ	קרב	approach	Dan 3:8
		שְׁלֵטוּ	שלט	rule	Dan 6:25
	2ms	רְשַׁמְתָּ	רשם	write	Dan 6:13, 14
		וּתְקֵפְתְּ	תקף	become strong	Dan 4:19
	1cs	קִרְבֵת	קרב	approach	Dan 7:16

STEM/CONJ.	PGN	WORD	ROOT	GLOSS(ES)	VERSE(S)
G PC	**3ms**	יִלְבַּשׁ	לבשׁ	*wear*	Dan 5:7
		וְיִסְבַּר	סבר	*intend*	Dan 7:25
		יִשְׁלַט	שׁלט	*rule*	Dan 5:7
		וְיִסְגֵּד	סגד	*prostrate oneself, bow down to the ground*	Dan 3:6, 10, 11
	3fs	תְּשַׁלַט	שׁלט	*rule*	Dan 2:39
	3mp	יִסְגְּדוּן	סגד	*prostrate oneself, bow down to the ground*	Dan 3:28
	3fp	יִשְׁכְּנָן	שׁכן	*dwell*	Dan 4:18
	2ms	תְּשַׁלַט	שׁלט	*rule*	Dan 5:16
		תִּלְבַּשׁ	לבשׁ	*wear*	Dan 5:16
		וְתִרְשֻׁם	רשׁם	*write*	Dan 6:9
	2mp	וְתִסְגְּדוּן	סגד	*prostrate oneself, bow down to the ground*	Dan 3:5, 15
	1cp	נִכְתֻּב	כתב	*write*	Ezra 5:10
		נִסְגֵּד	סגד	*prostrate oneself, bow down to the ground*	Dan 3:18
G JUSS	**3ms**	יִשְׁפַּר	שׁפר	*be pleasant, pleasing*	Dan 4:24
G IMV	**2ms**	פְּרֻק	פרק	*wipe away; ransom*	Dan 4:24
	2mp	שְׁבֻקוּ	שׁבק	*leave; (w/ לְ) leave smthg alone, unencumbered*	Dan 4:12, 20; Ezra 6:7
G PTCP	**ms**	קָטֵל	קטל	*kill*	Dan 5:19
		בָּרֵךְ	ברך I	*kneel*	Dan 6:11
		דָּלִק	דלק	*be on fire*	Dan 7:9

STEM/CONJ.	PGN	WORD	ROOT	GLOSS(ES)	VERSE(S)
	fs	כָּתְבָה	כתב	write	Dan 5:5
		בְּטֵלָא	בטל	intrans *cease(d)*	Ezra 4:24
		רָפְסָה	רפס	*trample*	Dan 7:7, 19
	mp	סָגְדִין	סגד	*prostrate oneself, bow down to the ground*	Dan 3:7, 12, 14
		שָׁפְטִין	שפט	*judge*	Ezra 7:25
		דָּבְקִין	דבק	*adhere, stick together*	Dan 2:43
		גָּזְרִין	גזר	*diviner*	Dan 2:27; 5:11
		וְגָזְרַיָּא	גזר	*diviner*	Dan 4:4; 5:7
		טָרְדִין	טרד	*drive away*	Dan 4:22, 29
		זָבְנִין	זבן	*buy*	Dan 2:8
	fp	וְכָתְבָן	כתב	write	Dan 5:5
G INF		לְמִפְשַׁר	פשר	*interpret*	Dan 5:16
		לְמִכְנַשׁ	כנש	*assemble*	Dan 3:2
		לְמִשְׁבַּק	שבק	*leave*	Dan 4:23
		וּכְמִקְרְבֵהּ	קרב	*approach* (w/ 3ms gen sx)	Dan 6:21
Gp SC	**3ms**	קְטִיל	קטל	*be killed*	Dan 5:30
		כְּתִיב	כתב	*be written*	Ezra 5:7; 6:2
		רְשִׁים	רשם	*be written*	Dan 5:24, 25; 6:11
		טְרִיד	טרד	*be driven away*	Dan 4:30; 5:21
	3fs	קְטִילַת	קטל	*be killed*	Dan 7:11
		פְּרִיסַת	פרס	*be divided*	Dan 5:28
	3mp	מְרִיטוּ	מרט	*be plucked*	Dan 7:4
		כְּפִתוּ	כפת	*be tied up*	Dan 3:21
	2ms	תְּקִילְתָּה	תקל	*be weighed*	Dan 5:27

STEM/CONJ.	PGN	WORD	ROOT	GLOSS(ES)	VERSE(S)
Gp PTCP	ms	בְּרִיךְ	II ברך	*blessed*	Dan 3:28
		גְּמִיר	גמר	*perfect, completed;* as adv *completely* (?)	Ezra 7:12
		וּזְקִיף	זקף	*raised*	Ezra 6:11
		שְׁלִם	שלם	*be finished*	Ezra 5:16
	fs	פְּלִיגָה	פלג	*divided*	Dan 2:41
		תְּבִירָה	תבר	*fragile, brittle*	Dan 2:42
tG SC	3fs	הִתְגְּזֶרֶת	גזר	*be cut out*	Dan 2:34
		אִתְגְּזֶרֶת	גזר	*cut out*	Dan 2:45
	2mp	הִזְדְּמִנְתּוּן	זמן	*conspire*	Dan 2:9
tG INF		לְהִתְקְטָלָה	קטל	*be killed*	Dan 2:13
D SC	3ms	קַטִּל	קטל	*kill*	Dan 3:22
		קַבֵּל	קבל	*receive*	Dan 6:1
		שַׁכֵּן	שכן	*cause to dwell, settle*	Ezra 6:12
		בָּרִךְ	II ברך	*bless*	Dan 2:19
	1cs	בָּרְכֵת	II ברך	*bless*	Dan 4:31
	3mp	בַּטִּלוּ	בטל	trans *stop*	Ezra 5:5
		וּבַטִּלוּ	בטל	trans *stop*	Ezra 4:23
		וּבַקַּרוּ	בקר	*search*	Ezra 4:19; 6:1
D PC	3ms	יְבַקַּר	בקר	*search*	Ezra 4:15
	2ms	וּתְקָרֵב	קרב	*offer*	Ezra 7:17
	3mp	וִיקַבְּלוּן	קבל	*receive*	Dan 7:18
		יְשַׁמְּשׁוּנֵּהּ	שמש	*minister, attend, serve* (w/ 3ms acc sx)	Dan 7:10

STEM/CONJ.	PGN	WORD	ROOT	GLOSS(ES)	VERSE(S)
	2mp	תְּקַבְּלוּן	קבל	receive	Dan 2:6
D JUSS	3ms	יְמַגַּר	מגר	overthrow	Ezra 6:12
D IMV	2mp	וּבַדַּרוּ	בדר	scatter	Dan 4:11
D PTCP	ms	מְפַשַּׁר	פשר	interpret	Dan 5:12
D INF		לְקַטְלָה	קטל	kill	Dan 2:14
		לְבַטָּלָא	בטל	trans stop	Ezra 4:21; 6:8
		לְבַקָּרָא	בקר	search	Ezra 7:14
		לְכַפָּתָה	כפת	tie up	Dan 3:20
		וּלְתַקָּפָה	תקף	make strong; enforce	Dan 6:8
Dp PTCP	ms	מְפָרַשׁ	פרש	separated, made distinct; translated; explained	Ezra 4:18
		מְבָרַךְ	ברך II	blessed	Dan 2:20
	mp	מְכַפְּתִין	כפת	tied up	Dan 3:23, 24
		מְסוֹבְלִין	סבל	maintained (?)	Ezra 6:3
	fp	וּמְסַתְּרָתָא	סתר I	hidden	Dan 2:22
tD JUSS	3ms	יִתְבַּקַּר	בקר	be searched	Ezra 5:17
tD PTCP	ms	מִשְׂתַּכַּל	שׂכל	contemplate	Dan 7:8
		מִשְׁתַּדַּר	שדר	exert, make every effort	Dan 6:15
	mp	מִתְקַטְּלִין	קטל	be killed	Dan 2:13
		מִתְכַּנְּשִׁין	כנשׁ	assemble	Dan 3:3
		וּמִתְכַּנְּשִׁין	כנשׁ	assemble	Dan 3:27

STEM/CONJ.	PGN	WORD	ROOT	GLOSS(ES)	VERSE(S)
H SC	3ms	הַדִּקוּ	דקק	*pulverize*	Dan 6:25
		וְהַשְׁלְטֵהּ	שלט	*make rule* (w/ 3ms acc sx)	Dan 2:48
		וְהַשְׁלְמַהּ	שלם	*complete, finish off* (w/ 3fs acc sx)	Dan 5:26
		וְהַשְׁלְטָךְ	שלט	*make rule* (w/ 2ms acc sx)	Dan 2:38
	3mp	וְהַלְבִּישׁוּ	לבש	*clothe*	Dan 5:29
		וְהַקְרִבוּ	קרב	*offer*	Ezra 6:17
		וְהַכְרִזוּ	כרז	*herald, proclaim*	Dan 5:29
		הַרְגִּזוּ	רגז	*enrage*	Ezra 5:12
		הַרְגִּשׁוּ	רגש	*throng* [= conspire (?)]	Dan 6:7, 12, 16
		הַקְרְבוּהִי	קרב	*present* (w/ 3ms acc sx)	Dan 7:13
	2ms	הַשְׁפֵּלְתָּ	שפל	*humble*	Dan 5:22
H PC	3ms	יְהַשְׁפִּל	שפל	*humble*	Dan 7:24
H IMV	2ms	הַשְׁלֵם	שלם	*fully deliver*	Ezra 7:19
H PTCP	ms	מַשְׁפִּיל	שפל	*bring low*	Dan 5:19
	mp	מְהַקְרְבִין	קרב	*offer*	Ezra 6:10
H INF		לְהַשְׁפָּלָה	שפל	*humiliate*	Dan 4:34
		לְהַשְׁמָדָה	שמד	*annihilate*	Dan 7:26
Hp SC	3fs	הָתְקְנַת	תקן	*be reestablished*	Dan 4:33

LIST #27: I-א VERBS

STEM/CONJ.	PGN	WORD	ROOT	GLOSS(ES)	VERSE(S)
G SC	3ms	אֲזַל	אזל	*go*	Dan 2:17, 24; 6:19, 20
		אֲמַר־	אמר	*say; order*	Dan 2:24, 25, 46; 3:13, 20; 5:2, 29; 6:17, 24; 7:1, 23
		וַאֲמַר	אמר	*say; order*	Dan 2:12; 6:25; 7:16; Ezra 5:15
		אֲתָה	אתה	*come*	Dan 7:22
		אֲתָא	אתה	*come*	Ezra 5:3, 16
	3fs	אָכְלָה	אכל	*eat*	Dan 7:7, 19
		וַאֲמֶרֶת	אמר	*say; order*	Dan 5:10
	3mp	אֲמַרוּ	אמר	*say; order*	Dan 4:23
		אֲכַלוּ	אכל	*eat*	Dan 6:25
		וַאֲכַלוּ	אכל	*eat*	Dan 3:8
		אֲזַלוּ	אזל	*go*	Ezra 4:23
		אֲתוֹ	אתה	*come*	Ezra 4:12
	1cs	אַמְרֵת	אמר	*say; order*	Dan 4:5
	1cp	אֲמַרְנָא	אמר	*say; order*	Ezra 5:4, 9
G PC	3ms	יֵאכֻל	אכל	*eat*	Dan 4:30
		יֵאמַר	אמר	*say; order*	Dan 3:29
		וְיֵאמַר	אמר	*say; order*	Dan 4:32
	3fs	וְתֵאכֻל	אכל	*eat*	Dan 7:23
	2mp	תֵּאמְרוּן	אמר	*say; order*	Jer 10:11
	1cp	נֵאמַר	אמר	*say; order*	Dan 2:36

STEM/CONJ.	PGN	WORD	ROOT	GLOSS(ES)	VERSE(S)
G JUSS	3ms	יֵאמַר	אמר	*say; order*	Dan 2:7
	3mp	יֵאבַדוּ	אבד	*perish*	Jer 10:11
G IMV	2ms	אֱמַר	אמר	*say; order*	Dan 2:4; 4:6, 15
		אֱזֶל־	אזל	*go*	Ezra 5:15
	2fs	אֲכֻלִי	אכל	*eat*	Dan 7:5
	2mp	אֱמַרוּ	אמר	*say; order*	Dan 2:9
		וֶאֱתוֹ	אתה	*come*	Dan 3:26
G PTCP	ms	אָמַר	אמר	*say; order*	Dan 4:4, 11
		וְאָמַר	אמר	*say; order*	Dan 2:5, 8, 15, 20, 26, 27, 47; 3:14, 19, 24, 25, 26, 28; 4:16, 20, 27; 5:7, 13, 17; 6:13, 17, 21; 7:2
		אָנֵס	אנס	*oppress, bother*	Dan 4:6
		אָתֵה	אתה	*come*	Dan 7:13
		אָמְרִין	אמר	*say; order*	Dan 3:4; 4:28; 6:6, 7; 7:5; Ezra 5:3
		וְאָמְרִין	אמר	*say; order*	Dan 2:7, 10; 3:9, 16, 24; 6:13, 14, 16
G INF		לְמִקְרֵא	קרא	*read*	Dan 5:8, 16
		לְמֵאמַר	אמר	*say; order*	Dan 2:9
		לְמֵמַר	אמר	*say; order*	Ezra 5:11
		לְמֵזֵא	אזה	*heat, stoke*	Dan 3:19
		לְמֵתֵא	אתה	*come*	Dan 3:2
		לְמֵזְיֵהּ	אזה	*heat, stoke* (w/ 3ms acc sx)	Dan 3:19
Gp PTCP	ms	אֲזֵה	אזה	*heat, stoke*	Dan 3:22
H SC	3ms	הֵימִן	אמן	*trust*	Dan 6:24
		הַיְתִי	אתה	*bring*	Dan 5:13

STEM/CONJ.	PGN	WORD	ROOT	GLOSS(ES)	VERSE(S)
	3mp	הֵיתָיו	אתה	*bring*	Dan 5:3, 23
		וְהַיְתִיו	אתה	*bring*	Dan 6:17, 25
		יְהֹבְדוּן	אבד	*kill*	Dan 2:18
H JUSS	2mp	תְּהוֹבֵד	אבד	*kill*	Dan 2:24
H INF		לְהוֹבָדָה	אבד	*kill*	Dan 2:12, 24
		וּלְהוֹבָדָה	אבד	*destroy*	Dan 7:26
		לְהַיְתָיָה	אתה	*bring*	Dan 3:13; 5:12
Hp SC	3ms	וְהוּבַד	אבד	*be destroyed*	Dan 7:11
	3fs	וְהֵיתָיִת	אתה	*be brought*	Dan 6:18
	3mp	הֵיתָיו	אתה	*be brought*	Dan 3:13
Hp PTCP	ms	מְהֵימַן	אמן	*trustworthy*	Dan 6:5
		וּמְהֵימַן	אמן	*trustworthy*	Dan 2:45

LIST #28: I-ע VERBS

STEM/CONJ.	PGN	WORD	ROOT	GLOSS(ES)	VERSE(S)
G SC	3ms	עֲבַד	עבד	*do, make*	Dan 3:1, 32; 5:1
		עַל	II עלל	*enter*	Dan 2:16, 24; 4:5; 6:11
	3fs	נֶגְדַת	עדה	*touch* (w/ בְּ); *pass* (w/ מִן) *out of*	Dan 3:27; 4:28
		עֲנָת	I ענה	*answer, reply; begin to speak*	Dan 5:10
		עַלַּת	II עלל	*enter*	Dan 5:10

STEM/CONJ.	PGN	WORD	ROOT	GLOSS(ES)	VERSE(S)
	3mp	עֲבַדוּ	עבד	*do, make*	Jer 10:11; Ezra 6:13
		וַעֲבַדוּ	עבד	*do, make*	Ezra 6:16
		עֲנוֹ	I ענה	*answer, reply; begin to speak*	Dan 2:7, 10; 3:9, 16; 6:14
	2ms	עֲבַדְתְּ	עבד	*do, make*	Dan 4:32
	1cs	עַבְדֵת	עבד	*do, make*	Dan 3:15; 6:23
G PC	3ms	יֶעְדֵּה	עדה	*pass away*	Dan 7:14
	3fs	תֶעְדֵּא	עדה	*be annulled; pass away*	Dan 6:9, 13
	2mp	תַעַבְדוּן	עבד	*do, make*	Ezra 6:8; 7:18
G PTCP	ms	עָבֵד	עבד	*do, make*	Dan 4:32; 6:11; Ezra 7:26
		וְעָבֵד	עבד	*do, make*	Dan 6:28
		עָנֵה	I ענה	*answer, reply; begin to speak*	Dan 2:5, 8, 15, 20, 26, 27, 47; 3:14, 19, 24, 25, 26, 28; 4:16 (*bis*), 27; Dan 5:7, 13, 17; 6:13, 17, 21; 7:2
	fs	עָבְדָה	עבד	*do, make*	Dan 7:21
	mp	עָבְדִין	עבד	*do, make*	Ezra 4:15
		עָנַיִן	I ענה	*answer, reply; begin to speak*	Dan 3:24
		עָלִין	II עלל	*enter*	Dan 4:4; 5:8
G INF		לְמֶעְבַּד	עבד	*do, make*	Ezra 4:22; 7:18
GP PTCP	ms	עֲשִׂית	עשׂת	*intend* active sense	Dan 6:4
tG SC	3fp	אֶתְעֲקַרָה	עקר	*be ripped out*	Dan 7:8

STEM/CONJ.	PGN	WORD	ROOT	GLOSS(ES)	VERSE(S)
tG PC	3ms	יִתְעֲבֵד	עבד	*be done; be turned into*	Dan 3:29; Ezra 6:11; 7:23
		יִתְעֲבִד	עבד	*be done; be turned into*	Ezra 7:21
	2mp	תִּתְעַבְדוּן	עבד	*be done; be turned into*	Dan 2:5
tG JUSS	3ms	יִתְעֲבֵד	עבד	*be done; be turned into*	Ezra 6:12
tG PTCP	ms	מִתְעֲבֵד	עבד	*be done; be turned into*	Ezra 7:26
		מִתְעֲבֶד־	עבד	*be done; be turned into*	Ezra 4:19
Dp PTCP	ms	מְעָרַב	ערב	*mixed*	Dan 2:41, 43
tD PTCP	ms	מִתְעָרַב	ערב	*intermingle*	Dan 2:43
	fs	מִתְעַבְדָא	עבד	*be done; be turned into*	Ezra 5:8
	mp	מִתְעָרְבִין	ערב	*intermingle*	Dan 2:43
H SC	3ms	הַנְעֵל	II עלל	*bring*	Dan 2:25; 6:19
	3mp	הֶעְדִּיו	עדה	*remove*	Dan 5:20
		הֶעְדִּיו	עדה	*remove*	Dan 7:12
H PC	3mp	יְהַעְדּוֹן	עדה	*remove*	Dan 7:26
H IMV	2ms	הַעֵלְנִי	II עלל	*bring* (w/ 1cs acc sx)	Dan 2:24
H PTCP	ms	מְהַעְדֵּה	עדה	*remove, depose*	Dan 2:21
H INF		לְהֶעָלָה	II עלל	*bring*	Dan 5:7
		לְהַנְעָלָה	II עלל	*bring*	Dan 4:3

STEM/CONJ.	PGN	WORD	ROOT	GLOSS(ES)	VERSE(S)
Hp SC	**3ms**	הֻעַל	II עלל	*be brought*	Dan 5:13
	3mp	הֻעַלּוּ	II עלל	*be brought*	Dan 5:15

LIST #29: I-ח VERBS

STEM/CONJ.	PGN	WORD	ROOT	GLOSS(ES)	VERSE(S)
G SC	**3ms**	חֲזָה	חזה	*see; perceive*	Dan 4:20; 7:1
		וְחַתְמַהּ	חתם	*seal* (w/ 3fs acc sx)	Dan 6:18
	2ms	חֲזַיְתָ	חזה	*see; perceive*	Dan 2:43, 45; 4:17
		חֲזַיְתָה	חזה	*be, become, exist; occur, happen*	Dan 2:41 (*bis*)
	2mp	חֲזַיְתוֹן	חזה	*see; perceive*	Dan 2:8
	1cs	חֲזֵית	חזה	*see; perceive*	Dan 2:26; 4:2, 6, 15
G PC	**3mp**	יַחְלְפוּן	חלף	*pass over*	Dan 4:20, 22, 29
	3mp	יַחִיטוּ	חוט	[possibly H stem] *repair*	Ezra 4:12
G JUSS	**3mp**	יַחְלְפוּן	חלף	*pass over*	Dan 4:13
G IMV	**2ms**	חֱיִי	חיה	*live*	Dan 2:4; 3:9; 5:10; 6:7, 22
G PTCP	**ms**	וְחָשֵׁל	חשל	*smash*	Dan 2:40
		חָזֵה	חזה	*see; perceive*	Dan 2:31, 34, 25; 4:7, 10; 5:5; 7:2, 4, 6, 7, 9, 11 (*bis*), 13, 21
	mp	חַשְׁחִין	חשח	*need*	Dan 3:16
		חָזַיִן	חזה	*see; perceive*	Dan 3:27; 5:23

STEM/CONJ.	PGN	WORD	ROOT	GLOSS(ES)	VERSE(S)
G INF		לְמֶחֱזֵא	חזה	see; perceive	Ezra 4:14
		בְּמְחַן	חנן	show mercy, grace	Dan 4:24
Gp PTCP	ms	חֲזֵה	חזה	seen = normal	Dan 3:19
	mp	חֲשִׁיבִין	חשב	be thought of	Dan 4:32
D SC	3mp	חַבְּלוּנִי	חבל	destroy (w/ 1cs acc sx)	Dan 6:23
D PC	3ms	יְחַוִּנַּה	חוה	show, make known, declare (w/ 3fs acc sx)	Dan 2:11
		יְחַוִּנַּנִי	חוה	make known (w/ 1cs acc sx)	Dan 5:7
	1cs	אֲחַוֵּא	חוה	show, make known, declare	Dan 2:24
	1cp	נְחַוֵּא	חוה	show, make known, declare	Dan 2:4
D IMV	3mp	וְחַבְּלוּהִי	חבל	destroy (w/ 3ms acc sx)	Dan 4:20
D INF		לְחַבָּלָה	חבל	destroy	Ezra 6:12
		לְחַטָּאָה	חטא	sin, make a sin offering	Ezra 6:17
tD SC	3ms	הִתְחָרַךְ	חרך	be singed	Dan 3:27
tD PC	3fs	תִּתְחַבַּל	חבל	be destroyed	Dan 2:44; 6:27; 7:14
tD PTCP	ms	וּמִתְחַנַּן	חנן	seek mercy, grace	Dan 6:12
H SC	3mp	הֶחֱסִנוּ	חסן	possess	Dan 7:22

STEM/CONJ.	PGN	WORD	ROOT	GLOSS(ES)	VERSE(S)
H PC	3ms	יְהַחֲוֵה	חוה	*make known*	Dan 5:12
	3mp	וְיַחְסְנוּן	חסן	*possess*	Dan 7:18
		יַחִיטוּ	חוט	*repair*	Ezra 4:12
	2mp	תְּהַחֲוֹן	חוה	*show, make known, declare*	Dan 2:6
		תְּהַחֲוַנַּנִי	חוה	*show, make known, declare (w/ 1cs acc sx)*	Dan 2:9
	1cp	נְהַחֲוֵה	חוה	*show, make known, declare*	Dan 2:7
H IMV	2mp	הַחֲוֹנִי	חוה	*show, make known, declare (w/ 1cs acc sx)*	Dan 2:6
H PTCP	ms	מַחֵא	חיה	*let live*	Dan 5:19
	fs	מְהַחְצְפָה	חצף	*be harsh*	Dan 2:15
		מַחְצְפָה	חצף	*be harsh*	Dan 3:22
H INF		לְהַחֲוָיָה	חוה	*show, make known, declare*	Dan 2:10, 16, 27; 3:32; 5:15
		וַאַחֲוָיַת	חוה	*make known*	Dan 5:12
Hp SC	3fs	הָחָרְבַת	חרב	*be laid waste*	Ezra 4:15

LIST #30: I-ה VERBS

STEM/CONJ.	PGN	WORD	ROOT	GLOSS(ES)	VERSE(S)
G SC	**3ms**	הֲוָה	הוה	*be, become, exist; occur, happen*	Dan 4:26; 5:19 (8x); 7:13
		הֲוָא	הוה	*be, become, exist; occur, happen*	Dan 6:4, 11, 15; Ezra 5:11
	3fs	הֲוָת	הוה	*be, become, exist; occur, happen*	Dan 2:35; 7:19; Ezra 5:5
		וַהֲוָת	הוה	*be, become, exist; occur, happen*	Ezra 4:24
	3mp	הֲווֹ	הוה	*be, become, exist; occur, happen*	Dan 5:19; 6:5; Ezra 4:20
		וַהֲווֹ	הוה	*be, become, exist; occur, happen*	Dan 2:35
	2ms	הֲוַיְתָ	הוה	*be, become, exist; occur, happen*	Dan 2:31, 34
	1cs	הֲוֵית	הוה	*be, become, exist; occur, happen*	Dan 4:1, 7, 10; 7:2, 4, 6, 7, 8, 9, 11 (*bis*), 13, 21
G PC	**3ms**	לֶהֱוֵה	הוה	*be, become, exist; occur, happen*	Dan 4:22
		לֶהֱוֵא	הוה	*be, become, exist; occur, happen*	Dan 2:28, 29 (*bis*), 41, 45; 5:29; 6:3; 7:23, 26
		יְהָךְ	הך	*reach*	Ezra 5:5; 7:13
	3fs	תֶּהֱוֵה	הוה	*be, become, exist; occur, happen*	Dan 2:41, 42 (*bis*)
		תֶּהֱוֵא	הוה	*be, become, exist; occur, happen*	Dan 2:40; 4:24; 7:23; Ezra 6:8
	3mp	לֶהֱוֹן	הוה	*be, become, exist; occur, happen*	Dan 2:43 (*bis*); 6:2, 3, 27; Ezra 6:10; 7:25

STEM/CONJ.	PGN	WORD	ROOT	GLOSS(ES)	VERSE(S)
G JUSS	**3ms**	לֶהֱוֵא	הוה	*be, become, exist; occur, happen*	Dan 2:20; 3:18; 4:12, 13; Ezra 5:8; 6:9; 7:26
		וִיהָךְ	הך	*go*	Ezra 6:5
	3fp	לֶהֶוְיָן	הוה	*be, become, exist; occur, happen*	Dan 5:17
G IMV	**2mp**	הֱווֹ	הוה	*be, become, exist; occur, happen*	Ezra 4:22
		הֱווֹ	הוה	*be, become, exist; occur, happen*	Ezra 6:6
G INF		לִמְהָךְ	הך	*go*	Ezra 7:13
D SC	**2ms**	הַדַּרְתָּ	הדר	*glorify*	Dan 5:23
	1cs	וְהַדְּרֵת	הדר	*glorify*	Dan 4:31
D PTCP	**ms**	מְהַלֵּךְ	הלך	*walk*	Dan 4:26
		וּמְהַדַּר	הדר	*glorify*	Dan 4:34
H PTCP	**mp**	מַהְלְכִין	הלך	*walk*	Dan 3:25; 4:34

LIST #31: I-י VERBS

STEM/CONJ.	PGN	WORD	ROOT	GLOSS(ES)	VERSE(S)
G SC	**3ms**	יְדַע	ידע	*know; learn; understand*	Dan 5:21; 6:11
		יְהַב־	יהב	*give*	Dan 2:37, 38, 48; 5:18, 19; Ezra 5:12, 16
		יְתִב	יתב	*sit*	Dan 7:9, 10

STEM/CONJ.	PGN	WORD	ROOT	GLOSS(ES)	VERSE(S)
	3mp	וִיהַבוּ	יהב	*give*	Dan 3:28
	2ms	יְדַעְתָּ	ידע	*know; learn; understand*	Dan 5:22
		יְהַבְתְּ	יהב	*give*	Dan 2:23
		יְכֵלְתָּ	יכל	*be able*	Dan 2:47
	1cs	יִדְעֵת	ידע	*know; learn; understand*	Dan 4:6
G PC	3ms	יֵיטַב	יטב	*be good* (w/ עַל־) *to*	Ezra 7:18
		יוּכַל	יכל	*be able*	Dan 2:10
		יִכֻּל	יכל	*be able*	Dan 3:29
		הַיִכֻל	יכל	*be able* (w/ interr ה)	Dan 6:21
	3mp	יִנְדְּעוּן	ידע	*know; learn; understand*	Dan 4:14
	2ms	תִּנְדַּע	ידע	*know; learn; understand*	Dan 2:30; 4:22, 23, 29
		וְתִנְדַּע	ידע	*know; learn; understand*	Ezra 4:15
		תִיכּוּל	יכל	*be able*	Dan 5:16
		תְּכוּל	יכל	*be able*	Dan 5:16
	1cs	וְאִנְדַּע	ידע	*know; learn; understand*	Dan 2:9
G IMV	2ms	דַּע	ידע	*know; learn; understand*	Dan 6:16
		הַב	יהב	*give*	Dan 5:17
G PTCP	ms	יָדַע	ידע	*know; learn; understand*	Dan 2:8, 22; Ezra 7:25
		יָהֵב	יהב	*give*	Dan 2:21
		יָכִל	יכל	*be able*	Dan 3:17; 4:34
	fs	וְיָכְלָה	יכל	*be more able, overpower*	Dan 7:21
		יָקִדְתָּא	יקד	*burn*	Dan 3:6, 11, 15, 17, 20, 21, 23, 26

STEM/CONJ.	PGN	WORD	ROOT	GLOSS(ES)	VERSE(S)
	mp	יָדְעִין	ידע	*know; learn; understand*	Dan 5:23
		יָדְעֵי	ידע	*know; learn; understand*	Dan 2:21; Ezra 7:25
		יָכְלִין	יכל	*be able*	Dan 2:27; 4:15; 6:5
		יָתְבִין	יתב	*dwell*	Ezra 4:17
		יָהֲבִין	יהב	*give*	Dan 6:3
		וְיָעֲטוֹהִי	יעט	*adviser* (w/ 3ms gen sx)	Ezra 7:15
		יָעֲטוֹהִי	יעט	*adviser* (w/ 3ms gen sx)	Ezra 7:14
Gp SC	3ms	יְהִיב	יהב	*be given*	Dan 7:4, 6, 14
		יְהִב	יהב	*be given*	Dan 7:22
	3fs	יְהִיבַת	יהב	*be given*	Dan 7:12, 27
		וִיהִיבַת	יהב	*be given*	Dan 5:28; 7:11
	3mp	וִיהִיבוּ	יהב	*be given*	Ezra 5:14
Gp PTCP	ms	יְדִיעַ	ידע	*be known; be learned; be understood*	Dan 3:18; Ezra 4:12, 13; 5:8
tG PC	3mp	וְיִתְיַהֲבוּן	יהב	*be given*	Dan 7:25
tG JUSS	3ms	יִתְיְהִב	יהב	*be given*	Dan 4:13
	3fs	תִּתְיְהִב	יהב	*be given*	Ezra 6:4
tG PTCP	ms	מִתְיְהֵב	יהב	*be given*	Ezra 4:20; 6:9
	fs	מִתְיַהֲבָא	יהב	*be given*	Ezra 6:8
	mp	מִתְיַהֲבִין	יהב	*be given*	Ezra 7:19
D PC	3ms	יְתִּב	יתב	*sit*	Dan 7:26

STEM/CONJ.	PGN	WORD	ROOT	GLOSS(ES)	VERSE(S)
D INF		לְיַצָּבָא	יצב	*ascertain, make certain of*	Dan 7:19
tD SC	3mp	אִתְיָעַטוּ	יעט	*consult together*	Dan 6:8
H SC	3ms	וְהוֹתֵב	יתב	*make dwell, settle*	Ezra 4:10
		וְהֵיבֵל	יבל	*bring*	Ezra 5:14; 6:5
		הוֹדַע	ידע	*make known, communicate*	Dan 2:15, 17, 45
		וְהוֹדַע	ידע	*make known, communicate*	Dan 2:28
		הוֹדְעָךְ	ידע	*make known, communicate* (w/ 2ms acc sx)	Dan 2:29
	2ms	הוֹדַעְתֵּנִי	ידע	*make known, communicate* (w/ 1cs acc sx)	Dan 2:23
		הוֹדַעְתֶּנָא	ידע	*make known, communicate* (w/ 1cp acc sx)	Dan 2:23
	1cp	וְהוֹדַעְנָא	ידע	*make known, communicate*	Ezra 4:14
H PC	3ms	יְהוֹדַע	ידע	*make known, communicate*	Dan 2:25
		יְהוֹדְעִנַּנִי	ידע	*make known, communicate* (w/ 1cs acc sx)	Dan 7:16
	3mp	יְהוֹדְעוּן	ידע	*make known, communicate*	Dan 2:30
		יְהוֹדְעִנַּנִי	ידע	*make known, communicate* (w/ 1cs acc sx)	Dan 4:3
	2mp	תְּהוֹדְעוּן	ידע	*make known, communicate*	Ezra 7:25
		תְהוֹדְעוּנַּנִי	ידע	*make known, communicate* (w/ 1cs acc sx)	Dan 2:5
		תְהוֹדְעֻנַּנִי	ידע	*make known, communicate* (w/ 1cs acc sx)	Dan 2:9
	1cs	אֲהוֹדְעִנֵּה	ידע	*make known, communicate* (w/ 3ms acc sx)	Dan 5:17

STEM/CONJ.	PGN	WORD	ROOT	GLOSS(ES)	VERSE(S)
H PTCP	**ms**	מְהוֹדֵא	ידה	*give thanks*	Dan 2:23
		וּמוֹדֵא	ידה	*give thanks*	Dan 6:11
	mp	מְהוֹדְעִין	ידע	*make known, communicate*	Dan 4:4, 16; 7:24
H INF		לְהוֹדָעָה	ידע	*make known, communicate*	Dan 5:8
		וּלְהֵיבָלָה	יבל	*bring*	Ezra 7:15
		לְהוֹדָעֻתַנִי	ידע	*make known, communicate* (w/ 1cs acc sx)	Dan 2:26; 4:15; 5:15, 16
		לְהוֹדָעוּתָךְ	ידע	*make known, communicate* (w/ 2ms acc sx)	Ezra 5:10
Hp SC	**3fs**	הוּסְפַת	יסף	*be added*	Dan 4:33

LIST #32: I-נ VERBS

STEM/CONJ.	PGN	WORD	ROOT	GLOSS(ES)	VERSE(S)
G SC	**3ms**	נְפַל	נפל	*fall*	Dan 2:46; 4:28
		נְפַק	נפק	*go out*	Dan 2:14
		וּנְשָׂא	נשא	*carry, lift*	Dan 2:35
	3fs	נֶפְקַת	נפק	*go out = be issued*	Dan 2:13
		נַדַּת	נדד	*flee*	Dan 6:19
	3mp	נְפַלוּ	נפל	*fall*	Dan 3:23
	3fp	נְפַקָה	נפק	*come out*	Dan 5:5
		וּנְפַלָה	נפל	*fall*	Dan 7:20
	1cs	נִטְלֵת	נטל	*lift*	Dan 4:31
		נִטְרֵת	נטר	*keep*	Dan 7:28

STEM/CONJ.	PGN	WORD	ROOT	GLOSS(ES)	VERSE(S)
G PC	3ms	יִנְתֵּן־	נתן	*give*	Dan 2:16
		יִפֵּל	נפל	*fall*	Dan 3:6, 10, 11
		יִפֵּל־	נפל	*fall*	Ezra 7:20
		יִתְּנִנַּהּ	נתן	*give* (w/ 3fs acc sx)	Dan 4:14, 22, 29
	3mp	יִנְתְּנוּן	נתן	*give*	Ezra 4:13
	2ms	תִּנְתֵּן	נתן	*give*	Ezra 7:20
	2mp	תִּפְּלוּן	נפל	*fall*	Dan 3:5, 15
G JUSS	3fs	תְּנֻד	נוד	*flee*	Dan 4:11
G IMV	2ms	שֵׂא	נשׂא	*carry, take*	Ezra 5:15
	2mp	פֻּקוּ	נפק	*go out*	Dan 3:26
G PTCP	ms	נָגֵד	נגד	*flow*	Dan 7:10
		וְנָפֵק	נפק	*go out*	Dan 7:10
		נָזִק	נזק	*come to grief* (*HALOT*); *be damaged*	Dan 6:3
		נָחִת	נחת	*descend*	Dan 4:10, 20
	mp	נָפְקִין	נפק	*go out*	Dan 3:26
		נָפְלִין	נפל	*fall*	Dan 3:7
		בָּנַיִן	בנה	*(re)build*	Ezra 4:12; 5:4; 6:14
		וּבָנַיִן	בנה	*(re)build*	Ezra 5:11
	fp	נָקְשָׁן	נקש	*knock*	Dan 5:6
Gp SC	3fs	וּנְטִילַת	נטל	*be lifted*	Dan 7:4
tG PC	3ms	יִתְנְסַח	נסח	*be pulled out*	Ezra 6:11

STEM/CONJ.	PGN	WORD	ROOT	GLOSS(ES)	VERSE(S)
D INF		לְנַסָּכָה	נסך	*pour out = offer*	Dan 2:46
tD SC	**3ms**	וְהִתְנַבִּי	נבא	*prophesy*	Ezra 5:1
	3mp	הִתְנַדַּבוּ	נדב	*volunteer*	Ezra 7:15
tD PTCP	**ms**	מִתְנַדַּב	נדב	*volunteer*	Ezra 7:13
		מִתְנַצַּח	נצח	*distinguish oneself, surpass*	Dan 6:4
	fs	מִתְנַשְּׂאָה	נשׂא	*rise up against*	Ezra 4:19
	mp	מִתְנַדְּבִין	נדב	*volunteer*	Ezra 7:16
H SC	**3ms**	הַנְפֵּק	נפק	*bring out*	Dan 5:2, 14 (*bis*); 6:5
	3mp	הַנְפִּקוּ	נפק	*bring out*	Dan 5:3
H PC	**3fs**	תְּהַנְזִק	נזק	*damage*	Ezra 4:13
	2ms	וְתַחֵת	נחת	*deposit*	Ezra 6:5
H IMV	**2ms**	אֲחֵת	נחת	*deposit*	Ezra 5:15
	2mp	אַתַּרוּ	נתר	*strip off*	Dan 4:11
H PTCP	**ms**	וּמַצֵּל	נצל	*deliver*	Dan 6:28
	fs	וּמְהַנְזְקַת	נזק	*damager*	Ezra 4:15
H INF		לְהַצָּלָה	נצל	*deliver*	Dan 3:29
		לְהַצָּלוּתֵהּ	נצל	*deliver* (w/ 3ms acc sx)	Dan 6:15
Hp SC	**3ms**	הָנְחַת	נחת	*be brought down, deposed*	Dan 5:20

STEM/CONJ.	PGN	WORD	ROOT	GLOSS(ES)	VERSE(S)
Hp PTCP	mp	מְהַחֲתִין	נחת	*deposited*	Ezra 6:1

LIST #33: II-א VERBS

STEM/CONJ.	PGN	WORD	ROOT	GLOSS(ES)	VERSE(S)
G SC	3ms	שְׁאֵל	שאל	*ask*	Dan 2:10
		טְאֵב	טאב	*be good to* (w/ עַל־) *X = X was glad*	Dan 6:24
		בְּאֵשׁ	באש	*be bad, evil to* (w/ עַל־)	Dan 6:15
	1cp	שְׁאֶלְנָא	שאל	*ask*	Ezra 5:9, 10
G PC	3ms	יִשְׁאֲלֶנְכוֹן	שאל	*ask* (w/ 2mp acc sx)	Ezra 7:21
G PTCP	ms	שָׁאֵל	שאל	*ask*	Dan 2:11, 27

LIST #34: II-ע VERBS

STEM/CONJ.	PGN	WORD	ROOT	GLOSS(ES)	VERSE(S)
G SC	3ms	זְעִק	זעק	*yell*	Dan 6:21
		וּבְעָה	בעה	*seek, request*	Dan 2:16
		בְּעָא	בעה	*seek, request*	Dan 2:49
	3mp	וּבְעוֹ	בעה	*seek*	Dan 2:13
	1cp	בְעֵינָא	בעה	*seek*	Dan 2:23

STEM/CONJ.	PGN	WORD	ROOT	GLOSS(ES)	VERSE(S)
G PC	**3ms**	יִבְעֵה	בעה	*request; seek*	Dan 6:8, 13
	3fs	וְתֵרֹעַ	רעע	*crush*	Dan 2:40
	1cs	אֶבְעֵא־	בעה	*seek*	Dan 7:16
G PTCP	**ms**	בָּעֵא	בעה	*seek*	Dan 6:12, 14
		בָעֵין	בעה	*seek*	Dan 6:5
	mp	וְיָעֲטוֹהִי	יעט	*adviser* (w/ 3ms gen sx)	Ezra 7:15
		יָעֲטֹהִי	יעט	*adviser* (w/ 3ms gen sx)	Ezra 7:14
G INF		לְמִבְעֵא	בעה	*seek*	Dan 2:18
D PC	**3mp**	יְטַעֲמוּן	טעם	*feed*	Dan 4:22, 29
		יִבְעוֹן	בעה	*seek*	Dan 4:33
		יְטַעֲמוּנֵּהּ	טעם	*feed* (w/ 3ms acc sx)	Dan 5:21
D PTCP	**ms**	מְרָעַע	רעע	*crush*	Dan 2:40
	mp	מְסָעֲדִין	סעד	*support*	Ezra 5:2
tD SC	**3mp**	אִתְיָעַטוּ	יעט	*consult together*	Dan 6:8

LIST #35: II-ח VERBS

STEM/CONJ.	PGN	WORD	ROOT	GLOSS(ES)	VERSE(S)
G SC	**3fs**	מְחָת	מחא	*strike*	Dan 2:35
		וּמְחָת	מחא	*strike*	Dan 2:34

STEM/CONJ.	PGN	WORD	ROOT	GLOSS(ES)	VERSE(S)
G PTCP	ms	נָחֵת	נחת	*descend*	Dan 4:10, 20
	mp	וְדָחֲלִין	דחל	*fear*	Dan 5:19; 6:27
Gp PTCP	ms	דְּחִיל	דחל	*feared*	Dan 2:31
	fs	דְּחִילָה	דחל	*feared*	Dan 7:7, 19
		וּשְׁחִיתָה	שחת	*corrupted, bad*	Dan 2:9; 6:5 (*bis*)
tG SC	3mp	הִתְרְחִצוּ	רחץ	*trust* (w/ עַל־) *in*	Dan 3:28
tG PC	3ms	יִתְמְחֵא	מחא	*be impaled*	Ezra 6:11
D PC	3ms	יְמַחֵא	מחא	*strike*	Dan 4:32
		וִידַחֲלִנַּנִי	דחל	*frighten* (w/ 1cs acc sx)	Dan 4:2
H PC	2ms	וְתַחֵת	נחת	*deposit*	Ezra 6:5
H IMV	2ms	אֲחֵת	נחת	*deposit*	Ezra 5:15
Hp SC	3ms	הָנְחַת	נחת	*be brought down, deposed*	Dan 5:20
Hp PTCP	mp	מְהַחֲתִין	נחת	*deposited*	Ezra 6:1

LIST #36: II-ה VERBS

STEM/CONJ.	PGN	WORD	ROOT	GLOSS	VERSE(S)
G SC	3ms	יְהַב־	יהב	*give*	Dan 2:37, 38, 48; 5:18, 19; Ezra 5:12, 16

STEM/CONJ.	PGN	WORD	ROOT	GLOSS	VERSE(S)
	3mp	וִיהַבוּ	יהב	*give*	Dan 3:28
	2ms	יְהַבְתְּ	יהב	*give*	Dan 2:23
G IMV	2ms	הַב	יהב	*give*	Dan 5:17
G PTCP	ms	כָּהֵל	כהל	*be able*	Dan 2:26; 4:15
		יָהֵב	יהב	*give*	Dan 2:21
	mp	כָּהֲלִין	כהל	*be able*	Dan 5:8, 15
		יָהֲבִין	יהב	*give*	Dan 6:3
Gp SC	3ms	יְהִיב	יהב	*be given*	Dan 7:4, 6, 14
		יְהִב	יהב	*be given*	Dan 7:22
	3fs	יְהִיבַת	יהב	*be given*	Dan 7:12, 27
		וִיהִיבַת	יהב	*be given*	Dan 5:28; 7:11
	3mp	וִיהִיבוּ	יהב	*be given*	Ezra 5:14
tG PC	3mp	וְיִתְיַהֲבוּן	יהב	*be given*	Dan 7:25
tG JUSS	3ms	יִתְיְהִב	יהב	*be given*	Dan 4:13
	3fs	תִּתְיְהִב	יהב	*be given*	Ezra 6:4
tG PTCP	ms	מִתְיְהֵב	יהב	*be given*	Ezra 4:20; 6:9
	fs	מִתְיַהֲבָא	יהב	*be given*	Ezra 6:8
	mp	מִתְיַהֲבִין	יהב	*be given*	Ezra 7:19

STEM/CONJ.	PGN	WORD	ROOT	GLOSS	VERSE(S)
D PC	**3mp**	יְבַהֲלוּנֵּהּ	בהל	*terrify* (w/ 3ms acc sx)	Dan 5:6
		יְבַהֲלַנֵּהּ	בהל	*terrify* (w/ 3ms acc sx)	Dan 4:16
		יְבַהֲלַנִּי	בהל	*terrify* (w/ 1cs acc sx)	Dan 4:2; 7:15, 28
D JUSS	**3ms**	יְבַהֲלָךְ	בהל	*terrify* (w/ 2ms acc sx)	Dan 4:16
	3mp	יְבַהֲלוּךְ	בהל	*terrify* (w/ 2ms acc sx)	Dan 5:10
tD PTCP	**ms**	מִתְבְּהַל	בהל	*be terrified*	Dan 5:9

LIST #37: II-ו VERBS

STEM/CONJ.	PGN	WORD	ROOT	GLOSS(ES)	VERSE(S)
G SC	**3ms**	הֲוָה	הוה	*be, become, exist; occur, happen*	Dan 4:26; 5:19 (8x); 7:13
		הֲוָא	הוה	*be, become, exist; occur, happen*	Dan 6:4, 11, 15; Ezra 5:11
		תְּוַהּ	תוה	*be astonished, startled, horrified*	Dan 3:24
		וְקָם	קום	*arise, get up; be established, endure*	Dan 3:24
		רָם	רום	*be high*	Dan 5:20
	3fs	הֲוָת	הוה	*be, become, exist; occur, happen*	Dan 2:35; 7:19; Ezra 5:5
		וַהֲוָת	הוה	*be, become, exist; occur, happen*	Ezra 4:24
		סָפַת	סוף	*be fulfilled*	Dan 4:30
	3mp	הֲווֹ	הוה	*be, become, exist; occur, happen*	Dan 5:19; 6:5; Ezra 4:20

STEM/CONJ.	PGN	WORD	ROOT	GLOSS(ES)	VERSE(S)
		וַהֲווֹ	הוה	be, become, exist; occur, happen	Dan 2:35
		קָמוּ	קום	arise, get up; be established, endure	Ezra 5:2
	2ms	הֲוַיְתָ	הוה	be, become, exist; occur, happen	Dan 2:31, 34
	1cs	הֲוֵית	הוה	be, become, exist; occur, happen	Dan 4:1, 7, 10; 7:2, 4, 6, 7, 8, 9, 11 (*bis*), 13, 21
G PC	3ms	לֶהֱוֵה	הוה	be, become, exist; occur, happen	Dan 4:22
		לֶהֱוֵא	הוה	be, become, exist; occur, happen	Dan 2:28, 29 (*bis*), 41, 45; 5:29; 6:3; 7:23, 26
		יְקוּם	קום	arise, get up; be established, endure	Dan 6:20; 7:24
		יְתוּב	תוב	intrans *return*	Dan 4:31, 33 (*bis*)
	3fs	תְּקוּם	קום	arise, get up; be established, endure	Dan 2:39, 44
		תְּדוּר	דור	dwell	Dan 4:18
		תֶּהֱוֵה	הוה	be, become, exist; occur, happen	Dan 2:41, 42 (*bis*)
		תֶּהֱוֵא	הוה	be, become, exist; occur, happen	Dan 2:40; 4:24; 7:23; Ezra 6:8
		וּתְדוּשִׁנַּהּ	דוש	*trample* (w/ 3fs acc sx)	Dan 7:23
	3mp	יְקוּמוּן	קום	arise, get up; be established, endure	Dan 7:10, 17
		יְקֻמוּן	קום	arise, get up; be established, endure	Dan 7:24
		לֶהֱוֹן	הוה	be, become, exist; occur, happen	Dan 2:43 (*bis*); 6:2, 3, 27; Ezra 6:10; 7:25
		יַחִיטוּ	חוט	[possibly H stem] *repair*	Ezra 4:12
	3fp	יְדוּרָן	דור	dwell	Dan 4:9

STEM/CONJ.	PGN	WORD	ROOT	GLOSS(ES)	VERSE(S)
G JUSS	**3ms**	לֶהֱוֵא	הוה	be, become, exist; occur, happen	Dan 2:20; 3:18; 4:12, 13; Ezra 5:8; 6:9; 7:26
	3fs	תְּנֻד	נוד	flee	Dan 4:11
	3fp	לֶהֶוְיָן	הוה	be, become, exist; occur, happen	Dan 5:17
G IMV	**2fs**	קוּמִי	קום	arise, get up; be established, endure	Dan 7:5
	2mp	הֱוֹו	הוה	be, become, exist; occur, happen	Ezra 4:22
		הֱוֹו	הוה	be, become, exist; occur, happen	Ezra 6:6
G PTCP	**ms**	קָאֵם	קום	arise, get up; be established, endure	Dan 2:31
	mp	וְקָיְמִין	קום	arise, get up; be established, endure	Dan 3:3
		קָאֲמַיָּא	קום	arise, get up; be established, endure	Dan 7:16
		זָיְעִין	זוע	tremble	Dan 5:19; 6:27
		דָּיְרִין	דור	dwell	Dan 2:38; 3:31; 6:26
		דָּיְרֵי	דור	dwell	Dan 4:32
		וְדָיְרֵי	דור	dwell	Dan 4:32
Gp SC	**3ms**	שְׁוִי	שוה	become like	Dan 5:21 (K)
tG PC	**3ms**	יִתְּזִין	זון	be fed	Dan 4:9
D SC	**3mp**	שַׁוִּיו	שוה	make the same as	Dan 5:21

STEM/CONJ.	PGN	WORD	ROOT	GLOSS(ES)	VERSE(S)
D PC	**3ms**	יְחַוִּנַּהּ	חוה	*show, make known, declare* (w/ 3fs acc sx)	Dan 2:11
		יְחַוִּנַּנִי	חוה	*make known* (w/ 1cs acc sx)	Dan 5:7
	1cs	אַחַוֵּא	חוה	*show, make known, declare*	Dan 2:24
	1cp	נְחַוֵּא	חוה	*show, make known, declare*	Dan 2:4
D PTCP	**ms**	וּמְרוֹמֵם	רום	*praise*	Dan 4:34
D INF		לְקַיָּמָה	קום	*set up, erect*	Dan 6:8
tD SC	**2ms**	הִתְרוֹמַמְתָּ	רום	*exalt oneself*	Dan 5:23
tD PC	**3ms**	יִשְׁתַּוֵּה	שׁוה	*be turned into*	Dan 3:29
H SC	**3ms**	הֲקֵים	קום	*raise, erect; found, establish; appoint*	Dan 3:2, 3 (*bis*), 5, 7
		וַהֲקִים	קום	*raise, erect; found, establish; appoint*	Dan 6:2
		הֲתִיב	תוב	trans *return*	Dan 2:14
		הֲקִימֵהּ	קום	*raise, erect; found, establish; appoint* (w/ 3ms acc sx)	Dan 5:11
		אֲקִימֵהּ	קום	*raise, erect; found, establish; appoint* (w/ 3ms acc sx)	Dan 3:1
	3mp	וַהֲקִימוּ	קום	*raise, erect; found, establish; appoint*	Ezra 6:18
		הֲתִיבוּנָא	תוב	trans *return* (w/ suffix) *to* (w/ 1cp acc sx)	Ezra 5:11
	2ms	הֲקֵימְתָּ	קום	*raise, erect; found, establish; appoint*	Dan 3:12, 18

STEM/CONJ.	PGN	WORD	ROOT	GLOSS(ES)	VERSE(S)
	1cs	הֲקֵימֶת	קום	*raise, erect; found, establish; appoint*	Dan 3:14
H PC	3ms	יְהַחֲוֵה	חוה	*make known*	Dan 5:12
		יְקִים	קום	*raise, erect; found, establish; appoint*	Dan 2:44; 4:14
		יְהָקֵים	קום	*raise, erect; found, establish; appoint*	Dan 5:21; 6:16
H PC	3fs	וְתָסֵיף	סוף	*bring to an end, annihilate*	Dan 2:44
	3mp	יְתִיבוּן	תוב	trans *return*	Ezra 5:5
		יַחִיטוּ	חוט	*repair*	Ezra 4:12
	2ms	תְּקִים	קום	*raise, erect; found, establish; appoint*	Dan 6:9
	2mp	תְּהַחֲוֺן	חוה	*show, make known, declare*	Dan 2:6
		תְּהַחֲוֻנַּנִי	חוה	*show, make known, declare* (w/ 1cs acc sx)	Dan 2:9
	1cp	נְהַחֲוֵה	חוה	*show, make known, declare*	Dan 2:7
H JUSS	3mp	יַהֲתִיבוּן	תוב	trans *return*	Ezra 6:5
H IMV	2mp	הַחֲוֺנִי	חוה	*show, make known, declare* (w/ 1cs acc sx)	Dan 2:6
H PTCP	ms	מְרִים	רום	*exalt*	Dan 5:19
		וּמְהָקֵים	קום	*raise, erect; found, establish; appoint*	Dan 2:21
	fp	מְגִיחָן	גוח	*stir up*	Dan 7:2

STEM/CONJ.	PGN	WORD	ROOT	GLOSS(ES)	VERSE(S)
H INF		לְהַחֲוָיָה	חוה	show, make known, declare	Dan 2:10, 16, 27; 3:32; 5:15
		וַאֲחַוִית	חוה	make known	Dan 5:12
		לְהָזָדָה	זוד	be arrogant; act presumptuously	Dan 5:20
		לַהֲקָמוּתֵהּ	קום	raise, erect; found, establish; appoint (w/ 3ms acc sx)	Dan 6:4
		לַהֲתָבוּתָךְ	תוב	trans give a reply (w/ suffix) to (w/ 2ms acc sx)	Dan 3:16
Hp SC	3fs	הֲקִימַת	קום	be set up, erected	Dan 7:4
		הֲקֵמַת	קום	be set up, erected	Dan 7:5

LIST #38: II-י VERBS

STEM/CONJ.	PGN	WORD	ROOT	GLOSS(ES)	VERSE(S)
G SC	3ms	וּבָת	בית	spend the night	Dan 6:19
		שָׂם	שים	put, place, lay	Dan 5:12; 6:14, 15; Ezra 5:3, 9, 13; 6:1, 3
		שָׂמֵהּ	שים	put, place, lay (w/ 3ms acc sx)	Ezra 5:14
	3mp	שָׂמוּ	שים	put, place, lay	Dan 3:12
	2ms	שָׂמְתָּ	שים	put, place, lay	Dan 3:10
	1cs	שָׂמֵת	שים	put, place, lay	Ezra 6:12
G IMV	2ms	חֱיִי	חיה	live	Dan 2:4; 3:9; 5:10; 6:7, 22
	2mp	שִׂימוּ	שים	put, place, lay	Ezra 4:21

STEM/CONJ.	PGN	WORD	ROOT	GLOSS(ES)	VERSE(S)
G PTCP	mp	דָּאיְנִין	דין	*judge*	Ezra 7:25
Gp SC	3ms	שִׂים	שׂים	*be put, placed, laid*	Dan 3:29; 4:3; 6:27; Ezra 5:17; 6:8, 11; 7:13, 21
	3fs	וְשֻׂמַת	שׂים	*be put, placed, laid*	Dan 6:18
tG PC	3ms	יִתְּשָׂם	שׂים	*be put; be turned into*	Ezra 4:21
	3mp	יִתְּשָׂמוּן	שׂים	*be put; be turned into*	Dan 2:5
tG PTCP	ms	מִתְּשָׂם	שׂים	*be put; be turned into*	Ezra 5:8
H PTCP	ms	מַחֵא	חיה	*let live*	Dan 5:19
Š SC	3ms	שֵׁיזִב	שׁיזב	*rescue*	Dan 6:28
		וְשֵׁיזִב	שׁיזב	*rescue*	Dan 3:28
		וְשֵׁיצִיא	שׁיציא	*complete*	Ezra 6:15
Š PC	3ms	יְשֵׁיזִב	שׁיזב	*rescue*	Dan 3:17
		יְשֵׁיזְבִנָּךְ	שׁיזב	*rescue* (w/ 2ms acc sx)	Dan 6:17
		יְשֵׁיזְבִנְכוֹן	שׁיזב	*rescue* (w/ 2mp acc sx)	Dan 3:15
Š PTCP	ms	מְשֵׁיזִב	שׁיזב	*rescue*	Dan 6:28
Š INF		לְשֵׁיזָבוּתֵהּ	שׁיזב	*rescue* (w/ 3ms acc sx)	Dan 6:15
		לְשֵׁיזָבוּתָךְ	שׁיזב	*rescue* (w/ 2ms acc sx)	Dan 6:21
		לְשֵׁיזָבוּתַנָא	שׁיזב	*rescue* (w/ 1cp acc sx)	Dan 3:17

LIST #39: III-א VERBS

STEM/CONJ.	PGN	WORD	ROOT	GLOSS(ES)	VERSE(S)
G SC	3ms	וּנְשָׂא	נשא	*carry, lift*	Dan 2:35
		מְטָא	מטא	*reach*	Dan 4:25
		מְטָה	מטא	*reach*	Dan 7:13, 22
	3fs	מְחָת	מחא	*strike*	Dan 2:35
		וּמְחָת	מחא	*strike*	Dan 2:34
		מְטָת	מטא	*reach*	Dan 4:21
		וּמְטָת	מטא	*reach*	Dan 4:19
		וּמְלָת	מלא	*fill*	Dan 2:35
	3mp	מְטוֹ	מטא	*reach*	Dan 6:25
G PC	3ms	יִמְטֵא	מטא	*reach*	Dan 4:8, 17
		יִשְׂגֵּא	שׂגא	*become big, grow*	Ezra 4:22
		יִקְרֵה	קרא	*read*	Dan 5:7
	3mp	יִקְרוֹן	קרא	*read*	Dan 5:15
	1cs	אֶקְרֵא	קרא	*read*	Dan 5:17
G JUSS	3ms	יִשְׂגֵּא	שׂגא	*become great, grow*	Dan 3:31; 6:26
	2ms	שֵׂא	נשא	*carry, take*	Ezra 5:15
G PTCP	ms	קָרֵא	קרא	*cry out, shout*	Dan 3:4; 4:11; 5:7
		לְשָׂנְאָךְ	שׂנא	*hater, enemy* (w/ 2ms acc sx)	Dan 4:16
G INF		לְמִקְרֵא	קרא	*read*	Dan 5:8, 16
Gp SC	3ms	קֱרִי	קרא	*be read*	Ezra 4:18, 23

STEM/CONJ.	PGN	WORD	ROOT	GLOSS(ES)	VERSE(S)
tG SC	3ms	הִתְמְלִי	מלא	*be filled*	Dan 3:19
tG PC	3ms	יִתְמְחֵא	מחא	*be impaled*	Ezra 6:11
D PC	3ms	יְמַחֵא	מחא	*strike*	Dan 4:32
D INF		לְחַטָּאָה	חטא	*sin, make a sin offering*	Ezra 6:17
tD SC	3ms	וְהִתְנַבִּי	נבא	*prophesy*	Ezra 5:1
tD JUSS	3ms	יִתְקְרֵי	קרא	*be called*	Dan 5:12
tD PTCP	fs	מִתְנַשְּׂאָה	נשא	*rise up against*	Ezra 4:19
Š SC	3ms	וְשֵׁיצִיא	שיציא	*complete*	Ezra 6:15

LIST #40: III-ע VERBS

STEM/CONJ.	PGN	WORD	ROOT	GLOSS(ES)	VERSE(S)
G SC	3ms	שְׁמַע	שמע	*hear*	Dan 6:15
		יְדַע	ידע	*know; learn; understand*	Dan 5:21; 6:11
	2ms	יְדַעְתָּ	ידע	*know; learn; understand*	Dan 5:22
	1cs	שִׁמְעֵת	שמע	*hear*	Dan 5:16
		וְשִׁמְעֵת	שמע	*hear*	Dan 5:14
		יִדְעֵת	ידע	*know; learn; understand*	Dan 4:6
G PC	3ms	יִשְׁמַע	שמע	*hear*	Dan 3:10

STEM/CONJ.	PGN	WORD	ROOT	GLOSS(ES)	VERSE(S)
	3fs	וְתֵרֹעַ	רעע	*crush*	Dan 2:40
	3mp	יִנְדְּעוּן	ידע	*know; learn; understand*	Dan 4:14
	2ms	תִּנְדַּע	ידע	*know; learn; understand*	Dan 2:30; 4:22, 23, 29
		וְתִנְדַּע	ידע	*know; learn; understand*	Ezra 4:15
	2mp	תִּשְׁמְעוּן	שמע	*hear*	Dan 3:5, 15
	1cs	וְאִנְדַּע	ידע	*know; learn; understand*	Dan 2:9
G IMV	2ms	דַּע	ידע	*know; learn; understand*	Dan 6:16
G PTCP	ms	יָדַע	ידע	*know; learn; understand*	Dan 2:8, 22; Ezra 7:25
	mp	שָׁמְעִין	שמע	*hear*	Dan 3:7; 5:23
		יָדְעִין	ידע	*know; learn; understand*	Dan 5:23
		יָדְעֵי	ידע	*know; learn; understand*	Dan 2:21; Ezra 7:25
		זָיְעִין	זוע	*tremble*	Dan 5:19; 6:27
Gp PTCP	ms	יְדִיעַ	ידע	*be known; be learned; be understood*	Dan 3:18; Ezra 4:12, 13; 5:8
D PTCP	ms	מְרָעַע	רעע	*crush*	Dan 2:40
	mp	מְצַבְּעִין	צבע	*drench*	Dan 4:22
tD PC	3ms	יִצְטַבַּע	צבע	*be soaked*	Dan 4:30
	3mp	וְיִשְׁתַּמְּעוּן	שמע	*hear, heed*	Dan 7:27
tD JUSS	3ms	יִצְטַבַּע	צבע	*be drenched*	Dan 4:12, 20; 5:21

STEM/CONJ.	PGN	WORD	ROOT	GLOSS(ES)	VERSE(S)
H SC	**3ms**	הוֹדַע	ידע	*make known, communicate*	Dan 2:15, 17, 45
		וְהוֹדַע	ידע	*make known, communicate*	Dan 2:28
		הוֹדְעָךְ	ידע	*make known, communicate* (w/ 2ms acc sx)	Dan 2:29
	2ms	הוֹדַעְתַּנִי	ידע	*make known, communicate* (w/ 1cs acc sx)	Dan 2:23
		הוֹדַעְתֶּנָא	ידע	*make known, communicate* (w/ 1cp acc sx)	Dan 2:23
	1cp	וְהוֹדַעְנָא	ידע	*make known, communicate*	Ezra 4:14
H PC	**3ms**	יְהוֹדַע	ידע	*make known, communicate*	Dan 2:25
		יְהוֹדְעַנִּי	ידע	*make known, communicate* (w/ 1cs acc sx)	Dan 7:16
	3mp	יְהוֹדְעוּן	ידע	*make known, communicate*	Dan 2:30
		יְהוֹדְעַנַּנִי	ידע	*make known, communicate* (w/ 1cs acc sx)	Dan 4:3
	2mp	תְּהוֹדְעוּן	ידע	*make known, communicate*	Ezra 7:25
		תְּהוֹדְעוּנַּנִי	ידע	*make known, communicate* (w/ 1cs acc sx)	Dan 2:5
		תְּהוֹדְעֻנַּנִי	ידע	*make known, communicate* (w/ 1cs acc sx)	Dan 2:9
	1cs	אֲהוֹדְעִנֵּה	ידע	*make known, communicate* (w/ 3ms acc sx)	Dan 5:17
H PTCP	**mp**	מְהוֹדְעִין	ידע	*make known, communicate*	Dan 4:4, 16; 7:24
H INF	**inf**	לְהוֹדָעָה	ידע	*make known, communicate*	Dan 5:8
		לְהוֹדָעֻתַנִי	ידע	*make known, communicate* (w/ 1cs acc sx)	Dan 2:26; 4:15; 5:15, 16
		לְהוֹדָעוּתָךְ	ידע	*make known, communicate* (w/ 2ms acc sx)	Ezra 5:10

LIST #41: III-ח VERBS

STEM/CONJ.	PGN	WORD	ROOT	GLOSS(ES)	VERSE(S)
G SC	3ms	שְׁלַח	שׁלח	send	Dan 3:2, 28; 6:23; Ezra 4:17; 5:6; 6:13
		פְּלַח־	פלח	serve	Dan 6:17, 21
	3mp	שְׁלַחוּ	שׁלח	send	Ezra 4:11; 5:7
	2mp	שְׁלַחְתּוּן	שׁלח	send	Ezra 4:18
	1cp	שְׁלַחְנָא	שׁלח	send	Ezra 4:14
		מְלַחְנָא	מלח	salt	Ezra 4:14
G PC	3ms	יִשְׁלַח	שׁלח	send	Ezra 5:17; 6:12
	3mp	יִפְלְחוּן	פלח	serve	Dan 3:28; 7:14, 27
G PTCP	ms	פָּלַח־	פלח	serve	Dan 6:17, 21
	mp	דָּבְחִין	דבח	sacrifice	Ezra 6:3
		פָּלְחִין	פלח	serve	Dan 3:12, 14, 17, 18
		וּפָלְחֵי	פלח	servant	Ezra 7:24
		חַשְׁחִין	חשׁח	need	Dan 3:16
Gp SC	3ms	שְׁלִיחַ	שׁלח	sent	Dan 5:24
	3mp	פְּתִיחוּ	פתח	be opened	Dan 7:10
Gp PTCP	ms	שְׁלִיחַ	שׁלח	sent	Ezra 7:14
	fp	פְּתִיחָן	פתח	be opened	Dan 6:11
tG SC	3ms	הִשְׁתְּכַח	שׁכח	be found	Dan 2:35; 6:24
		וְהִשְׁתְּכַח	שׁכח	be found	Ezra 6:2

STEM/CONJ.	PGN	WORD	ROOT	GLOSS(ES)	VERSE(S)
	3fs	הִשְׁתְּכַחַת	שכח	*be found*	Dan 5:11, 12, 14; 6:5, 23
	2ms	וְהִשְׁתְּכַחַתְּ	שכח	*be found*	Dan 5:27
tG PC	3ms	יִתְנְסַח	נסח	*be pulled out*	Ezra 6:11
D SC	2ms	שַׁבַּחְתָּ	שבח	*praise*	Dan 5:23
	1cs	שַׁבְּחֵת	שבח	*praise*	Dan 4:31
	3mp	וְשַׁבַּחוּ	שבח	*praise*	Dan 5:4
D PTCP	ms	מְשַׁבַּח	שבח	*praise*	Dan 4:34
		וּמְשַׁבַּח	שבח	*praise*	Dan 2:23
tD PTCP	ms	מִתְנַצַּח	נצח	*distinguish oneself, surpass*	Dan 6:4
H SC	3ms	הַצְלַח	צלח	*promote*	Dan 3:30; 6:29
	3mp	וְהַשְׁכַּחוּ	שכח	*find*	Dan 6:12; Ezra 4:19
	1cs	הַשְׁכַּחַת	שכח	*find*	Dan 2:25
	1cp	הַשְׁכַּחְנָה	שכח	*find*	Dan 6:6
H PC	2ms	תְהַשְׁכַּח	שכח	*find*	Ezra 7:16
		וּתְהַשְׁכַּח	שכח	*find*	Ezra 4:15
	1cp	נְהַשְׁכַּח	שכח	*find*	Dan 6:6
H PTCP	ms	וּמַצְלַח	צלח	*prosper*	Ezra 5:8
	mp	וּמַצְלְחִין	צלח	*prosper*	Ezra 6:14

STEM/CONJ.	PGN	WORD	ROOT	GLOSS(ES)	VERSE(S)
	fp	מְגִיחָן	גוח	*stir up*	Dan 7:2
H INF		לְהַשְׁכָּחָה	שכח	*find*	Dan 6:5

LIST #42: III-ה VERBS

STEM/CONJ. PGN	PGN	WORD	ROOT	GLOSS(ES)	VERSE(S)
G SC	**3ms**	רְבָה	רבה	*grow*	Dan 4:8, 17, 30
		אֲתָה	אתה	*come*	Dan 7:22
		אֲתָא	אתה	*come*	Ezra 5:3, 16
		וּבְעָה	בעה	*seek, request*	Dan 2:16
		מְנָה־	מנה	*count*	Dan 5:26
		חֲזָה	חזה	*see; perceive*	Dan 4:20; 7:1
		הֲוָה	הוה	*be, become, exist; occur, happen*	Dan 4:26; 5:19 (8x); 7:13
		הֲוָא	הוה	*be, become, exist; occur, happen*	Dan 6:4, 11, 15; Ezra 5:11
		בְּעָא	בעה	*seek, request*	Dan 2:49
		בְּנֵהִי	בנה	*(re)build (w/ 3ms acc sx)*	Ezra 5:11
	3fs	רְבַת	רבה	*grow, become great*	Dan 4:19
		עֲדָת	עדה	*touch (w/ בְּ); pass (w/ מִן) out of*	Dan 3:27; 4:28
		עֲנָת	I ענה	*answer, reply; begin to speak*	Dan 5:10
		הֲוָת	הוה	*be, become, exist; occur, happen*	Dan 2:35; 7:19; Ezra 5:5
		וַהֲוָת	הוה	*be, become, exist; occur, happen*	Ezra 4:24

STEM/CONJ. PGN	WORD	ROOT	GLOSS(ES)	VERSE(S)
3mp	אֲתוֹ	אתה	*come*	Ezra 4:12
	וּבְנוֹ	בנה	*rebuild*	Ezra 6:14
	וּבְעוֹ	בעה	*seek*	Dan 2:13
	רְמוֹ	רמה	*throw*	Dan 6:25
	וּרְמוֹ	רמה	*throw*	Dan 6:17
	עֲנוֹ	עֲנה I	*answer, reply; begin to speak*	Dan 2:7, 10; 3:9, 16; 6:14
	שְׁנוֹ	שנה	intrans *change*	Dan 3:27
	הֲווֹ	הוה	*be, become, exist; occur, happen*	Dan 5:19; 6:5; Ezra 4:20
	וַהֲווֹ	הוה	*be, become, exist; occur, happen*	Dan 2:35
	אִשְׁתִּיו	שתה	*drink*	Dan 5:4
	וְאִשְׁתִּיו	שתה	*drink* (w/ בְּ) *from*	Dan 5:3
	שְׁנוֹהִי	שנה	intrans *changed on him* (w/ 3ms acc sx)	Dan 5:6
2ms	הֲוַיְתָ	הוה	*be, become, exist; occur, happen*	Dan 2:31, 34
	חֲזַיְתָ	חזה	*see; perceive*	Dan 2:43, 45; 4:17
	חֲזַיְתָה	חזה	*be, become, exist; occur, happen*	Dan 2:41 (*bis*)
	רְבִית	רבה	*grow, become great*	Dan 4:19
	חֲזַיְתוֹן	חזה	*see; perceive*	Dan 2:8
1cs	צְבִית	צבה	*desire, wish*	Dan 7:19
	הֲוֵית	הוה	*be, become, exist; occur, happen*	Dan 4:1, 7, 10; 7:2, 4, 6, 7, 8, 9, 11 (*bis*), 13, 21
	חֲזֵית	חזה	*see; perceive*	Dan 2:26; 4:2, 6, 15
	בֱּנַיְתַהּ	בנה	*(re)build* (w/ 3fs acc sx)	Dan 4:27
1cp	רְמֵינָא	רמה	*throw*	Dan 3:24
	בְּעֵינָא	בעה	*seek*	Dan 2:23

STEM/CONJ. PGN		WORD	ROOT	GLOSS(ES)	VERSE(S)
G PC	3ms	יִבְעֵה	בעה	request; seek	Dan 6:8, 13
		יֶעְדֵּה	עדה	pass away	Dan 7:14
		יִשְׁנֵא	שנה	be different	Dan 7:24
		יִצְבֵּא	צבה	desire, wish	Dan 4:14, 22, 29; 5:21
		לֶהֱוֵה	הוה	be, become, exist; occur, happen	Dan 4:22
		לֶהֱוֵא	הוה	be, become, exist; occur, happen	Dan 2:28, 29 (bis), 41, 45; 5:29; 6:3; 7:23, 26
	3fs	תִּשְׁנֵא	שנה	intrans change; be different	Dan 6:18; 7:23
		תֶּהֱוֵה	הוה	be, become, exist; occur, happen	Dan 2:41, 42 (bis)
		תֶּהֱוֵא	הוה	be, become, exist; occur, happen	Dan 2:40; 4:24; 7:23; Ezra 6:8
		תֶעְדֵּא	עדה	be annulled; pass away	Dan 6:9, 13
	3mp	וְיִשְׁתּוֹן	שתה	drink (w/ בְּ) from	Dan 5:2
		לֶהֱוֹן	הוה	be, become, exist; occur, happen	Dan 2:43 (bis); 6:2, 3, 27; Ezra 6:10; 7:25
	2ms	תִּקְנֵא	קנה	buy	Ezra 7:17
	1cs	אֶבְעֵא־	בעה	seek	Dan 7:16
G JUSS	3ms	לֶהֱוֵא	הוה	be, become, exist; occur, happen	Dan 2:20; 3:18; 4:12, 13; Ezra 5:8; 6:9; 7:26
	3mp	יִבְנוֹן	בנה	rebuild	Ezra 6:7
	3fp	לֶהֶוְיָן	הוה	be, become, exist; occur, happen	Dan 5:17
G IMV	2ms	חֱיִי	חיה	live	Dan 2:4; 3:9; 5:10; 6:7, 22

STEM/CONJ. PGN		WORD	ROOT	GLOSS(ES)	VERSE(S)
	2mp	וֶאֱתוֹ	אתה	*come*	Dan 3:26
		הֲווֹ	הוה	*be, become, exist; occur, happen*	Ezra 4:22
		הֲווֹ	הוה	*be, become, exist; occur, happen*	Ezra 6:6
G PTCP	**ms**	צָבֵא	צבה	*desire, wish*	Dan 5:19 (4x)
		שָׁתֵה	שתה	*drink*	Dan 5:1
		גָּלֵא	גלה	*reveal*	Dan 2:22, 28
		וְגָלֵא	גלה	*revealer*	Dan 2:29
		וְגָלֵה	גלה	*reveal*	Dan 2:47
		דָּמֵה	דמה	*resemble*	Dan 3:25
		בָּעֵא	בעה	*seek*	Dan 6:12, 14
		חָזֵה	חזה	*see; perceive*	Dan 2:31, 34, 25; 4:7, 10; 5:5; 7:2, 4, 6, 7, 9, 11 (*bis*), 13, 21
		עָנֵה	I ענה	*answer, reply; begin to speak*	Dan 2:5, 8, 15, 20, 26, 27, 47; 3:14, 19, 24, 25, 26, 28; 4:16 (*bis*), 27; Dan 5:7, 13, 17; 6:13, 17, 21; 7:2
		אָתֵה	אתה	*come*	Dan 7:13
	fs	דָּמְיָה	דמה	*resemble*	Dan 7:5
		שָׁנְיָה	שנה	*be different*	Dan 7:19
	mp	בָּנַיִן	בנה	*(re)build*	Ezra 4:12; 5:4; 6:14
		וּבָנַיִן	בנה	*(re)build*	Ezra 5:11
		חָזַיִן	חזה	*see; perceive*	Dan 3:27; 5:23
		שָׁתַיִן	שתה	*drink* (w/ בְּ) *from*	Dan 5:23
		שָׁנַיִן	שנה	intrans *changed*	Dan 5:9
		בָּעַיִן	בעה	*seek*	Dan 6:5
		עָנַיִן	I ענה	*answer, reply; begin to speak*	Dan 3:24
	fp	שָׁנְיָן	שנה	*be different*	Dan 7:3

STEM/CONJ. PGN		WORD	ROOT	GLOSS(ES)	VERSE(S)
G INF		לְמִגְלֵא	גלה	reveal	Dan 2:47
		לְמִבְעֵא	בעה	seek	Dan 2:18
		לְמֶחֱזֵא	חזה	see; perceive	Ezra 4:14
		לְמִבְנֵא	בנה	rebuild	Ezra 5:2, 17; 6:8
		לִבְּנֵא	בנה	rebuild	Ezra 5:3, 13
		לְמִבְנְיָה	בנה	rebuild	Ezra 5:9
		לְמִשְׁרֵא	שרה	loosen	Dan 5:16
		לְמִרְמֵא	רמה	throw	Dan 3:20; Ezra 7:24
		לְמֵזֵא	אזה	heat, stoke	Dan 3:19
		לְמֵתֵא	אתה	come	Dan 3:2
		לְמֵזְיֵהּ	אזה	heat, stoke (w/ 3ms acc sx)	Dan 3:19
		וּכְמִצְבְּיֵהּ	צבה	desire, wish (w/ 3ms gen sx)	Dan 4:32
Gp SC	3ms	שְׁוִי	שוה	become like	Dan 5:21 (K)
		גְּלִי	גלה	be revealed	Dan 2:19
		גְּלִי	גלה	be revealed	Dan 2:30
	3mp	רְמִיו	רמה	be placed	Dan 7:9
		וּרְמִיו	רמה	be thrown	Dan 3:21
Gp PTCP	ms	חֲזֵה	חזה	seen = normal	Dan 3:19
		בְּנֵה	בנה	(re)build	Ezra 5:11
		אֲזֵה	אזה	heat, stoke	Dan 3:22
		שְׁרֵא	שרה	dwell	Dan 2:22
	mp	שְׁרַיִן	שרה	untied	Dan 3:25
tG SC	3fs	אֶתְכְּרִיַּת	כרה	be distressed, troubled, disturbed	Dan 7:15
tG PC	3ms	יִתְרְמֵא	רמה	be thrown	Dan 3:6, 11; 6:8, 13

STEM/CONJ. PGN		WORD	ROOT	GLOSS(ES)	VERSE(S)
	3fs	תִּתְבְּנֵא	בנה	*be rebuilt*	Ezra 4:13, 16, 21
	2mp	תִּתְרְמוֹן	רמה	*be thrown*	Dan 3:15
tG JUSS	3ms	יִתְבְּנֵא	בנה	*be rebuilt*	Ezra 5:15; 6:3
tG PTCP	ms	מִתְבְּנֵא	בנה	*being rebuilt*	Ezra 5:8, 16
D SC	3ms	מַנִּי	מנה	*appoint*	Dan 2:24
		וּמַנִּי	מנה	*appoint*	Dan 2:49
		רַבִּי	רבה	*make great, promote*	Dan 2:48
	2ms	מַנִּיתָ	מנה	*appoint*	Dan 3:12
	3mp	וְשָׁרִיו	שרה	*begin*	Ezra 5:2
		שַׁנִּיו	שנה	trans *change = violate*	Dan 3:28
		שַׁוִּיו	שוה	*make the same as*	Dan 5:21
D PC	3ms	יְבַלֵּא	בלה	*harass, wear out*	Dan 7:25
		יְחַוִּנַּה	חוה	*show, make known, declare* (w/ 3fs acc sx)	Dan 2:11
		יְחַוִּנַּנִי	חוה	*make known* (w/ 1cs acc sx)	Dan 5:7
	1cs	אַחַוֵּא	חוה	*show, make known, declare*	Dan 2:24
	3mp	יְבַעוֹן	בעה	*seek*	Dan 4:33
	1cp	נְחַוֵּא	חוה	*show, make known, declare*	Dan 2:4
D JUSS	3mp	יְשַׁנּוֹן	שנה	trans *change*	Dan 4:13

STEM/CONJ. PGN		WORD	ROOT	GLOSS(ES)	VERSE(S)
D IMV	2ms	מֶנִּי	מנה	*appoint*	Ezra 7:25
D PTCP	ms	וּמְצַלֵּא	צלה	*pray*	Dan 6:11
		וּמְשָׁרֵא	שרה	*loosen*	Dan 5:12
	mp	וּמְצַלַּיִן	צלה	*pray*	Ezra 6:10
	fp	מְשַׁנְיָה	שנה	*be different*	Dan 7:7
tD SC	3ms	אֶשְׁתַּנִּי	שנה	intrans *change*	Dan 3:19
tD PC	3ms	יִשְׁתַּוֵּה	שוה	*be turned into*	Dan 3:29
		יִשְׁתַּנֵּא	שנה	intrans *change*	Dan 2:9
	3mp	יִשְׁתַּנּוֹן	שנה	*be changed*	Dan 7:28
tD JUSS	3mp	יִשְׁתַּנּוֹ	שנה	*be changed*	Dan 5:10
tD PTCP	mp	מִשְׁתָּרַיִן	שרה	*giving way*	Dan 5:6
H SC	3ms	הַיְתִי	אתה	*bring*	Dan 5:13
		הַגְלִי	גלה	*deport, exile*	Ezra 4:10; 5:12
	3mp	הֶעְדִּיו	עדה	*remove*	Dan 5:20
		הֶעְדִּיו	עדה	*remove*	Dan 7:12
		הַיְתִיו	אתה	*bring*	Dan 5:3, 23
		וְהַיְתִיו	אתה	*bring*	Dan 6:17, 25
H PC	3ms	יְהַחֲוֵה	חוה	*make known*	Dan 5:12
		יְהַשְׁנֵא	שנה	trans *change*	Ezra 6:11
	3mp	יְהַעְדּוֹן	עדה	*remove*	Dan 7:26

STEM/CONJ. PGN		WORD	ROOT	GLOSS(ES)	VERSE(S)
	2mp	תְּהַחֲוֹן	חוה	show, make known, declare	Dan 2:6
		תְּהַחֲוֻנַּנִי	חוה	show, make known, declare (w/ 1cs acc sx)	Dan 2:9
	1cp	נְהַחֲוֵה	חוה	show, make known, declare	Dan 2:7
H IMV	2mp	הַחֲוֹנִי	חוה	show, make known, declare (w/ 1cs acc sx)	Dan 2:6
H PTCP	ms	מְהַעְדֵּה	עדה	remove, depose	Dan 2:21
		מְהַשְׁנֵא	שנה	trans change	Dan 2:21
		מַחֵא	חיה	let live	Dan 5:19
		מְהוֹדֵא	ידה	give thanks	Dan 2:23
		וּמוֹדֵא	ידה	give thanks	Dan 6:11
H INF		לְהַשְׁנָיָה	שנה	trans change	Dan 6:9, 16; 7:25; Ezra 6:12
		לְהַיְתָיָה	אתה	bring	Dan 3:13; 5:12
		לְהַחֲוָיָה	חוה	show, make known, declare	Dan 2:10, 16, 27; 3:32; 5:15
		וַאַחֲוָיַת	חוה	make known	Dan 5:12
Hp SC	3fs	וְהֵיתָיִת	אתה	be brought	Dan 6:18
	3mp	הֵיתָיוּ	אתה	be brought	Dan 3:13

LIST #43: GEMINATE ROOTS

STEM/CONJ.	PGN	WORD	ROOT	GLOSS(ES)	VERSE(S)
G SC	3ms	עַל	II עלל	*enter*	Dan 2:16, 24; 4:5; 6:11
	3fs	עַלַּת	II עלל	*enter*	Dan 5:10
	3mp	דָּקוּ	דקק	*break*	Dan 2:35
G PC	3fs	וְתֵרֹעַ	רעע	*crush*	Dan 2:40
G PTCP	mp	עָלִין	II עלל	*enter*	Dan 4:4; 5:8
G INF		בְּמִחַן	חנן	*show mercy, grace*	Dan 4:24
D SC	3ms	מַלִּל	מלל	*speak*	Dan 6:22
D PC	3ms	יְמַלִּל	מלל	*speak*	Dan 7:25
D IMV	2mp	וְקַצִּצוּ	קצץ	*cut off, lop off*	Dan 4:11
D PTCP	ms	מְמַלִּל	מלל	*speak*	Dan 7:8, 20
		מְרָעַע	רעע	*crush*	Dan 2:40
	fs	מְמַלְּלָה	מלל	*speak*	Dan 7:11
tD PC	1cs	אֶשְׁתּוֹמַם	שמם	*be appalled*	Dan 4:16
tD PTCP	ms	וּמִתְחַנַּן	חנן	*seek mercy, grace*	Dan 6:12
H SC	3ms	הַדִּקוּ	דקק	*pulverize*	Dan 6:25
		הַנְעֵל	II עלל	*bring*	Dan 2:25; 6:19
	3fs	וְהַדֵּקֶת	דקק	*pulverize*	Dan 2:34, 35

STEM/CONJ.	PGN	WORD	ROOT	GLOSS(ES)	VERSE(S)
	3mp	אֶשְׁכְלִלוּ	שכלל	*finish*	Ezra 4:12 (K)
H PC	3fs	תַּטְלֵל	טלל	*find shade*	Dan 4:9
		תַּדִּק	דקק	*pulverize*	Dan 2:40, 44
		וְתַדְּקִנַּה	דקק	*pulverize* (w/ 3fs acc sx)	Dan 7:23
H IMV	2ms	הַעֵלְנִי	עלל II	*bring* (w/ 1cs acc sx)	Dan 2:24
H PTCP	ms	מְהַדֵּק	דקק	*pulverize*	Dan 2:40
	fs	מַדֶּקָה	דקק	*pulverize*	Dan 7:19
		וּמַדֶּקָה	דקק	*pulverize*	Dan 7:7
H INF		לְהֶעָלָה	עלל II	*bring*	Dan 5:7
		לְהַנְעָלָה	עלל II	*bring*	Dan 4:3
Hp SC	3ms	הֻעַל	עלל II	*be brought*	Dan 5:13
	3mp	הֻעַלּוּ	עלל II	*be brought*	Dan 5:15
Š SC	3ms	וְשַׁכְלְלֵהּ	כלל	*finish* (w/ 3ms acc sx)	Ezra 5:11
	3mp	שַׁכְלִלוּ	כלל	*finish*	Ezra 4:12
		וְשַׁכְלִלוּ	כלל	*finish*	Ezra 6:14
Š INF		לְשַׁכְלָלָה	כלל	*finish, complete*	Ezra 5:3, 9
Št PC	3mp	יִשְׁתַּכְלְלוּן	כלל	*be finished*	Ezra 4:13, 16

LIST #44: METATHESIZING ROOTS

STEM/CONJ.	PGN	WORD	ROOT	GLOSS(ES)	VERSE(S)
tG SC	3ms	הִשְׁתְּכַח	שכח	be found	Dan 2:35; 6:24
		וְהִשְׁתְּכַח	שכח	be found	Ezra 6:2
	3fs	הִשְׁתְּכַחַת	שכח	be found	Dan 5:11, 12, 14; 6:5, 23
	2ms	וְהִשְׁתְּכַחַתְּ	שכח	be found	Dan 5:27
tG PC	3fs	תִּתְבְּנֵא	בנה	be rebuilt	Ezra 4:13, 16, 21
		תִּשְׁתְּבִק	שבק	be left (w/ לְ) to	Dan 2:44
tD SC	3ms	אֶשְׁתַּנִּי	שנה	intrans change	Dan 3:19
tD PC	3ms	יִצְטַבַּע	צבע	be soaked	Dan 4:30
		יִשְׁתַּוֵּה	שוה	be turned into	Dan 3:29
		יִשְׁתַּנֵּא	שנה	intrans change	Dan 2:9
	3mp	וְיִשְׁתַּמְּעוּן	שמע	hear, heed	Dan 7:27
		יִשְׁתַּנּוֹן	שנה	be changed	Dan 7:28
	1cs	אֶשְׁתּוֹמַם	שמם	be appalled	Dan 4:16
tD JUSS	3ms	יִצְטַבַּע	צבע	be drenched	Dan 4:12, 20; 5:21
	3mp	יִשְׁתַּנּוֹ	שנה	be changed	Dan 5:10
tD PTCP	ms	מִשְׂתַּכַּל	שׂכל	contemplate	Dan 7:8
		מִשְׁתַּדַּר	שדר	exert, make every effort	Dan 6:15
	mp	מִשְׁתָּרַיִן	שרה	giving way	Dan 5:6
		מִשְׁתַּבְּשִׁין	שבש	be perplexed	Dan 5:9

LIST #45: THE ROOT סלק

STEM/CONJ.	PGN	WORD		GLOSS	VERSE(S)
G SC	**3fs**	סִלְקַת	*come up*		Dan 7:20
		סִלְקָת	*come up*		Dan 7:8
	3mp	סְלִקוּ	*come up*		Dan 2:29; Ezra 4:12
G PTCP	**fp**	סָלְקָן	*come up*		Dan 7:3
H SC	**3mp**	הַסִּקוּ	*bring up*		Dan 3:22
H INF		לְהַנְסָקָה	*bring up*		Dan 6:24
Hp SC	**3ms**	וְהֻסַּק	*be brought up*		Dan 6:24

VERBS BY FREQUENCY OF ATTESTED FORM AND NUMBER OF STEMS

LIST #46: VERBS BY FREQUENCY OF ATTESTED FORM

There are 691 unique verb forms attested in Biblical Aramaic. Of these, 534 (= 77%) occur only once. The 157 forms that occur more than once are listed here, in order of the frequency with which they occur. If one includes repeated forms, there are 1078 verb forms in Biblical Aramaic. Therefore, the following list accounts for about half of the total verb forms that appear.

	WORD	PARSING	FREQ.
1	וְאָמַר	G ptcp ms abs אמר *say; order*	23
2	עָנֵה	G ptcp ms abs I ענה *answer, reply; begin to speak*	23
3	חָזֵה	G ptcp ms abs חזה *see; perceive*	15
4	הֲוָא	G sc 3ms הוה *be, become, exist; occur, happen*	14
5	חֲזֵית	G sc 1cs חזה *see; perceive*	14
6	הֲוֵית	G sc 1cs הוה *be, become, exist; occur, happen*	13
7	אֲמַר	G sc 3ms אמר *say; order*	11
8	הֲוָה	G sc 3ms הוה *be, become, exist; occur, happen*	10
9	לֶהֱוֵא	G pc 3ms הוה *be, become, exist; occur, happen*	9
10	שָׂם	G sc 3ms שׂים *put, place, lay*	8
11	יָקֵדְתָּא	G ptcp fs emph יקד *burn*	8
12	וְאָמְרִין	G ptcp mp abs אמר *say; order*	8
13	שִׂים	Gp sc 3ms שׂים *be put, placed, laid*	8
14	יְהַב־	G sc 3ms יהב *give*	7
15	לֶהֱוֺן	G pc 3mp הוה *be, become, exist; occur, happen*	7
16	לֶהֱוֵא	G juss 3ms הוה *be, become, exist; occur, happen*	7
17	שְׁלַח	G sc 3ms שׁלח *send*	6
18	אָמְרִין	G ptcp mp abs אמר *say; order*	6
19	עֲנוֹ	G sc 3mp I ענה *answer, reply; begin to speak*	5
20	חֱיִי	G imv 2ms חיה *live*	5
21	הִשְׁתְּכַחַת	tG sc 3fs שׁכח *be found*	5

	WORD	PARSING	FREQ.
22	הֲקֵים	H sc 3ms קום *raise, erect; found, establish; appoint*	5
23	לְהַחֲוָיָה	H inf חוה *show, make known, declare*	5
24	אֲזַל	G sc 3ms אזל *go*	4
25	וַאֲמַר	G sc 3ms אמר *say; order*	4
26	עַל	G sc 3ms II עלל *enter*	4
27	יִצְבֵּא	G pc 3ms צבה *desire, wish*	4
28	תֶּהֱוֵא	G pc 3fs הוה *be, become, exist; occur, happen*	4
29	תִּנְדַּע	G pc 2ms ידע *know; learn; understand*	4
30	צָבֵא	G ptcp ms abs צבה *desire, wish*	4
31	פָּלְחִין	G ptcp mp abs פלח *serve*	4
32	יְדִיעַ	Gp ptcp ms ידע *be known; be learned; be understood*	4
33	יִתְרְמֵא	tG pc 3ms רמה *be thrown*	4
34	הַנְפֵּק	H sc 3ms נפק *bring out*	4
35	לְהַשְׁנָיָה	H inf שנה trans *change*	4
36	לְהוֹדָעֻתַנִי	H inf ידע *make known, communicate* (w/ 1cs acc sx)	4
37	עֲבַד	G sc 3ms עבד *do, make*	3
38	רְבָה	G sc 3ms רבה *grow*	3
39	הֲוָת	G sc 3fs הוה *be, become, exist; occur, happen*	3
40	הֲווֹ	G sc 3mp הוה *be, become, exist; occur, happen*	3
41	חֲזַיְתָ	G sc 2ms חזה *see; perceive*	3
42	וְיִסְגֻּד	G pc 3ms סגד *prostrate oneself, bow down to the ground*	3
43	יְתוּב	G pc 3ms תוב intrans *return*	3
44	יִפֵּל	G pc 3ms נפל *fall*	3
45	יִתְּנִנַּהּ	G pc 3ms נתן *give* (w/ 3fs acc sx)	3
46	תֶּהֱוֵה	G pc 3fs הוה *be, become, exist; occur, happen*	3
47	יִפְלְחוּן	G pc 3mp פלח *serve*	3
48	יַחְלְפוּן	G pc 3mp חלף *pass over*	3
49	אֱמַר	G imv 2ms אמר *say; order*	3
50	שְׁבֻקוּ	G imv 2mp שבק *leave;* (w/ לְ) *leave smthg alone, unencumbered*	3
51	עָבֵד	G ptcp ms abs עבד *do, make*	3
52	קָרֵא	G ptcp ms abs קרא *cry out, shout*	3
53	יָדַע	G ptcp ms abs ידע *know; learn; understand*	3
54	סָגְדִין	G ptcp mp abs סגד *prostrate oneself, bow down to the ground*	3
55	יָכְלִין	G ptcp mp abs יכל *be able*	3

	WORD	PARSING	FREQ.
56	בָּנֵין	G ptcp mp abs בנה (re)build	3
57	דָּיְרִין	G ptcp mp abs דור dwell	3
58	לְמִבְנֵא	G inf בנה rebuild	3
59	רְשִׁים	Gp sc 3ms רשם be written	3
60	יְהִיב	Gp sc 3ms יהב be given	3
61	וּשְׁחִיתָה	Gp ptcp fs שחת corrupted, bad	3
62	יִתְעֲבֵד	tG pc 3ms עבד be done; be turned into	3
63	תִּתְבְּנֵא	tG pc 3fs בנה be rebuilt	3
64	יְבַהֲלֻנַּנִי	D pc 3mp בהל terrify (w/ 1cs acc sx)	3
65	תִּתְחַבַּל	tD pc 3fs חבל be destroyed	3
66	יִצְטַבַּע	tD juss 3ms צבע be drenched	3
67	הוֹדַע	H sc 3ms ידע make known, communicate	3
68	הַרְגִּשׁוּ	H sc 3mp רגש throng [= conspire (?)]	3
69	מְהוֹדְעִין	H ptcp mp ידע make known, communicate	3
70	כְּתַב	G sc 3ms כתב write	2
71	שְׁפַר	G sc 3ms שפר be pleasant, pleasing	2
72	וּתְקֵף	G sc 3ms תקף become strong	2
73	פְּלַח־	G sc 3ms פלח serve	2
74	יְדַע	G sc 3ms ידע know; learn; understand	2
75	יָתֵב	G ptcp ms abs יתב sit	2
76	נְפַל	G sc 3ms נפל fall	2
77	מְטָה	G sc 3ms מטא reach	2
78	אֲתָא	G sc 3ms אתה come	2
79	חֲזָה	G sc 3ms חזה see; perceive	2
80	אָכְלָה	G sc 3fs אכל eat	2
81	עֲדָת	G sc 3fs עדה touch (w/ בְּ); pass (w/ מִן) out of	2
82	סְלִקוּ	G sc 3mp סלק come up	2
83	שְׁלַחוּ	G sc 3mp שלח send	2
84	עֲבַדוּ	G sc 3mp עבד do, make	2
85	רְשַׁמְתָּ	G sc 2ms רשם write	2
86	הֲוַיְתָ	G sc 2ms הוה be, become, exist; occur, happen	2
87	חֲזַיְתָה	G sc 2ms חזה be, become, exist; occur, happen	2
88	עַבְדֵת	G sc 1cs עבד do, make	2
89	אֲמַרְנָא	G sc 1cp אמר say; order	2

	WORD	PARSING	FREQ.
90	שְׁאֶלְנָא	G sc 1cp שאל *ask*	2
91	יִשְׁלַח	G pc 3ms שלח *send*	2
92	יִמְטֵא	G pc 3ms מטא *reach*	2
93	יִבְעֵה	G pc 3ms בעה *request; seek*	2
94	יְקוּם	G pc 3ms קום *arise, get up; be established, endure*	2
95	יְהָךְ	G pc 3ms הך *reach*	2
96	תְּקוּם	G pc 3fs קום *arise, get up; be established, endure*	2
97	תִּשְׁנֵא	G pc 3fs שנה intrans *change; be different*	2
98	תֶעְדֵּא	G pc 3fs עדה *be annulled; pass away*	2
99	יְקוּמוּן	G pc 3mp קום *arise, get up; be established, endure*	2
100	וְתִסְגְּדוּן	G pc 2mp סגד *prostrate oneself, bow down to the ground*	2
101	תִּשְׁמְעוּן	G pc 2mp שמע *hear*	2
102	תַּעַבְדוּן	G pc 2mp עבד *do, make*	2
103	תִּפְּלוּן	G pc 2mp נפל *fall*	2
104	יִשְׂגֵּא	G juss 3ms שגא *become great, grow*	2
105	גֹּדּוּ	G imv 2mp גדד *chop down*	2
106	כָּהֵל	G ptcp ms abs כהל *be able*	2
107	שָׁאֵל	G ptcp ms abs שאל *ask*	2
108	נָחֵת	G ptcp ms abs נחת *descend*	2
109	אָמַר	G ptcp ms abs אמר *say; order*	2
110	יָכִל	G ptcp ms abs יכל *be able*	2
111	גָּלֵא	G ptcp ms abs גלה *reveal*	2
112	בָּעֵא	G ptcp ms abs בעה *seek*	2
113	רָפְסָה	G ptcp fs abs רפס *trample*	2
114	גָּזְרִין	G ptcp mp abs גזר *diviner*	2
115	וְגָזְרַיָּא	G ptcp mp emph גזר *diviner*	2
116	טָרְדִין	G ptcp mp abs טרד *drive away*	2
117	שָׁמְעִין	G ptcp mp abs שמע *hear*	2
118	וְדָחֲלִין	G ptcp mp abs דחל *fear*	2
119	כָּהֲלִין	G ptcp mp abs כהל *be able*	2
120	יָדְעֵי	G ptcp mp cstr ידע *know; learn; understand*	2
121	חָזַיִן	G ptcp mp abs חזה *see; perceive*	2
122	זָיְעִין	G ptcp mp abs זוע *tremble*	2
123	עָלִּין	G ptcp mp abs II עלל *enter*	2

	WORD	PARSING	FREQ.
124	לְמֶעְבַּד	G inf עבד *do, make*	2
125	לְמִקְרֵא	G inf קרא *read*	2
126	לִבְנֵא	G inf בנה *rebuild*	2
127	לְמִרְמֵא	G inf רמה *throw*	2
128	טְרִיד	Gp sc 3ms טרד *be driven away*	2
129	קֱרִי	Gp sc 3ms קרא *be read*	2
130	יְהִיבַת	Gp sc 3fs יהב *be given*	2
131	וִיהִיבַת	Gp sc 3fs יהב *be given*	2
132	דְּחִילָה	Gp ptcp fs דחל *feared*	2
133	הִשְׁתְּכַח	tG sc 3ms שכח *be found*	2
134	יִתְבְּנֵא	tG juss 3ms בנה *be rebuilt*	2
135	מִתְיְהֵב	tG ptcp ms יהב *be given*	2
136	מִתְבְּנֵא	tG ptcp ms בנה *being rebuilt*	2
137	וּבַקַּרוּ	D sc 3mp בקר *search*	2
138	יְטַעֲמוּן	D pc 3mp טעם *feed*	2
139	מְמַלִּל	D ptcp ms מלל *speak*	2
140	לְבַטָּלָא	D inf trans בטל *stop*	2
141	מְעָרַב	Dp ptcp ms ערב *mixed*	2
142	מְכַפְּתִין	Dp ptcp mp כפת *tied up*	2
143	וְהֵיבֵל	H sc 3ms יבל *bring*	2
144	הַגְלִי	H sc 3ms גלה *deport, exile*	2
145	הַנְעֵל	H sc 3ms II עלל *bring*	2
146	וְהַדֵּקֶת	H sc 3fs דקק *pulverize*	2
147	וְהַשְׁכַּחוּ	H sc 3mp שכח *find*	2
148	הַיְתִיו	H sc 3mp אתה *bring*	2
149	וְהַיְתִיו	H sc 3mp אתה *bring*	2
150	הֲקֵימְתָּ	H sc 2ms קום *raise, erect; found, establish; appoint*	2
151	יְקִים	H pc 3ms קום *raise, erect; found, establish; appoint*	2
152	יְהָקֵים	H pc 3ms קום *raise, erect; found, establish; appoint*	2
153	תַּדֵּק	H pc 3fs דקק *pulverize*	2
154	מַהְלְכִין	H ptcp mp הלך *walk*	2
155	לְהוֹבָדָה	H inf אבד *kill*	2
156	לְהַיְתָיָה	H inf אתה *bring*	2
157	לְשַׁכְלָלָה	Š inf כלל *finish, complete*	2

LIST #47: ROOTS BY NUMBER OF STEMS IN WHICH THEY OCCUR

	WORD	GLOSS(ES)	FREQ.

ROOTS OCCURRING IN 5 STEMS

1	שׁנה	(H) trans *change* [6x]; (G) *be different* [4x]; intrans *change* [2x]; (w/ 3ms suffix) intrans *changed on him* [1x]; (G ptcp) intrans *changed* [1x]; (tD) intrans *change* [2x]; *be changed* [2x]; (D) trans *change* [1x]; trans *change = violate* [1x]; (Dp) *be different* [1x]	21
2	קטל	(Gp, tG, tD) *be killed* [4x]; (G, D) *kill* [3x]	7

ROOTS OCCURRING IN 4 STEMS

1	קום	(G) *arise, get up; be established, endure;* (H) *raise, erect; found, establish; appoint;* (Hp) *be set up, erected;* (D) *set up, erect*	35
2	שרה	(G) *loosen* [1x]; (D) *loosen* [1x]; *begin* [1x]; (Gp) *dwell* [1x]; *untied* [1x]; (tD) *giving away* [1x]	6
3	II ברך	(G, D) *bless* [2x]; (Gp, Dp) *blessed* [2x]	4
4	רום	(G) *be high* [1x]; (D) *praise* [1x]; (H) *exalt* [1x]; (tD) *exalt oneself* [1x]	4

ROOTS OCCURRING IN 3 STEMS

1	אתה	(G) *come* [7x]; (H) *bring* [7x]; (Hp) *be brought* [2x]	16
2	II עלל	(G) *enter* [7x]; (H) *bring* [5x]; (Hp) *be brought* [2x]	14
3	רמה	(tG) *be thrown* [5x]; (G) *throw* [4x]; *throw = impose* [1x]; (Gp) *be thrown* [1x]; *be placed* [1x]	12
4	גלה	(G) *reveal* [3x]; (G ptcp) *revealer* [2x]; (Gp) *be revealed* [2x]; (H) *deport, exile* [2x]	9
5	קרב	(G) *approach* [5x]; (H) *offer* [2x]; *present* [1x]; (D) *offer* [1x]	9
6	סלק	(G) *come up* [5x]; (H) *bring up* [2x]; (Hp) *be brought up* [1x]	8
7	אבד	(H) *kill* [4x]; *destroy* [1x]; (G) *perish* [1x]; (Hp) *be destroyed* [1x]	7
8	כלל	(Š) *finish, complete* [4x + 1x Qere]; (Št) *be finished* [2x]; (H) *finish* [1x, Ketiv]	7
9	דחל	(Gp ptcp) *feared* [3x]; (G) *fear* [2x]; (D) *frighten* [1x]	6
10	נחת	(G) *descend* [2x]; (H) *deposit* [2x]; (Hp) *be brought down, deposed* [1x]; *deposited* [1x]	6
11	יתב	(G) *sit* [2x]; *dwell* [1x]; (D) *sit* [1x]; (H) *make dwell, settle* [1x]	5
12	כפת	(Gp) *be tied up* [1x]; (D) *tie up* [1x]; (Dp ptcp) *tied up* [2x]	4
13	מחא	(G, D) *strike* [3x]; (tG) *be impaled* [1x]	4

	WORD	GLOSS(ES)	FREQ.
14	שׁוה	(Gp) *become like* [1x, Ketiv]; (D) *make the same as* [1x, Qere] (tD) *be turned into* [1x]	2

ROOTS OCCURRING IN 2 STEMS

	WORD	GLOSS(ES)	FREQ.
1	ידע	(G) *know, learn; understand;* (H) *make known, communicate*	47
2	חזה	(G) *see, perceive;* (Gp ptcp) *proper, customary*	31
3	יהב	(G) *give;* (tG) *be given*	28
4	עבד	(G) *do, make;* (tG) *be done; be turned into*	28
5	שׁים	(G) *put, place, lay;* (tG) *be put; be turned into*	26
6	בנה	(G) *rebuild* [10x]; *(re)build* [5x]; (tG) *be rebuilt* [5x]; (tG ptcp) *being rebuilt* [2x]	22
7	שׁכח	(tG) *be found* [9x]; (H) *find* [8x]	17
8	חוה	(H) *show, make known, declare* [11x]; (D) *show, make known, declare* [4x]	15
9	שׁלח	(G) *send* [12x]; (Gp) *sent* [2x]	14
10	בעה	(G) *seek, request* [11x]; (D) *seek* [1x]	12
11	נפק	(H) *bring out* [5x]; (G) *go out* [4x]; *go out = be issued* [1x]; *come out* [1x]	11
12	קרא	(G) *read* [5x]; *be read* [2x]; *cry out, shout* [3x]; (tD) *be called* [1x]	11
13	דקק	(H) *pulverize* [9x]; (G) *break* [1x]	10
14	עדה	(H) *remove, depose* [4x]; (G) *pass away, be annulled* [3x]; *touch* (w/ בְּ) [1x]; *pass* (w/ מִן) *out of* [1x]	9
15	שׁמע	(G) *hear* [8x]; (tD) *hear, heed* [1x]	9
16	בהל	(D) *terrify* [7x]; (tD) *be terrified* [1x]	8
17	כתב	(G) *write* [6x]; (Gp) *be written* [2x]	8
18	תוב	(G) intrans *return* [3x]; (H) trans *return* [3x]; trans *return* (w/ suffix) *to* [1x]; trans *give a reply* (w/ suffix) *to* [1x]	8
19	רשׁם	(G) *write* [4x]; (Gp) *be written* [3x]	7
20	שׁלט	(G) *rule* [4x]; *have power* (w/ בְּ) *over* [1x]; (H) *make rule* [2x]	7
21	בטל	(D) trans *stop* [4x]; (G) intrans *cease(d)* [2x]	6
22	גזר	(G ptcp) *diviner* [4x]; (tG) *cut out* [1x]; *be cut out* [1x]	6
23	חבל	(D) *destroy* [3x]; (tD) *be destroyed* [3x]	6
24	חיה	(G) *live* [5x]; (H) *let live* [1x]	6
25	צלח	(H) *prosper* [3x]; *promote* [1x]; (D) *pray* [2x]	6
26	רבה	(G) *grow* [3x]; *grow, become great* [2x]; (D) *make great, promote* [1x]	6
27	בקר	(D) *search* [4x]; (tD) *be searched* [1x]	5

	WORD	GLOSS(ES)	FREQ.
28	מנה	(D) *appoint* [4x]; (G) *count* [1x]	5
29	צבע	(tD) *be drenched* [3x]; *be soaked* [1x]; (D) *drench* [1x]	5
30	שבק	(G) *leave* [3x]; *leave* (w/ לְ) smthg *alone, unencumbered* [1x]; (tG) *be left* (w/ לְ) *to* [1x]	5
31	תקף	(G) *become strong* [4x]; (D) *make strong; enforce* [1x]	5
32	טרד	(G) *drive away* [2x]; (Gp) *be driven away* [2x]	4
33	ערב	(Dp) *mixed* [2x]; (tD) *intermingle* [2x]	4
34	אמן	(H) *trust* [1x]; (Hp ptcp) *trustworthy* [2x]	3
35	הלך	(D, H) *walk* [3x]	3
36	יעט	(G ptcp) *adviser* [2x]; (tD) *consult together* [1x]	3
37	כנש	(G, tD) *assemble*	3
38	לבש	(G) *wear* [2x]; (H) *clothe* [1x]	3
39	נזק	(G) *come to grief* (HALOT); *be damaged* [1x]; (H) *damage* [1x]; (H ptcp) *damager* [1x]	3
40	נשא	(G) *carry, lift* [1x]; *carry, take* [1x]; (tD) *rise up against* [1x]	3
41	שלם	(H) *complete, finish off* [1x]; *fully deliver* [1x]; (Gp) *be finished* [1x]	3
42	חנן	(G) *show mercy, grace* [1x]; (tD) *seek mercy, grace* [1x]	2
43	מלא	(G) *fill* [1x]; (tG) *be filled* [1x]	2
44	נטל	(G) *lift* [1x]; (Gp) *be lifted* [1x]	2
45	סוף	(G) *be fulfilled* [1x]; (H) *bring to an end, annihilate* [1x]	2
46	פשר	(G, D) *interpret*	2
47	רעע	(G, D) *crush*	2
48	שכן	(G) *dwell* [1x]; (D) *cause to dwell, settle* [1x]	2

ROOTS OCCURRING IN ONLY 1 STEM

1	אמר	(G) *say; order*	71
2	הוה	(G) *be, become, exist; occur, happen*	71
3	ענה I	(G) *answer, reply; begin to speak*	30
4	יכל	(G) *be able* [11x]; *be more able, overpower* [1x]	12
5	נפל	(G) *fall*	11
6	סגד	(G) *prostrate oneself, bow down to the ground*	11
7	פלח	(G) *serve* [9x]; (G ptcp) *servant* [1x]	10
8	צבה	(G) *desire, wish*	10
9	שיזב	(Š) *rescue*	9

	WORD	GLOSS(ES)	FREQ.
10	יקד	(G) burn	8
11	מטא	(G) reach [7x]; arrive [1x]	8
12	אזל	(G) go	7
13	אכל	(G) eat	7
14	דור	(G) dwell	7
15	נתן	(G) give	7
16	שאל	(G) ask	6
17	מלל	(D) speak	5
18	שבח	(D) praise	5
19	שתה	(G) drink [2x]; drink (w/ בְּ) from [3x]	5
20	הך	(G) go [3x]; reach [1x]	4
21	חלף	(G) pass over	4
22	כהל	(G) be able	4
23	שפל	(H) humble [2x]; humiliate [1x]; bring low [1x]	4
24	אזה	(G) heat, stoke	3
25	הדר	(D) glorify	3
26	טעם	(D) feed	3
27	יבל	(H) bring	3
28	נדב	(tD) volunteer	3
29	נצל	(H) deliver	3
30	קבל	(D) receive	3
31	רגש	(H) throng [= conspire (?)]	3
32	שגא	(G) become great, grow [2x]; become big, grow [1x]	3
33	שחת	(Gp ptcp) corrupted, bad	3
34	שפר	(G) be pleasant, pleasing	3
35	גדד	(G) chop down	2
36	דמה	(G) resemble	2
37	זוע	(G) tremble	2
38	חסן	(H) possess	2
39	חצף	(H) be harsh	2
40	ידה	(H) give thanks	2
41	פתח	(Gp) be opened	2
42	רפס	(G) trample	2
43	אנס	(G) oppress, bother	1

	WORD	GLOSS(ES)	FREQ.
44	באש	(G) *be bad, evil to* (w/ עַל־)	1
45	בדר	(D) *scatter*	1
46	בית	(G) *spend the night*	1
47	בלה	(D) *harass, wear out*	1
48	בנס	(G) *be enraged*	1
49	ברך I	(G) *kneel*	1
50	גוח	(H) *stir up*	1
51	גמר	(Gp ptcp) *perfect, completed*; as adv *completely* (?)	1
52	דבח	(G) *sacrifice*	1
53	דבק	(G) *adhere, stick together*	1
54	דוש	(G) *trample*	1
55	דין	(G) *judge*	1
56	דלק	(G) *be on fire*	1
57	זבן	(G) *buy*	1
58	זוד	(H) *be arrogant; act presumptuously*	1
59	זון	(tG) *be fed*	1
60	זמן	(tG) *conspire*	1
61	זעק	(G) *yell*	1
62	זקף	(Gp ptcp) *raised*	1
63	חוט	(G/H) *repair*	1
64	חטא	(D) *sin, make a sin offering*	1
65	חרב	(Hp) *be laid waste*	1
66	חרך	(tD) *be singed*	1
67	חשב	(Gp) *be thought of*	1
68	חשח	(G) *need*	1
69	חשל	(G) *smash*	1
70	חתם	(G) *seal*	1
71	טאב	(G) *be good to* (w/ עַל־) X = *X was glad*	1
72	טלל	(H) *find shade*	1
73	יטב	(G) *be good* (w/ עַל־) *to*	1
74	יסף	(Hp) *be added*	1
75	יצב	(D) *ascertain, make certain of*	1
76	כרה	(tG) *be distressed, troubled, disturbed*	1
77	כרז	(H) *herald, proclaim*	1

	WORD	GLOSS(ES)	FREQ.
78	מגר	(D) *overthrow*	1
79	מלח	(G) *salt*	1
80	מרט	(Gp) *be plucked*	1
81	נבא	(tD) *prophesy*	1
82	נגד	(G) *flow*	1
83	נדד	(G) *flee*	1
84	נוד	(G) *flee*	1
85	נטר	(G) *keep*	1
86	נסח	(tG) *be pulled out*	1
87	נסך	(D) *pour out = offer*	1
88	נצח	(tD) *distinguish oneself, surpass*	1
89	נקש	(G) *knock*	1
90	נתר	(H) *strip off*	1
91	סבל	(Dp) *maintained (?)*	1
92	סבר	(G) *intend*	1
93	סגר	(G) *close, shut*	1
94	סעד	(D) *support*	1
95	I סתר	(Dp ptcp) *hidden*	1
96	II סתר	(G) *destroy*	1
97	עקר	(tG) *be ripped out*	1
98	עשת	(Gp) *intend* active sense	1
99	פלג	(Gp ptcp) *divided*	1
100	פרס	(Gp) *be divided*	1
101	פרק	(G) *wipe away; ransom*	1
102	פרש	(Dp ptcp) *separated, made distinct; translated; explained*	1
103	קנה	(G) *buy*	1
104	קצף	(G) *be furious*	1
105	קצץ	(D) *cut off, lop off*	1
106	רגז	(H) *enrage*	1
107	רחץ	(tG) *trust (w/ עַל־) in*	1
108	שכל	(tD) *contemplate*	1
109	שנא	(G ptcp) *hater, enemy*	1
110	שבש	(tD) *be perplexed*	1
111	שדר	(tD) *exert, make every effort*	1

	WORD	GLOSS(ES)	FREQ.
112	שִׁיצִיא	(Š) *complete*	1
113	שְׁמד	(H) *annihilate*	1
114	שׁמם	(tD) *be appalled*	1
115	שׁמשׁ	(D) *minister, attend, serve*	1
116	שׁנה	(H) *change*	1
117	שׁפט	(G) *judge*	1
118	תבר	(Gp ptcp) *fragile, brittle*	1
119	תוה	(G) *be astonished, startled, horrified*	1
120	תקל	(Gp) *be weighed*	1
121	תקן	(Hp) *be reestablished*	1

PRONOMINAL SUFFIXES

LIST #48: WORDS WITH 3MS SUFFIXES

	WORD	LEX. FORM	GLOSS(ES)	FREQ.
MASCULINE SINGULAR NOUNS				
1	פִּשְׁרֵהּ	פְּשַׁר	*interpretation*	14
2	פִּשְׁרֵא	פְּשַׁר	*interpretation*	2
3	שְׁמֵהּ	שֻׁם	*name*	7
4	בַּיְתֵהּ	בַּיִת	*house; palace; temple*	6
5	אֱלָהֵהּ	אֱלָהּ	*God; god, deity*	5
6	רוּמֵהּ	רוּם	*height*	5
7	שָׁלְטָנֵהּ	שָׁלְטָן	*empire; dominion*	5
8	אִנְבֵּהּ	אֶנֶב	*fruit*	3
9	אַתְרֵהּ	אֲתַר	*place*	3
10	לִבְבֵהּ	לְבַב	*heart*	3
11	עָפְיֵהּ	עֳפִי	*leaves*	3
12	גִּשְׁמֵהּ	גְּשֵׁם	*body*	2
13	חֲלָקֵהּ	חֲלָק	*portion, lot*	2
14	מַלְאֲכֵהּ	מַלְאַךְ	*angel*	2
15	פְּתָיֵהּ	פְּתָי	*width*	2
16	צַוְּארֵהּ	צַוַּאר	*neck*	2
17	רֵאשֵׁהּ	רֵאשׁ	*head*	2
18	רֵוֵהּ	רֵו	*appearance*	2
19	אֲבוּהִי	אַב	*father*	1
20	בְּרֵהּ	II בַּר	*son*	1
21	גַּוֵּהּ	גּוּ	*midst*	1
22	הֵיכְלֵהּ	הֵיכַל	*palace*	1
23	זִיוֵהּ	זִיו	*brightness, radiance*	1
24	חֲדוֹהִי	חֲדֵה	*chest*	1

	WORD	LEX. FORM	GLOSS(ES)	FREQ.
25	חַיְלֵהּ	חַיִל	*power; army*	1
26	חַרְצֵהּ	חֲרַץ	*hip*	1
27	כָּרְסְיֵהּ	כָּרְסֵא	*throne*	1
28	לְבוּשֵׁהּ	לְבוּשׁ	*clothing*	1
29	מְדוֹרֵהּ	מְדוֹר	*dwelling*	1
30	מִשְׁכְּבֵהּ	מִשְׁכַּב	*bed*	1
31	מִשְׁכְּנֵהּ	מִשְׁכַּן	*dwelling*	1
32	שַׂעֲרֵהּ	שְׂעַר	*hair*	1

FEMININE SINGULAR NOUNS

1	מַלְכוּתֵהּ	מַלְכוּ	*kingdom*	6
2	יְדֵהּ	יַד	*hand*	4
3	חֲזוֹתֵהּ	חֲזוֹת	*visibleness, ability to be seen* (?); *branches, canopy of a tree* (?)	2
4	בָּעוּתֵהּ	בָּעוּ	*request*	1
5	עִזְקְתֵהּ	עִזְקָה	*signet ring*	1
6	עִלִּיתֵהּ	עִלִּי	*upstairs room*	1
7	רַגְלֵהּ	רְגַל	*foot*	1
8	רוּחֵהּ	רוּחַ	*wind*	1
9	שְׁנָתֵהּ	שְׁנָה II	*sleep*	1

MASCULINE PLURAL NOUNS

1	רַבְרְבָנוֹהִי	רַבְרְבָנִין	*lord*	6
2	עַבְדוֹהִי	עֲבֵד	*slave, servant*	4
3	עַנְפוֹהִי	עֲנַף	*bough, branches*	4
4	חַבְרוֹהִי	חֲבַר	*friend, companion*	3
5	שָׁרְשׁוֹהִי	שְׁרֹשׁ	*root*	3
6	אַנְפּוֹהִי	אֲנַף	*face*	2
7	בְּנוֹהִי	בַּר II	*son*	2
8	זִיוֹהִי	זִיו	*splendor, radiance*	2
9	רַעְיֹנֽוֹהִי	רַעְיוֹן	*thought*	2
10	אֻשּׁוֹהִי	אֹשׁ	*foundation*	1
11	אָתוֹהִי	אָת	*sign*	1
12	גַּלְגִּלּוֹהִי	גַּלְגַּל	*wheel*	1

	WORD	LEX. FORM	GLOSS(ES)	FREQ.
13	הַדָּבְרוֹהִי	הַדָּבַר	*companion*	1
14	כָּהֲנוֹהִי	כָּהֵן	*priest*	1
15	מַעֲבָדוֹהִי	מַעֲבָד	*work, deed*	1
16	מְעוֹהִי	מְעֵה	*belly*	1
17	קַרְצוֹהִי	קְרַץ	*bits*	1
18	תִּמְהוֹהִי	תְּמַה	*wonder*	1

FEMININE PLURAL NOUNS

	WORD	LEX. FORM	GLOSS(ES)	FREQ.
1	לְחֵנָתֵהּ	לְחֵנָה	*consort*	2
2	רַגְלוֹהִי	רְגַל	*feet*	2
3	שֵׁגְלָתֵהּ	שֵׁגַל	*second-tier wife; concubine*	2
4	אֹרְחָתֵהּ	אֹרַח	*path*	1
5	אַרְכֻבָּתֵהּ	אַרְכֻבָּא	*knee*	1
6	בִּרְכוֹהִי	בְּרֵךְ	*knee*	1
7	דְּרָעוֹהִי	דְּרַע	*arm*	1
8	טִפְרוֹהִי	טְפַר	*nail*	1
9	יַרְכָתֵהּ	יַרְכָה	*thigh*	1
10	כְּנָוָתֵהּ	כְּנָת	*associate, colleague*	1
11	שָׁקוֹהִי	שָׁק	*shin, leg*	1

PREPOSITIONS

	WORD	LEX. FORM	GLOSS(ES)	FREQ.
1	לֵהּ	לְ	*to, for, belonging to*	18
2	בֵּהּ	בְּ	*in, into; by, through, with*	13
3	מִנֵּהּ	מִן	*from, away from, out of, some of, because of; than*	4
4	עֲלוֹהִי	עַל-	*on, upon, over, concerning, about, against; to, toward*	12
5	עֲלֵהִי	עַל-	*on, upon, over, concerning, about, against; to, toward*	1
6	קֳדָמוֹהִי	קֳדָם	*before, in the presence of*	4
7	קֳדָמוֹהִי	קֳדָם	*before, in the presence of*	3
8	וּקֳדָמוֹהִי	קֳדָם	*before, in the presence of*	1
9	תְּחֹתוֹהִי	תְּחוֹת	*under*	2
10	תַּחְתּוֹהִי	תְּחוֹת	*under*	1
11	עִמֵּהּ	עִם	*with*	1

WORD	LEX. FORM	GLOSS(ES)	FREQ.

PARTICLE

1	אִיתוֹהִי	אִיתַי	*it is*	1

VERBS

1	סַתְרֵהּ	II סתר	[G sc 3ms] *destroy*	1
2	בְּנָהִי	בנה	[G sc 3ms] *(re)build*	1
3	שָׂמֵהּ	שׂים	[G sc 3ms] *put, place, lay*	1
4	שְׁנוֹהִי	שׁנה	[G sc 3mp] intrans *changed on him*	1
5	יָעֲטֹהִי	יעט	[G ptcp mp] *adviser*	1
6	וְיָעֲטוֹהִי	יעט	[G ptcp mp] *adviser*	1
7	וּכְמִקְרְבֵהּ	קרב	[G inf] *approach*	1
8	וּכְמִצְבְּיֵהּ	צבה	[G inf] *desire, wish*	1
9	לְמֵזֵיהּ	אזה	[G inf] *heat, stoke*	1
10	וְהַשְׁלְטֵהּ	שלט	[H sc 3ms] *make rule*	1
11	הֲקִימֵהּ	קום	[H sc 3ms] *raise, erect; found, establish; appoint*	1
12	אֲקִימֵהּ	קום	[H sc 3ms] *raise, erect; found, establish; appoint*	1
13	הַקְרְבוּהִי	קרב	[H sc 3mp] *present*	1
14	אֲהוֹדְעִנֵּהּ	ידע	[H pc 1cs] *make known, communicate*	1
15	לְהַצָּלוּתֵהּ	נצל	[H inf] *deliver*	1
16	לַהֲקָמוּתֵהּ	קום	[H inf] *raise, erect; found, establish; appoint*	1
17	יְבַהֲלוּנֵּהּ	בהל	[D pc 3mp] *terrify*	1
18	יְבַהֲלֻנֵּהּ	בהל	[D pc 3mp] *terrify*	1
19	יְטַעֲמוּנֵּהּ	טעם	[D pc 3mp] *feed*	1
20	יְשַׁמְּשׁוּנֵּהּ	שׁמשׁ	[D pc 3mp] *minister, attend, serve*	1
21	וְחַבְּלוּהִי	חבל	[D imv 2mp] *destroy*	1
22	וְשַׁכְלְלֵהּ	כלל	[Š sc 3ms] *finish*	1
23	לְשֵׁיזָבוּתֵהּ	שׁיזב	[Š inf] *rescue*	1

LIST #49: WORDS WITH 3FS SUFFIXES

	WORD	LEX. FORM	GLOSS(ES)	FREQ.

MASCULINE SINGULAR NOUNS

1	גַּוַּהּ	גַּו	*midst*	2
2	גַּבַּהּ	גַּב	*side (HALOT), back (NRSV, NJPS)*	1
3	גַּפַּהּ	גַּף	*wing*	1
4	גִּשְׁמַהּ	גְּשֵׁם	*body*	1
5	חֶזְוַהּ	חֱזוּ	*appearance*	1
6	פֻּמַּהּ	פֻּם	*mouth*	1
7	רֵאשַׁהּ	רֵאשׁ	*head*	1

FEMININE SINGULAR NOUNS

1	שִׁנַּהּ	שֵׁן	*tooth*	2
2	חַבְרָתַהּ	חַבְרָה	*companion*	1
3	טִפְרַהּ	טְפַר	*claw*	1
4	רַגְלַהּ	רְגַל	*foot*	1

PREPOSITIONS

1	לַהּ	לְ	*to, for, belonging to*	8
2	בַּהּ	בְּ	*in, into; by, through, with*	6
3	מִנַּהּ	מִן	*from, away from, out of, some of, because of; than*	2
4	עֲלַהּ	עַל־	*on, upon, over, concerning, about, against; to, toward*	2
5	קֳדָמַהּ	קֳדָם	*before, in the presence of*	2
6	קָדָמַהּ	קֳדָם	*before, in the presence of*	1

VERBS

1	יִתְּנִנַּהּ	נתן	[G PC 3ms] *give*	3
2	וְחַתְמַהּ	חתם	[G SC 3ms] *seal*	1
3	בֱּנַיְתַהּ	בנה	[G SC 1cs] *(re)build*	1
4	וּתְדוּשִׁנַּהּ	דוש	[G PC 3fs] *trample*	1
5	יְחַוִּנַּהּ	חוה	[D PC 3ms] *show, make known, declare*	1
6	וְהַשְׁלְמַהּ	שלם	[H SC 3ms] *complete, finish off*	1
7	וְתַדְּקִנַּהּ	דקק	[H PC 3fs] *pulverize*	1

LIST #50: WORDS WITH 3MP SUFFIXES

	WORD	LEX. FORM	GLOSS(ES)	FREQ.

MASCULINE SINGULAR NOUNS

	WORD	LEX. FORM	GLOSS(ES)	FREQ.
1	אֱלָהֲהוֹן	אֱלָה	God; god, deity	3
2	אֱלָהֲהֹם	אֱלָה	God; god, deity	2
3	גֶּשְׁמְהוֹן	גְּשֵׁם	body	2
4	יֶדְהֹם	יַד	hand	1
5	כָּלְהוֹן	כֹּל	all, each, every, the whole, the entirety	1
6	מְדָרְהוֹן	מְדוֹר	dwelling	1
7	רֵאשְׁהוֹן	רֵאשׁ	head	1
8	שָׁלְטָנְהוֹן	שָׁלְטָן	empire; dominion	1

MASCULINE PLURAL NOUNS

	WORD	LEX. FORM	GLOSS(ES)	FREQ.
1	כְּנָוָתְהוֹן	כְּנָת	associate, colleague	6
2	סַרְבָּלֵיהוֹן	סַרְבָּל	trousers (?); coat (?)	2
3	בְּנֵיהוֹן	בַּר II	son	1
4	יוֹמֵיהוֹן	יוֹם	day	1
5	גַּרְמֵיהוֹן	גְּרַם	bone	1
6	לְבֻשֵׁיהוֹן	לְבוּשׁ	clothing	1
7	נִסְכֵּיהוֹן	נְסַךְ	libation	1
8	פַּטְּשֵׁיהוֹן	פְּטִישׁ	garment; shirt (?); trousers (?)	1
9	קַרְצֵיהוֹן	קְרַץ	bits	1
10	רָאשֵׁיהֹם	רֵאשׁ	head	1
11	שְׁמָהָתְהֹם	שֻׁם	name	1

FEMININE PLURAL NOUNS

	WORD	LEX. FORM	GLOSS(ES)	FREQ.
1	כַּרְבְּלָתְהוֹן	כַּרְבְּלָה	cap, hat	1
2	בְּמַחְלְקָתְהוֹן	מַחְלְקָה	section, course, division	1
3	מִנְחָתְהוֹן	מִנְחָה	grain offering	1
4	נְשֵׁיהוֹן	נְשִׁין	wives	1
5	פְּלֻגָּתְהוֹן	פְּלֻגָּה	division	1

	WORD	LEX. FORM	GLOSS(ES)	FREQ.

PREPOSITIONS

	WORD	LEX. FORM	GLOSS(ES)	FREQ.
1	לְהוֹן	לְ	*to, for, belonging to*	7
2	לְהֹם	לְ	*to, for, belonging to*	5
3	לְהוֹם	לְ	*to, for, belonging to*	1
4	בְּהוֹן	בְּ	*in, into; by, through, with*	6
5	מִנְּהוֹן	מִן	*from, away from, out of, some of, because of; than*	2
6	עֲלֵיהוֹן	עַל-	*on, upon, over, concerning, about, against; to, toward*	2
7	עֲלֵיהֹם	עַל-	*on, upon, over, concerning, about, against; to, toward*	1
8	אַחֲרֵיהוֹן	אַחֲרֵי	*after*	1
9	עִמְּהוֹן	עִם	*with*	1
10	קֳדָמֵיהוֹן	קֳדָם	*before, in the presence of*	1

NUMBER

	WORD	LEX. FORM	GLOSS(ES)	FREQ.
1	תְּלָתֵּהוֹן	תְּלָת	*the three of them*	1

PARTICLE

	WORD	LEX. FORM	GLOSS(ES)	FREQ.
1	יָתְהוֹן	יָת	*whom*	1

LIST #51: WORDS WITH 3FP SUFFIXES

	WORD	LEX. FORM	GLOSS(ES)	FREQ.

MASCULINE SINGULAR NOUN

	WORD	LEX. FORM	GLOSS(ES)	FREQ.
1	כָּלְּהֵין	כֹּל	*all, each, every, the whole, the entirety*	1

PREPOSITIONS

	WORD	LEX. FORM	GLOSS(ES)	FREQ.
1	מִנְּהֵין	מִן	*from, away from, out of, some of, because of; than*	5
2	מִנְּהֶן	מִן	*from, away from, out of, some of, because of; than*	1
3	בֵּינֵיהֶן	בֵּין	*between*	2

LIST #52: WORDS WITH 2MS SUFFIXES

WORD	LEX. FORM	GLOSS(ES)	FREQ.

MASCULINE SINGULAR NOUNS

	WORD	LEX. FORM	GLOSS(ES)	FREQ.
1	אֱלָהָךְ	אֱלָה	God; god, deity	10
2	אֲבוּךְ	אַב	father	4
3	לִבְבָךְ	לְבַב	heart	2
4	מִדְרָךְ	מְדוֹר	dwelling	2
5	מִשְׁכְּבָךְ	מִשְׁכַּב	bed	2
6	עַבְדָךְ	עֲבֵד	slave, servant	2
7	רַעְיוֹנָךְ	רַעְיוֹן	thought	2
8	אֲחָךְ	אַח	brother	1
9	זִיוָיךְ	זִיו	radiance	1
10	חֲטָאָךְ	חֲטִי	sin	1
11	חֶלְמָךְ	חֵלֶם	dream	1
12	עָרָךְ	עָר	adversary	1
13	צַוְּארָךְ	צַוַּאר	neck	1
14	קָבְלָךְ	קֳבֵל	before you	1
15	רֵאשָׁךְ	רֵאשׁ	head	1
16	שָׁלְטָנָךְ	שָׁלְטָן	empire; dominion	1

FEMININE SINGULAR NOUNS

	WORD	LEX. FORM	GLOSS(ES)	FREQ.
1	יְדָךְ	יַד	hand	4
2	מַלְכוּתָךְ	מַלְכוּ	kingship, sovereignty; reign; kingdom, realm	4
3	נִשְׁמְתָךְ	נִשְׁמָה	breath	1
4	רְבוּתָךְ	רְבוּ	greatness	1
5	שְׁלֵוְתָךְ	שְׁלֵוָה	ease, serenity	1

MASCULINE PLURAL NOUNS

	WORD	LEX. FORM	GLOSS(ES)	FREQ.
1	אֲבָהָתָךְ	אַב	father	1
2	רַבְרְבָנָךְ	רַבְרְבָנִין	lord	1

WORD	LEX. FORM	GLOSS(ES)	FREQ.

FEMININE PLURAL NOUNS

	WORD	LEX. FORM	GLOSS(ES)	FREQ.
1	אֹרְחָתָךְ	אֲרַח	*path*	1
2	לְחֵנָתָךְ	לְחֵנָה	*consort, concubine, prostitute*	1
3	מַתְּנָתָךְ	מַתְּנָה	*gift*	1
4	נְבִזְבְּיָתָךְ	נְבִזְבָּה	*present, reward*	1
5	עֲוָיָתָךְ	עֲוָיָה	*iniquity*	1
6	שֵׁגְלָתָךְ	שֵׁגַל	*second-tier wife; concubine*	1

PREPOSITIONS

	WORD	LEX. FORM	GLOSS(ES)	FREQ.
1	לָךְ	לְ	*to, for, belonging to*	13
2	עֲלָךְ	עַל־	*on, upon, over, concerning, about, against; to, toward*	8
3	מִנָּךְ	מִן	*from, away from, out of, some of, because of; than*	5
4	בָּךְ	בְּ	*in, into; by, through, with*	4
5	קָדָמָךְ	קֳדָם	*before, in the presence of*	2
6	בָּתְרָךְ	בָּאתַר	*after*	1
7	לְוָתָךְ	לְוָת	*with*	1
8	עִמָּךְ	עִם	*with*	1

PARTICLE

	WORD	LEX. FORM	GLOSS(ES)	FREQ.
1	אִיתָךְ	אִיתַי	[with interr ה] *are you?*	1

VERBS

	WORD	LEX. FORM	GLOSS(ES)	FREQ.
1	לְשָׂנְאָךְ	שׂנא	[G ptcp ms] *hater, enemy*	1
2	יְבַהֲלָךְ	בהל	[D juss 3ms] *terrify*	1
3	יְבַהֲלוּךְ	בהל	[D juss 3mp] *terrify*	1
4	וְהַשְׁלְטָךְ	שׁלט	[H sc 3ms] *make rule*	1
5	הוֹדְעָךְ	ידע	[H sc 3ms] *make known, communicate*	1
6	לְהוֹדָעוּתָךְ	ידע	[H inf] *make known, communicate*	1
7	לַהֲתָבוּתָךְ	תוב	[H inf] trans *give a reply* (w/ suffix) *to*	1
8	יְשֵׁיזְבִנָּךְ	שׁיזב	[Š pc 3ms] *rescue*	1
9	לְשֵׁיזָבוּתָךְ	שׁיזב	[Š inf] *rescue*	1

LIST #53: WORDS WITH 2MP SUFFIXES

	WORD	LEX. FORM	GLOSS(ES)	FREQ.
MASCULINE SINGULAR NOUNS				
1	אֱלָהֲכֹם	אֱלָה	*God; god, deity*	2
2	אֱלָהֲכוֹן	אֱלָה	*God; god, deity*	1
3	שְׁלָמְכוֹן	שְׁלָם	*peace*	2
FEMININE SINGULAR NOUN				
1	דָּתְכוֹן	דַּת	*verdict*	1
MASCULINE PLURAL NOUN				
1	בָּתֵּיכוֹן	בַּיִת	*house; palace; temple*	1
PREPOSITIONS				
1	לְכֹם	לְ	*to, for, belonging to*	3
2	לְכוֹן	לְ	*to, for, belonging to*	1
PARTICLE				
1	אִיתֵיכוֹן	אִיתַי	*you are*	2
VERBS				
1	יִשְׁאֲלֶנְכוֹן	שׁאל	[G PC 3ms] *ask*	1
2	יְשֵׁיזְבִנְכוֹן	שׁיזב	[Š PC 3ms] *rescue*	1

LIST #54: WORDS WITH 1CS SUFFIXES

	WORD	LEX. FORM	GLOSS(ES)	FREQ.
MASCULINE SINGULAR NOUNS				
1	רֵאשִׁי	רֵאשׁ	*head*	4
2	מִשְׁכְּבִי	מִשְׁכַּב	*bed*	3

	WORD	LEX. FORM	GLOSS(ES)	FREQ.
3	אֱלָהִי	אֱלָהּ	God; god, deity	2
4	מַנְדְּעִי	מִנְדַּע	knowledge	2
5	מָרִי	מָרֵא	lord	2
6	הַדְרִי	הֲדַר	majesty	2
7	אַבִי	אַב	father	1
8	בֵּיתִי	בַּיִת	house; palace; temple	1
9	הֵיכְלִי	הֵיכַל	palace	1
10	זִוִי	זִיו	splendor	1
11	חֶזְוִי	חֱזוּ	vision	1
12	חֶלְמִי	חֵלֶם	dream	1
13	חִסְנִי	חֱסֵן	power, might	1
14	מִלְכִּי	מְלַךְ	advice	1
15	לִבִּי	לֵב	heart	1
16	תַּלְתִּי	תַּלְתָּא	triumvir (official of the third rank), *rank third*	1

FEMININE SINGULAR NOUNS

1	מַלְכוּתִי	מַלְכוּ	kingship, sovereignty; reign; kingdom, realm	4
2	רוּחִי	רוּחַ	spirit	1

MASCULINE PLURAL NOUNS

1	אֲבָהָתִי	אַב	father	1
2	אֱלָהַי	אֱלָהּ	God; god, deity	1
3	הַדָּבְרַי	הַדָּבַר	companion	1
4	זִיוַי	זִיו	splendor, radiance	1
5	רַבְרְבָנַי	רַבְרְבָנִין	lord	1
6	רַעְיוֹנַי	רַעְיוֹן	thought	1

FEMININE PLURAL NOUNS

1	יְדָי	יַד	hand	1
2	עַיְנַי	עַיִן	eye	1

	WORD	LEX. FORM	GLOSS(ES)	FREQ.

PREPOSITIONS

	WORD	LEX. FORM	GLOSS(ES)	FREQ.
1	מִנִּי	מִן	from, away from, out of, some of, because of; than	10
2	קָדְמַי	קֳדָם	before, in the presence of	8
3	לִי	לְ	to, for, belonging to	7
4	עֲלַי	עַל-	on, upon, over, concerning, about, against; to, toward	4
5	בִּי	בְּ	in, into; by, through, with	1
6	עִמִּי	עִם	with	1

VERBS

	WORD	LEX. FORM	GLOSS(ES)	FREQ.
1	לְהוֹדָעֻתַנִי	ידע	[H inf] make known, communicate	4
2	יְבַהֲלֻנַּנִי	בהל	[D pc 3mp] terrify	3
3	חַבְּלוּנִי	חבל	[D sc 3mp] destroy	1
4	וִידַחֲלִנַּנִי	דחל	[D pc 3ms] frighten	1
5	יְחַוִּנַּנִי	חוה	[D pc 3ms] make known	1
6	הוֹדַעְתַּנִי	ידע	[H sc 2ms] make known, communicate	1
7	יְהוֹדְעִנַּנִי	ידע	[H pc 3ms] make known, communicate	1
8	יְהוֹדְעֻנַּנִי	ידע	[H pc 3mp] make known, communicate	1
9	תְהוֹדְעוּנַּנִי	ידע	[H pc 2mp] make known, communicate	1
10	תְהוֹדְעֻנַּנִי	ידע	[H pc 2mp] make known, communicate	1
11	תְּהַחֲוֻנַּנִי	חוה	[H pc 2mp] show, make known, declare	1
12	הַעֵלְנִי	עלל	[H imv 2ms] bring	1
13	הַחֲוֻנִי	חוה	[H imv 2mp] show, make known, declare	1

LIST #55: WORDS WITH 1CP SUFFIXES

	WORD	LEX. FORM	GLOSS(ES)	VERSE
MASCULINE SINGULAR NOUN				
1	אֱלָהַנָא	אֱלָה	God; god, deity	Dan 3:17
MASCULINE PLURAL NOUN				
1	אֲבָהָתַנָא	אַב	father	Ezra 5:12
PARTICLE				
1	אִיתַנָא	אִיתַי	we are	Dan 3:18
PREPOSITIONS				
1	עֲלֶינָא	עַל־	on, upon, over, concerning, about, against; to, toward	Ezra 4:12
2	לַנָא	לְ	to, for, belonging to	Ezra 4:14
VERBS				
1	הוֹדַעְתֶּנָא	ידע	[H sc 2ms] make known, communicate	Dan 2:23
2	לְשֵׁיזָבוּתַנָא	שׁיזב	[Š inf] rescue	Dan 3:17
3	הֲתִיבוּנָא	תוב	[H sc 3mp] trans return (w/ suffix) to	Ezra 5:11

EASILY CONFUSED WORDS

LIST #56: HOMONYMNS

	WORD	GLOSS(ES)	POS	FREQ.
1	II בַּר	*son*	noun	19
2	I בַּר	*field*	noun	7
3	I שָׁנָה	*year*	noun	7
4	II שֵׁנָה	*sleep*	noun	1
5	II ברך	(G, D) *bless* [2x]; (Gp, Dp) *blessed* [2x]	verb	4
6	I ברך	(G) *kneel*	verb	1
7	II לָהֵן	*except*	prep	4 (7)
		but [2x], *unless* [1x]	disj	3 (7)
8	I לָהֵן	*therefore*	conj	3
9	I סתר	(Dp ptcp) *hidden*	verb	1
10	II סתר	(G) *destroy*	verb	1

LIST #57: CONSONANTAL HOMOGRAPHS

	WORD	GLOSS(ES)	POS	FREQ.
1	מִן־	*from, away from, out of, some of, because of; than*	adv	119
		from, away from, out of, some of, because of; than	prep	
2	מַן	*whoever* [6x]; *who?* [4x]	pron	10

	WORD	GLOSS(ES)	POS	FREQ.
3	אֱלָהּ	God; god, deity	noun	95
4	אֵלֶּה	these	pron	2
5	אמר	(G) say; order	verb	71
6	אִמַּר	lamb	noun	3
7	בַּיִת	house; palace; temple	noun	45
8	בית	(G) spend the night	verb	1
9	פְּשַׁר	interpretation	noun	33
10	פשר	(G, D) interpret	verb	2
11	קֳבֵל	because	conj	32
		that which is in front	noun	
		facing, opposite, corresponding to	prep	
12	קבל	(D) receive	verb	3
13	I ענה	(G) answer, reply; begin to speak	verb	30
14	עֲנֵה	poor, miserable	adj	1
15	עבד	(G) do, make; (tG) be done; be turned into	verb	28
16	עֲבֵד	slave, servant	noun	7
17	עִם	with	prep	22
18	עַם	people	noun	15
19	גְּבַר	man, person [20x]; man [1x]	noun	21
20	גִּבָּר	hero, warrior, strong man	noun	1
21	שנה	(H) trans change [5x]; (G) be different [4x]; intrans change [2x]; (w/ 3ms suffix) intrans changed on him [1x]; (G ptcp) intrans changed [1x]; (tD) intrans change [2x]; be changed [2x]; (D) trans change [1x]; trans change = violate [1x]; (Dp) be different [1x]	verb	20

	WORD	GLOSS(ES)	POS	FREQ.
22	I שָׁנָה	*year*	noun	7
23	II שָׁנָה	*sleep*	noun	1
24	כְּתָב	*writing, instruction*	noun	12
25	כתב	(G) *write* [6x]; (Gp) *be written* [2x]	verb	8
26	אֻמָּה	*nation*	noun	8
27	אַמָּה	*cubit*	noun	4
28	דֵּךְ	*that*	adj	6
29	דֵּךְ	*that*	adj	6
30	חבל	(D) *destroy* [3x]; (tD) *be destroyed* [3x]	verb	6
31	חֲבָל	*harm*	noun	3
32	סָפַר	*scribe*	noun	6
33	סְפַר	*book*	noun	5
34	פָּרַס	*Persia*	GN	6
35	פְּרֵס	volume measure *peres*, weight measure *one-half a mina; one-half shekel*	noun	2
36	פרס	(Gp) *be divided*	verb	1
37	דִּין	*judgment, justice* [3x]; *court* [2x]	noun	5
38	דין	(G) *judge*	verb	1
39	סוֹף	*end*	noun	5
40	סוף	(G) *be fulfilled* [1x]; (H) *bring to an end, annihilate* [1x]	verb	2
41	רוּם	*height*	noun	5
42	רום	(G) *be high* [1x]; (D) *praise* [1x]; (H) *exalt* [1x]; (tD) *exalt oneself* [1x]	verb	4

	WORD	GLOSS(ES)	POS	FREQ.
43	תְּקֵף	(G) *become strong* [4x]; (D) *make strong; enforce* [1x]	verb	5
44	תְּקָף	*strength, might*	noun	1
45	תְּקֹף	*strength*	noun	1
46	זְמָר	*musical instrument*	noun	4
47	זַמָּר	*singer*	noun	1
48	רְבוּ	*greatness*	noun	4
49	רִבּוֹ	*myriad, 10,000*	num	2
50	שְׁלָם	*peace*	noun	4
51	שׁלם	(H) *complete, finish off* [1x]; *fully deliver* [1x]; (Gp) *be finished* [1x]	verb	3
52	שׁפל	(H) *humble* [2x], *humiliate* [1x], *bring low* [1x]	verb	4
53	שְׁפַל	*low, lowest*	noun	1
54	תַּמָּה	*there*	adv	4
55	תְּמַה	*wonder*	noun	3
56	אָחֳרִי	*another*	adj	5 (6)
		another	noun	1 (6)
57	אַחֲרֵי	*after*	prep	3
58	אַל	*not*	part	3
59	אֵל	*these*	adj	1 (Q)
60	הדר	(D) *glorify*	verb	3
61	הֲדַר	*majesty*	noun	3
62	הלך	(D, H) *walk* [3x]	verb	3
63	הֲלָךְ	*field* or *produce tax*	noun	3

	WORD	GLOSS(ES)	POS	FREQ.
64	מֶלַח	salt	noun	3
65	מלח	(G) salt	verb	1
66	מֶלֶךְ	king	noun	180
67	מְלַךְ	advice	noun	1
68	עִקַּר	stump	noun	3
69	עקר	(tG) be ripped out	verb	1
70	חסן	(H) possess	verb	2
71	חֱסֶן	power, might	noun	2
72	קַיָּם	enduring, established	adj	2
73	קְיָם	statute	noun	2
74	תְּקֵל	weight measure *shekel*, or pun on תקל תְּקִיל Gp ptcp ms *weighed*	noun	2
75	תקל	(Gp) be weighed	verb	1
76	אִדַּר	threshing floor	noun	1
77	אֲדָר	Adar	MN	1
78	נגד	(G) flow	verb	1
79	נֶגֶד	toward	prep	1
80	פלג	(Gp ptcp) divided	verb	1
81	פְּלַג	half	noun	1
82	קצף	(G) be furious	verb	1
83	קְצַף	fury, wrath	noun	1

LOANWORDS

LIST #58: PERSIAN LOANWORDS

	WORD	GLOSS(ES)	POS	FREQ.
1	דָּת	*law* [11x]; *decree* [2x]; *verdict* [1x]	noun	14
2	אֲחַשְׁדַּרְפַּן	*satrap*	noun	9
3	רָזָה	*secret, mystery*	noun	9
4	אָסְפַּרְנָא	*diligently*	adv	7
5	פִּתְגָם	*word, answer* [3x]; *sentence* [1x]; *report* [1x]; *edict* [1x]	noun	6
6	סְרַךְ	high official *president*	noun	5
7	הַדָּבַר	*companion*	noun	4
8	המונך	*necklace, chain*	noun	3
9	נִשְׁתְּוָן	*letter*	noun	3
10	פַּרְשֶׁגֶן	*copy*	noun	3
11	אֲדַרְגָּזַר	*counselor*	noun	2
12	אַזְדָּא	*publicly known* thus *irrevocable*	adj	2
13	אֲפַרְסְכָי	[or Akk. lw] *official title, apharsechai-official; or a people, Apharsechite*	noun	2
14	אֻשַׁרְנָא	[or Akk. lw] *shrine* (?), *structure* (?), *furnishings* (?)	noun	2
15	דְּתָבַר	*judge*	noun	2
16	הַדָּם	*limb*	noun	2
17	סַרְבָּל	*trousers* (?); *coat* (?)		2
18	אֲרִיךְ	*worthy of an Aryan, i.e., proper, fitting*	adj	1
19	כָּרוֹז	*herald*	noun	1
20	נֶבְרְשָׁה	*lampstand*	noun	1
21	נִדָן	*sheath = body*	noun	1
22	שְׁרֹשׁוּ	*rooting out = banishment*	noun	1
23	אַפְתֹם	[or Akk. lw] *surely* (?), *certainly* (?), *finally* (?)	adv	1

	WORD	GLOSS(ES)	POS	FREQ.

POSSIBLE PERSIAN LOANWORDS

	WORD	GLOSS(ES)	POS	FREQ.
1	פְּטִישׁ	*garment; shirt* (?); *trousers* (?)	noun	1
2	שׁוּשַׁנְכִי	*Susaite*	noun	1

LIST #59: SUMERIAN LOANWORDS

	WORD	GLOSS(ES)	POS	FREQ.
1	אֹשׁ	*foundation*	noun	3
2	נְכַס	*property, wealth*	noun	2

LIST #60: AKKADIAN LOANWORDS

	WORD	GLOSS(ES)	POS	FREQ.
1	אַתּוּן	*furnace*	noun	10
2	כְּנָת	*associate, colleague*	noun	7
3	אַשָּׁף	*conjurer; exorcist*	noun	6
4	מִדָּה	*tribute, tax*	noun	4
5	אַרְגְּוָן	*purple*	noun	3
6	בְּלוֹ	*tax* paid in kind, *produce tax*	noun	3
7	הֲלָךְ	*field* or *produce tax*	noun	3
8	לְחֵנָה	*consort, concubine, prostitute*	noun	3
9	שֵׁגַל	*second-tier wife; concubine*	noun	3
10	אֲפַרְסְכָי	[or Pers. lw] official title, *apharsechai-official*; or a people, *Apharsechite*	noun	2
11	פְּרֵס	volume measure *peres*, weight measure *one-half a mina; one-half shekel*	noun	2
12	קְרָץ	*bits*	noun	2
13	אֲשַׁרְנָא	[or Pers. lw] *shrine* (?), *structure* (?), *furnishings* (?)	noun	2

	WORD	GLOSS(ES)	POS	FREQ.

POSSIBLE AKKADIAN LOANWORDS

	WORD	GLOSS(ES)	POS	FREQ.
1	אִגְּרָה	*letter*	noun	3
2	גְּוָלוּ	*dunghill; latrine pit*	noun	3

LIST #61: AKKADIAN CALQUES

	WORD	GLOSS(ES)	POS	FREQ.
1	תִּלְתָּא	*triumvir* (official of the third rank), *rank third*	noun	3
2	בְּעֵל־טְעֵם	*chancellor, chief government official*	collocation	3

LIST #62: GREEK LOANWORDS

	WORD	GLOSS(ES)	POS	FREQ.
1	פְּסַנְתֵּרִין	*psalterion*	noun	4
2	קִיתָרֹס	*kitharos, zither*	noun	4
3	סוּמְפֹּנְיָה	*symphonia*	noun	3

LIST #63: HEBREW LOANWORD

	WORD	GLOSS	POS	FREQ.
1	עֶלְיוֹן	*most high*	noun	4

א

אֱדַיִן coordinating conj, *then*
temp. adv, *then*

אֱלָה noun m (emph אֱלָהָא; = Heb אֱלוֹהַּ),
God; god, deity

אמר verb (= Heb), G, *say; order*

אֱנָשׁ noun m (emph אֲנָשָׁא; = Heb אֱנוֹשׁ),
individual *person, human being;*
coll *people, humanity*

אֲנָשָׁא see אֱנָשׁ

ב

בְּ prep (= Heb), *in, into; by, through,*
with

בָּבֶל GN (= Heb), *Babylon*

בַּיִת noun m (emph בַּיְתָא; = Heb), *house;*
temple

ד

דִּי rel pron, *who, which, that;*
in gen construction, *(that) of;*
subordinating conj, *that;*
introduces final clauses, *so that*

דְּנָה prox dem adj and pron, *this*

דָּנִיֵּאל PN (= Heb), *Daniel*

ה

הוה verb (= Heb היה, II הוה), G, *be,*
become, exist; occur, happen

הוי see הוה

ו

וַ coordinating conj and disj (= Heb),
and, but

ח

חזה verb (= Heb), G, *see; perceive;*
Gp ptcp, *proper, customary*

חזי see חזה

ט

טְעֵם noun m (emph טַעְמָא, cstr טְעֵם, טַעַם;
= Heb טַעַם), *good taste, tact,*
sophistication; statement;
command; advice, report

טַעַם see טְעֵם

טַעְמָא see טְעֵם

י

ידע verb (= Heb), G, *know; learn;*
understand; H, *make known,*
communicate

יהב verb (= Heb), G, *give;* tG, *be given*

יְרוּשְׁלֵם GN (= Heb יְרוּשָׁלַם), *Jerusalem*

יִשְׂרָאֵל GN (= Heb), *Israel*

כ

כְּ prep (= Heb), *like, as; about,*
approximately; according to,
corresponding with;
conj (w/ inf) *as soon as*

כֹּל noun m (e כְּלָא; = Heb), *all, each, every,*
whole, entirety

כָּל־ in כָּל־קֳבֵל, = לְ + כְּ, **not** noun m כֹּל
HALOT s.v. קֳבֵל

ל

לְ prep (= Heb), *to, for, belonging to*

לָא neg part (= Heb לֹא), *no, not*

לֶהֱוֵא verb G pc 3ms or juss 3ms הוה

לִי prep לְ w/ 1cs gen sx

לְקֳבֵל see קֳבֵל

ק

קְבֵל — noun m קְבֵל *that which is in front;*
prep, *facing, opposite,*
corresponding to;
subordinating conj, *because;*
לְקָבֵל *because (of); in front of*

קֳדָם — prep, *before, in the presence of*

קום — verb (= Heb), G, *arise, get up;*
be established, endure;
H, *raise, erect; found,*
establish; appoint; Hp, *be set up,*
erected; D, *set up, erect*

שׂ

שׂים — verb (= Heb), G, *put, place, lay;*
tG, *be put; be turned into*

שׁ

שְׁמַיִן — noun m (emph שְׁמַיָּא; = Heb שָׁמַיִם),
sky, heaven

שְׁמַיָּא — see שְׁמַיִן

מ

מֶלֶךְ — noun m (emph מַלְכָּא; = Heb), *king*

מַלְכָּא — noun ms emph מֶלֶךְ

מַלְכוּ — noun f (emph מַלְכוּתָא; = Heb מַלְכוּת),
kingship, sovereignty; reign;
kingdom, realm

מַלְכוּתָא — noun fs emph מַלְכוּ

מַלְכוּתָה — noun fs emph מַלְכוּ

מִן־ — prep and adv (= Heb), *from, away*
from, out of, some of, because
of; than

מִנִּי — prep מִן w/ 1cs gen sx

נ

נְבוּכַדְנֶצַּר — PN (= Heb), *Nebuchadnezzar II*

ע

עבד — verb (= Heb I עשׂה), G, *do, make;*
tG, *be done; be turned into*

עַד־ — prep (= Heb III עַד), *as far as,*
until, up to; during, within;
conj, *until*

עַל־ — prep (= Heb. plus the meaning
of Heb אֶל־), *on, upon, over,*
concerning, about, against;
to, toward

עִם — prep (= Heb), *with*

ענה I — verb (= Heb), G, *answer, reply;*
begin to speak

פ

פְּשַׁר — noun m (emph פִּשְׁרָא), *interpretation*

פְּשַׁר — noun ms cstr

פִּשְׁרָא — noun ms emph פְּשַׁר

M000239520